GERMAN MEMORIALS, MOTIFS, AND MEANINGS

A VOLUME IN THE SERIES
Public History in Historical Perspective

EDITED BY
Marla R. Miller

GERMAN MEMORIALS, MOTIFS, AND MEANINGS

A CULTURAL HISTORY IN
BRONZE, WOOD, AND STONE

JENNIFER HANSEN-GLUCKLICH

University of Massachusetts Press
Amherst and Boston

Copyright © 2025 by University of Massachusetts Press
All rights reserved

ISBN 978-1-62534-882-1 (paper); 883-8 (hardcover)

Designed by Sally Nichols
Set in Minion
Printed and bound by Books International, Inc.

Cover design by adam b. bohannon
Cover photo by Jennifer Hansen-Glucklich, *Hohensyburg Castle Memorial.*
Courtesy of the photographer.

Library of Congress Cataloging-in-Publication Data
A catalog record for this book is available from the Library of Congress.

British Library Cataloguing-in-Publication Data
A catalog record for this book is available from the British Library.

For Ariel
mori va-ahuvi

Contents

Illustrations ix
Acknowledgments xi

INTRODUCTION
1

CHAPTER ONE
The Original German *Volk*
Autochthony and Primal Origins
14

CHAPTER TWO
The German *Volk* as *Waldvolk*
The Mythic Forest in German Culture
43

CHAPTER THREE
Lebensmale (Living Memorials)
Nature's Monuments to Peace, Unification, the Departed, and the Extraordinary
73

CHAPTER FOUR
From Giants' Graves, Stone Dances, and Devils' Stones to the Twenty-First Century
Findlinge in German Memorialization
103

CHAPTER FIVE
To Perish on a Hill of Sacrifice
Meaningful Death, Self-Transcendence, and Violence
142

CHAPTER SIX
Für Herd und Heimat (For Hearth and Home)
Memorializing Sacrifice in the Fatherland
167

CHAPTER SEVEN
Bitte Gott, Mache die Seele von Pein Wieder Frei
Wayside Memorials of Admonishment, Remembrance, and Atonement
218

CHAPTER EIGHT
From Medieval Blood Feuds to Modern Genocide and Refugees
Memorials of Collective Atonement, Reconciliation, and Reorientation
254

CONCLUSION
287

Notes 295
Index 351

Illustrations

FIGURE 1. Fragments of Innere Festigung, by Jupp Rübsam, Düsseldorf. Photo: Wikipedia Commons. 5

FIGURE 2. *Varus* by Anselm Kiefer, Collection Van Abbemuseum, Eindhoven. Photography: Peter Cox, Eindhoven. 70

FIGURE 3. Ring-shaped *Heldenhain*: linden in the center with forty oaks, a protective wall of trees, a ditch, stones bearing the names of the fallen, and benches. Designed by Willy Lange. Lange, *Deutsche Heldenhaine* (Leipzig, 1915). 86

FIGURE 4. Memorial in Martin Luther Church cemetery in Trittau. Photo: Marlise Appel, Ev. Akademie der Nordkirche. 117

FIGURE 5. Reunification monument in Baden-Baden. 130

FIGURE 6. Karberg Memorial Hall, Ehrenfriedhof am Haddebyer Noor. Photo: Wikipedia Commons. 137

FIGURE 7. Honor Grove Kunduz, Forest of Remembrance in Schwielowsee. Photo: Wikipedia Commons. 140

FIGURE 8. Memorial in Großholthausen cemetery. 169

FIGURE 9. Memorial in Erfelden. 173

FIGURE 10. Hohensyburg Castle Memorial. 177

FIGURE 11. Hohensyburg Castle Memorial (alternate view). 177

FIGURE 12. Hofgarten Memorial, Munich. 179

FIGURE 13. Memorial in Dußlingen. 180

FIGURE 14. Sigmaringen Tholos Tomb (external view). 181

FIGURE 15. Sigmaringen Memorial (internal view). 182

FIGURE 16. Memorial in Oberhaching. 183

FIGURE 17. Memorial in Neu-Isenburg. 185

FIGURE 18. Memorial in Wanne-Eickel. 187

FIGURE 19. Memorial in Gießen. 187

FIGURE 20. Lüdenscheid Memorial model. 188

FIGURE 21. Memorial in Lüdenscheid. 189

FIGURE 22. Memorial in Odenheim. 190

FIGURE 23. Memorial in Weinheim. 191

FIGURE 24. Memorial in Kley/Oespel (Dortmund). 192

FIGURE 25. Reeser Platz Memorial, Düsseldorf. 194

FIGURE 26. Memorial in Memmingen at the Mariä Himmelfahrt Church. 198

FIGURE 27. Memorial in Pang (Rosenheim). 201

FIGURE 28. Memorial in Deusen (Dortmund). 205

FIGURE 29. Memorial in Markt Schwaben. 208

FIGURE 30. Memorial in Waldkirch-Kollnau. 216

FIGURE 31. Original glass plate photograph (taken between 1900 and 1910) of Eiserne Händl, Neustadt a.d. Donau. Photo: Stadtarchiv Abensberg. 248

FIGURE 32. Horst Hoheisel, "The Crushed Brandenburg Gate," proposed memorial for the murdered Jews of Europe, 1994. © 2024. Photo: Artists Rights Society (ARS), New York / VG Bild-Kunst, Bonn. 274–75

FIGURE 33. Sea of Tears memorial, Dresden. Photo: Wikipedia Commons. 281

FIGURE 34. Memorial in Langendreer (Bochum). 288

Acknowledgments

It is with great pleasure that I thank those who have helped me in so many ways with the research, writing, and publication of this book. I would first like to thank Matt Becker of University of Massachusetts Press for his belief in and support of this book, and for his remarkable responsiveness, engagement, and guidance through every stage of this project. I would also like to thank Ben Kimball and Ivo Fravashi for their fine work during the final stages of publication. I owe a special thanks to Jonathan Skolnik and Daniel Reynolds for their early positive feedback on the project proposal, and a particular debt of gratitude to Jonathan for all his intellectual and academic support since I studied with him so many years ago. I would also like to thank the two anonymous readers for University of Massachusetts Press for their careful reading and helpful suggestions. Thank you as well to Andrea Meckley, the Interlibrary Loan magician at University of Mary Washington, who secured for me dozens of obscure texts, and to UMW for granting me a Waple Professorship in support of the final stages of this project. I am grateful as well to all those in Germany (mentioned in endnotes throughout the book) who shared with me documents and helped me secure photographs of memorials I could not visit in person.

I would like to thank my dear friends and colleagues who have given me their generous support in a variety of ways, from debating titles and offering substantive comments to simply asking for updates, showing warm interest, and encouraging my further progress: Michal Aharony, Maysoon Al-Sayed Ahmad, María Laura Bocaz-Leiva, Gonzalo Campos-Dintrans, Antonia Delgado-Poust and Brad Gething, Elvira and George Evangelauf, Eric Gable, Jeff Grossman, Jason James, Scott Powers and

Alex Mejia, Maria Ramos and John Carroll, Kristan and Eli Sternberg, Marcel Rotter, Rabbi Menachem Sherman, and Melissa Wiser. I owe a special debt to Selma Erdogdu-Volmerich for hosting me in Dortmund and for helping me with tricky translations, and a special thanks to Oliver Volmerich for an enlightening tour of Dortmund memorials and monuments and for sharing with me his limitless knowledge of Dortmund history. A warm thanks to my family for their love and encouragement: to my mother and stepfather, Linette and Chuck Dugo, my sister Erica Mumford, and my grandmother Norma Haag, *z"l*, who did not live to see the publication of this book but whose belief in me, interest, and love helped make it possible.

I owe my greatest debt, as always, to Ariel Glucklich, my beloved husband, teacher, steadfast supporter, and attentive, tireless reader, who has stood by me unwaveringly throughout the many years of this project, exploring Germany's memorial landscape with me (and occasionally getting lost with me while searching for tucked-away memorials in out-of-the-way villages), encouraging me without fail, and helping me with every aspect of this book, from initial conception to final edits. Words cannot express my boundless gratitude and love.

GERMAN MEMORIALS, MOTIFS, AND MEANINGS

INTRODUCTION

From beneath a stone shroud atop a black marble catafalque extends the tightly clenched fist of a German memorial soldier. This memorial, designed by Franz Dorrenbach (1924/25) and dedicated to the fallen soldiers and sons of the fourth Queen Augusta Guards Grenadier Regiment of World War I, stands in the Columbiadamm Cemetery in Neukölln, Berlin. On top of the shroud lie the fallen soldier's bayonet, a laurel wreath, and his iconic *Stahlhelm* (steel helmet). From the other side of the memorial, viewers may glimpse a second clenched fist peeking out from beneath the death shroud. The memorial's message rings clear: although temporarily defeated, the German army will rise again to avenge the humiliated German nation. An inscription engraved above the memorial's dedication reads: "Wir starben, auf dass Deutschland lebe, so lasset uns leben in Euch!" ("We died so that Germany might live, so let us live through you"). These words link the survival of Germany to the self-sacrifice of its soldiers; but they also stake a claim on the future by obligating future generations to remember and honor that sacrifice as an outstanding debt demanding repayment through the currency of remembrance.

This is a book about monuments and memorials and the ways in which they create binding, enduring cultural memories. The question that motivates this book is the question of why certain motifs and symbols have endured, and continue to endure, in German memorialization despite vast political, social, and cultural changes over time, including the founding and collapse of empires, two world wars, occupation by foreign powers, division, and reunification. As the description of the Columbiadamm memorial suggests, this book is, above all, a book about stories—stories of suffering and loss but also stories of ancient Germanic communities and rituals, of mythical origins, magical trees, and enchanted stones, of bloody forest battles against Roman legions, of heroic, self-sacrificing soldiers, and of repentance, atonement, and national, cultural renewal. Together, these memorial and monument stories create a rich, creative, at times dangerous but always intriguing topography of memory.

Creating and sharing stories is fundamental to human experience. In a discussion of the features of folk psychology,[1] renowned psychologist Jerome Bruner explains that we as human beings organize our experiences into narrative forms—an unconscious process similar to converting visual input into figure and ground and a feature, perhaps, of our linguistic or psychological capacities.[2] When we are born into our native cultures, we absorb our native folk psychology and its narratives in the same way that we acquire our native tongues: both are necessary for seamless participation in communal life. The narratives of our folk psychology order our experiences; they tell us not only what "is" but what "should be." They give us, in other words, our "plot" or fabula.[3]

Monuments and memorials, like folk psychology, are narrative driven—they are, in essence, narratives depicted and written in stone. The relevance of these narratives to those who erected the structures is clear: but why should these stories continue to be told long after the communities who created them have disappeared? Why should we, citizens of the twenty-first century, listen to the stories of monuments and memorials constructed in many cases not merely years and decades but centuries ago? We have much to learn from monuments and memorials. With their inscriptions, forms, symbols, and iconography, they speak to us with a variety of voices: they boast and mourn, celebrate and admonish. In the words of archaeologist Richard Bradley, monuments embody "ideas about the world."[4] Their topographical locations, too, tell stories, revealing the intended audiences of monuments and memorials. A memorial tucked away in a quiet wooded grove speaks to a public different from the one imagined for a memorial displayed in the pedestrian zone of a bustling city.

Monuments and memorials tell us many things if we care to listen. They are *lieux de mémoire*, in the words of Pierre Nora—objects in which memory has taken "root in the concrete" or places where memory "crystallizes and secretes itself."⁵ Monuments and memorials speak to us from the times of their origins, presenting as consensual and binding the values and beliefs of the nations, institutions, communities, and persons who designed and erected them, including their sufferings, losses, hopes for the future, and founding myths. Monuments and memorials tell us how a community sees itself and what it holds sacred. They dictate what should be remembered and what is better left forgotten; they speak of shared triumph or defeat, and they translate individual grief into public mourning, rendering death comprehensible and meaningful. They offer compensation and reparation to those who have suffered loss, and they determine who is worthy of being labeled a victim, a hero, a martyr, or who shall be branded an enemy. They immortalize, sacralize, and serve as sites of pilgrimage. Monuments and memorials also ennoble and legitimize power, justifying and normalizing the past. They repair breaches by overcoming conflicts in society and they mobilize citizens. They bolster chosen narratives of the past and silence others. They obligate the living as well as future generations to uphold the values and remember and honor the sacrifices of those for whom they claim to speak.

With their alchemy of symbols and signs, words and matter, monuments and memorials possess extraordinary power: they are capable of rewriting history, transforming catastrophe and chaos into order and cohesion. They venerate and heroize, exalting figures and events from the past; but they also accuse and deny. They defame and erase those deemed unworthy of inclusion in their imagined communities. Monuments often declare new beginnings, promising resurrection and renewal. Monuments and memorials unify and tear apart. They lie. Sometimes, as in late twentieth- and early twenty-first-century Germany, monuments and memorials educate and admonish. They mourn, atone, ask forgiveness, and seek reconciliation with their nation's victims.

Above all, monuments and memorials create, stabilize, and eternally fix in stone, steel, glass, and bronze narratives of the past, of shared collective memory, of community and identity. The work of monuments and memorials, supported by social memorial practices such as dedications and memorial rituals, help to shape a people's national identity. French scholar Ernst Renan offers insight into the phenomenon of national identity when he describes the nation as "a soul, a spiritual principle" and argues that "the nation, like the individual, is the culmination of a long history of effort, sacrifice, and of devotion. . . . A heroic past, great figures, glory . . . this is the social capital upon which we base a national idea." As Aleida Assmann further explains, Renan understands the word "soul" in this context to mean "communal memory"—that is, memory consisting of "national memories" of a "shared heritage of glory and regret" as well as "acts of mourning," for "shared suffering unites."[6]

The concept of shared memories is crucial, for the voices of monuments and memorials are the voices of fabricated consensus: a collective "we" imagined and spoken against (usually unnamed but often implied) enemies, be they internal or external. Exclusion is as fundamental to memorialization as inclusion. Walter Benjamin famously declared that "there is no document of civilization which is not at the same time a document of barbarism."[7] Monuments and memorials, too, as cultural artifacts of civilizations, are documents of barbarism: they silence the dissenting voices of those who fail to align with their preferred narratives.

Monuments and memorials do not merely speak of the times in which they were created: they or their traces also tell us stories about the times since their births—their "afterlives," in the words of archaeologist Christopher Evans[8]—during which they were celebrated or vandalized, destroyed or dismantled, permitted to disintegrate and sink into the earth or preserved and renovated, left in situ or relocated to museums, or—as is often the case in Germany—allowed to remain standing but supplemented with new inscriptions or explanatory plaques providing context and disavowing militaristic, nationalistic, or revanchist iconography.

Occasionally, the life story of a monument or memorial mirrors the disruptions and upheavals of its environment, offering a window into the changes and shifts of a country as it descends, for example, from a first attempt at democracy—Germany's post–World War I Weimar Republic—into the totalitarianism of the Third Reich, and finally emerges as the strong democracy and economic powerhouse of today's Federal Republic of Germany. Josef "Jupp" Rübsam's World War I Memorial for the Fallen Soldiers of the Lower-Rhine Füsilier-Regiment Nr. 39 of General Ludendorff[9] is such a memorial. Titled Innere Festigung (Inner Fortification), the memorial was erected and dedicated on Sedantag,[10] September 2, 1928, in Düsseldorf in front of the Tonhalle (the city concert hall, formerly known as the Rheinhalle).[11] Jewish citizens of Düsseldorf as well as Jewish relatives of members of the 39th Fusilier Regiment itself were not invited to the dedication, including those who had helped finance the memorial with donations.

Rübsam's memorial featured two colossal stone soldiers in poses evocative of sphinxes—mythological creatures with the bodies of lions, eagles' wings, and human heads—as depicted in Egyptian and Greek art. The sphinx-soldiers lay prone, shoulder to shoulder, propped up on their elbows, with their massive bodies stretching out behind them. One soldier wore a helmet and the other a head bandage; they gazed forward, presumably toward the front.

Sharply defined cheekbones; straight, wide noses; arched eyebrows; and thick lips lent an exotic, dramatic quality to their aspects. The helmeted soldier's left hand rested on the right hand of his comrade. The men symbolized power and strength (they were men but also more than mere men: superhuman beings with mythological strength like that of the mythological creatures they resembled); they were courageous and loyal

FIGURE 1. Fragments of Innere Festigung, by Jupp Rübsam, Düsseldorf. Photo: Wikipedia Commons.

to their country and each other (they faced the enemy at the front and supported each other); and they were resilient (although one soldier was injured, he continued to fight).

Despite the fact that Rübsam (1896–1978) was a former volunteer soldier in the thirty-ninth regiment and former prisoner of war of the French in North Africa, he was not spared Nazi censure: his memorial was declared "degenerate' (*entartet*) and his career sabotaged. The memorial, to be sure, had its detractors from the beginning, including German nationalist and National Socialist groups who condemned the memorial as "far eastern," "unheroic," "Jewish," and a "mockery of front-line soldiers." Among others, Erich Ludendorff himself, former commander of the thirty-ninth regiment and later participant in several putsch attempts during the Weimar Republic, publicly opposed Rübsam's memorial, repeatedly demanding that his name be removed from the memorial inscription and denigrating the memorial soldiers as "two recumbent savages in field-gray coats" and "ungainly half-animals of inferior race" (*niederrassische Halbtiere*). The memorial, he concluded, revealed a "Jewish worldview" and, as such, was to be disparaged.

Although both Rübsam and his memorial were vigorously defended by the Young Rhineland (Das Junge Rheinland) artists' group, of which Rübsam was a member, Innere Festigung was repeatedly vandalized by right-wing forces and finally removed and stored away by the National Socialists in March 1933. In 1939, a replacement memorial, still standing today (discussed in chapter 6), was erected at the Reeser Platz in Düsseldorf. In 1942, Rübsam's memorial was largely destroyed by a bomb. The career of Rübsam's memorial, however, was not yet over. Two surviving fragments—the head and shoulders of the helmeted soldier and a small segment of the bandaged soldier's torso—were reerected near the memorial's original site after the artist's death in 1978. A new inscription on the brick plinth supporting the fragments identifies them as the remains of the original memorial and notes that they were "newly erected in 1978 as a warning against terror and intolerance on the site of the original memorial"—thereby recasting the former war memorial as a *Mahnmal* (a memorial of admonishment).[12]

A final chapter in the memorial's afterlife came to pass in 2020, when the Art Commission of the City of Düsseldorf, in cooperation with the Film Workshop and Regional Representation 01,[13] presented a three-dimensional digital reconstruction of the original memorial. After downloading the free application "Düsseldorf Augmented," visitors can see an image of the intact memorial in its original location in front of the concert hall and learn about the memorial's history.[14]

From its origins to the present, Innere Festigung has been celebrated, despised, vandalized, dismantled, destroyed, reerected, and reimagined. Now, thanks to twenty-first-century technology, it has been virtually resurrected. Rübsam's memorial recalls Pierre Nora's description of *lieux de mémoire* as objects, sites, or other entities with the "capacity for metamorphosis, an endless recycling of their meaning and an unpredictable proliferation of their ramifications."[15] Endlessly changing, *lieux de mémoire* "escape from history"; they are not restricted to a single moment in time but are rather sites "forever open to the full range of [their] possible significations."[16] Today's visitors to Innere Festigung encounter a *lieu de mémoire*: a century of history condensed and crystallized into a single, pregnant moment and image.

Memorial stories like the one just recounted offer a glimpse into the rich and unpredictable careers of some of the more interesting monuments and memorials in German history. Unlike most studies of German memorials, this book transcends the focus on specific historical periods to illuminate the continuity of symbols and motifs derived from myth, folklore, medieval imagery, Christianity, and national iconography across historical boundaries. It takes, therefore, great leaps in time, venturing from pagan, early Christian, and medieval times to the twentieth and twenty-first centuries, only to return in later chapters to examples of memorials from intervening centuries. The focus of the book on thematic endurance and its transhistorical perspective allows and even encourages a flexibility that in other contexts might be seen as indiscriminate or promiscuous by historians. This approach to memorials does have precedence, however. Renowned German historian Reinhart Koselleck argues that although each individual memorial points to the "social and political circumstances" in which it was created, "the iconography and aesthetic forms of memorials cannot be entirely accounted for by examining the conditions of their coming into being. They have their own history; their repetitions possess different temporal rhythms than those of the events that memorials immortalize."[17] Therefore, Koselleck continues, "it shouldn't surprise us that the arsenal of forms and the iconography of political *Totenmale* (monuments to the dead), unscathed by historical events, remain relatively stable across periods of time all the way into our current century." Details and styles change, of course, but the most insistently recurrent topoi—the victorious or dying soldier who rises again, comforting gods, angels, and saints, mythological animals, crosses, and weapons, and a mixture of iconography and inscriptions gleaned from antiquity and Christianity—reappear again and again.[18]

The idea of enduring motifs raises the question of the transmission of culture through material objects—an issue of central concern to the disciplines of anthropology and archeology as well as memory and cultural studies. Anthropologist Michael Rowlands, drawing on the works of Francis Yates and E. H. Gombrich, explains that the "duration of objects as a mnemonic device" is central to cultural transmission in the European tradition of monumental built environments.[19] Durable objects, Rowlands avers, "assert their own memories" and "possess their own personal trajectories," playing a central role in what Rowlands calls the "work" of memory itself, which is "inseparable from the motive to memorialize."[20] The key to this efficacy of durable objects in the work of remembrance, Rowlands explains, lies in the belief, according to European classical tradition, in the linear nature of cultural memory—a belief still basic to our Western sense of "personal and group integrity and coherence."[21] If, following Platonic tradition, "identity is prefigured in sameness and all future events correspond in their essence to origins," then "identity, truth, authenticity require a return to an original state of being, manifested in the repetition of form" carried out by and in durable material objects.

This repetition of form is fundamental to the conservative transmission of culture from generation to generation; the successful transmission of culture is thus most likely to occur in places where successive generations are "exposed constantly to highly visible examples of material objects invested with authoritative credibility,"[22] for example, in rural areas where cultural life tends to be rooted in traditional mores, beliefs, and rituals to a greater degree than in urban ones. Monuments and memorials that point to an original state of being—for example, those resurrecting or otherwise recalling prehistoric monumental objects, as discussed in the first section of this book—reinforce this sense of the linear nature of memory and identity rooted in origins.

It is crucial to add at this point a few caveats. As Aleida Assmann has pointed out, nations—like other collectives—"do not 'have' a memory; rather, they 'make' one with the assistance of memorial signs and symbols."[23] In arguing for cultural continuity in German memorialization, I do not reify German memory and consciousness as fixed and objective; nor do I subscribe to the idea of an innate, essential *Germanentum* (Germanness) or *deutsches Wesen* (German being). I am, however, arguing that select cultural symbols and motifs, including myths of nature and origins, concepts of sacrifice, and ideas of atonement and penance endure through time, and that they do so thanks to the power of material objects to transmit cultural memory and meaning from generation to generation.

To speak of cultural memory is to speak of collective memory—a much-discussed and -debated concept, especially since the 1990s. For Maurice Halbwachs, the influential late nineteenth- and early twentieth-century sociologist, collective memory emerges from social contexts and is embedded in social frameworks: "it is in society that people normally acquire their memories," Halbwachs writes, and "it is also in society that they recall, recognize, and localize their memories."[24] Contributing to the conversation on collective memory, Jay Winter and Emmanuel Sivan define collective remembrance as the "act of gathering bits and pieces of the past, and joining them together in public"[25]—a definition that highlights the role of selection and collaboration in collective remembrance. Stefan Goebel, similarly, in the context of writing about war remembrance in Germany, maintains that collective memory "arose out of a dialogue between high politics and vernacular culture; from a dialogue between agents working within state institutions and civil society,"[26] thereby stressing both the collaborative process of collective memory as well as the diversity of voices (elite and popular, institutional / public and private) that contribute to creating that memory.

As Aleida Assmann further argues, the cultural dimension of memory—the "field of interaction" supported by "signs and media" that helps to "sustain and stabilize biological memory"—is carried and expanded from generation to generation by means of material representations (transferable cultural artifacts such as texts, images, monuments, memorials) and symbolic practices (festivals and rituals). These media of cultural memory possess "stability and duration"; as "carriers of memory" they are "externalized and objectivized" and "can be taken in and appropriated" by members of later generations who play no role in creating the artifacts themselves. The "temporal scope" of such cultural artifacts is thus not limited to a "human lifespan but can potentially be extended indefinitely," conceivably stretching across centuries with the help of institutions that "extend the lifespan of those objects beyond that of finite human individuals, thus securing their long-term validity."[27]

Of course, the endurance of cultural artifacts bearing cultural memory depends on human actors to acknowledge as significant and embrace not only the inherited artifacts themselves but also the cultural identities those artifacts help to shape. The environment that nurtures and preserves the life spans of cultural artifacts is thus the "group that creates its identity by means of these symbols"—a "group that is always engaged in changing, renewing, and revitalizing this cultural pool."[28] Like Rowlands, Assmann stresses the essential role of repetition in the process of stabilizing and transmitting cultural memory across generations. Objects like monuments and memorials "secure transgenerational memory by means of material signs or regular repetition. They offer occasions for later generations to grow into a collective memory" as they are "brought together with living memories and appropriated by these memories. Appropriating this content by freely identifying with it allows the individual to achieve his or her cultural identity"—in this case, an identity as part of a group of people sharing a past history and common future defined in national terms.[29]

OVERVIEW OF CHAPTERS

The first four chapters of this book explore the role of nature and natural forms in German monuments and memorials. The book begins with a chapter focusing on conceptions of the German *Volk* (people or nation) as an autochthonous *Volksgemeinschaft* (ethnic community) with origins in the primordial, primeval forest. Chapter 2 turns to an examination of the German people as a *Waldvolk* (a people of the forest) while exploring the twin concepts defining forests—infinity and eternity—and the auratic, totemic qualities of trees in German folk psychology. Chapter 3 shifts from myths and legends of Germanic forests to actual living monuments: the *Lebensmale* that illustrate the auratic and totemic properties of trees previously discussed. Chapter 4 moves from trees to stones; it explores the role of *Findlinge* (glacial erratics) as memorials and monuments, both those standing alone and those used in a variety of arrangements such as *Hünengräber* (dolmens) and within *Ahnenstätten* (non-Christian cemeteries).

With the next two chapters, the book pivots from natural forms of memorialization to the iconography of sacrifice on German war memorials. Chapter 5 focuses on theories of sacrifice that include ideas of martyrdom, moral debt, myths of sacrifice, and sacrificial ritual in Germanic history, and the meaning of sacrifice in war memorialization in modern Germany. Chapter 6 turns to memorials that demonstrate the symbolism of sacrifice with a focus on how a soldier's sacrifice as an act enabling the rebirth of the nation and redemption of the fatherland is depicted. The final two chapters of the book focus on memorials expressing regret and penance. Chapter 7 considers wayside memorials erected in medieval and early modern Germanic communities to mark and atone for unnatural death, while chapter 8 considers collective rather than individual atonement in both the medieval and early modern as well as modern periods, with a particular focus on post–World War II memorials of atonement and moral reorientation. The book concludes with the argument that monuments and memorials of reorientation present a unique opportunity in German memorialization: they accept responsibility for the past and declare a commitment to democracy and multiculturalism while avoiding the potential pitfalls of a victim-identified memory culture.

Ironically, in order to unpack and understand memory, one does *not* turn to history. Although memory appears to operate in time, its structure is above all symbolic. The time of memory is always a collage of phenomena that may have originated in a certain past—but functions or provides meaning in a pregnant, present moment. This book is attentive, above all, to the dimension of memory by offering a phenomenology of memory without pretending to offer a would-be "objective" history of memorials.

A robust body of scholarly literature already exists on German monuments and memorials and continues to grow. Much of this literature focuses on specific time periods, such as the boom in monument building during the Second Empire,[30] the World War I and Weimar Republic period,[31] the post–World War II and Holocaust era,[32] and the years since Germany's reunification.[33] Other studies concentrate on notable trends in German memorialization, including Stefan Goebel's book on medievalism and World War I memorials, James E. Young's work on countermonuments and memorials, and Stephan Scholz's investigation of memorials to German expellees in the wake of World War II.[34] A third category of scholarly works focus on German memorialization in specific locations: Brian Ladd's architectural study of Berlin as well as books by Bernhard Losch, Hartmut Schmied, and Heinz Köber, which explore memorials and their legends in particular rural regions in Germany, are noteworthy.[35] Finally, a few scholarly studies span vast time periods and regions—Meinhold Lurz's unsurpassed six-volume catalogue and analysis of German war memorials from the early nineteenth-century Wars of Liberation to the memorials of the Federal Republic of Germany is notable—or, in the case of the scholarship of Reinhart Koselleck, offer a comprehensive, theoretical analysis of the European memorial landscape with a focus on the way in which memorials belong to and reflect political culture.[36]

While deeply indebted to these scholars and their seminal works, this book also adds a new and unique voice to the ongoing conversation on German memorialization. Although previous scholarly works, including those already mentioned, analyze the iconography and forms of memorials, treating them as texts that may be read and interpreted within their political and historical contexts to reveal deeper truths about German society and culture, this book is singular in treating as its main subject of investigation the recurring motifs in German memorialization themselves—those motifs, namely, that endure across time. The sources and meanings of these motifs are then pursued beyond the memorials themselves to be traced, found, and uncovered as they appear in the visual arts, myth, literature, and in political, theological, economic, and scientific discourse. It is worth noting that many of the memorials discussed in this book have not often attracted the attention of scholars. Such memorials were not erected as a result of high-profile planning committees of elite citizens cognizant of the eyes of the world on them and soliciting proposals from world famous artists and architects in international competitions; rather, these memorials are often the modest products of local parish and veteran association committees or individual village and town denizens, financed by local fund raising and donations. As such, these memorials more often than not express a conservative perspective as well as traditional beliefs more common to rural than urban areas, although exceptions may also be found.

While the discussions of monuments and memorials within these pages are always carefully grounded in the specific political, social, and cultural contexts in which they were conceived and erected, the memorials examined here also tell a longer, more enduring story of German cultural ideas of death and rebirth, violence and redemption, nature and culture, identity and community. These enduring narratives are transmitted via memorials to new generations; the memorials themselves perform the cultural work of transmission by not only embodying but also creating lasting memory. This book pursues, in short, a balancing act between the general and the specific, the eternal and the contemporary. It paints a portrait of German memorialization in broad strokes that move between centuries and generations. To this end, chapters are arranged around enduring, vivid motifs of forests and trees, ancient communities and sacred groves, *Findlinge* (glacial erratics) and stone circles, raised fists, warrior saints, and praying monks.

The messages of the memorials described in this book transcend specific moments because they are essential to human experience: guilt; regret; sorrow; loss; sacrifice; atonement; debt; the quest for political, social, and cultural unity; the hope for a better future; the dream of an organic, stable, integrated community; and the deep need for the past to make sense. The forms that these concepts, beliefs, and experiences take are shaped by German history and culture; the narratives delineated in this book are German stories, but they are also human stories that will resonate with all of us.

This book, finally, focuses on the visual and visceral qualities of memorials, many of which have not attracted the attention paid to iconic German memorials, such as the Memorial to the Murdered Jews of Europe in Berlin or the famous, behemothic monuments of the Second Empire. At the heart of each discussion of a memorial or monument is a richly detailed description of form and consideration of how the aesthetics of memorials and monuments contribute to their narratives. As such, this book takes the reader on a vivid journey through Germany's memory culture by way of some of its most unusual—and in many cases, forgotten or unknown but abiding—creations.

CHAPTER ONE
The Original German "Volk"
Autochthony and Primal Origins

INTRODUCTION: A MEMORIAL IN EFFELDER

In a small community in Thuringia, deep in the green heart of Germany, stands a great tree carved from stone, its bared roots jutting from a thick trunk beneath billowing foliage. This tree is neither beech nor spruce nor pine—all natural choices for the region—but rather an oak, the original Teutonic tree[1] worshipped by ancient Germanic tribes and honored by Friedrich Hölderlin, Johann Gottfried von Herder, and a myriad of other German writers, philosophers, and poets throughout the ages.

This oak, carved in stone, reaches a height of almost seven feet while resting on a wide base of irregularly shaped boulders. A tombstone-shaped edifice next to the tree bears an inscription that reads: "Nicht nur Bäume haben Wurzeln, auch Menschen brauchen ihre Heimat ("Not only trees have roots; human beings also need their home"). Around these words appear the coats of arms belonging to eight former territories from which Germans and ethnic Germans (*Volksdeutsche*) were expelled as a result of World War II. Variegated in shape, size, and color, the stones arranged in a heap before the oak suggest a ritual site—reminiscent, perhaps, of the burial mounds that according to scholars of the Viking Age served as a dwelling and resting place for the gods.[2]

A nearby plaque mirrors the tombstone marker with its displayed coats of arms but also informs us: This memorial stone was dedicated by the Federation of Expellees [*Bund der Vertriebenen*], Eichsfeld Chapter, on May 5, 1996. The circle in front of the memorial contains 229 stones from thirteen different regions of expulsion, laid in remembrance and as a warning. Three years after its dedication, a document was placed in the memorial's foundation calling for the right to one's homeland and for just treaties for Germany and for Germans. This revanchist response followed the German-Polish Border Treaty of November 1990, which finalized under international law the Oder-Neiße border of the earlier Treaty of Warsaw (1970). A perimeter of plain paving stones encircling the heap of stones creates two discrete spaces: the sacred mound of relics harvested from Germany's former eastern territories and, beyond the boundary wall of stones, the profane landscape of present-day Effelder, Germany.

The Effelder memorial to the expellees stands at the Roman Catholic Saint Alban Church (known as the *Eichsfelder Dom*) in the small community of Effelder within the district of Eichsfeld. A festive atmosphere marked the memorial's dedication on May 5, 1996, led by Father Borkowski and Pastor Opitz and attended by local political and church representatives. Father Borkowski's sermon on the fate of the German expellees received great acclaim and was followed by a concert.[3] Eight hundred Catholics and Protestants attended this community event—an impressive number considering that the town of Effelder itself, as of 2008, had a population of less than fifteen hundred people. The Effelder memorial is no mere passive monument: it was designed to play a role in civic life and to serve as the site for observing *Tag der Heimat* (Homeland Day), a day of remembrance for German expellees from the east. Homeland Day was first observed in 1950 in West Germany[4] and continues to be celebrated every year throughout Germany on the first Sunday of September. Each year, the *Bund der Vertriebenen* (Federation of Expellees), the organizer of Homeland Day, declares a new motto. A few examples of mottos from previous years include "Menschenrechte auch für die Deutschen" ("Human rights also for Germans," 1977), "Deutschland geht nicht ohne uns!" ("There is no Germany without us!" 2014), and "Vertreibungen sind Unrecht—gestern wie heute" ("Expulsions are unjust—yesterday as well as today," 2015).

The tree and rock imagery of the Effelder memorial evoke the natural world, but the memorial's imagery moves beyond facile nature metaphors, drawing on the myths of pagan Germanic tribes to create a rich, densely layered narrative of identity, history, and memory. Although images of crosses and other Passion symbols such as crowns of thorns commonly ornament expellee memorials, trees and roots are particularly popular because they evoke two powerful ideas: first, that a natural, organic connection exists between a people and its land, and second, that a group of people may enjoy "a natural right" to a certain piece of land.[5] A memorial stone in the new cemetery of Lingen, a town in Lower Saxony, echoes the symbolism of the Effelder memorial with its depiction of a *Lebensbaum* (tree of life) with exposed roots and coats of arms of former German territories. Similarly, a memorial in Augsburg, Bavaria, in the shape of a tree, dedicated in 1952, stands next to a plaque bearing the inscription: "Was durch Haß getrennt wurde, kann nur durch die Liebe wieder vereint werden. Den Toten des deutschen Ostens zum Gedenken" ("What has been torn asunder by hate can only be reunited through love. Dedicated to the dead of the German East"). Not only images of trees but actual living trees transplanted to towns in Germany from former eastern territories memorialize expellees and lost homelands. In 1952, a willow from Brezg, Poland (previously part of Prussia and later the German Empire), was planted in Goslar, Lower Saxony. This willow serves as a memory tree and symbol of loyalty to the lost homeland of Brezg. A Pomeranian linden, finally, has stood since 1975 at Ostlandplatz in Itzehoe, Schleswig-Holstein. A memorial stone, added in 1976, declares: "Recht auf die Heimat—ein Menschenrecht" ("The right to one's home: a human right").[6]

It is perhaps surprising for a book focusing on German memorialization across the centuries to begin with a discussion of the memorial in Effelder—a memorial erected only recently, at the turn of the twenty-first century. As this chapter progresses, however, it will become clear that this choice serves to emphasize the continuity of German memorial culture and the ideas and concepts on which this culture is based—ideas and concepts present in the very earliest articulations of Germanic identity and nationhood as well as the most recent. This chapter offers, in effect, a window into one of the most complex and richest sources of German memorial culture—the myth of a Germanic primal origin and its ties to the forest.

Forests and trees, like the tree depicted in the Effelder memorial, have long served in German folk psychology and cultural discourse as a canvas on which ideas about origins, community—the *Volk*—and an essential "Germanness" (*Germanentum*) are projected. Germanic myth, ritual, literature, and art have for centuries articulated a mystical bond between the Germanic peoples and their natural landscape. This chapter traces the threads of this conception from its premodern imaginings up to its twenty-first-century expression. This will serve not only as an explanation for the forms of memorial objects but will also elucidate ideological-political, religious, and militaristic implications.

Memorials embodying the values attached to forests invite a bifocal analytical approach. The materialist, causal, theorizing approach looks at economy, ecology, and even military history. A discursive approach interprets memorials as objects of mystery, magic, and cosmology. Both approaches will serve this chapter, which begins with a consideration of Germanic pagan rituals and myths of Germanic origin. Autochthonous beliefs linking the Germanic "race" to the primeval forest, as we shall see, have led to both positive and negative outcomes in German history. We shall then consider the concept of the *Volksgemeinschaft* (ethnic community) through the lens of Anthony Smith's writings on the "ethnie" and nostalgia for kin and territory. Nostalgia for an idealized Germanic past has often been accompanied by autochthonous and racist sentiments, as witnessed, for example, in *Heimat* discourse and the *Heimat* movement. After discussions of *Heimat* discourse and the sacred nature of the tree in Germanic folk psychology, the chapter turns to the seminal, nation-building creation myth of German history: the Battle of the Teutoburg Forest. This discussion leads to the final two sections of the chapter: rituals of sacrifice, including the myth of Odin and the cosmic ash tree Yggdrasil, and the metaphysical significance of trees in both pagan and modern German culture.

GERMANIC PAGAN RITUALS AND MYTHS OF GERMANIC ORIGIN

Early Germanic Pagan Practice

The Germanic peoples were Christianized quite early by the Romans, mainly during the third and fourth centuries, and by the end of the sixth century most Germanic peoples had adopted Christian practice without, however, wholly abandoning their pagan religious practices and beliefs. Early conversion in addition to the Germanic migrations (375–568 CE) and the fact that pagans left behind few written records helps to explain why most historical knowledge about pagan practice comes to us from Scandinavia, where paganism survived into the tenth, eleventh, and twelfth centuries.[7] The most detailed descriptions of Germanic pagan ritual reach us, therefore, not from the pens and parchment of the pagans themselves but rather through the gaze of outsiders, namely, through classical texts in Greek or Latin, often composed by Christian monks. The cultural perspectives and agendas of these observers influenced their views on the Germanic tribes and their religious practices. The famous text *Germania* (98 CE), written by Roman historian and politician Tacitus, and Caesar's *De bello Gallico* (58–50 BCE) are prime examples. Other texts on ancient Germanic life were composed by medieval chroniclers such as Thietmar of Merseburg (975–1018) and Adam of Bremen (before 1050–1081/1085). Additional sources on pagan practice, and the best sources on the Indo-European worship of sacred trees, are found in the descriptions of pagan Norse mythology from the thirteenth century—the *Elder* or *Poetic Edda* and the *Younger* or *Prose Edda*, the latter written by Icelandic historian and poet Snorri Sturluson.[8]

A Myth of Primal Origins

Particularly valuable for our understanding of pagan Germanic culture are the writings of Roman historian Tacitus, who traces the origins of the Germanic *Volk* back to the forested groves of the primeval Germanic landscape. As told in the myths of ancient ballads, the primeval ancestor of the Germans, the god Tuisto,[9] sprung directly from the earth into being. Tuisto begot a son named Mannus, who in turn begot three sons, whose names are borne by three categories of peoples: the Ingaevones, who dwelt by the ocean; the Herminones, who dwelt in the middle country, and the Instaevones, the remainder of the Germanic peoples. Tuisto and his son Mannus are thus "the fathers and founders" of the German nation.[10] Tacitus also offers a theory of the "original" Germanic race: "a people pure, and independent, and resembling none but themselves" with "eyes stern and blue, yellow hair, [and] huge bodies." This race, Tacitus explains, is "nowise mixed with different nations," having never "mingled by inter-marriage" thanks to a topography "hideous and rude, under a rigorous climate, dismal to behold or to manure (cultivate)."[11] In Tacitus's depiction, an inhospitable climate reveals itself as a curious kind of blessing for having protected the original German *Volk* from adulteration.

According to this autochthonous folk narrative, the Germanic *Volk* is an "original" *Volk*, rooted in the soil from which it emerged and unique among peoples. In a passage from *Germania* describing a custom followed by Germanic tribes when entering a sacred grove where human sacrifice was performed, Tacitus emphasizes the curious rituals and autochthonous beliefs of the tribes: "No one enters it otherwise than bound with ligatures, thence professing his subordination and meanness, and the power of the Deity there. If he fall down, he is not permitted to rise or be raised, but grovels along upon the ground. And of all their superstition, this is the drift and tendency; that from this place the nation drew their original, that here God, the supreme Governor of the world, resides, and that all things else whatsoever are subject to him and bound to obey him."[12]

As the birthplace of the Germanic *Volk*, the primeval forest (the *Urwald*) evokes reverence and continues still to this day, in many contexts, to "symbolize Germany's heritage—the stronghold of its cultural origins, of its ancient bonds of community, and of its collective national possession."[13] The Hercynian Forest in particular serves as the imagined site of the Germanic *Volk*'s origin—unimaginably ancient, populated by oaks, and once allegedly stretching, according to Pliny the Elder, from west to east all the way from the Rhine to perhaps as far as the Elbe and across the Danube.[14]

The Germanic Origin Myth in German Cultural History

Tacitus's portrayal of the mythic birth of the German race in the primeval forest has held seductive power over the German popular imagination throughout history, peaking during the late eighteenth, nineteenth, and early twentieth centuries.[15] In the twentieth century, autochthonous beliefs linking the Germanic *Volk* to a primordial forest landscape have been used to nefarious purpose. National Socialists cynically exploited such folk narratives to bolster a racist ideology that labeled "Aryan" Germans as "natural" and thus worthy of belonging to the new German order while "non-Aryan" Germans were judged as "foreign" and excluded. A useful lens for viewing the role of the forest in Nazi ideology is offered by Michael Imort: for the three National Socialist paradigms of *Volk*, race, and *Lebensraum* (living space), Imort correlates the three functions of the forest—as model for the new German *Volksgemeinschaft* (ethnic community), as "indicator of the spatial extent of race," and as a means for acquiring new spaces fit for German settlement.[16]

Representations of the German forest—already coded to signify "German nature" and "German race"—not only helped National Socialists articulate racist ideas of "Germanness" and "otherness" but also helped ready the German population to wage battle against the inferior "other" and justify eastward expansion.[17]

Imagining the forest as a site of sacred origin has been used for productive as well as destructive purposes, however, by helping to garner support for nature preservation groups. The writings of conservative folklorist and social theorist Wilhelm Heinrich Riehl (1823–1897) on the forest created a link between nationalism and environmental preservation, exercising a profound influence on Germany's *Naturschutz* and *Heimatschutz* (nature protection and homeland protection) movements.[18] While true that Germany's earliest landscape preservation groups, emerging in the 1880s, were largely motivated by nationalism in response to French occupation, such preservation groups were also motivated by middle-class anxiety over urbanization and industrialization, and by the fear that a disfigured natural landscape would lead to moral decline and a loss of German national character. In this fear we glimpse a perceived analogy between the health of the German peoples and the health of the German forests (to be discussed further in chapter 2). Trees in particular were perceived as "'national monuments' that anchored the organic foundation of national identity," while forests in general bore marks of the "primordial homeland" settled by the original Germanic tribes.[19]

THE VOLKSGEMEINSCHAFT AND GERMANIC ETHNIE

The Concept of the Ethnie

In Germanic folk psychology, myths of origin and *Volk* merge into a single nostalgic vision of an organic, coherent, ethnically integrated community (the *Volksgemeinschaft*). Our understanding today of the ethnic dimension of community owes a great debt to Anthony Smith, who describes the ethnic community, or *ethnie*, as largely mythic and symbolic, and residing in a "quartet of myths, memories, values, and symbols."[20] The dimensions of the ethnie include a collective name, a common myth of descent (a myth of origin), a shared history (even if this history is not entirely based in fact), a distinctive, shared culture (language, customs, folklore, food, religion), an association with a specific territory (a sacred habitat and homeland to which a people may symbolically return), and a sense of solidarity.[21]

Dimensions of the ethnie are evoked by the earliest monuments of European prehistory from the Neolithic period: namely, a common myth of descent and origin and an association with a sacred territory and homeland. These early monuments incorporated circular shapes, similar to the circle of sacred stones at the Effelder memorial, emphasizing the monument's role "as the centre of a dispersed community" and linking the living community to a mythical settlement once inhabited by founding ancestors. Such monuments offered prehistoric communities, in the words of archaeologist Richard Bradley, a "testimony of attachment" both to the mythical origin of the community and to the contemporary community. At sites such as these, history and myth merge, creating a connection to the past concretized and intensified through the ancestral relics deposited there. A stone circle transforms an encircled object into a monument, declaring it the center of the world—an axis mundi or universal pillar—linking the three cosmic regions of underworld, earth, and heaven.[22] Encircling an object with stones in pagan practice thus created not only a boundary but an entirely new world apart—a discrete world possessing a complex and sacred geography.[23]

Nostalgia for Kinship and Territory

Characteristic of the myths, memories, values, and symbols associated with an ethnie is the experience of nostalgia. Conceptions of the forest in the Germanic folk tradition as the setting of a once ideal community imbue the forest with a strong feeling of nostalgia in the German imagination. This nostalgia ebbs and flows in resonance with societal, economic, and political realities. Nostalgia, explains Smith, appears in two forms: nostalgia for kinship (the *Volksgemeinschaft*) and nostalgia for territory (the sacred habitat and homeland). In Germany, nostalgia for kinship has often manifested as the desire for a coherent and unified ethnic community (epitomized in the concept of the original *Volk*). Such myths of community are often tied to geography; they locate a people's origins in a "mysterious and primordial time" when forefathers occupied ancestral terrain at once mysterious, remote, and inaccessible.[24] Nostalgia for territory in Germany has predominantly appeared, as already discussed, in the idealization of the forest as the *Volk*'s site of origin;

but rivers, too, have effectively evoked nostalgia in German history. The Rhine River, for example, inspired the nineteenth-century literary and aesthetic movement of Rhine Romanticism, which included influential artists and writers such as Clemens Brentano, Caspar David Friedrich, and Heinrich Heine.[25]

Nostalgic efforts to resurrect traditional Germanic folk culture—whether motivated by political, social, or cultural interests—have repeatedly turned to Germany's arboreal, medieval past to find a model for a unique culture rooted in a singular soil. Jacob Grimm's *Deutsche Mythologie* (*Teutonic Mythology*, 1835) and Jacob and Wilhelm Grimm's *Altdeutsche Wälder* (*Old German Forests*, 1813), a journal of medieval poetry, legends, songs, and fables, are two examples of such efforts. Indeed, *Altdeutsche Wälder* "explicitly linked German forests to the genesis and continuity of authentic German culture," thereby addressing the need for a common cultural heritage.[26] The Grimm brothers' seven-volume collection of local forest laws (*Weisthümer*, 1840–78), meanwhile, "sought to resurrect . . . the eclipsed spirit and laws of the German people."[27] It was the Grimm brothers' collection of fairy tales, however, titled *Kinder- und Hausmärchen* (*Children's and Household Tales*), published in two volumes in 1812 and 1815, that most successfully preserved German folk culture. Through these tales, many of which are set in the forest, the Grimm brothers sought to capture the "pure" voice of the German *Volk* and preserve this voice in writing as oral storytelling traditions were disappearing due to urbanization and industrialization.[28] For the Grimm brothers, the "most natural and pure forms of culture—those which held the community together—were linguistic and were to be located in the past."[29]

This heady, nostalgic mixture of ethnicity, culture, and landscape with potent autochthonous undertones also served a political purpose by transcending the often-disappointing reality confronting the not-yet-unified German states in the years leading up to 1871. It comes as no surprise that nostalgic visions of kin and territory united the embrace of vernacular culture and the veneration for the forest that characterized German Romanticism during the late eighteenth and early nineteenth centuries. Indeed, the German Romantic idolized "distant realms" and "native customs," while longing for "a newer and more virile Germanism" reminiscent of old Germanic culture.[30]

Autochthony and Racism

The longing for a lost, idealized Germanic community and culture has at times inspired indulgence in whimsical activities with autochthonous undertones: a group of students at the University of Göttingen, for example, formed a Hainbund (Grove League) in 1772 and spent a night in an ancient oak grove, their hands linked together with garlands made of oak leaves.[31] In contrast, insidious, even toxic consequences of such nativist imaginings manifest in ideas of purity in the context of national identity, seen, for example, in the conviction that French "civilization" was inferior to pure, organic German "culture." Nostalgia tinged with autochthonous undertones has assumed in German history infamous racist dimensions as well. The reverence for the forest and opposition to deforestation promoted by Wilhelm Riehl, mentioned earlier, went hand in hand with a deep hostility toward modernism and urbanism as well as a tendency toward antisemitism, encapsulated in the image of the rootless, unnatural, alien "wandering Jew."

Heimat Discourse and the Heimat Movement

The pairing of ideologies such as antiurbanism with antisemitism and nationalism with environmental preservation is typical of *Heimat* discourse—a discourse of beliefs and values concerning ideas of home, homeland, and issues of identity and belonging. *Heimat*—a notoriously difficult word to translate—may not be rendered simply as "home" or "homeland," although the word may be used to refer to both of these; rather, *Heimat* evokes emotionally charged images of a nourishing and sacred piece of earth possessing rich deposits of memory, identity, and tradition that in turn shape national and local character.

Heimat discourse has politically conservative origins in Germany but has taken a variety of forms throughout history; as such, it has not always been tied to an exclusively reactionary or xenophobic outlook. Rather, a range of interpretations and meanings have adhered to the concept, including regional and pluralistic perspectives.[32] At the heart of the *Heimat* movement was the belief that landscape reveals a people's unique memory and culture, and that collective identity is deeply impacted by environment.[33] Within *Heimat* discourse, the concept of the "natural" and what qualifies as "natural" has shifted dramatically over the years to resonate with changing political realities.[34]

During the late nineteenth and early twentieth centuries, the *Heimat* movement attempted to unite historical, preservationist, cultural, and environmentalist groups coming together to protect the German homeland. Increasingly during this time, *Heimat* discourse became a convenient means for attacking cultural modernism and mass society as well as particular groups of people as "unnatural" and antithetical to the "authentic" Germanic being and way of life. Such discourse fed the cancer of *völkisch* (populist, nationalist, racist) ethnonationalism and xenophobia; indeed, this *völkisch*, right-wing aspect of *Heimat* discourse dominated during World War I and the subsequent years of the Weimar Republic as environmental politics increasingly radicalized.[35]

Aspects of *Heimat* discourse together with kinship and territorial nostalgia and concepts of ethnic and cultural purity would soon become key aspects of National Socialist ideology, helping drive the Germans eastward in quest of *Lebensraum*. Members of early landscape conservation groups would later become some of the more passionate supporters of the *Blut und Boden* (blood and soil) mysticism of National Socialism, an ideology neatly combining kinship and territorial nostalgia in its quest to create an organic German *Volksgemeinschaft* as the basis for the German nation.[36] The enthusiasm among members of landscape conservation groups for National Socialism has unfortunately burdened the German environmental movement with "an ambiguous political and moral legacy."[37] At least in theory, no German government took the protection of the German forests more seriously than the Third Reich.[38] In practice, however, National Socialist development projects such as the *Autobahn* as well as rearmament, land reclamation, and dam building initiatives caused massive environmental damage.[39]

Nostalgia rooted in the concept of *Heimat* and evoking a lost, idealized community has characterized German folk psychology for centuries. Because the German forest of the Middle Ages offers an ideal setting for romanticized images of a traditional folk culture, it presents itself as a resonant symbol of the unique cultural identity of an imagined, homogenous German *Volk*. The longing in German folk psychology for a unified community reveals a primordial "trauma of division"—but like all nostalgia, this nostalgia expresses a longing for a past that never was. "It is not an exaggeration to say," Robert Pogue Harrison writes, "that the myth of a lost unity holds sway over modern German history as a whole . . . [it] could be characterized as a prolonged attempt at cultural, national, social, spiritual, or racial reunification."[40] At the heart of these myths of an ideal Germanic community stands the unified *Volk*, at home in the primeval forest.

Born from the Forest: The Germanic Volk

In Germanic folk narratives, the power of the *Volk* lies in its inherent nature as a *Waldvolk* (people of the forest), born from the forest and carrying within it the forest's powers of strength, rebirth, and renewal. Wilhelm Heinrich Riehl describes the forest as the very soul of Germany and the secret to the German future.[41] In contrast to the French, Italians, and English, who, according to Riehl, had squandered their futures by taming their forests into fields and meadows, the Germans would continue to draw energy and power from their woods.[42] The Effelder memorial, discussed earlier, relies on two natural forms to communicate its message: stones and an oak tree. Stones evoke ragged mountain ranges and wild, rocky landscapes. In Germanic pagan practice, as in other pagan communities, stones were sacred and embodied the power of place. Early anthropologist James Frazer describes a pagan custom of swearing an oath on a stone—a practice based in part on the belief that a stone magically lends its strength to an oath.[43] It was trees in particular, however, that pagan communities invested with sacred power.

The Sacred Nature of Trees

With their tall, vertical stance, cyclical existence, and myth-like longevity, trees were ideal symbols for the human, natural, and divine realms. Some trees live not only hundreds but even thousands of years, presenting an image of eternity and timelessness and figuring prominently in creation and origin myths from around the world.[44] Believing that trees harnessed natural and divine power, pagans used trees both as the stage and as actors in their theaters of religious practice. As embodiments of the sacred, trees were imagined as the site of what historian of religion Carole Cusack calls the "primeval hierophany"[45]—a concept based on Mircea Eliade's well-known description of the hierophany as a break or rupture in the homogeneity of space, through which the sacred is made manifest. As Eliade argues, "Every sacred space implies a hierophany, an irruption of the sacred that results in detaching a territory from the surrounding cosmic milieu and making it qualitatively different."[46]

Trees in Germanic Pagan Practice

Invested with sacred meaning, trees were essential to the rituals of Germanic tribes. Germanic pagans, like other pagan peoples, believed that trees revealed profound truths about the nature of the world and the universe; they worshipped trees as well as the deities they believed to be dwelling within. The belief that divine spirits dwelt within trees, however, as Ken Dowden has explained, was merely a way of accommodating tree worship into a religious world that was increasingly shifting toward a worship of personal divinities.[47] Ancient Germanic tribes, in other words, did not need to believe that gods dwelt within trees in order to find the trees sacred and worthy of worship.

Germanic tribes also viewed trees as oracles and as the means for communicating with divine beings.[48] In *Germania*, Tacitus describes the divining rituals of tribes involving the manipulation of twigs from fruit trees,[49] while pyres of particular woods such as oak, beech, pine, and juniper were used for cremating important tribal figures, reaffirming the bonds between the deceased and the forest.[50] As a tribute to their power and sacredness, trees were often bedecked by Germanic tribes with tokens of worship and respect,[51] and in German tradition trees have long been believed to possess the power to safeguard and protect: guardian trees, for example, once commonly planted beside dwellings (a practice that continued into the nineteenth century), safeguarded families under the cover of their spreading branches.[52] Such practices have not disappeared entirely: the custom of hanging votive offerings with *vitta* (woolen bands like tinsel) on trees to mark their sanctity finds its echo in the practice of modern-age Christians who decorate trees with images of the Virgin Mary.[53]

Trees, finally, have long been imagined to be a source of power by pagan as well as modern-day Germans because they appear to embody not only natural but also human and divine characteristics. Symbolic of the divine thanks to their long lives and periods of rebirth, the tree is invested with the powers of life, regeneration, and self-renewal. The growth patterns of trees, furthermore, have provided observers with a sense of directionality that is at once irreversible and humanizing: trees are thus "vehicles of power" thanks to the symbolism of their natural growth.⁵⁴ The correspondence between the human and the arboreal may be seen in the custom of using tree forms for mapping kinship and tribal relations—a custom still practiced today in the form of the family tree.⁵⁵ "From the family tree to the tree of knowledge, from the tree of life to the tree of memory," writes Robert Pogue Harrison, "forests have provided an indispensable resource of symbolization in the cultural evolution of humankind."⁵⁶

THE MYTHIC BATTLE OF THE TEUTOBURG FOREST

One legend above all others locates the origin of the Germanic *Volk* in the primeval forest: the legend of the Roman soldier Arminius (later known as Hermann the Cherusker), famous for leading the ancient Germanic tribes in uprising against Varus Quinctilius and his Roman legions in the Teutoburg Forest in 9 CE.⁵⁷ Tacitus describes this famous battle in his *Annals*, a history of the Roman Empire from the reign of Tiberius to Nero. Although not the first account of the battle, Tacitus's version would become "the first decisive literary passage that turned the conqueror of 9 AD into an immortal hero."⁵⁸

The Battle of the Teutoburg Forest and Nation Building

The legend of Arminius's revolt against Varus possesses all the elements of an immortal myth: Arminius was born to a Germanic tribal (Cherusci) chief named Sigimer, who had been captured by the Romans. Like Moses, Arminius was raised by strangers but returned to his people to liberate them from oppression. Tacitus paints a portrait of Arminius—a Roman citizen and traitor, actually, who lured three Roman legions into an ambush ending in extermination—as the paradigmatic German hero not only for his defeat of Varus but for his triumph over the political tyranny of Rome. With his victory,⁵⁹ Arminius allegedly prevented the Romanization of the Germanic tribes, and the myth of the Battle of the Teutoburg Forest thus evolved into the tale of a nascent people fighting for its sovereignty against foreign oppressors and became a founding myth of the German nation.

Mythologization, explains Aleida Assmann, is one of the two paths to nation building.⁶⁰ Nations require a "collective will that is oriented toward the future," but this "will must be strengthened by the construction of a collective past. It is this collective memory that makes the present meaningful as one stage in the course of a necessary and long-term development. The potential for the national memory of a historical event to act as a *Mythomotorik* (mythomotor) lies precises in this temporal orientation: it endows the present with orientation and meaning insofar as it is revealed to be an intermediate stage of a motivating narrative that includes the past and the future." The nineteenth century, Assmann concludes—the age in which, it is important to note, the popularity of the myth of the Battle of the Teutoburg Forest peaked—was the age in which national myths emerged "that appropriated the past to the present by focusing on particular moments that [supported] an identity-constructing narrative."[61] The Battle of the Teutoburg Forest is such a nation myth: one that acts as a *Mythomotorik* in the development of Germany's national identity.

Other ancient accounts of the Battle of the Teutoburg Forest vary from Tacitus's telling by portraying Arminius in less glowing terms. Roman scholar Velleius Paterculus (*Compendium of Roman History*, 2.117.2–120.5), for example, describes Arminius's opponent Varus as a well-intentioned man lacking in judgment, "slow in mind as he was in body," and Arminius himself as treacherous although "brave in action and alert in mind, possessing an intelligence quite beyond the ordinary barbarian." Varus, although forewarned by his loyal chief Segestes, was, in the words of Velleius, blinded by fate and destined for a reversal of fortune. Lulled into a sense of security by the scheming Germanic tribes, he and his legions presented an easy target.[62] Varus, furthermore, is described as possessing "more courage to die than to fight" and as following the example of his father and grandfather before him by committing suicide in the face of disaster.[63]

Indeed, so badly prepared were the Romans in this account that the conflict was more slaughter than battle: "Hemmed in by forests and marshes and ambuscades, [the Roman army] was exterminated almost to a man by the very enemy whom it had always slaughtered like cattle."[64] A report by Roman historian Florus (*Epitome of Roman History* 2.30 [4.12.29–39]) describes the battle as surpassing all others in its cruelty and carnage, with the barbarians putting out the Romans' eyes, cutting off their hands, and sewing one man's mouth shut after having removed his offending tongue.[65]

An account of the battle by Roman historian Cassius Dio (*Roman History*, 56.19–22.2) presents a unique perspective: in Dio's telling, the forest terrain itself actively supports the Germanic tribes in battle. Within the "impenetrable forests" the tribes reveal themselves to be "enemies instead of subjects," emerging from the "densest thickets" to surround the Romans on all sides. The surface of the mountains is described as uneven and broken by ravines, and the trees, tall and huddled close together, block the Romans' passage. The forest floor is slippery due to heavy rains, and tree roots and logs jut forth treacherously from the ground, tripping up the Romans and causing them to collide with the trees, whose upper branches are constantly breaking off and crashing down on the hapless soldiers.[66] Dio's narrative thus presents trees and roots, logs and forest floor as brothers-in-arms, conspiring with the tribes to trap, confuse, and cripple the enemy.

Ancient historians as well as modern German historians such as Karl-Wilhelm Welwei, Theodor Mommsen, Leopold von Ranke, and Dieter Timpe have debated not only the facts of the battle but its actual historical significance as well. Such doubts, however, are merely of a factual nature, for "no doubts remain about the legendary or mythical aspects of how such facts came to be interpreted."[67] Throughout the ages, in times of need, the Arminius myth has repeatedly returned—a mythic Barbarossa emerging from his sleep in the Kyffhäuser hills to rescue his threatened countrymen.[68]

The Battle of the Teutoburg Forest in German History

The myth of the Battle of the Teutoburg Forest has endured for centuries because it is much more than a tale of bravery and victory: it is a myth of creation—*cultural* creation—in which the forest, a primordial substance, is presented as the chaos from which German civilization emerged. The Arminius myth combines several elements valuable to German folk narratives: first, the battle took place in the ancient Germanic forest, locating the crucial act of tribal / national independence at the site of the imagined origin of the *Volk* itself. Second, the leader of the uprising, Arminius, was an original member of the *Volk* as the son of a Cherusci chief but also a man at home in Roman military culture, intimately versed in the ways and customs of the enemy. Finally, Arminius's triumph allegedly saved the tribes not merely from death or slavery but also from collective, cultural obliteration by preserving the unique Germanic ethnie.

Ulrich von Hutten

A few examples from German history illustrate the salience and flexibility of the Arminius myth as well as its ideological, national, and political implications. German scholar and Protestant reformer Ulrich von Hutten (1488–1523) declared Arminius to be the father of the German nation and "first German hero" who offered proof of a Germanic national tradition and consciousness, but von Hutten also interpreted Arminius's rebellion against Rome as a symbol of the "German struggle against the Roman papacy."[69] In his dialogue *Arminius*, Hutten goes so far as to describe Tacitus being summoned by the god Mercury in order to appear before the judge Minos in the pagan underworld and testify that Arminius was a superior warrior to Scipio, Hannibal, and Alexander the Great.[70]

Konrad Celtis

Other examples from German history illustrate not only the resilience of the myth but also the power of Tacitus's characterization of the ancient Germanic tribes in his ethnographic tract *Germania*, a text that helped give birth to the myth of Germanic ethnic and cultural purity.[71] During the fifteenth century, Tacitus's portrait of Germanic tribal life exerted considerable influence on German-language culture thanks to the efforts of the Franconian Renaissance scholar and poet Konrad Celtis (1459–1508). Celtis's reception of Tacitus popularized the text among German humanists, who found the text useful for bolstering support of a German Reformation. Celtis used the *Germania*, in short, as evidence that the German-speaking lands differed in their very essence from Latin Europe, drawing on Tacitus's characterizations of the ancient Germanic tribes to strengthen his argument that the Germanic future did not lie under the papal yoke.

In his sensationalistic portrait in *Germania*, Tacitus depicts the primordial Germanic tribes as savages dwelling in swamps and woods, clad only in animal skins or tree bark. Tacitus also invested these "ferocious primitives," however, with "natural nobility through their instinctive indifference to the vices that had corrupted Rome: luxury, secrecy, property, sensuality, [and] slavery."[72] Tacitus portrayed the Germanic tribes, moreover, as pure and honest, virile and self-reliant—offering a moral reproach and alternate life model for his fellow Romans, whom he judged as decadent and corrupted by overindulgence in pleasure.[73] But Tacitus was not only seeking to admonish his own flawed society; he was also, perhaps, providing justification for Rome's shift from expansionism to fixed imperial boundaries.[74] Indeed, Tacitus describes the German lands in *Germania* as *informem terris*—shapeless and dismal[75]—a description hardly encouraging of further Roman incursion.

Drawing on Tacitus's complimentary characterizations of the tribes, Celtis argued that present-day Germans should seek the roots of their unique identity in their pagan past and their land's great forests.[76] Just as Tacitus used his *Germania* to critique his decadent coevals, so did Celtis, centuries later, use the *Germania* to critique the decadent "Italian sensuality" of the south.[77] The *Germania*'s portrayal of an ancient Germanic people with a distinct culture, system of laws, and religious practices also supported early nationalism by equating "Germanic" with "German," thereby allowing nationalists to claim "two thousand years of Germanic *cum* German history."[78] Daniel Casper von Lohenstein of Breslau followed this pattern with his unfinished seventeenth-century work on Arminius, which describes the Roman empire, against which his hero battled, in such a way as to reveal that he was really writing, in code, about the French—namely, the empire of Louis XIV (1638–1715), which had expanded to the extent that German princes briefly bonded together in unity against the Sun King.[79]

Arminius from the Nineteenth Century to Today
German writers resurrected the Arminius myth during the period of Romanticism as well as an effective response to the military supremacy and perceived cultural superiority of the French during the Napoleonic Wars. In the face of French aggression, Arminius offered the German states an urgently needed collective identity as a *Kulturnation* (cultural nation) instead of as a political one.[80] After the defeat of Napoleon at Waterloo in 1815, the Arminius myth transformed into a story about German political unity, and in the years after German unification in 1871, the myth—now of interest mainly to Prussian Protestants—shifted its focus from external (French) enemies to internal—Catholic, Social Democrat, and Jewish—ones.[81]

After Germany's demoralizing defeat in World War I, Arminius reemerged once more: this time as the unifier of the defeated German people. In 1925, the Deutsche Turnerschaft (German Gymnastic Federation) organized the first Hermannslauf (Hermann Race) to Detmold, North

Rhine–Westphalia, site of the great Hermann Monument (Hermannsdenkmal) by Joseph Ernst von Bandel, dedicated in August 1875. The massive Hermann Monument features an imposing bronze statue of Hermann in winged helmet, standing on the cupola of a circular temple with ten columns and holding aloft his sword. The monument stands on the mountain peak Grotenburg within the Teutoburg Forest and faces not south, in the direction of Italy, as might be expected, but rather west toward France. Excerpts from Tacitus's *Annals* and inscriptions commemorating the Wars of Liberation against Napoleon and subsequent wars with France in 1870 and 1871 appear in niches between the pillars of the temple. These inscriptions not only equate Hermann with Kaiser Wilhelm I but also compare the ancient Germanic tribes' battle against Varus with Germany's wars against France. Hermann's sword, twenty-three feet long and weighting over twelve hundred pounds, bears the words "Deutsche Einigkeit Meine Staerke / Meine Staerke Deutschlands Macht" ("German unity is my strength / My strength is Germany's might") and his shield reads, "Treufest" ("Always faithful").[82] As a symbol for the freedom and unity of the German people, the Hermann Monument is one of the few national monuments of its period that was not initiated by a monarch or state institution but rather by the artist and funded through donations. As such, it may be seen as a true reflection of the will of the populace and expression of the *Volk*.[83]

The Hermannslauf served as a reminder to modern Germans that they were the "sons of their fatherland" who could master their past and future only if they remained "united and true."[84] The race, it is worth noting, still takes place each spring on the last Sunday of April, but is now an athletic event purged of politics; during the run, thousands of Germans run just over thirty-one kilometers from the Hermann Monument to Sparrenberg Castle in Bielefeld.

Unsurprisingly, National Socialists, too, hurried to appropriate the figure of Arminius, fetishizing classic dramas about the mythic battle by Heinrich von Kleist (1808) and Christian Dietrich Grabbe (1838) as well as promoting new texts by Paul Albrecht and Bodo Ernst that valorized the ancient hero.[85] The Hermann Monument itself became a central site for Nazi pageantry, serving as the backdrop for rallies, processions, and speeches, and appearing on Nazi posters and placards.[86] After World War II, during the 1950s, the monument became a symbol for West German hopes for future German unification.[87] Only the far right, the ultranationalist *Nationaldemokratische Partei Deutschlands* (National Democratic Party of Germany, NPD) resurrected Arminius as a symbol of *völkisch* ideology, while other nationalist groups used the Hermann Monument as the site for their secret meetings under the cloak of darkness.[88] In East Germany, the Battle of the Teutoburg Forest retained a certain amount of value as a demonstration of how a superior society with primitive communist ideals triumphed over an imperialistic empire.[89]

During the last few decades, Arminius's presence has persisted mainly through his monumental form in Detmold, no longer fomenting nationalistic aspirations but rather attracting tourists and starring in advertisements—helping to sell Salzgitter steel and Zimbo sausage and, in 1999, donning a giant soccer jersey emblazoned with the name of a local beer—Herforder Pils. The year 2009 marked the two-thousand-year anniversary of the Battle of the Teutoburg Forest, a historic milestone celebrated at the Kalkriese Museum and Park in Bramsche, district of Osnabrück with a retrospective and historical reenactments. Still today, Arminius lingers in the consciousness of the far right, as witnessed in the name of the small ultranationalist German party ARMINIUS-Bund des deutschen Volkes (Arminius-League of the German People). This anti-abortion, anti-immigration, anti–European Union (in its current form) and anti-Euro party founded in 2013 is sufficiently radical that it calls for the dissolution of Germany's Grundgesetz (Basic Law for the Federal Republic of Germany).

Arminius has enjoyed quite an impressive career for almost half a century as a screen onto which national hopes and dreams have been projected.[90] He is the quintessential warrior—a convenient and inspiring "mold of one hero [who] fits all kinds of political or military figures," including, depending on the context, the Holy Roman Emperor Frederick I. Barbarossa (1155–1190), Holy Roman Emperor Leopold I (1658–1705), Kaiser Wilhelm I (1797–1888), Otto von Bismarck (1815–1898), and even Adolf Hitler.[91] Like the French Revolution or the Spanish Reconquista, the Battle of the Teutoburg Forest transcends normal, historical time, acquiring a messianic quality that fills history with meaning.[92] Such potent moments allow the fate of a people to emerge; they possess what Walter Benjamin famously described as *Jetztzeit* (now-time)—moments ripe with revolutionary potential, torn from the homogenous, ceaseless flow of historical time. We might also consider the Battle of the Teutoburg Forest to be, in the language of Pierre Nora, a "great event," that is, an event "on which posterity retrospectively confers the greatness of origins, the solemnity of inaugural ruptures." The Teutoburg Forest itself offers an example of what Nora designates as *lieu de mémoire*: a site "where memory crystallizes and secretes itself" and which "return[s] in the cycles of memory."[93]

The triumph of Arminius over Rome's legions is a transcendent event in the German cultural imagination, and part of a larger mythic vision of an autochthonous ethnie rooted in the primordial forests of the Germanic lands.[94] German poet Reinhold Schneider captures the power of the mythic battle when he writes that at the site of the Hermann Monument in Detmold the traces of primordial times reappear: as the Germanic Cherusci pour from the woods, he declares, it is as if the forest itself had risen up to fight alongside its marshes and ravines, recalling the narrative of Cassius Dio.[95] From the Battle of the Teutoburg Forest a legend was born, and from this legend developed an enduring *Schicksalsgemeinschaft* (a community of destiny or fate) and *Seelenlandschaft* (mindset or, literally, "landscape of the soul").[96]

RITUALS OF SACRIFICE IN TEUTOBURG FOREST AND BEYOND

The tale of the Battle of the Teutoburg Forest is a myth of cultural creation and origin. But the myth of Arminius's battle possesses another crucial dimension essential to our analysis of the myth of the original Germanic *Volk*: the role of the ritual of sacrifice in the service of social solidarity and ethnic community.[97] Clifford Geertz's definition of ritual captures the sense in which ritual both reflects the reality and reveals the dreams of ritual actors: "In ritual, the world as lived and the world as imagined, fused under the agency of a single set of symbolic forms, turns out to be the same world."[98] In the ritual-like retelling of the myth of the Battle of the Teutoburg Forest throughout the centuries, generations of Germans have reenacted this primordial declaration of autonomy and sovereignty, both celebrating and reconfirming the ultimate good of the individual's sacrifice for the collective *Volk*.

The element of ritual sacrifice in the Battle of the Teutoburg Forest manifests concretely as well as metaphorically. During the Roman campaign of 15–17 CE, six years after Varus's defeat, Germanicus, the nephew of the emperor Tiberius, returned to Teutoburg Forest. There, as Tacitus describes in his *Annals*, Germanicus discovered the grisly remains of Varus's slaughtered men from six years earlier: "In the middle of the plain there were whitening bones, scattered or piled up.... Nearby lay fragments of weapons and horses' limbs, and also, on the trunks of trees, skulls were impaled. In the neighboring groves were barbarian altars, at which they had sacrificed tribunes and first-rank centurions."[99] These are no mere "coincidental atrocities but a view of warfare as sacrifice and the appropriate form of dedication of the sacrifice is to hang it in a tree or on an artificial one, the gallows."[100]

Self-Sacrifice of the Soldier in German Culture

The virtue of self-sacrifice for a greater good—be it for king or Kaiser, community or nation—has long been valorized in German culture. From the warrior values of the ancient Germanic tribes and the code of chivalry of medieval *Rittertum* (knighthood) to the volunteer citizen-soldier fighting the "people's crusade" against Napoleon, the idealistic World War I soldier, and the World War II soldier dying for *Volk*, *Führer*, and *Vaterland*, the path of virtue for German men has repeatedly been imagined as one of self-sacrifice. Representations of self-sacrifice shift over time: poems and songs celebrating the early nineteenth-century Wars of Liberation presented the "joyous self-sacrifice" of soldiers who fought for the national cause,[101] while in the wake of World War I, the "Myth of the War Experience," described by George Mosse in his seminal work *Fallen Soldiers: Reshaping the Memory of the World Wars*, presented self-sacrifice through the "cult of the fallen soldier." In Mosse's words, "The Myth of the War Experience," particularly in defeated nations, "was designed to mask war and to legitimize the war experience; it was meant to displace the reality of war. The memory of the war was refashioned into a sacred experience which provided the nation with a new depth of religious feeling, putting at its disposal ever-present saints and martyrs, places of worship, and a heritage to emulate."[102] Drawing on ideas of resurrection and martyrdom, the "cult of the fallen soldier" (part of the "the Myth of the War Experience"), sought to transcend death by reframing it as self-sacrifice in imitatio Christi, leading to both personal and national regeneration. Often depicted lying, in Passion-inspired imagery, in the arms of Jesus, soldiers became martyrs in the post–World War I "religion of nationalism."[103]

The Third Reich, in turn, valorized and demanded the virtue of self-sacrifice not only from soldiers but also from civilians back home. With the unconditional surrender of Germany in 1945 and no postwar myth to rescue German honor from the ignominy of defeat, representations of self-sacrifice became more complicated; there was little honor to be had for soldiers who died for a discredited, criminal war instigated by Germany.[104] Postwar journals and popular literature thus depicted World War II soldiers as having sacrificed for their comrades rather than for the Third Reich, describing the fallen soldiers as dying for solidarity and loyalty rather than patriotism.[105]

Despite changing forms of expression, modern notions of sacrifice share a fundamental characteristic: they are based on the ideal of reciprocity.[106] In exchange for sacrificing one's youth, health, and often life, a soldier reaps the rewards of honor and glory—or, at least, camaraderie. The principle of sacrifice also played a central role in ancient Germanic tribal custom—here, however, sacrifice was visual and concrete as well as conceptual. Pagans offered up sacrificial gifts of decapitated horse and cow heads to their gods Tiwaz, Thor, and Odin, hanging their offerings from tree branches in ancient forest groves.[107] As in modern times, sacrificial rituals were based on reciprocity—here, social and religious reciprocity. Pagans often performed sacrifices before and after battle to win favor from the gods or as thank offerings for a victory.[108] Sacrifices also served as the means of communal bonding, with the ritual slaughter and consumption of an animal marking the climax of pagan ritual. Such community events channeled aggression and dispersed guilt while uniting the group and reinforcing communal identity through social bonding.[109] Pagan tribes such as the Saxons, Hermunduri, and Goths sacrificed human beings, too, as a means of unloading impurity or to please their gods (usually Odin/Wodan or Tiwaz).[110]

Odin's Sacrifice and the Cosmic Ash Tree Yggdrasil

By staging ritual sacrifices in forest groves and displaying sacred offerings in the branches of trees, pagans reenacted a central myth of Norse mythology: the sacrifice of the god Odin on the great cosmic ash tree Yggdrasil (mentioned in both "Der Seherin Gesicht" and "Grimnirlied" as well as in Jacob Grimm's *Deutsche Mythologie*). According to legend, Yggdrasil was a magnificent tree—immensely strong, immortal, and self-renewing. At once a guardian tree to the gods and the fixed and eternal center of the world (axis mundi), Yggdrasil possessed a trunk that reached to the heavens, branches that stretched out over the entire universe, and roots that extended below to the underworld, connecting the realms of the gods, giants, mankind, and the dead. This view of the world tree as a ladder, stretching from the underworld to the heavens, resonates with the idea of a road between worlds—a common conception in shamanistic religions.[111] The god Odin, according to myth, pierced himself with a spear on the boughs of Yggdrasil to gain power over the runes and acquire their secret, magical knowledge.[112] With the power of the runes, Odin liberated himself and was born anew as a rejuvenated, powerful being. This image of a suffering, self-sacrificing god bears clear phenomenological similarity to scriptural narratives of the crucifixion in Christianity, while the association between sacrifice and rejuvenation resonates with modern conceptions, including those apparent at the start of World War I.

Both the pagan, ritual act of sacrifice and the modern self-sacrifice of the soldier shape narratives of Germanic folk psychology, narrative, and memory. As will be discussed in later chapters, memorials to fallen soldiers often incorporate natural objects like trees and rocks as well as groves into their forms, evoking centuries-old resonances between a *Volk*, its primeval forests, and sacrifice.

DEATH, REBIRTH, AND THE FOREST

As mentioned earlier, the myth and ritual rooted in the primeval arboreal landscape draw inspiration from qualities perceived as inherent to trees and forests, including, most prominently, the idea of rebirth following death. Trees and forests are intimately linked in the cultural imagination of German-language cultures with death and what follows. During World War I, Austrian military authorities designed special cemeteries on foreign soil to honor the "sacrificial death" (*Opfertod*) of Austro-Hungarian soldiers. The sites chosen for these places of "purification and elevation" were often the forest, for forest cemeteries (*Waldfriedhöfe*) are perceived to "fit organically" into the landscape and to express "the deepest connection to nature."[113]

Many German poets, furthermore, have composed verse dedicated to eternally renewing trees. Johann Gottfried von Herder and Heinrich Heine write of winter trees waiting for the return of life with spring in "An die Bäume in Winter" ("To the Trees in Winter") and "Neuer Frühling" ("New Spring"), respectively, while Friedrich Hölderlin depicts trees as immortal beings—namely, as "sons of the mountain," "a nation of Titans," and "gods belonging only to themselves and to the heavens"—in "Die Eichbäume" ("The Oak Trees"). Hermann Hesse, born in the Black Forest town of Calw, ascribes to trees the power to "preach, undeterred by particulars, the ancient law of life. A tree says: A kernel is hidden in me, a spark, a thought, I am life from eternal life.... I was made to form and reveal the eternal in my smallest special detail."[114] From Wilhelm Müller's linden tree and Goethe's ginkgo biloba to Oscar Loerke's birch and Eduard Mörike's beech, the tree in German poesy is itself ever-renewing.

The Metaphysical Significance of Trees

Traditional Germanic values concerning death, rebirth, and eschatology—both pagan and modern—are too wide-ranging and complex to recount here; however, a few examples of how Germanic folk psychology invests trees with metaphysical significance will suffice to give an indication of the richness of association between trees and concepts of death and rebirth. Germanic pagan peoples commonly worshipped trees as divine and powerful beings, and still today, tree imagery and tree-shaped statuary are commonly found on German memorials.

Deciduous trees such as oaks and lindens are popular in memorialization because they shed and grow new leaves in rhythm with the seasons, illustrating nature's cyclical processes of decline and renewal, death and rebirth. Cyclical renewal offers a reassuring contrast to the human conception of linear time and mortality—a phenomenon noted by scholars Wilhelm Mannhardt, Gerard Van der Leeuw, and Gilbert Durand, among others.[115] Jeffrey K. Wilson's analysis of the German magazine *Gartenlaube*'s "Curious Trees" series demonstrates that the evocative power of trees in the German imagination lay in their status as "living witnesses to the past": "Trees could transcend the individual and link one to past and future generations ... the *Gartenlaube* endorsed ancient trees as suitable monuments to reflect on the past."[116] The fruits of trees, moreover, figure prominently in creation and immortality myths from Germanic lands as well as from around the world: in Chinese mythology, peaches of immortality offer eternal life, while in Norse mythology apples grant eternal youth, and in Greek myth ambrosia stills the hunger of the immortal gods.

Yggdrasil, the glorious ash tree mentioned earlier, exists at the heart of pagan eschatology and tree symbolism. According to myth, a time of natural disasters and a great battle (known as Ragnarök) was predicted to one day devastate the earth. When this time drew near, Yggdrasil would shake and tremble in warning.[117] During Ragnarök itself, Yggdrasil would provide solace for one man and one woman, who would hide within the tree and later reemerge to repopulate the earth. A source of new life and unborn souls, Yggdrasil stands at the center of mythic cycles of creation and destruction, offering a form of defiance before the finality of death.[118]

Tree Metaphysics in Modern German Culture

Centuries later, National Socialism would link the rebirth and renewal of the German nation and *Volk* to the rebirth and renewal of the German forest. In the film *Ewiger Wald* (*Eternal Forest*, 1936), the film's narration repeatedly equates the German people with trees and forests. The words "Eternal forest, eternal nation. / The tree lives like you and I. / It reaches for space like you and I. / Its death and creation are woven together in time. / The nation—like the forest—stands in eternity," for example, accompany an image of two intertwined trees.[119] In another scene, depictions of burial featuring hollowed-out logs as caskets are followed by those of dancers encircling a maypole (symbolic of Yggdrasil). The narration declares: "We originated in the forest. / We live like the forest. . . . What is the meaning of death? / After every death there is new life."[120] A third scene, set in the medieval period, presents impoverished farmers reseeding a German forest with cones. The narration states: "The farmer is dead! / The nation in calamity. / The destroyed fields and forests are / Complaints from the homeland in the wind. / The seed is looking forward to the new deed / So that new forest will rise from spring soil."[121] Death and creation, decline and renewal are thus portrayed as inevitable, natural cycles that encompass both *Volk* and forest.

Contemporary German culture continues to ascribe to trees the symbolism of immortality and rebirth. A burial ritual in Germany that acknowledges such symbolism is *Baumbestattung* (tree burial). With few exceptions, German states must obey Germany's *Friedhofszwang*—a regulation stipulating that the remains of the dead be buried or otherwise kept in cemeteries; burial at sea and other methods of natural burial—for example, burial in an approved site in the forest—are also permitted. With *Baumbestattung*, a deceased's ashes are mixed with soil into humus, into which a tree of the deceased's choice is then planted—a magnolia, Japanese flowering cherry tree, weeping birch, linden, oak, or ginkgo. To comply with cemetery regulations, this process may take place in Holland, the Czech Republic, or Switzerland. Once the deceased's ashes have been fully absorbed by the roots of the tree, the tree is returned to Germany and planted. Antje Körner, owner of the funeral home Bestattungshaus Körner in Walsrode, Lower Saxony, calls this process a *Lebensbaumbestattung* (tree of life burial); it allows the deceased to live on in the form of a tree and remain within the natural cycle of life. In her words, "Es gibt ein Leben nach dem Tod" ("There is life after death").

CONCLUSION

Since World War II and the Holocaust, certain leitmotifs common in German folk psychology have fallen under suspicion or been altogether discredited. Belief in an *Urvolk* based on racial, ethnonationalist principles, for example, has been abandoned by all but the most extreme right-wing factions during most of the second half of the twentieth and the early twenty-first century.

What is the fate, then, of the German forest and its symbolism in post–World War II folk psychology? During the years of scarcity immediately following Germany's defeat, the forest acquired a new meaning for people in desperate need of fire for heating and cooking. Germans scoured the woods, chopping down thousands of trees for firewood and leaving a ravaged forest landscape in their wake. In response to this widespread destruction, the Schutzgemeinschaft Deutscher Wald (Association for the Protection of the German Forest) was founded in 1947. On a conceptual level, the bond between German identity and the forest since World War II has, despite National Socialism's exploitation of forest symbolism, largely remained intact—so much so that author Elias Canetti could write in 1960: "In no other modern country has the forest-feeling [*Waldgefühl*] remained as alive as it has in Germany.... The Germans still seek the forest in which their forefathers lived, and feel at one with the trees."[122] This *Waldgefühl*, however, has not gone unexamined: in the decades since World War II, artists Joseph Beuys (1921–1986) and Anselm Kiefer (born 1945), among others, have interrogated the legacy of German forest myths, seeking in these myths redemptive potential or questioning the continuities of German myths, icons, and landscape memory.[123]

By the 1970s, German conceptions of trees and forests were changing once again as forests of spruce and fir appeared to be in mortal danger due to pollution. Environmental groups rushed to address the crisis, the green movement emerged, and the word *Waldsterben* (forest death) entered the German lexicon, largely thanks to the efforts of forestry scientist Bernhard Ulrich. In the early 1980s, tens of thousands of Germans demonstrated in the streets, and Die Grünen, the Green Party, won in 1983 its first seats in the Bundestag, the West German parliament.[124] *Waldsterben*, happily, has not come to pass as predicted, but the passionate response of so many Germans not only from the Green Party but from across the political spectrum, as well as the growing popularity of the Green Party today, testify to the vital role the forest continues to play in the values and identities of many Germans. As Richard Hayman explains, "The German Greens are the most successful of all the ecological political parties in Europe, partly because of the potency of German nature myths."[125] This is not in any way to diminish the radical differences between National Socialist forest ideology and German environmentalism today: after all, the Green Party is deeply committed to pacifism and human rights as well as environmental protection. Wilson thus warns us not to conflate the two ideologies despite a shared belief that the fate of the German nation and the forest are linked, and despite common roots in nineteenth-century discourses of the German forest. Rather, Wilson suggests that we might "think about both the blood-and-soil rhetoric and the anxiety over acid rain as two (very distinct) branches of the same tree."[126]

This chapter began with a description of a stone oak memorial to German expellees in Effelder, Germany. The Effelder memorial draws its potency from a rich history of myth and autochthonous beliefs linking the German people to their soil and forests; it resonates with those at home in a particular version of German culture—one whose musical score is rich in the leitmotifs of forest imagery and nature mysticism. For such persons, the Effelder memorial evokes a world at once vivid and tenebrous, like flashes of a distant, remembered dream. A great oak with exposed roots, a heap of stones, and a stone circle: together, these elements tell a story of attachment and belonging that ends in homesickness and mourning for a lost *Heimat*. As professor of forestry Karl Rebel declares in his work *Der Wald in der Deutscher Kultur* (1934), "Forest, *Heimat*, and Fatherland are one to the Germans."[127] As the imagined site of the Germanic *Volk*'s mythic, primal origin, as well as the battlefield on which the original Germanic tribes vanquished their primordial enemy, wresting their freedom and future from foreign hands, the forest embodies powerful notions of ethnic community, autonomy, and peoplehood. Such potent symbolism has not diminished with time; rather, it endures in ever-new forms and fantasies. Despite its conceptual shapeshifting, the voice of the forest—of immortal oaks witnessing the passage of centuries and dense thickets helping to defeat a mortal enemy—still speaks in tones resonant and full of promise to those who know how to listen.

CHAPTER TWO

Germanic Volk as Waldvolk
The Mythic Forest in German Culture

The German people are by nature a people of the forest, and this origin is still reflected in the essence of their being.
—Carl Wilhelm Neumann, *Das Buch vom deutschen Wald* (1937)

INTRODUCTION: THE IVENACK OAKS

In the Ivenack Oak Park of Mecklenburg-Vorpommern stand Germany's famous "thousand-year-old oaks." These giants with massive trunks, luxuriant crowns, gnarled burl knots, elegant forks, and labyrinthine clusters of branches are among the oldest and grandest trees of Europe. The park's largest oak boasts a circumference of almost thirty-eight feet and a height of over 116 feet. This oak—one of the largest and oldest in Germany[1]—has lived at least eight hundred and perhaps as long as a thousand years, witnessing epochs of upheaval and stability, division and unification. The Ivenack oaks are living monuments: in 2016 Germany declared them the country's first *Nationales Naturdenkmal* (national nature monument).[2] Approximately fifty thousand tourists travel each year to visit these legendary trees.

A magical tale enhances the mystique of the Ivenack oaks. According to legend, a young woman, though engaged to be married, was assigned to a convent in Ivenack by her family. The reluctant nun planted what would become the greatest of the oaks, placing her engagement ring around the tender stem of the sapling. As years passed, the sapling grew into a magnificent oak, and with it expanded and grew, magically, the ring. Still today—though invisible to the eye—the ring is said to span the colossal trunk, encircling within its band the seemingly limitless life force of an immortal being.³

The Ivenack oaks illustrate how trees may communicate a rich array of meanings at once secular and sacred, natural-historical and magical / mythic. They are one example among many nature monuments thriving in Germany today. This chapter expands further on a theme introduced in chapter 1: the symbolism of trees and the forest in German cultural history. The symbolic power of tree monuments emerges from the salience of trees, especially oaks and lindens but also ash trees, in German folk psychology and myth as well as in political and sociocultural discourse. Tree memorials and monuments such as *Gedenkbäume* (memorial trees); *Friedenslinden* and *Friedenseichen* (peace lindens and peace oaks); *Heldenhaine* (heroes' groves); *Naturdenkmale* (nature monuments); and *Einheitsbäume* (unification trees), all of which will be discussed in chapter 3, reveal the significance of trees in ancient and modern Germany.⁴

This chapter does not argue that traditional, mythical beliefs about the forest constitute, in the words of Albrecht Lehmann, a lasting mental paradigm defining German culture today. As Lehmann points out, to argue that the intellectual power and political dynamics of a modern, industrialized society like Germany derive from ancient forests of oak, and that a "subterranean current of thought and feeling" persists unbroken from prehistoric times to our modern age, as argued by Eugen Mogk and Friedrich von der Leyen,⁵ among others, would be problematic.⁶ Rather, this chapter argues that ever-shifting and metamorphosing cultural leitmotifs of the forest and trees may be traced through the products of artistic and intellectual German culture for centuries. These motifs endure. They do so in the form of seductive narratives of origin, freedom, community, and renewal that serve powerful psychological, social, and political needs. These motifs are, however, not inherent to German consciousness and thought as implied by the idea of a "lasting mental paradigm"—a notion that presupposes a reified notion of "Germanness." Rather, enduring cultural motifs and memories are transmitted through time and across generations via enduring cultural forms that include literature, art, music, and other texts.

We shall begin by looking at forest motifs and metaphors followed by nature myths of Indo-European and particularly Norse mythology. We shall then examine the idea of the German people as a *Waldvolk*, and the forest as the source of an idealized Germanic essence. Theories on the healing properties of trees as well as theories of nature as conceived by Johann Wolfgang von Goethe and Alexander von Humboldt enrich our portrait of the role of trees and the forests in German folk psychology. We shall also consider how the concept of the *Waldvolk* has manifested and been exploited in German culture, most notably during the years of National Socialism. Finally, this chapter considers the post–World War II legacy of forest symbolism and mythology in German culture and art.

FOREST MOTIFS AND METAPHORS

Swiss scholar Rainer Guldin argues that three metaphors of the forest may be traced throughout German culture: the forest as an exterritorial reservoir or source of power; the forest as a sacred, light-flooded cathedral; and the forest as a standing or marching army. The German forest, particularly the legendary Hercynian forest of ancient times, is the prime example of a symbolically potent forest: its mythic image presents a "primordial perfection and abundance" lost to modern man and evokes a longing to annul the territorial fragmentation and division that has plagued the German-speaking lands over the centuries.[7]

The Forest as Testimony

The symbolic potency of the forest in German cultural life renders it a powerful form for memorialization. Memorials and monuments fulfill many functions: preeminent is their power to connect communities to their pasts, both real and imagined. This function may be traced back to some of our species' earliest monuments: in a study of Neolithic and Bronze Age Europe, Richard Bradley analyzes prehistoric enclosures, which count among the earliest monuments of Northwest Europe. Despite the passage of time, communities continued to build enclosures in traditional forms for many years, as if citing earlier enclosure structures of Neolithic times. These monuments, Bradley postulates, were built in such a way as to recall settlements of the past and "the wider community" that once lived there. They offer testimony, in short, to a "people's attachment to place."[8]

Now, centuries later, tree monuments and memorials of the modern age share with these prehistoric enclosure monuments their power to act as forms of testimony. Trees are living witnesses in unique ways. To paraphrase German physician and psychiatrist Johannes Baptista Friedreich (1796–1862), trees are witnesses to the past and act as memorials to the centuries. But they are also witnesses to time itself: a tree is at once a symbol of the year—due to its natural, cyclical rhythms—and a symbol of a particular span of years. And yet, trees also transcend time; they "stretch upward toward the light of heaven and bathe themselves in infinity."[9]

The Infinite, Eternal Forest

Limitlessness in space and time—infinity and eternity—are the twin concepts that dominate descriptions of the forest in German poesy and prose. In the words of German writer Manfred Hausmann (1898–1986), it is the sound of *Ewigkeit* (eternity) that fills the endless stillness of the woods.[10] Eternity and infinity also characterize descriptions of the forest in the writings of German historian and philosopher Oswald Spengler (1880–1936). In his magnum opus *The Decline of the West* (1918–22), Spengler ascribes to the forest a transcendent, mystical power to evoke philosophical musings: "The rustle of the woods . . . stands with its secret questions 'whence? whither?' [and] its merging of presence into eternity, in a deep relation with Destiny, with the feeling of History and Duration, with the quality of Direction that impels the anxious, caring, Faustian soul toward infinitely-distant Future."[11] Throughout German and even classical cultural history, the space of the German woods itself has been perceived as infinite: Caesar famously marveled in his *De bello Gallico* at the vastness of the Hercynian forest, claiming that a man might travel east for sixty days without reaching its edge,[12] while Austrian writer Heimito von Doderer imagined a forest with mythical dimensions that might be traversed not in days, weeks, or months but in thousands of years in his novella *Das letzte Abenteuer* (*The Last Adventure*).

Evoking the infinite and the eternal, trees and tree monuments root communities in the spaces and places of distant and remote ancestral communities. By facilitating such attachment, tree monuments help contemporary peoples bond to their own actual, living communities, simultaneously reaffirming their current communities as well as the enduring essence of their original (ancestral) communities. Two concepts help explain this power to facilitate attachment: aura and the totemic principle.

Aura and Totem

The source of the power of testimony, to which Bradley refers in the context of prehistoric enclosures, lies in the authenticity of an object. Like Neolithic enclosures, tree monuments testify to unique times and places; they possess presence and aura. In his seminal essay "The Work of Art in the Age of Mechanical Reproduction" (1936), German-Jewish philosopher Walter Benjamin argues that the authenticity of a work of art depends on "the presence of the original"—that is, its "presence in time and space, its unique existence at the place where it happens to be."[13] At the heart of this unique quality of authenticity lies an object's ability to bear testimony to the "history which it has experienced." When authenticity is compromised, the authority or the "aura" of the artwork "withers" and is lost.[14]

Benjamin explains the aura of historical objects by turning to the aura of natural objects, such as a mountain range or a branch. He describes the aura of these objects as "the unique phenomenon of a distance, however close it may be."[15] The distance of the natural object is the distance of an object or being that cannot be reduced to our experience or consumption of it. To experience an object's aura is to experience that object's authenticity—its unique being and power to return our gaze, allowing us to experience a "continual and unending face to face encounter" with it.[16] Irreplicable and unique in its solitary existence, the natural object evokes an ethical subjectivity in the viewer, rooted in contemplation and visual dialogue rather than voyeurism.

The concept of aura helps elucidate the power of tree monuments. To stand before the Ivenack oaks is to experience awe before witnesses to centuries of life—a time span positively mythic compared to our paltry human sense of time. Although part of this story, aura alone cannot explain the attachment that has bound Germans to trees throughout the ages. The pagan religions of ancient Germanic tribes do not technically qualify as totemic, but Émile Durkheim's theory of the totemic principal in his influential work *The Elementary Forms of Religious Life* (1912) nevertheless casts light on two essential aspects underlying the prehistoric, medieval, and modern German attachment to trees.

First, Durkheim's theory of the totem helps explain how a natural object like a tree may function as a totemic object by symbolically representing the primordial Germanic ethnic community (*Volksgemeinschaft*).

Second, Durkheim reveals the dynamic by which a society perceives the qualities of a totem animal or plant as merging with the qualities of that society itself, so that totem and society share "one and the same essence."[17] In this case, a member of the *Volksgemeinschaft* shares essential "Germanic" characteristics (loyalty, strength, rejuvenescence) with the totemic object—the tree. A variety of Germanic cultural activities and art forms, including festivals, dance, art, and literature, testify to the abiding belief that members of the *Volksgemeinschaft* share an essential nature with trees, especially oak trees. Indeed, the *Stammtisch*, the most paradigmatic of German traditions (literally "tree trunk table," a fixed place where friends regularly gather for socializing), hearkens back to the gathering of Germanic tribes beneath their totem linden, oak, and fir trees.[18]

The totem itself is a plant or animal sacred to a particular clan. This plant or animal may be neither picked nor eaten.[19] These prohibitions protecting the totem are present as well in ancient Germanic customs relating to trees: only the initiated were permitted to enter the sacred oak groves of Germanic tribes; others who dared enter or who desecrated the grove by breaking off even a single twig suffered loss of life and property.[20] A trace of this practice may be seen in laws forbidding the cutting down of particular trees—fruit trees, beech, and oaks—during later years.[21] The excessive punishment of tree vandals in Germanic custom also testifies to the sacred status of certain trees. Both Dr. Paul Wagler, citing a law in Hesse-Homburg from 1401,[22] and James Frazer[23] relate a gruesome penalty for those who vandalize trees: the offenders' stomachs were to be slit open and their intestines pulled out and nailed to the violated tree. The *Frevler* (evildoer or blasphemer) was then led repeatedly in a circle around the tree until his intestines had wound about and covered the damaged trunk.[24]

The totem, furthermore, fulfills a vital social function by marking the distinctiveness of a social group.[25] In Durkheim's analysis, the totem is both a concrete object and symbol; above all, the totem embodies the clan itself, transfigured and imagined in the physical form of the totemic plant or animal.[26] An individual's transcendent feeling toward his or her community—the sense of belonging to something greater than oneself, feelings of dependence, and an awareness of the force of the clan and its intangible substance as a community—attaches to the totem and becomes conscious of itself.[27] The energy or force of these emotions and states of mind is not mortal; it endures across generations, remaining "always present, alive, and the same. It animates the generations of today as it animated those of yesterday and will animate those of tomorrow."[28] The totem thus affirms moral unity and stabilizes social feelings rooted in the community; it not only expresses the awareness a society has of itself but also "serves to create—and is a constitutive element of—that awareness."[29]

The sacred nature of the totem abides in its parts as well, which possess the "same powers and efficacy" as the whole.[30] This principle holds true for certain trees, namely oaks and lindens, in German cultural symbolism. The Iron Cross (*Eiserne Kreuz*), for example—a medal instituted by Frederick William III of Prussia for bravery during the early nineteenth-century Wars of Liberation—bore an image of a cluster of three oak leaves together with the Teutonic cross. Numerous war memorials erected during the Imperial and post–World War I periods were ornamented with oak leaves and acorns and erected in the shade of oak or linden trees; after World War II, images of oak leaves imprinted every newly minted coin.[31] To understand, however, why the tree (especially the oak tree) possesses the cultural gravitas that it does in German culture, including its auratic and totemic properties, requires a closer look at the symbolic power of trees and their roles in Germanic myths.

NATURE MYTHS

Nature myths are common to both the Germanic and Asiatic Indo-Europeans, and myths attributing the creation of man from trees appear in both Indo-Iranian and Teuton traditions.[32] In the narrative of human creation related in chapter 5 of Icelandic historian Snorri Sturluson's *Gylfaginning*, part of his thirteenth-century *Prose Edda*, human beings are created from two trees found lying by the sea shore: "As Bor's sons (the god Odin and his god-brothers Hœner and Loder) went along the sea-strand, they found two trees. These trees they took up and made men of them. The first gave them spirit and life; the second endowed them with reason and power of motion; and the third gave them form, speech, hearing and eyesight. They gave them clothes and names; the man they called Ask, and the woman Embla. From them all mankind is descended." The names "Ask" and "Embla" are understood to refer to the trees from which they were created: the ash and elm tree.[33] In other myths, such as the myth of the apple-bearing Scandinavian goddess Idunn, the fruits of trees offer an approximation of immortal life by granting eternal youth.[34]

Nature myths—often imagined to be part of a distant past—continue to thrive in modern as well as traditional cultures. As religion scholar Bruce Lincoln argues, it is the narrative form of myth that makes myths so attractive and memorable, so efficacious in naturalizing and legitimizing our taxonomies along with their inherent discriminations and hierarchies. Myth, Lincoln explains, is essentially "ideology in narrative form."[35] Religion scholarship shows that such myths endure because they harness the power of the natural world, offering an abiding image of regenerative life and an eternal life source that transcends the limitations of human mortality. The symbolism of regenerative life force offers more, however, than consolation for death or an answer to the threat of meaninglessness in modern, industrialized society. Nature myths offer a world where we may imagine ourselves as part of a greater narrative, in which each life derives from and returns to a single, knowable source. In the words of German novelist Hermann Hesse, the predictable, seasonal rhythms in the life of a tree reveal "das Geheimnis des Seins" ("the secret of being") and "das unruhvolle Spiel des Lebens" ("the restless play of life").[36] The existential power of the nature myth underlies its political, social, and cultural efficacy.

The Powers of Trees in Indo-European Myths

Trees in particular have often functioned in Indo-European myths as homologues for humans, the world, and the universe.[37] As such, the tree becomes an image of the world (*imago mundi*) as well as the center or world pillar (axis mundi), bridging multiple worlds by connecting the earth with the heavens and underworld and human beings with their gods.[38] With their cyclical patterns of decline and growth, dormancy and renewal, trees offer an ideal symbol for healing and rebirth and often possess magical and regenerative powers of healing in myths. The religious theme of the sacred tree with magical powers may be found across a variety of religious traditions, including the ancient Sumerian and Akkadian religions.[39] One of the most famous mythical trees—the Tree of Life—plays a seminal role in Near Eastern myth and ritual as well as folklore around the world.[40] In Genesis, the Tree of Life (Etz Chaim), most likely a date palm, grows in the Garden of Eden—its fruits, which transmit the gift of eternal life, are guarded by cherubim. The Tree of Life appears again in the book of Revelation in the Christian Bible, now growing in New Jerusalem and bearing fruit whose leaves will heal the nations (Revelation 22:2). Sacred trees of other traditions, such as the Haoma tree of Zoroastrianism and Persian mythology, the Banyan and Neem trees of Hinduism, the Tuba tree of Islam, and the Bodhi tree of Buddhism, are believed to possess special properties of health and healing.

Mythic Trees in Norse Mythology

A definition of myth by theologian Don Cupitt, in truncated form, declares: "A myth is typically a traditional sacred story of anonymous authorship and archetypal and universal significance which is recounted in a certain community and is often linked with a ritual . . . myth-making is evidently a primal and universal function of the human mind as it seeks a more-or-less unified vision of the cosmic order, the social order, and the meaning of the individual's life."[41] German philosopher Ernst Cassirer's rather early analysis of the mythical mind, in turn, ties myth to the sort of work that memorials suggest. In his important work *Language and Myth*, Cassirer quotes Max Müller's description of myth: "Mythology is inevitable, it is natural, it is an inherent necessity of language . . . it is in fact the dark shadow which language throws upon thought."[42] Noting that such definitions of myth have long been abandoned by etymology and comparative mythological research, Cassirer maintains that such attitudes are nevertheless "ever recurrent": they depict the mythical world as, essentially, "a world of illusion—but an illusion that finds its explanation whenever the original, necessary self-deception of the mind, from which the error arises, is discovered."[43] But, Cassirer continues, "if myth be really . . . nothing but the darkening shadow which language throws upon thought, it is mystifying indeed that this shadow should appear ever as in an aura of its own light, should evolve a positive vitality and activity of its own, which tends to eclipse what we commonly call the immediate reality of *things*, so that even the wealth of empirical, sensuous experience pales before it."[44]

And so, indeed, does Yggdrasil, the cosmic ash tree of Norse mythology—home to an eagle that knows many things, a hawk named Vedfolner, and a squirrel named Ratatoskr who scurries up and down its trunk delivering "words of envy" between the eagle and the dragon or devil Nidhug, who gnaws the tree's root from below—reveal a strange and wonderful world. Although rotting at the side, bitten by stags, gnawed on by Nidhug, and surrounded by serpents, Yggdrasil thrives: its branches, which "spread over all the world and reach up above heaven," host the council meetings of the gods. Water from the sacred fountain of Urd—water so sacred that any object that touches it becomes as white as the film of an eggshell—nourishes the tree, so that from its branches "come the dews that fall in the dales"—a dew that feeds the bees and bears the magical name "honey-fall." "Green forever" stands Yggdrasil, beset by destruction but eternally blooming and feeding the world.[45] A second glorious tree of Norse mythology called Lerad stands near Valhalla, the home of the god Odin and all valiant warriors who have fallen in battle since the beginning of the world. The heroes dwelling in Valhalla drink mead (an alcoholic drink of fermented honey and water) given by the she-goat Heidrun, who feeds on the leaves of Lerad: "From her teats runs so much mead that she fills every day a vessel in the hall from which the horns are filled."[46]

The myths of Yggdrasil and Lerad fulfill the functions of myth as outlined by Cupitt. The former offers a vision of cosmic order: though "bearing distress greater than men know,"[47] Yggdrasil flourishes with the help of magical waters to sustain the creatures of the earth and connect the three realms of heaven, earth, and underworld. Lerad, meanwhile, offers a coherent social order in which heroic actions are rewarded with ceaselessly flowing mead and the individual warrior's life acquires meaning in the duty of self-sacrifice.

The symbolic meanings of trees, both in Germanic pagan rituals of the past[48] and in enduring folk narratives, resonate with the descriptions of special trees in Norse mythology: they embody ideas of the sacred, provide nourishment, and symbolize an idealized image of the Germanic *Volk*, communal identity, and ethnie. Among the oak, yew, ash, and linden, all valued as sacred in pagan ritual, the oak and linden today still possess symbolic power.[49] The special meanings of trees and the forest in German national identity will be discussed in the next section.

THE WALDVOLK (PEOPLE OF THE FOREST)

The trees and forest hold a sacred place in Germanic mythology and national identity; indeed, the Germanic primeval forest may be considered mythic in its own right.⁵⁰ In Germanic folk narratives, trees, groves, and the primeval forest possess a magical aura and occupy a singular and sacred space. The forest possesses a poetic dimension that transforms a simple wooded grove into a poetic landscape essential to Germanic myths of community and evocative of a mysterious and primordial time.⁵¹

The Forest as Symbol and Essence of Being

Klaus Schriewer, expert on the cultural history of the German forest, describes the forest as a symbol in modern German mythology. Together with project director Albrecht Lehmann at the University of Hamburg, Schriewer conducted a research project called "Lebensstichwort Wald"⁵² (1995–98).⁵³ As part of this project, more than one hundred Germans from Hamburg, the Harz region, and Osnabrück were interviewed about their experiences with and their ideas about the forest.⁵⁴ Uniting an otherwise diverse range of attitudes and beliefs is what Schriewer calls the idea of the *Ursprünglichkeit* (primordial nature) of the forest.⁵⁵

Given the essential role that the forest has long played (and continues to play) in German culture, it is not surprising that German natural scientist and writer Carl Wilhelm Neumann described the German *Volk* as a *Waldvolk* whose origin is still reflected in the essence of their being: "The tree worship of the Germanic tribes and their faith in the forest . . . in a word, their spiritual condition (*Seelenverfassung*), was shaped by their dense forest environment, and continues to live on in their blood— the blood of their ancestors."⁵⁶ With these words Neumann expresses the abiding belief that the unique nature of the Germanic *Volk* may be traced back to the forest-dwelling Germanic tribes. A modern formulation of the sentiment Neumann expresses may be found in the popular idea of the forest as a symbol in the German "collective unconscious"—a concept that appeals to the populace in times of need. The concept of the *Waldvolk* reappeared with particular élan during the late 1970s and 1980s as part of the previously mentioned discourse of *Waldsterben* (forest death or forest decline).⁵⁷

In German folk psychology, mythic trees primarily inhabit the past, but they also predict and celebrate the future. The Babisnauer Pappel (a black poplar), planted in 1808 in Babisnau, Saxony, is believed to augur peace with its blossoming rhythms. As related by German scholar and diarist Victor Klemperer, the blooming of the tree predicts the end of war and return to peace. The poplar allegedly bloomed in 1870, foretelling the end of the Franco-Prussian War in 1871, then bloomed again in 1918 and 1945 to mark the ends of World War I and World War II.[58] In 2008 the Babisnauer Pappel celebrated its bicentennial birthday with more than five hundred visitors.

It is worth noting that the integrity of the German people, their health and sovereignty, has long been bound to the integrity of the forest in German folk psychology even into the twentieth century. The preface to an art portfolio assembled to raise money for the protection and preservation of the central German forest in August 1924,[59] for example, explicitly links the precarious state of the German forest to the precarious state of post–World War I Germany. The first lines of the preface lament the loss of German forestland to causes such as tree diseases, pollution, deforestation, and insects. But the first source of harm listed is the loss of German forest to Germany's enemies due to war: "Almost a tenth of the German forest along the former east and west boundaries of the German state has fallen into the hands of our enemies and, in the Pfalz [Palatinate] and Rhine- and Ruhr- regions, [the German forest] lies abandoned and defenseless in their clutches."

The forest, the preface continues, is the "common property of all Germans and must be protected as the fountain of health [*Gesundbrunnen*] of our people [*Volk*]." Here, the health of the German *Volk* is directly correlated to the health of the forest. The preface closes by declaring that in the future, the "German forest will once again enchant a free and happy people."[60] Words mourning the loss of German woodlands to its enemies and words predicting a corrective to this injustice thus bookend the preface, extending a plea for preserving the forest into a condemnation of the Treaty of Versailles and a call for revision of boundaries.[61]

While other cultural traditions imbue the forest with sacred meaning, Germanic folk psychology is unique in imagining the forest to be the very *source* of Germanic being—a magical and mystical wellspring of the singular Germanic nature that reveals itself in the *Volksgemeinschaft* (organic, ethnically coherent community). As the realization of an essential and unchanging Germanic nature, the ethnic community is linked to a particular Germanic destiny—a *Schicksalsgemeinschaft*, as described in chapter 1 in reference to the Battle of the Teutoburg Forest.

Although ideas of an essential "Germanness" had long been associated with the *Urwald* (the primordial forest), it was Wilhelm Riehl, introduced in the previous chapter, who first developed a systematic nationalistic ideology linking German identity with the forest.[62] Riehl argued that national character emerges organically from topography, and that a people's landscape is a "repository of collective memory."[63] For "Germany to stay German" and for the "pulse of the German *Volk* to continue to beat warmly and cheerfully," Riehl argues, the forest must be preserved—for in the untamed forest lies the "natural, raw substance of the original Germanic *Volk* from which the German people today may draw strength."[64] A people must die off, Riehl concludes, if it loses its recourse to the forest dwellers.[65]

The Healing Properties of Trees

In Germanic folk history, oak, linden, and ash trees reign supreme: their symbolism colors every aspect of cultural history from politics and the arts to memorializing rituals. Indeed, the *urmächt'ge Eichen* (most powerful and primordial oaks)[66] are among the most venerated trees of the early Indo-European peoples, thanks in part to their ubiquity in the middle-European forests of antiquity,[67] but also because the natural products of the oak from bark to blossoms have for centuries supplied humankind with herbal remedies.

As the *Gesundbrunnen* of the German *Volk*, trees and their products have long been valued for their healing powers. According to the literature of ancient remedies, the bark of the oak tree treats a wide range of ailments, including acne and dandruff, while oak bark bath supplements heal hemorrhoids, ulcers, and boils. Oak bark milk counteracts the toxic effects of poisoning, and oak bark coffee cures swollen glands. Oak gallnuts, one of the earliest herbal remedies known to man, were used during the Middle Ages to stop bleeding, heal wounds, and neutralize lead, copper, and other kinds of metal poisoning. Sixteenth-century botanist and herbalist Jacobus Theodorus, known as Tabernaemontanus, declared everything on the oak tree—bark, leaves, and acorns—to possess natural astringent properties, making oak products ideal for treating skin and digestive disorders.[68] Oak tree products have also been used to treat frostbite, loose teeth, diarrhea, and internal bleeding.[69]

Oaks featured in magical *Heilkunde* (art of healing) during the Middle Ages as well. Incantations spoken beneath oak trees were believed to heal gout, fever, broken limbs, and toothaches. To cure mouth ulcers, for example, the afflicted should stand within a cluster of three oak trees, rub a twig from one of the trees across his teeth three times, and recite: "Mundfäul geh hin und wieder / Geh aus allen meinen Gliedern / Und komm nie wieder" ("Vanish, mouth ulcers / Leave all my limbs / And never return again"). Similar incantations existed to cure headaches and fever.[70] The afflicted also crawled through hollow oaks in the hopes of shedding their illnesses, or metaphorically stuffed their sicknesses into oaks by gouging holes in the trunks, inserting hair or finger- or toenails within, and then sealing the holes with wood. The oak was, finally, believed to offer an antidote to impotence. A man of the Middle Ages suffering from erectile disfunction was instructed to bore a hole in an oak trunk and insert his penis within while reciting the words: "O Eiche, so wie dein Herz gesund ist, so möge mein Glied gesund sein" ("Oh oak tree, as healthy as your heart is, so may my penis also be").[71]

Lindens, too, have a rich history of providing natural remedies for Germanic peoples. When brewed as tea, linden tree blossoms were used to treat colds and the flu; when mixed with wine, they were said to counteract lead poisoning.[72] In the Middle Ages, incantations recited beneath lindens allegedly cured gout by transferring the condition to the linden, while linden seeds, leaves, and blossoms treated headaches, burns, ulcers, epilepsy, urinary retention, mouth ulcers, and even broken hearts.[73] Mistreating a linden could lead to unpleasant consequences; a man who urinated against a linden might be struck with punishing styes—an affliction cured, in turn, by linden leaves.[74]

Belief in the healing powers of trees may also be witnessed in the European pagan custom of hanging objects associated with recovery and healing, such as crutches, from tree branches.[75] The practice of hanging pieces of clothing belonging to the sick on oak trees similarly testifies to the conviction that trees possess the power to heal.[76] A modern echo of this practice continues still today in German parks, for example, in the Westfalen Park in Dortmund, North Rhine-Westphalia, in the form of a *Schnullerbaum*—a tree on which children hang their pacifiers, signifying the children's maturation and auguring success for future development. In these examples, strength and renewal are imagined to be flowing from the tree to the human subject, revealing magical thinking.

Trees and forests possess the power of rejuvenation and healing in ways at once physical, spiritual, social, and cultural in German folk psychology. Like the primeval forest itself—a complex living, breathing organism whose survival depends on the strength and health of its trees as well as millions of smaller organisms—Germans have for centuries imagined their communities as drawing strength from its people, just as the German people have drawn strength from the primordial forest. In the natural rhythms of deciduous trees resides a regenerative power that makes a powerful promise: mortality is but a precursor to new life, and German culture and community will follow the forest's cyclical patterns of decline and renewal.

THEORIES OF NATURE: JOHANN WOLFGANG VON GOETHE AND ALEXANDER VON HUMBOLDT

To deepen our understanding of the meaning of trees in German cultural history, it is helpful to consider the seminal theories of nature presented by two of Germany's preeminent writers and thinkers: Johann Wolfgang von Goethe (1749–1832) and Alexander von Humboldt (1769–1859). Both men were passionate observers of plant life and authored influential writings on the natural world; their insights shed light on the development of certain strands of thought concerning nature and botany.

Goethe

Johann Wolfgang von Goethe, a great lover of trees,[77] conceived of nature as an endless process of becoming. Metamorphosis, he writes, is the "key to the whole alphabet of nature," and nature exists in a state of becoming and ceaseless flux.[78] The apex of constant metamorphosis emerges in the perfection of plants and animals into two forms: the tree (a "magical structure") and man: "The plant . . . [is] ultimately glorified, fixed and rigid, in the tree; and the animal, with utmost mobility and freedom, in mankind."[79] Tree and man thus stand in a special, kinship-like relation to one another as twin climactic forms of transformation.

The idea of a homology between tree and human being in German-language letters precedes Goethe. More than two centuries earlier, the Swiss physician, alchemist, and philosopher Paracelsus (born Theophrastus von Hohenheim, 1493–1541) developed the concept of the doctrine of signatures, a theory according to which herbs heal the parts of the body that they resemble. Paracelsus depicted the homology between man and tree in striking terms: "This plant resembles man. It has his skin, which is the bark; his head and hair are its roots; it has his figure and his signs, his senses and his sensitivity in its stem which, if damaged, will cause death. It is adorned with foliage, blossoms, and fruits as is man with his sense of hearing, his face, and language."[80]

In a similar vein, the late-seventeenth-century Dutch copper engraving *Der Pflanzenmensch* (*The Plant Man*) (from the *Compendium anatomicum nova method institutum*, Amsterdam, 1696) depicts a naked man with legs spread and extended, uplifted arms; roots protrude from his feet and leafy branches from his veins—specifically, from phlebotomy points.[81] As Margit Stadlober notes, the ancient north-of-the-Alps Germanic belief of the close connection between the fate of men and trees, which lasted into the sixteenth century, emerged from the belief that humans originally grew on trees.[82] Internal attributes similar to humans have been attributed to trees as well: in the mythologist and folklorist writings of Wilhelm Mannhardt on the forest cults of the ancient Germanic tribes (*Wald- und Feldkulte*, 1875), all trees are animated with souls, trees bleed when wounded, and the fate of sylvan spirits is bound to their host trees.[83]

Belief merges with practice in the Germanic traditions of *Lebensbäume* (life trees) and *Schicksalsbäume* (fate or destiny trees). Inspired by the concept of the *Doppelgängerbeziehung* (Doppelgänger relationship) between man and tree, life trees and destiny trees are planted when babies are born. When Goethe was born, for example, his grandfather planted a pear tree in his garden. Such trees are envisioned as lifelong companions for a newborn child, with tree and child sharing a common fate: "Stirbt der Baum, stirbt auch der Mensch" ("If the tree dies, so too will the person") and vice versa.[84] Though no longer as common a practice as formerly, the custom still exists in new, modern forms: the Marienstift Hospital in Braunschweig, Lower Saxony, for example, pledged to plant a new tree in the Schulwald in Neuerkerode for every baby born during the year 2020. Approximately one thousand new trees were planted.

Humboldt

Like those of Goethe, the influential works of Alexander von Humboldt testify to the unity of nature and the connections between plant life and human beings. Humboldt's concept of "the web of life" depicts earth as one great living organism in which all living things are connected.[85] In his seminal work

Views of Nature (*Ansichten der Natur*, 1808), Humboldt describes organic life as a great force "unceasingly occupied with connecting to new forms those elements liberated by death," thereby contributing to the "richness of life and its renewal" in nature.[86]

Humboldt also argues that each zone of the earth possesses its own distinct character or "physiognomy" based on what he calls "the old and profound power of organization . . . [that] binds all animal and vegetable life forms to firm, perpetually returning types."[87] Just as one may speak of a "physiognomy in individual organic beings," Humboldt writes, "so too is there a physiognomy of nature." This physiognomy or "natural character" of different parts of the world "is connected in the most intimate way to the history of humanity and to that of its culture, including the character of a people" who inhabit a particular landscape.[88] Humboldt thus presents a vision of life in which the moral world is influenced directly by the physical world, and in which the sensory and the extrasensory are interconnected realms.[89] In Humboldt's vision, the physiognomy of a landscape shapes the physiognomy—culture, history, and identity—of a people, so that nature and human nature—*Wald* and *Volk*—are organically linked.

THE WALDVOLK CONCEPT IN CULTURE

The concept of the *Waldvolk* has a long and rich history in German culture, assuming at times radical contours. The German journalist, writer, and founder of the *Volkshochschule* (adult education center) Ehm Welk (1884–1966), for example, argued that the German love for the forest—unique among peoples—is not merely cultural but racial, arising from mysterious powers that he claims have survived for thousands of years in German blood and will continue to do so for all time. From the "Germanic ancestors of prehistory," Welk writes, "flows a single current of nature-bound nationhood . . . and the breath of eternity flows with this current: from the days of awakened human consciousness in the forest to the powerful coming into being of a people [*Volk*] to the Sunday outings of the city folk and beyond into immortality."[90]

From Caspar David Friedrich's paintings *Hermanns Grab* (*Hermann's Grave*, 1812) and *Der Chasseur im Walde* (*The Chasseur in the Forest*, 1814) and Carl Wilhelm Kolbe's etching *Waldstück mit knorriger Eiche* (*Woodland Scene with Gnarled Oak*, 1800) to Joseph Freiherr von Eichendorff's nature and patriotic poetry, the primeval forest evokes an ancient, idealized Germanic world. The German forest has also played a starring role in German opera: consider Wagner's *Parsifal* as well as his *Siegfried*, with its famous *Waldweben* (forest weaving) motif, or Carl Maria von Weber's *Der Freischütz* (*The Marksman*). The poem "Wotan-Bismarck" by philologist and writer Gottfried Doehler (1863–1943) is emblematic of *Waldvolk*-inspired texts: it depicts Wotan, the mythical Germanic god also known as Odin, as protector of the German people and fatherland who reappears throughout history to help the German *Volk* in times of need, assuming the forms of Karl der Große (Charlemagne), Barbarossa (Holy Roman Emperor Frederick I), and Martin Luther. In paintings, the forest is often paired with other symbols of prehistoric tribal life such as a dolmen or cairn / megalithic tomb of the Neolithic period, thereby anchoring the forest in prehistory. Heinrich Schilking's (1815–1895) *Das Hünengrab im Walde* (*The Giant's Grave in the Forest*, 1841), and Caspar David Friedrich's *Hünengrab im Schnee* (*Cairn in Snow*, 1807) both code forests as ancient through the presence of a *Hünengrab*, which, in the words of German classicist and poet Johann Heinrich Voß (1751–1826), belong to the *Vorwelt* (the primeval world).[91]

As a leitmotif in Germanic folk psychology, the primeval forest appears in quotidian beliefs concerning myths of origins and ideas of community and peoplehood as well. Jeffrey K. Wilson offers a close examination of the deep roots of the forest in the German folk imagination by analyzing the "sylvan discourse" of German civil society.[92] This discourse originated in the nationalism of the early nineteenth century and relied on the "German reverence for the woods, rooted in their barbarian past"; it was perpetuated by foresters, botanists, geographers, historians, lawyers, and politicians as well as artists of all kinds and was exploited by multiple groups for various political ends.[93] In Wilson's words, "The woods served as a flexible, malleable symbol, transcending Germany's myriad divisions to encompass the entire nation . . . unit[ing] a landscape and a history splintered by internecine struggles." Sylvan discourse constructed Germans, in effect, as a *Waldvolk*, offering "a national landscape and a national memory" rooted in a "Teutonic past."[94]

The symbolic potency of the forest in German culture reveals itself even in the German language itself. Words such as *Waldgesinnung* (forest mindset), *Waldanschauung* (forest worldview), and *Waldeinsamkeit* (forest solitude) hint at the special bond between Germans and their forests. Indeed, *Waldeinsamkeit* emerged as a popular concept during the German Romantic period, appearing in poems and stories by Ludwig Tieck, Heinrich Heine, and Joseph Freiherr von Eichendorff, in a woodcut by Ludwig Richter (*Waldeinsamkeit*, 1861), and, notably, in Albrecht Altdorfer's *Sankt Georg und der Drache* (*Saint George and the Dragon*, 1510). In the latter, dense, lush green forest dominates the picture, radiating a sense of mystery and power that overshadows the human subject—a knight at the bottom of the picture, tiny and insignificant against the oaks, evergreens, and ferns that the frame barely contains.

The Sanctity of the Forest

Because sacred trees played vital roles in pagan ritual and worship, they were often targeted for destruction by ambitious Christian missionaries, who mutilated and chopped down the trees, often using their wood to build chapels and churches. This cruel practice sought to eradicate pagan belief by destroying the pagans' objects of worship. According to the monk Willibald in the *Vita Bonifatii*, Saint Boniface chopped down the splendid oak of Jupiter in the eighth century while endeavoring to convert the pagans of Hesse.[95] As legend relates, the Jupiter oak fell into four pieces of equal length with the first superficial cut of Saint Boniface's axe—a miracle so wondrous that the Hessian pagans willingly converted on the spot. The wood of the Jupiter oak was then used to build an oratory dedicated to Saint Peter.[96] Similarly, Charlemagne felled the Irminsul (a pillar of wood dedicated to the Germanic god Irmin), sacred to the Saxons as their axis mundi, during the eighth-century Saxon Wars.[97] The Irminsul was so influential that it inspired German domestic architecture; wooden houses in late antiquity and the early Middle Ages often contained a central column in imitation of the great sacred pillar.[98]

Other groups of missionaries employed gentler means of persuasion by adapting and incorporating tree worship into Christian practice. *Marieneichen* (oaks of Mary), *Marienlinden*[99] (lindens of Mary), and *Baumbilder* ("tree images"—wooden tabernacles affixed to trees displaying locally venerated saints and passion imagery), as well as a variety of other tree shrines that thrived during the Baroque era in particular, testify to the continued sacredness of trees long after the defeat of paganism.[100] Joseph von Führich's painting *Einführung des Christentums in den deutschen Urwäldern* (*The Introduction of Christianity into the Primeval Forests of Germany*, 1864) depicts this gentler vision of conversion with a scene depicting pagans and Christians occupying peacefully, if still separately, a wooded grove.

In many aspects of German society, trees and forests have inspired, and continue to inspire, a vague sense of religiosity in the form of a nebulous sacredness. Mystical language and imagery evoking the mysterious, secret, and inexpressible reveal the sacred nature of trees in art and literature. German-language poet Nikolaus Lenau (1802–1850) describes in his poem "Der Eichwald" ("The Oak Forest," 1830) a sacred, somber oak forest in which the author is seized by sweet dread in the presence of mysterious rustling; the forest is about to reveal the very meaning of God's love before it falls still again, cowed by God's nearness.[101]

The sacrality of the forest may even speak, via the medium of poetry, in its own voice, as in the poem "Der Wald und der Wanderer" ("The Forest and the Wanderer") by Johann Gottfried von Herder (1744–1803). The poem describes a hiker, who, while wandering through a forest, hears a bardic tone emerging from an oak; it is the voice of the forest itself, promising shade, tranquility, vitality, and courage. Sacred symbolism infuses the unfolding scene: the tips of the spruces reach heavenward, and the trees, the spirits of paradise, transform into a choir singing sacred blessings.[102]

Not only German poets but artists as well have imbued the forest with sacred, often Christian religious feeling: a vast number of artworks depict religious scenes set in lush wooded landscapes, including W. Hecht's (1843–1920) etching *Anachoret* (*Anchorite*), Caspar David Friedrich's *Kreuz im Walde* (*Cross in the Forest*, 1812), Carl Spitzweg's (1808–85) *Marterl* (*Wayside Cross*), and Jakob Götzenberger's fresco *Allerheiligen* (*All Saint's Day* , 1844), the latter two of which depict young women praying in wooded scenes, their slender figures surrounded by dense forest. Arnold Schulten's *Waldlandschaft mit Betenden* (*Forest Landscape with Praying Figures*, 1868) also depicts an image of piety, but the praying figures are miniscule, eclipsed by the towering, majestic trees surrounding them. In these paintings, the forest is a natural cathedral; the grandeur of its lush greenery and separation from the world of men encourage pious feeling, while the sunlight filtering through the delicate branching patterns of the trees evokes the prismatic beauty of light cast through stained-glass windows. The figures are contemplative or praying; they are still, quiet and at peace. The cathedral-like aesthetics of the forest are perhaps best captured by Spengler in the following passage:

> The character of the Faustian cathedral is that of the *forest*. The mighty elevation of the nave above the flanking aisles ... the transformation of the columns ... into pillars and clustered-pillars that grow up out of the earth and spread on high into an infinite subdivision and interlacing of lines and branches; the giant windows by which the wall is dissolved and the interior filled with mysterious light—these are the architectural actualizing of a world-feeling that had found the first of all its symbols in the high forest of the Northern plains, the deciduous forest with its mysterious tracery, its whispering of ever-mobile foliage over men's heads, its branches straining through the trunks to be free of earth.[103]

For Spengler, the shape and structure of trees inspire sacred feelings: oaks, beeches, and lindens, "with the fitful light-specks playing in their shadow-filled volume[,] are felt as bodiless, boundless, spiritual," while the oak "seems, ever restless and unsatisfied, to strain beyond its summit."[104] The great cosmic tree of Norse mythology, Yggdrasil (discussed in chapter 1), is an ash tree—perhaps, as Spengler speculates, because the ash itself displays the "victory of the upstriving branches over the unity of the crown" and appears to be at once "dissolving" and "expanding into space,"[105] just as Yggdrasil was said to extend its branches across the entire universe, connecting the heavens with the earth and underworld. For Spengler, "the endless, lonely, twilight wood became and remained the secret wistfulness in all Western building-forms," so that the very structures we inhabit still today whisper to us with the voices of the forest.

Autochthony, National Socialism, and Völkisch Culture

Mit Waldheil und Heil Hitler! (Hail the forest and Hitler!)
—Required greeting of the Palatinate Forest Association during the Third Reich

Beyond its evocative aesthetics and vague religiosity, the forest possesses another wellspring of sacrality in German cultural history: the forest as the source of the Germanic *Volk* itself, as discussed in chapter 1.[106] The concept of an autochthonous Germanic *Volk* rooted in a primeval forest landscape has long possessed both inspiring and destructive potential.

Autochthonous themes may be likened to a refrain, a seductive leitmotif adopting new guises as it endures throughout the centuries—from nineteenth-century Romantic nationalism to agrarian and *völkisch* youth groups such as the Artamanen-Gesellschaft (Artaman League, 1923–34) to National Socialism and post–World War II environmentalism.[107]

The positive power of autochthonous symbolism lies in its ability to harness romantic and nostalgic energy to promote healing and resurrection; autochthonous symbolism may draw on images of the life-affirming renewal and rebirth present in nature to signify new beginnings and reconciliation after great loss. Such symbolism is common in German literature: Romantic poet Achim von Arnim declares the forest in his poem "Stolze Einsamkeit" ("Proud Solitude," 1813) to be the place of his rebirth following his death: "Here I die," he writes, "and here I am born."

Autochthonous symbolism, with its rhetoric of cultural renewal couched in organic metaphors, possesses a darker side as well. It may draw power from a malignant vision of the past—one obsessed with the birth of a great and "pure" race in holy groves, with bloody battles in primeval forests fought to preserve the unique Germanic *Volk*, and with sacrificial rituals strengthening Germanic tribal warriors. And it may be, and has been, exploited in the service of revanchist fantasies and dreams of territorial expansion and cultural revisionism during the nineteenth and early twentieth centuries—especially during the years of National Socialism. A particularly toxic aspect to autochthonous thought is the destructive ideal of the *Volksgemeinschaft* (ethnic community), which leads to ethnic nationalism and xenophobia. In the words of German historian Hagen Schulze, "It is not the idea of the nation that needs to be overcome in Europe, rather the fiction of the fateful, objective, inescapable unity of *Volk*, nation, history, language, and state."[108]

The toxicity of nineteenth- and early twentieth-century autochthonous beliefs seeps from a variety of sources, both literary and nonfiction. Particularly poisonous are the writings of Prussian forester Rudolf Düesberg (1856–1926). Like other German writers previously discussed, Düesberg draws an analogy between man and tree, but in Düesberg's racist reckoning it was no longer "mankind" who shared the pinnacle of development with the tree, but rather, and exclusively, the German. In his book *Der Wald als Erzieher* (1910) (*The Forest as Educator*), Düesberg declares the natural social order of the German forest to be a cure for urbanizing, nomadic, parasitic Jewish tendencies, arguing that the German forest shares its essence with the German *Volk*—an affinity extending into the very fiber of Germans' innermost beings. *Volk* and forest share a unique character, Düesberg argues, for they are the product of the same *Heimat*; both are autochthonous, rooted in the earth, and both have matured while struggling against a harsh climate and unfruitful soil.[109]

Düesberg's intellectual kin, the nineteenth-century writer and folklorist Wilhelm Heinrich Riehl, also exploited tree symbolism to promote nationalist and racist ideas. Riehl argued that the German nature and character were directly tied to the history of the German people as a *Waldvolk*: from the primordial Germanic freedom of the erstwhile tribes dwelling deep within the woods, he writes, flows a deep influence on the character and customs of all classes of Germans.[110] For Riehl, "it was from the forest and its primeval population that Germany again and again received the strength and character that made and sustained it as a nation."[111]

German ethnographer and geographer Friedrich Ratzel (1844–1904) shared these beliefs in the "folkish, social-hygienic function of the forest for the German nation."[112] Ratzel describes *"Waldvölker"* like the Germans in his book *Anthropogeographie* (1891) as living in such an intimate relationship to the forest that "the nature of the forest interlaced with their entire being."[113] Underlying such amorphous musings is the belief in an essential Germanic nature and being that exists, objectified and totem-like, in the form of trees in the forest. Forestry scientist Dr. Eduard Zentgraf (1882–1973) goes so far as to trace exemplary "German" virtues back to the forest: *Treue* (loyalty), *kriegerischer Geist* (warrior spirit) and *Heimatliebe* (love of homeland), he argues, are inextricably bound to the German forest. Zentgraf even explains the popularity of "un-Germanic Bolshevism" in certain regions of Germany to be the direct result of an either missing or flawed forestry practice.[114]

None less than Germany's Iron Chancellor agreed, declaring that one who destroys an ancient tree betrays a Slavic rather than German character, as if acknowledging and protecting the sanctity of trees were an ethnic trait.[115] As Micheal Imort demonstrates, up until the end of the nineteenth century the forest served the purpose of "nationalizing nature"; that is, the forest became the "quintessential German landscape" and symbol for the German nation. After the turn of the century, however, the 'Germanized' forest became a tool for "naturalizing the nation," acting as a model for a "natural" and "timeless" model for Germany.[116]

The manipulation of forest feeling among Germans reached its apex during the 1930s and early 1940s as Nazi demagogues exploited autochthonous ideology to violent purpose. Functionaries active in the Nazi research institute *Das Ahnenerbe* (ancestral heritage), founded by Heinrich Himmler and dedicated to exploring racial theories, showed particular interest in *völkisch* theories of the forest.[117] National Socialists in general were eager to appropriate Riehl's *völkisch* writings, discovering in Riehl's dichotomy between forest and field a fertile metaphor for depicting Germans as a healthy, superior race.[118] The Germanic race—a "natural" race rooted in its land and soil—could then be usefully contrasted to the "urbanized" and "morally decadent" other—be it the French, Italians, English, or, especially, the Jews—those soulless, forestless "races" that had emasculated their forests into fields and thereby squandered their futures.

The discourse of Riehl and his followers, as well as other *völkisch* writers such as Ernst Moritz Arndt, helped promote a "nascent mood of racism in Germany that ran parallel with an unprecedented interest in nature conservation."[119] Arndt, for example, wrote in 1820 that the preservation of the forest was a precondition for the survival of the German *Volk*, arguing that caring for and sustaining the forest was a sacred duty.[120] Popular literature, finally, bolstered *völkisch* forest theories. *Heimatromane* (*Heimat* novels)—a genre of lowbrow literature idealizing simple, wholesome, rural life in contrast to life in the big city—is a prime example. Ludwig Ganghofer (1855–1920), an author of *Heimat* novels, wrote in *Das Schweigen im Wald* (*Silence in the Forest*): "If one could only exist as the forest, rejecting the weak and the low and only tolerating what is strong and healthy."[121] Here once again we see the conflation of man and tree, and an imagining of the forest as a model for human community.

Such views reach a climax in the photographs of German biologist and nature conservationist Walther Schoenichen, director of the Reichsstelle für Naturschutz in Berlin. Deeply influenced by the writings of Riehl, Schoenichen created in 1934 a series of photographs called *Urwaldwildnis in deutschen Landen* (*Primeval Wilderness in German Lands*). Schoenichen's photographs of forest scenes are accompanied by titles steeped in militaristic language: "Spruce and maple unite in loyal camaraderie"; "Far-reaching tangles of branches characterize the combat zone's spruce forest"; and "Battle-hardened spruces are forward posts in the highlands."[122] Schoenichen's 1939 *Biologie der Landschaft* (*Biology of Landscape*), similarly, drew on Riehl's *völkisch* theories of the forest and repeated Riehl's conviction that without its forest, German culture would be unimaginable.[123]

Building on the foundation of nationalistic, racist forest ideology from the nineteenth century, Nazi ideology popularized the idea of the forest community as a model for a new Germany based on ethnic purity and so-called Germanic values.[124] The forest thus served as a persuasive link between modern Germans and their ancient heritage, acting as a symbol that could be exploited to promote values like self-sacrifice for the collective as well as strength, resilience, and rootedness in the soil (*Bodenständigkeit*), while also justifying the expansion of the German Reich.[125]

Ewiger Wald (Eternal Forest)

Film emerged during the years of the Third Reich as a powerful medium for the spreading of *völkisch* theories about the forest. The film *Ewiger Wald* (1936), produced by the Nationalsozialistische Kulturgemeinde (National Socialist Cultural Organization) and briefly discussed in chapter 1, both sacralizes and militarizes the forest.[126] The film strives to evoke the forest feelings of the German people in order to transfer that attachment from the forest to the nation. Tree trunks and soldiers are visually matched in the film, while the forest itself, as a single entity, stands for the *Volk*, which, "like the forest, would enter a transcendent, eternal realm, realized in Nazi strength and pride."[127] Throughout the film, the forest and the German *Volk* together suffer hardship and celebrate triumph in various historical scenes, including the Battle of the Teutoburg Forest, defeat in World War I (where a field of tree stumps symbolizes countless German lives lost), and finally the joyous arrival of National Socialism. *Ewiger Wald* essentially proclaims that the "individual German was rooted in the soil as a symbolic tree in the forest of the *Volksgemeinschaft*."[128] But *Ewiger Wald* also suggests that in order to realize their ideal nation, the German people must make sacrifices, including routing out the enemies that threaten to destroy the German *Volk* from within. The narration states: "We cultivate the waiting soil / Cut out what is sick and of foreign race.... The eternal forest which will build the new society / And a new society based on the eternal forest."[129] A reference to felling trees that are "sick and of foreign race" is, of course, a thinly veiled reference to eliminating peoples coded in National Socialist ideology as being of inferior and foreign race.

Although offering the most explicit example of its kind, *Ewiger Wald* is not unique. An exhibition on forests in Berlin in 1936, called *Der Wald* (*The Forest*), condemned foreign trees and denigrated "Slavic steppe people" and "Jewish desert people" in contrast to "German forest people." A few years later, signs appeared along the edges of German forests reading, "Jews are not welcome in our German forests."[130] If the forest and the German people were one, then the purity of the forest correlated to the purity of the *Volk*. As Nazi functionary and *Reichsforstmeister* (Reich Master of the Forests), Hermann Göring declared in a speech of 1936 to foresters in Stettin (now Poland): "The forest and the German *Volk*, in the National Socialist view, share a similar nature. The *Volk*, too, is a community, a great, organic, eternal being.... The eternal forest and the eternal *Volk* belong together."[131]

The film *Ewiger Wald* and the exhibition *Der Wald* are part of a larger cultural pattern described by Elias Canetti in his important book *Masse und Macht* (*Crowds and Power*, 1960). Here, Canetti notes that the German people absorb the romantic mythology of the German forest from hundreds of songs and poems and analyzes the confluence of forest and army imagery in German thought, arguing that the crowd symbol of the Germans was

> more than just the army; it was the *marching forest*. In no other modern country has the forest-feeling remained as alive as it has in Germany. The parallel rigidity of the upright trees and their density and number fill the heart of the German with a deep and mysterious delight. To this day he loves to go deep into the forest where his forefathers lived; he feels at one with the trees.... Its [the tree's] steadfastness has much in common with the same virtue in a warrior. In a single tree the bark resembles a coat of mail; in a whole forest ... it suggests rather the uniforms of an army ... for the German ... army and forest transfused each other in every possible way.[132]

Scholar Rainer Guldin agrees, noting that the metaphorical connection between tree and soldier has long been a powerful force in Germanic culture: the German love for the forest and its trees is simultaneously the love for one's comrades on the front, so that mourning falling trees is also an act of mourning fallen soldiers.[133]

During the years of National Socialism, the racist, *völkisch* theories of the German forest and German *Volk*, popularized during the nineteenth and early twentieth centuries, experienced a renaissance. The eternal *Volk* and the eternal forest, in the words of Hermann Göring, found resonance in the image of a primordial, premodern, ethnically pure *Volksgemeinschaft*. This brand of racism, epitomized in the *Blut und Boden* (blood and soil) ideology of National Socialism and in the writings of Nazi ideologue Richard Walther Darré, would eventually find its apotheosis in the conviction that certain persons were not only "unnatural" and toxic to an essential "Germanness" but therefore also unworthy of life.

POSTWAR TREE SYMBOLISM IN GERMANY

In the decades since World War II and the Holocaust, German artists have grappled with the complex legacy of tree and forest symbolism in German cultural history.[134] One of the best-known of these engagements is *Varus*[135] (1976) by Anselm Kiefer, born 1945. *Varus* is one of several works in which Kiefer confronts the myth of Arminius (Hermann) and its role in Germany's catastrophic nationalism. *Varus*, an allegorical oil and acrylic painting on burlap, features a darkly charred, apocalyptic forest. The eye follows a dead-end path through a wintry forest of deep reds, browns, and blacks; a series of wounds scattered across the path drip blood against a thin cover of snow that barely restrains the black and dark red tones pushing out from beneath.

Across this desolate, burnt, wasted wooded scene scrawls in black charcoal the name "Varus." The names of other influential German figures, "the makers ... memorialists and decorators of the primal myth" of the Battle of the Teutoburg Forest—"the primal symbol of Germany's cultural identity"—appear written in white against the trees.[137] Among others are the names Hermann, Friedrich Gottlieb Klopstock, Heinrich von Kleist, Rainer Maria Rilke, Joseph Christian Dietrich Grabbe, Johann Gottlieb Fichte, (General) von Schlieffen, Friedrich Daniel Schleiermacher, Friedrich Hölderlin, Königin Luise (Queen of Prussia), Martin (Heidegger), and Stefan (George).[138] Matthew Rampley reads *Varus* and Kiefer's related pieces *Ways of Worldly Wisdom* (1976–77) and *Ways of Worldly Wisdom—The Hermanns-Schlacht* (1978–80) as a "melancholy mourning of the disaster of German history," an "interrogation of a particular view of 'Germanness,'" and a recognition that "myth and violence have always been latent possibilities in German culture."[139]

FIGURE 2. *Varus*, by Anselm Kiefer, Collection Van Abbemuseum, Eindhoven. Photography: Peter Cox, Eindhoven.

A second German artist, Arnulf Rainer, born in 1929, has also turned to the forest to interrogate the toxic consequences of German nationalism. In his investigations of trees as a symbol of Germany and German identity, Rainer seeks to expose and deconstruct the dangerous entanglements between nationalism and tree imagery. Appalled by the way that the German oak has featured in aggressive nationalist discourse, Rainer created a series of drawings titled *Eichen* (*Oaks*, 1986) depicting leaves of non-German oaks.[140] With this series, Rainer not only uncouples the oak from its Germanic associations but also exposes the absurdity of such associations in the first place by drawing our attention to the folly of attributing nationalistic characteristics to plant species—a direct repudiation of the *völkisch* theories discussed earlier.

A myriad of other postwar German artists, including Nikolaus Lang, Michael Badura, Norbert Stück, Harald Finke, Dieter Appelt, Herman Prigann,[141] Sigmar Polke, and Reinhart Heinsdorff engage forest imagery in their art from a variety of perspectives, including the ecological and conservationist. A brief look at the works by two of these artists gives a sense of the unique approaches to the forest in postwar German art. *Walddenkmal* (*Forest Memorial*, 1982) by Reinhart Heinsdorff depicts three opulent masses of foliage bursting forth three-dimensionally from a series of three nested wooden frames. Beneath the foliage, resting on the bottom of the second frame, lies a single paintbrush. The foliage is alive and lush, and so luxuriant that the frames cannot contain it: here, the dead wood of the frames meets the irrepressible life force of the greenery. The number "three"—three trees burst forth, three frames fail to contain them—is a sacred number in both Christianity and in pagan religions, signifying rebirth, renewal, and resurrection. Here, raw, powerful life cannot be contained—even by art.

A second example is the installation *Abhörung des Waldrandes* (1987) (*Listening to the Edge of the Forest*) by German photographer, painter, sculptor, and video artist Dieter Appelt. *Listening to the Edge of the Forest* integrates photography, sound, and video to create a complex sensory experience of the forest. Appelt began his project with a series of photographs of "ascending and descending silhouettes" of several forests from staggered distances and in measured intervals. He then scanned the photographs to detect their tonal images. These tonal images emerged as "rhythmic drum-like music"; this "monotonous aural layer" accompanies as a soundtrack an abstract, black and yellow video playing in the exhibition. This video is taken from the sound studio control monitor; it depicts in visual images the "sound," that is, the tonal images, of the forest.

Appelt's installation stages "the technical process of eavesdropping on the edge of the forest, and only shows us the hard shadows of nature. The motif of the forest serves as a mysterious, mythical space that the artist seeks to approach with these image-based scores."[142] The audience effectively *listens* to the forest while also *watching*, through the play of images, the very process of listening to the forest. The observer's participation thus becomes part of the work itself, and the forest emerges within a quicksilver play of perceptions, sights, and sounds.

CONCLUSION

A preoccupation with the German forest continues into the twenty-first century. The exhibition *Unter Bäumen: Die Deutschen und der Wald* (*Beneath the Trees: The Germans and the Forest*, December 2, 2011–March 4, 2012) explores the forest as a *Projektionsfläche* (projection surface) on which German dreams, fears, and ideals are cast. In the exhibition catalogue, Benjamin Ziemann describes the exhibition's presentation of the emotional relationship between tree and soldier, as well as the perceived collective *Schutzfunktion* (protective function) of the forest as a form of security for soldiers on the front.[143]

To quote the words of scholar Dieter Borchmeyer: "For Germans, the forest poses nothing short of a landscape of longing.... Forest consciousness in Germany is a phenomenon that has spanned all generations [and] social classes as well as ideological and political leanings since the Romantic period ... one fruit of this phenomenon has been the birth and sustenance of a constant that has pervaded and still pervades German culture."[144] The legacy of the forest in German cultural history is richly multifaceted. As part of this history, the tree emerges as an infinitely complex being with vast symbolic power: at once mythic and sacred, Doppelgänger and auratic object, emblem and totem, form of testimony and vehicle for human memory. In the next chapter, we will examine tree monuments themselves through a cultural anthropological lens.

CHAPTER THREE
Lebensmale (Living Memorials)
Nature's Monuments to Peace, Unification,
the Departed, and the Extraordinary

INTRODUCTION: DIESSEITS AND JENSEITS

In a small, extraordinary book titled *Trees: Reflections and Poems*, German author Hermann Hesse—son of the Black Forest town Calw, Baden-Württemberg—draws on sacred language to plumb the depths of the multifaceted nature of trees. Hesse's vignettes present trees as sanctuaries (*Heiligtümer*) and the most penetrating preachers (*die eindringlichsten Prediger*). They possess God's divinity while pursuing their sacred purpose—to preach the primordial law of life (*das Urgesetz des Lebens*). Hesse's trees are creatures of both *Diesseits* (this world) and *Jenseits* (the beyond): the "world rustles" in the tips of their branches while their roots "rest in infinity."[1] They are thus part of our world, the natural world, but also part of the divine, eternal world beyond that defies our senses and understanding. When one wanders through the old oak groves of Westphalia, Heinrich Heine writes, one hears the voices of prehistory and the echo of profound magical spells.[2] With their evocative forms, astoundingly long lives, and seasonal rhythms, trees resonate with human conceptions of the divine while also embodying the power of the natural world.

The perceived twin nature of the tree as both natural and divine makes it an ideal form for memorials and monuments seeking to connect us, as mortal beings rooted in a specific time and place, not only with the departed but also with eternal ideas and principles that precede and outlive us. Fittingly, these living memorials and monuments have been called *Lebensmale* (living memorials or monuments). The German language is remarkably rich when it comes to words denoting memorial forms. The lexicon includes *Denkmal*, *Mahnmal*, *Ehrenmal*, and *Gedenkstätte*. *Denkmal*, a compound of *denken* (to think about) and *Mal* (symbol or sign), refers to both monuments and memorials, while *Mahnmal* (from *mahnen*, to warn or admonish), restricts itself to memorials. An *Ehrenmal* (from *ehren*, to honor) refers, again, to memorials but also to cenotaphs, while the more formal-sounding *Gedenkstätte* (a memorial place or site) consists of *gedenken* (to commemorate) and *Stätte* (a site or place). The rather eccentric term *Lebensmal* (created from the words *Leben* [life] and the already-mentioned *Mal*) is not found in dictionaries. Indeed, this word is seldom used, but it does appear in a speech given by Erich Schmidt at the unveiling of the Theodor Fontane memorial by Max Wiese in Neuruppin (Brandenburg) on June 8, 1907. In his speech, Schmidt used the word *Lebensmal* to stress that, although deceased, Fontane—or rather, his spirit—would continue to linger among the living.[3] A *Lebensmal*, in both Schmidt's and our context, is a *Denkmal* possessing the quality of life—either metaphorically, as in the case of the Fontane memorial, or literally, when memorials are actual living beings, such as trees.

Both memorials and monuments will be discussed in this chapter. Distinctions between these two forms are often blurred. Philosopher and art critic Arthur Danto, however, offers helpful distinctions between the two: "We erect monuments so that we shall always remember, and build memorials so that we shall never forget." Moreover, "monuments commemorate the memorable and embody the myths of beginnings. Memorials ritualize remembrance and mark the reality of ends."[4] This chapter begins with a discussion of the concept of the *Naturdenkmal* (nature monument) and looks at a few examples of nature monuments, namely, extraordinary trees possessing particular aesthetic qualities and accompanied by myths and legends. We then turn to perhaps the most salient example of memorial trees: the *Heldenhaine* (heroes' groves) designed and planted to honor the fallen of World War I. The remainder of this chapter considers three additional categories of living monuments and memorials: peace oaks and lindens, memorial trees that commemorate the lives of notable figures in German history, and—most recently—unification trees, planted to mark the joyous reunification of Germany.

NATURDENKMALE (NATURE MONUMENTS)

Geographer, explorer, and naturalist Alexander von Humboldt, born in Berlin in 1769, was the first to use the term *Naturdenkmal*. Humboldt coined this term at the turn of the nineteenth century to describe a *Zamang del Guayre*, an extraordinary mimosa tree he encountered while traveling in Venezuela.[5] Humboldt described this magnificent tree—an object of reverence and admiration by local inhabitants—as sublime and imposing.[6] But Humboldt saw in this mimosa tree more than mere beauty and stature, and declared it a monument of nature. With this novel concept of the *Naturdenkmal*, Humboldt created a new paradigm for understanding how trees of historic significance and extraordinary beauty harness symbolic power to act as memorials and monuments.

Approximately a century later, botanist and nature conservationist Hugo Conwentz, born in 1855 near Danzig, established the Prussian State Office for Nature Monument Preservation, thereby expanding the goals of *Denkmalpflege* (historical monument preservation) to *Naturdenkmalpflege* (preservation of nature monuments).[7] In so doing, Conwentz effectively argued that the state should treat trees of a certain age as "historical monuments worthy of protection."[8] Yet another century later, the category of "national nature monuments" (*Naturdenkmale*) became protected under article twenty-four of Germany's Federal Nature Conservation Act. Article twenty-four defines *Naturdenkmale* as objects or areas that "for reasons of science, natural history, cultural history or national heritage, and because of their rarity, special characteristics or beauty are of outstanding importance. National nature monuments are to be protected in the same manner as nature conservation areas."[9]

Naturdenkmale and Naturschutz

The principles behind protecting *Naturdenkmale*, like the Ivenack oaks described at the beginning of chapter 2, hearken back to the landscape preservation movements that emerged in Germany during the late nineteenth century. The *Naturschutz* (nature conservation) and *Heimatschutz* (homeland protection)[10] movements of this time revealed the anxieties of middle-class Germans as they confronted issues of national identity, a changing environment due to industrialization and urbanization, and the destruction of rural beauty.[11] Important to note is that these concerns were primarily rooted in *nationalist* rather than *ecological* anxieties and reflected the belief that German identity and the German landscape were intimately bound to one another. Conflating German identity with the German landscape meant that the disfigurement of the natural environment would result in the disfigurement of national character, resulting in moral decline.[12] In light of these beliefs, the *Naturdenkmal* offered a longed-for palliative remedy by anchoring national identity in a beloved landscape symbolic of a primordial Germanic past. Later, the Deutscher Wald e. V., Bund zur Wehr und Weihe des Waldes (German Forest Association for the Defense and Consecration of the Forest), founded in 1923 in the wake of Germany's defeat in World War I, would contribute, in the words of Dieter Borchmeyer, to the "chauvinist forest propaganda"[13] exploited by right-wing nationalists in their efforts to define German identity as organic and rooted in the German topography.

Initial efforts to preserve *Naturdenkmale* revealed politically conservative tendencies; this is not surprising, considering the motivation to preserve what was perceived as German national identity.[14] It is also important to note that the concept of the *Naturdenkmal* was not an esoteric one limited to nature conservationists; rather, an entire literature of *Naturdenkmale* emerged during the nineteenth and early twentieth centuries, including *Baumbücher* (tree books), tourist guides, postcards, maps, picture books, and catalogues of noteworthy trees in particular regions, such as Hugo Conwentz's *Forest Botanical Notebook* (1900).[15]

Today, one may discover beautiful thousand-year-old trees with the help of twenty-first-century technology and the brothers Stefan and Uwe Kühn, creators of Germany's Deutsches Baumarchiv (German Tree Archive).[16] The brothers' website includes a list of 1,750 nationally significant trees sorted by type, location, trunk circumference, type of trunk, and name of the tree discoverer; individuals who share their knowledge of a tree of appropriate age and value may become local, regional, or even national *Baum-Entdecker* (tree-discoverers) and appear in the LNBB (Liste national bedeutsamer Bäume) (list of nationally significant trees).

Strange and Wonderful Trees: Lebensmale of the Late Nineteenth Century

A lower-tech source documenting remarkable trees in Germany is the late nineteenth- and early twentieth-century article series "Deutschlands merkwürdige Bäume" (Germany's Curious Trees). The descriptions of these miraculous and often magical trees were published in a series of fifty-three articles between 1883 and 1905 in *Die Gartenlaube—Illustriertes Familienblatt* (*The Garden Arbor—Illustrated Family Journal*), an extremely popular mass-circulation German magazine published between 1853 and 1944.[17] The ancient giants featured in these articles are often contorted and broken by age, but their tortured contours only intensify their beauty and individuality. These trees act as memorials to vanished ages; they testify to lost times and communities while their legends offer us nostalgic visions of the past. A few examples will suffice to suggest how trees may act as memorials to times past.

The Kaditz Linden[18]

The Kaditz linden lives in the town of Kaditz, Saxony, not far from Dresden. As described in *Die Gartenlaube*, the Kaditz linden has survived at least one thousand years and boasts a girth of thirty-six feet. It stands today among graves between the Emmaus church and rectory and presents an unusual visage: a fire in the early nineteenth century split the trunk in two; multiple, massive secondary trunks developed in the wake of this damage to support the tree. The trunk itself is hollow and spacious enough that tables and chairs could be set up within, proving to be such a temptation that the community had to install a lock to prevent youthful village dwellers from using the hollow trunk for mischief. The survival of the Kaditz linden after the traumatic fire testifies to the rejuvenating power of trees: although the bark on one side has broken off, exposing the tree to the elements and risking its health, a new cover of bark has grown within the tree along its hollow inner walls, restoring the tree to life.

No mere scenic backdrop, the Kaditz linden has actively participated in the lives of the generations of Germans who have treasured its presence. Resonating with the Germanic custom of designating a village linden tree as a gathering point, the Kaditz linden has witnessed discussions of community business as well as joyous occasions like dances, festivals, and feast days. Such a dance beneath the branches of a linden appears in David Kandel's illustration *Tanz unter der Linde* (*Dance beneath the Linden Tree*), which appears in German botanist, physician, and minister Hieronymus Bock's work *Kreutterbuch* (*Book of Herbs*), 1572. But the Kaditz linden has also served darker, punitive purposes; legend has it that the Kaditz linden functioned as a pillory and effective means of castigating and humiliating gossipy women and similar miscreants. Indeed, according to *Die Gartenlaube*, an ingrown piece of iron—the remnant of a hinged iron collar that once held the necks of evil-tongued women—still lies embedded in the trunk of the tree. According to the legend, the offending women sat, shackled, against the linden while churchgoers passed by on their way to worship at the local church, presenting a pretty object of scorn for the *Schadenfreude* of the pious. The disciplinary function of the Kaditz linden echoes the ancient traditions of the *Femelinden* (punishment linden) and *Galgenbaum* (hanging tree).[19]

The Kaditz linden symbolizes enduring strength and life; its form tells a tale of survival, renewal, and rebirth. Its aura emerges as well from its ability to bear testimony; it whispers a story that engages its visitors in an intimate relationship to the past, while the fragment of embedded iron offers a physical trace of a long-abandoned Germanic custom, helping a modern, contemporary community imagine and connect with a medieval, ancestral one.

The Puch Linden[20]

Many of the trees described in the "Curious Trees" series exhibit a similar auratic power to bridge the modern visitor to the long-distant past. A thousand-year-old linden in Puch, Bavaria, plays a central role in the tale of the blessed recluse and saint Edigna von Puch, who is said to have lived in the linden's hollow trunk for thirty-five years until her death. According to legend, Puch—the virginal daughter of Henry I, King of the Franks—fled her home to avoid marriage, relinquishing a life of wealth and privilege to pursue a life of poverty, austerity, and good deeds. A series of three signs led the fugitive Edigna to her future linden home: her oxen suddenly stopped walking, a bell rang, and her rooster crowed. These three simultaneous events occurred before the Puch linden tree, and so Edigna accepted God's signs and stayed. After Edigna's death, a miraculous oil with the power of healing is said to have oozed from the Puch linden, magically continuing the work of good deeds practiced by the tree's virtuous occupant. A site of pilgrimage and, in the words of the article's author, a true miracle of God's nature, the *Edignalinde* (Edigna linden) possesses the aura of an object at once natural and supernatural, sacred and magical.

Numerous other trees immortalized in the pages of the *Gartenlaube*'s series evoke themes of renewal and rebirth. The Prior linden in Hagen-Priorei, North Rhine–Westphalia, for example, is a fascinating, candelabrum-shaped tree described by Hugo Kruskopf as a "mute witness to gray prehistoric times when the ancient Germanic tribes still sacrificed to their gods."[21] Not far from the Prior linden, Kruskopf writes, an igneous rock with runes was discovered; perhaps, he suggests, this rock had been used as an *Opferstein* (altar stone) in ancient rituals. Such references to the medieval and ancient are common in tales of trees in the *Gartenlaube* series: some trees possess enormous hollow trunks in which the early municipal court (*Gemeindegericht*) was said to gather or are described as witnesses to the primeval forest (*Urwald*). Others are described as symbols for the unification of the Germanic tribes, or as resting places for Charlemagne. Uniting these otherwise unique trees is the singular power to offer testimony to the past and to bind a living community to a distant, primordial one.

The Bridegroom's Oak

Some *Naturdenkmale*, such as the *Bräutigamseiche* (Bridegroom's Oak) outside the town of Eutin in the Dodau Forest in Schleswig-Holstein, are beloved sites that continue to play an active role in contemporary life. This approximately five-hundred-year-old oak has its own postal address: a hole high in the trunk, reachable only by ladder, serves as a postbox for love seekers—a tradition that traces back to a young couple, the daughter of a forester and the son of a chocolate maker, in the nineteenth century. The secret lovers used the hole as a drop box for their love letters until they were permitted to marry. This romantic oak has received love letters from six continents and has acted as matchmaker in more than one hundred marriages. The *Bräutigamseiche* was itself married to another tree with a postal address as well: the relatively youthful, one-hundred-and-fifty-year-old chestnut named *Jüchtwind*, which lived in the Himmelgeist quarter of Düsseldorf. Sadly, *Jüchtwind* had to be felled in 2015; the surviving trunk was shaped by chainsaw sculptor Jörg Bäßler into a sculpture of a female tree spirit—a nod to traditional myths of tree-dwelling spirits.

The *Naturdenkmale* discussed in this section are remarkable beings: thanks to their long lives, unique physical forms and aesthetic qualities, and locations, they have inspired myths and stories that have been passed down through generations. Other *Lebensmale* emerge and acquire enduring significance in a radically different way: these trees were planted with the specific purpose of creating a symbolically rich memorial landscape for Germany's fallen heroes.

HEROES' GROVES

> Deutsches Volk, du herrlichstes vor allen, deine Eichen stehn, du bist gefallen!
> (German Volk, most splendid of all, your oaks still stand, you have fallen!)
>
> —Theodor Körner, "Die Eichen" (1811)

Arguably the most explicit illustration of how tree memorials and monuments reveal sacred beliefs about the forest is the phenomenon of the *Heldenhain*, or heroes' grove, of the World War I era. These wooded memorial groves, modeled on fabled Germanic prehistoric forest groves, draw on a rich weave of symbolism and myth to create a unique memory landscape that is fundamentally nostalgic and reactionary. Although the focus here is on *Heldenhaine*, plans to feature forests in World War I memorials were not restricted to these memorial groves. Friedrich Ebert, the first German president who served from 1919 to 1925, proposed in 1924 the erection of a national memorial for fallen soldiers of World War I in a forest—the "primordial origin" and "power source" of the German people.[22] Ebert's proposal was never realized, but the intention reveals similar ideological assumptions and ideas to those that inspired the *Heldenhaine*, groves declared by Karl von Seeger to be "authentically German, ancient, [and] religious."[23]

The Symbolism of Groves

Nestled within the primeval forest of Germanic prehistory was the sacred wooded grove—a magical and otherworldly space that has colored the imaginations of so many German intellectuals and artists, from Romantic poets, patriots, and philosophers to Nazi demagogues. The sacrality of the grove as a wooded cult site is a universal feature of Indo-European pagan religion. Groves have been known by many names, including *lucus*, deriving from the more general *"loukos"* in Indo-European for open meadowland; *nemus* (forest or grove); and the Germanic *"harug."* Viewed as inviolable by prehistoric peoples, groves served as spaces of asylum and protection as well as the stages for worship and ritual. Thanks to their sacred status, entrance to groves was restricted and subject to taboos.[24]

Within the protected, shadowed refuge of groves, ancient Germanic tribes such as the Cimbri, Alci, Saxons, and Semnones offered sacrifices to their pagan gods, whom they believed to dwell within. Renowned Roman historian Tacitus describes the outdoor worship of the Germanic tribes with admiration: "They [the tribes] judge it altogether unsuitable to hold the Gods enclosed within walls"; rather, "they consecrate whole woods and groves, and by the names of the Gods they call these recesses."[25] Centuries later, German writer Johann Jakob Wilhelm Heinse would describe the forest grove as the model for the Christian cathedral: "What are domes," he asks, "other than the arches of linden and oak trees? One enters a cathedral as one enters a sacred grove: through a refreshing corridor of eminently high, expansive shade-trees."[26]

But why were forest groves chosen as sites for sacred initiations and ritual ceremonies in the first place? How did groves emerge as the stage for world- and time-renewing sacrifices? The sacrality of the grove, as Ken Dowden explains, derives from a range of factors, including its shape and geography.[27] A typically small, densely wooded area with limited undergrowth, a forest grove features a center surrounded by trees that demarcate its boundaries.[28] By the virtue of these boundaries, the grove invites a certain reverence: it naturally sets itself apart, a quality described by religion historians and theorists such as Mircea Eliade as a prerequisite of the sacred.[29]

In Northern European pagan belief, groves belonged to an entirely other reality: they were ancient places "untamed and dangerous" where "human control runs out." Roman philosopher Pliny the Elder described groves as "uncorrupted by the passage of time" and thus as pure spaces separate from the profane world.[30] Robert Pogue Harrison offers another perspective, delineating the grove as a space that signifies the beginning of human agency against the background of wilderness in the primeval forest. The "first human families," Harrison explains, "had to clear the oak trees in order to plant another kind of tree: the genealogical tree. To burn out a clearing in the forest and to claim it as the sacred ground of the family—that, according to [political philosopher Giambattista] Vico, was the original deed of appropriation that first opened the space of civil society."[31] A burnt-out clearing or open space within a grove, as Vico explains, "was called a *lucus*, in the sense of an eye." According to myth, the heavy foliage of the forest concealed divine intentions until the god Vulcan set fire to the forest and thereby "opened the eye" to the sky. Man might thereafter "read the auspices," that is, god's hidden intentions, by deciphering the signs written on the skies. Harrison concludes, therefore, that the clearing of the grove is "the original site of our theologies and cosmologies, our physics and metaphysics, in short, our 'contemplations.'"[32]

Pagan peoples sacralized groves not only in religious and metaphysical but also in legal and political contexts. A notable example is the role of the forest grove as the site for communal decision making and nation building at the ancient Germanic assembly called the Thing (*das Ding*), a practice common to all early Germanic peoples. These ancient assemblies of legations from tribal villages created a first sense of nationhood among the tribes; representatives from the one hundred villages of the Semnones, for example, are known to have held their meetings in forest groves.[33] The grove thus acquired the symbolism of a site of unification—a space where the first, early steps toward nationhood and peoplehood, and thus the very formation of the Germanic *Volk*—took place.

GROVES IN THE TWENTIETH CENTURY: *HELDENHAINE*

Willy Lange's Vision of the *Heldenhain*

The symbolic power of the grove has not restricted itself to premodern times. In the early twentieth century, the grove experienced a revival in collective cultural life thanks to landscape architect Willy Lange's popular and widely supported conception of the *Heldenhaine* (heroes' groves): sacred memorial groves of oak trees dedicated to the fallen soldiers of World War I.[34] Lange first introduced his concept of the *Heldenhain* to the public in an article titled "Heldeneichen und Friedenslinden" ("Heroes' Oaks and Peace Lindens," 1914) in the daily newspaper *Tägliche Rundschau*. Lange subsequently elaborated on his idea in a 1915 volume *Deutsche Heldenhaine* (*German Heroes' Groves*) published by the Arbeitsgemeinschaft für Deutschlands Heldenhaine,[35] the association Lange created to establish his heroes' groves. In addition to Lange's own writings, the 1915 volume includes essays by other contributors, including, among others, Willy Pastor, a historian, *völkisch* writer, and editor at the *Tägliche Rundschau*, and a number of letters, poems, and songs praising oaks and supporting the *Heldenhain* concept.

Lange's vision for *Heldenhaine* was not an entirely original conception; rather, it belonged to a new nationalistic trend in German horticulture that emerged in the early twentieth century. This horticultural movement sought to define a *German* horticulture independent of the influential French and English models. The new German horticulture should be, in the words of Karl Heicke, editor of the journal *Die Gartenkunst* (*The Art of Gardening*), essentially *German*, expressing a uniquely German nature and character. German horticulture discourse became increasingly nationalistic during this time, acquiring to today's ears a ludicrously expansionist and aggressive tone. In a speech to the Deutsche Gesellschaft für Gartenkunst (German Association for Garden Art) in 1915, Heicke declared that German horticulture in all its artistic, economic, and social significance would conquer the world and be a model and leading voice for all other countries.[36] Similarly, landscape gardener Leberecht Migge waxed enthusiastically in 1915 about the inevitable dominance of German horticulture over the French, English, and American varieties. The world, Migge declared hyperbolically, would become infused with German *Wesen* (nature or being) by means of its gardening practices.[37]

Horticulture as a form of cultural imperialism was rooted in the conviction that German gardening practices were inherently superior to those of other nations. Following this line of thought, Lange presents *Heldenhaine* as a superior, fundamentally German memorial practice reflecting a superior and uniquely Germanic mindset. Unlike the "steppe nomads," he writes, the Germans are a *Volk* of the woods and meadows and are thus the only people that could imagine or produce the *Heldenhain*.[38] Art and garden historian Franz Hallbaum (1893–1939) agreed with this sentiment, declaring that while other peoples chose to memorialize the departed in stone, only the Germans drew on the living material of nature to remember their dead.[39]

Concepts of horticultural and memorial exceptionalism resonate with Lange's overall vision for the *Heldenhain*—a nostalgic conception infused with traces of ethnonationalism. Lange envisioned *Heldenhaine* as more than mere memorials; these groves were to be nothing less than mythic spaces recreating premodern Germanic grove culture. Within his vision, oak trees were to replace the heroes' memorials of antiquity and the Middle Ages.[40] Lange and his contributors stress throughout their writings in the 1915 volume the transformative power of the primeval, sacred forest for the Germanic race. Willy Pastor, for example, praises the worship of trees and the forest as a source of pure and benevolent power from old, as yet unconfused times that would reawaken loyalty, courage, and beauty in the modern German *Volk*.[41] The *Heldenhain* volume's essays, finally, are sprinkled with references to Siegfried, Parsifal, Freya, and the sacred festivals of Germanic mythology, clearly framing *Heldenhaine* as part of a continuous and vital Germanic mythology.[42] Predictably, a *Heldenhain* was proposed for Mount Donnershaugk, a site belonging to the realm of the Norse mythological god of thunder, Donar-Thor, in the Thuringian forest.[43]

Guidelines for *Heldenhain* creation are laid out in meticulous detail across the 112 pages of Lange's *Heldenhain* volume. An oak tree (referred to as a *Lebens-Eiche* (oak of life) and *Lebensmal*) was to be planted for each fallen soldier or, in the language of Lange, each "Siegfried."[44] Regardless of rank, all soldiers were to be honored and memorialized together as German brothers in heroes' groves. Stones inscribed with the names of each fallen soldier would accompany the oak trees.

Although *Heldenhaine* would primarily honor the dead, Lange and his collaborators imagined the sites to be places of celebration, resurrection, and hope as well; within these groves, fallen soldiers would be resurrected and live for centuries in the form of oak trees. The groves would be places of pilgrimage and community; here, locals would gather for holidays, "resurrection festivals" in the spring, gymnastics, shooting practice, athletic competitions, and fests dedicated to the fatherland.[45] But heroes' groves would also offer something longer lasting: a corrective to modern, urban life for the Germanic forest soul (*Waldseele*) in the form of a space dedicated to the eternal youth and rejuvenation of the German *Volk* through nature.[46] This rejuvenation and rebirth, Lange and his collaborators argue, would provide a much-needed alternative to the toxic, urban societies and Renaissance cultures of southern civilizations.[47]

In this vein, contributor Dr. Johannes Speck emphasizes themes of decline and renewal as well as the importance of *Heldenhaine* to young Germans. If youthful Germans were to engage in outdoor games in imitation of the ancient Germans, he argues, and were to learn military virtues (such as self-sacrifice and loyalty), remembering (and imitating) through military exercises and games the heroes of the past, then a rebirth of the German *Volk* could take place.[48] The *Heldenhain* would thus help create new generations of duty-bound, patriotic Germans. Drawing on traditional, conservative gender roles, Lange visualizes children coming to the *Heldenhain* and wandering through the stillness of the grove, where they would become aware of how many Siegfrieds had died for German women and girls; the girls, in turn, would learn what they must do in order to be worthy of the Siegfrieds' self-sacrificing love.[49]

The Design and Structure of *Heldenhaine*

Given the crucial role *Heldenhaine* were to play in the renewal of the German *Volk*, the rules for their establishment needed to be precise and well-planned. Like the ancient Germanic groves, these groves, too, would be protected and held sacred: the picking of flowers or carving of tree trunks within *Heldenhaine* was to be strictly forbidden and punishable. Only oaks (and in some cases, a linden) were to be planted in *Heldenhaine*. All oaks were to be not only similar but utterly identical in shape and stature, standing in orderly rows and equidistant from one another so as to evoke the impression of an orderly army of equals.[50] This, too, lacks originality; oaks have often been imagined as young men, especially soldiers, in German literature. Romantic poet Clemens Brentano, for example, describes oak trees in a forest as friends who stand together and share a common goal, and who would sacrifice themselves for each other (*Godwi oder das Steinerne Bild der Mutter*), while Elias Canetti, as mentioned earlier, analyzed the German crowd symbol (*Massensymbol*) as a marching forest.

The spatial organization of the *Heldenhain*, like the rules governing its arrangement, was carefully prescribed: at the center of the *Heldenhaine* would stand a *Kaiser-* and *Friedenslinde* (Kaiser- and peace linden), surrounded by a wall of field stones with concentric rings of oak trees extending outward.[51]

Lange describes the *Friedenslinde* as a symbol of peace, security, homeland, and tranquility.[52] It is essential, Lange explains, that each oak have a close relationship to the center of the grove where the elevated *Kaiser-* and *Friedenslinde*, dedicated to Kaiser Wilhelm II, stands. In this way, soldier oaks might metaphorically rally about the Kaiser.[53] The *Friedenslinde* was also intended to create a link between modern German communities and their ancient forefathers by recalling the *Gemeindelinde* (community linden tree) of medieval Germanic settlements.[54]

A protective wall, together with borders of trees, ditches, trenches, and embankments, was to separate the sacred space of the *Heldenhain* from the surrounding, profane world. These protective walls and borders would highlight the sacred otherness of the grove while also evoking images of a protected German homeland.[55] Embankments and trenches, furthermore, recall the forms of prehistoric graves, strengthening the line of continuity that Lange sought to draw between modern and prehistoric Germanic life. Ultimately, as the *Heldenhaine* volume explains, the goal of the heroes' groves was to evoke a sense of *Urwüchsigkeit* (autochthony): the groves would restore the lost bond between modern, twentieth-century Germany—a product of the destructive forces of industrialization and urbanization—and the sacred, primordial Germanic homeland.[56]

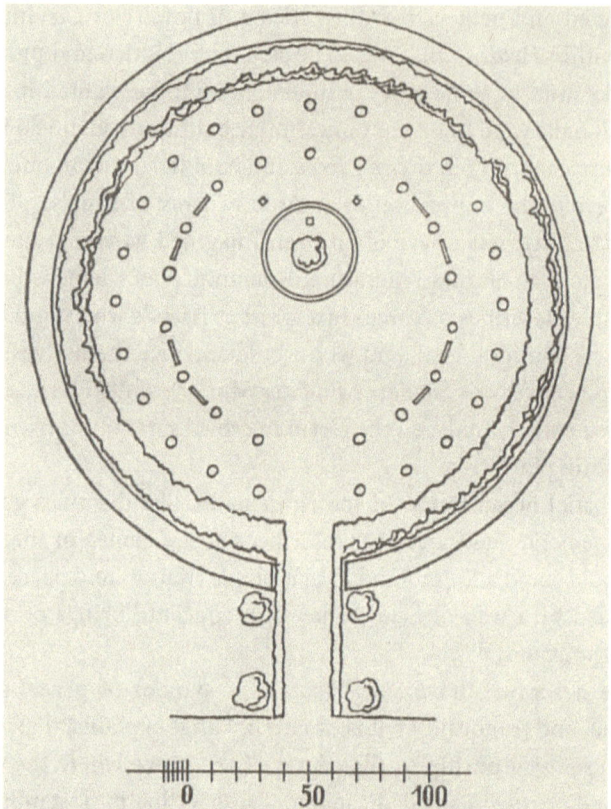

FIGURE 3. Ring-shaped *Heldenhain*: linden in the center with forty oaks, a protective wall of trees, a ditch, stones bearing the names of the fallen, and benches. Designed by Willy Lange. Lange, *Deutsche Heldenhaine* (Leipzig, 1915).

In essence, *Heldenhaine* were to adhere to a ring-shaped pattern, which appealed to Lange for two reasons: first, rings were used to symbolize the sun and the course of its perceived movement across the sky in the rituals of sun worship practiced by prehistoric Germanic tribes.[57] The ring formation also suggests a militaristic function by recalling a standard method of defense against foreign armies.[58] Other elements of the *Heldenhain* encourage a political, nationalistic interpretation: Lange refers to *Heldenhain* oaks as *Stammesbäume* (family trees)—a designation that frames oaks as symbols of Germanic ethnicity across the ages. The oak, Lange continues, is the "Einheits-Sinnbild der deutschen Stämme" (symbol of unification of the Germanic tribes).[59] By presenting oak groves as the spaces where the first efforts at unification of the Germanic tribes took place, both Lange and Willy Pastor create a continuity within Germanic history based on a centuries-long striving toward unification and nationhood.[60]

The *Heldenhain* as Link to an Idealized Past

The nature of the *Heldenhain* as a slow-growing, ever-evolving living memorial resonates, finally, with Lange's reactionary wish to evoke a feeling of continuity between modern-age Germans and a remote, preindustrial, Teutonic past. Thanks to the centuries-old oaks that would gradually fill the groves, new generations of Germans could imagine the long-distant primeval forest. Such historical continuity was particularly important in the wake of World War I, which, as the first mass-industrialized war, was experienced as a rupture with the past and as a force of dislocation and discontinuity.[61] By creating a bond with a premodern past, the trauma of war might be transformed into a coherent narrative rooted in an alternative model of time and community.[62] Nostalgia would offer comfort and reassurance in a time of upheaval.

But the *Heldenhain* concept also possessed darker roots, namely, the dangerous, autochthonous ideas of a primordial Germanic race. Landscape architecture scholar Gert Groening stresses the nationalistic, monarchist, racist, and aggressively militaristic intention of Lange's *Heldenhaine*. The language employed by the *Heldenhain* volume contributors to describe *Heldenhaine* oaks eerily prefigures the very language that National Socialists would later use to dehumanize their victims. Dr. Möller, for example, a contributor to the volume, argues that those planting trees in the heroes' groves must be careful to notice the *Heimat und Herkunft* (home and heritage) of the trees; there must be no *Krüppelbäume* (crippled or disfigured trees), he writes, and special attention must be paid that only local German trees—and certainly no trees of "foreign ancestry," such as Slavic oaks–be permitted within heroes' groves.[63] This obsession with purity and provenance when selecting oak trees resonates with the essentially racist ideology of Lange's memorial groves: if the groves were indeed to shape the bodies, minds, and souls of future generations of Siegfrieds, then German children must be nourished by the presence of purely German oaks.

Lange imagined that *Heldenhaine* would be erected in every German town that suffered the loss of soldiers during the war, creating a coherent and homogenous landscape of memory that would unify Germans and their memories of the war throughout all lands where the German language was spoken—in Lange's words, "so weit die deutsche Zunge klingt."[64] Lange's

Heldenhain proposal received enthusiastic support from thousands of Germans, many of whom wrote Lange effusively grateful letters. Some of these letters, proudly quoted in the *Heldenhain* volume, were written by soldiers on the front. These praising voices from the trenches provided a powerful recommendation to the project, as these men were essentially approving the heroes' groves that might conceivably memorialize their own deaths.[65] "The beautiful thought," one letter declares, "that young heroes will transform into oak trees and live on, as in a fairytale, brings comfort"—a sentiment recalling the Germanic myth that souls of the dead inhabit trees.[66] "Only a German mind could conceive such an idea," extols a second, while a third—written by a squadron minister—effuses that the "*Heldenhain* is the only worthy way to honor German soldiers because it resonates with German nature itself."[67]

The *Heldenhain* proposal excited enthusiastic support among not only the general population but also the highest levels of government. When Lange revealed his idea for the *Heldenhaine* in 1914, Germans still believed that a swift and victorious outcome to the war lay ahead, and the idea of memorializing all soldiers as equals, regardless of rank, appealed to a country awash in patriotic feeling. Indeed, a veritable wave of community-focused activity swept Germany during 1914: enthusiastic young men volunteered to fight, women rushed forward to work in military and base hospitals, and numerous donation campaigns and relief efforts such as the *Liebesgabenaktion* (care package program) testified to widespread and passionate support of the troops. Communities rallied to support wives, mothers, and children left behind at home and local charity groups supported needy families. It was this context of euphoric togetherness, bolstered by faith in a short and successful war, that galvanized many communities to begin planning local *Heldenhaine*.[68]

The Legacy of the *Heldenhain*

Although Lange's dream of a comprehensive and unifying network of *Heldenhaine* was not to be realized, due in part to the unexpectedly high number of German casualties that rendered the project of planting one oak tree for each fallen soldier untenable, the success of Lange's vision should not be underestimated.[69] The *Volksbund Deutsche Kriegsgräbersorge* (German War Graves Commission) adopted the idea of the *Heldenhaine* for cemeteries abroad,[70] and within Germany itself a number of *Heldenhaine* were created, notably in Soltau, Lower Saxony; Neumünster, Schleswig-Holstein;

Ludwigslust, Mecklenburg-Vorpommern; Essenerberg, Lower Saxony; and Lehmkuhlen-Hohenhütten, Schleswig-Holstein, among others. Smaller *Heldenhaine* as well as *Heldenhaine*-inspired cemeteries or memorials, often called *Ehrenhaine* (honor groves), are exceedingly common in Germany, appearing in the countless towns, villages, and hamlets that lost men to the first world war.[71]

The aesthetics and philosophy of Lange's *Heldenhain*, furthermore, have influenced designers and architects of many later German memorial spaces. The Ohlsdorf Cemetery in Hamburg (established 1877), the largest park cemetery in the world, features an *Ehrenhain* dedicated to fifty-five antifascist resistance fighters from Hamburg who were murdered or died as a result of their imprisonment. Johannes Wilhelm Cordes, the first architect of the cemetery, echoed core principles of Lange's *Heldenhain* in his unrealized idea for a *Heldenpark* (heroes' park) dedicated to fallen soldiers—a park designed to feature a circular grove of oak trees.[72]

In recent years, select German towns and cities have begun renaming their *Heldenhaine*—a symbolic gesture reflecting the efforts of community leaders to distance themselves from a word and concept associated with the political far right. These decisions also indicate a more general pattern of turning away from a memorial culture that glamorized war by venerating heroism and self-sacrifice for the homeland. Post–World War II German memory culture tends to posit peace as its ideal and looks to mourn the fallen rather than worship Siegfried-like figures.

The town of Deggendorf in Bavaria, for example, renamed its *Heldenhain* on the Geiersberg a *Gefallenenhain* (grove for the fallen) in 2012. The symbolism of this change did not escape the notice of local veterans' associations, who were initially upset by the decision. At the same time, memorial plaques bearing the names of fallen Waffen-SS at the grove were removed. Changing the name has not been enough to deter right-wing extremists, however, who continue to visit the *Gefallenenhain* in Deggendorf. A group of *niederbayerische Nationalisten* (lower-Bavarian nationalists) arrived at the Deggendorf *Gefallenenhain* on March 16, 2014, wielding black flags and torches to honor the war dead. It should come as no surprise that right-wing extremists, perceiving an attack on their beliefs and values, have opposed the renaming of *Heldenhaine*. The far right and neo-Nazi German political party Der Dritte Weg (The Third Path) has condemned the decision to rechristen Deggendorf's *Heldenhain* as *Gefallenenhain* as *ahnenfeindlich* (hostile to one's ancestors).[73] Similarly, local veterans' and expellees' associations in Neumünster protested the renaming of a *Heldenhain* erected in 1921 as a *Friedenshain* (peace grove) in 1987.[74]

The symbolic efficacy of the oak-centered *Heldenhain*—its widespread appeal to early twentieth-century Germans and adoption by numerous communities—also reflects the totemic status of the oak in German cultural history, as discussed in chapter 2. In the language of Durkheim, the oak symbolically represents the primordial Germanic community and simultaneously shares with that community a singular, unique essence. The qualities ascribed to oak trees themselves in German literature and art (strength, longevity, a rootedness in German history and landscape), as previously discussed, are believed to echo and mirror the qualities of Germany's fallen soldiers, who were strong and loyal to each other and to their *Heimat* and *Volksgemeinschaft*. Unlike vulnerable human beings, however, the oak appears to defy mortality with its centuries-long lifespan; it thus animates, to recall Durkheim's description of the totem, "the generations of today as it animated those of yesterday and will animate those of tomorrow."[75] Lange's *Heldenhain* oaks, finally, fulfill further functions of the totem by fostering moral unity and social stability, and by seeking to create a coherent, integrated community rooted in the original Germanic *Volksgemeinschaft*. The *Heldenhain* itself—in its creators' eyes a uniquely *German* form of memorialization—would thus echo the power of the totem as a marker of distinctiveness by symbolically embodying a unique and singular community.

FRIEDENSEICHEN AND FRIEDENSLINDEN (PEACE OAKS AND PEACE LINDENS)

> Deutschland hat ewigen Bestand, (Germany survives eternally),
> Es ist ein kerngesundes Land! (It is a hale and hearty country!)
> Mit seinen Eichen, seinen Linden (With its oaks, with its lindens)
> Werd ich es immer wiederfinden. (I will always find it again.)
> —Heinrich Heine, "Nachtgedanken" (1843)

Rich with symbolic significance, oaks and lindens are the trees of choice for celebrating and commemorating watershed events in German history. A striking example is the hundreds of *Friedenseichen* (peace oaks) planted in German communities to commemorate the Franco-Prussian War (July 19, 1870—May 10, 1871) and the long-yearned-for unification of

Germany.⁷⁶ A typical *Friedenseiche* grows in Auernheim (Treuchtlingen), Bavaria; this magnificent oak was planted in 1870 by soldiers returning home from war. Today, a memorial to the victims of World War I and World War II stands near the oak. Other peace oaks or accompanying boulders (glacial erratics [*Findlinge*], to be discussed in chapter 4) bear plaques praising peace. A peace oak in Flintbek, Schleswig-Holstein, is emblematic: it bears a plaque reading, "Friede. 10. Mai 1871" (Peace. May 10, 1871). Similarly, a plaque attached to a boulder near a peace oak in Sande, Lower Saxony, reads, "Friedenseiche / Gepflanzt am 18. Juni 1871" (Peace oak / planted on June 18, 1871).

A third example, in Sterup, Schleswig-Holstein, is accompanied by a boulder engraved with the words "Zum Gedächtnis des glorreichen Friedens 1871 und der tapferen Krieger ist dieser Gedenkstein unter der Friedenseiche errichtet" ("This commemorative stone is raised in memory of the glorious peace of 1871 and the brave warriors"). Verses ten and thirteen of Psalm 85, a Psalm of returned exiles, follow: "Gottes Hülfe ist nahe bei denen, die ihn fürchten, dass in unserm Lande Ehre wohne, dass uns auch der Herr Gutes thue, damit unser Land sein Gewächs gehe" ("Surely his salvation is nigh them that fear Him; that glory may dwell in our land; Yea, the Lord will give that which is good; and our land shall yield her produce"). The Franco-Prussian War, instigated by the formation of the North German Confederation in the wake of the Austro-Prussian War of 1866 and a French demand for a return to the borders of 1814, is here equated with the Babylonian exile of the First Temple, while the peace of 1871 and subsequent unification of German states into a Prussian-dominated German nation is framed as the manifestation of God's glory and greatness on earth.

Like *Friedenseichen*, *Friedenslinden* (peace lindens) have also been traditionally planted to honor peace and freedom in the German nation. A group of school children together with their teacher and pastor of the Saint Johannes Church in Gittelde, Lower Saxony, planted a peace linden on October 18, 1913, for example, to mark the one hundredth anniversary of the Battle of Leipzig, also known as the Battle of the Nations— the decisive battle of the nineteenth-century Wars of Liberation against Napoleon. Citizens planted peace lindens in 1871, too, in Darmstadt-Eberstadt, Bronnweiler, and Passau, Bavaria, and indeed all across the new German nation. Many of these peace lindens, as in Gittelde and

Passau, were adapted into war memorials—a common and logical practice, given the symbolism of the peace linden.

As discussed in chapter 2, certain trees—the oak in particular but also the linden—act as powerful symbols in German folk psychology and cultural history. Since chapter 2 addresses both the healing properties of oaks and lindens and the preponderance of forests and trees in select German artistic works, this section will restrict itself to a few, brief, previously unmentioned observations.[77]

Oaks (Quercus)

Oaks (of the genus *Quercus*) have long possessed sacred meaning in Germanic folk history, beginning with their veneration in northwestern European paganism.[78] German writers from Theodor Lessing to Friedrich Gottlieb Klopstock and Heinrich von Kleist, as well as lesser-known authors such as Johannes Trojan and Max von Schenkendorf, have declared the oak to be the "German tree" par excellence and to embody the German *Volk* itself. In the 1842 poem "Bundeszeichen" (the symbol of a community or group), German poet August Heinrich Hoffmann von Fallersleben (1798–1874), author of the German national anthem, declares the oak tree to be the symbol of the German people. Like the oak tree, he declares, which stands free, strong, and unflappable in the midst of a storm, the German people must not falter or waver but remain courageous in deed and thought.[79]

Oak trees, moreover, have repeatedly appeared as symbols in the service of political causes. During the Wars of Liberation (1813–14), German artists of the period such as Georg Friedrich Kersting painted oaks to conjure up a pure, primordial *Germanentum*(Germanness) that bespoke patriotism, courage, strength, and freedom in pictures that thematized the wars, including *Auf Vorposten* (*Outpost Duty*, 1815) and *Die Kranzwinderin* (*The Wreath-Weaver*, 1815). A few decades later, as the failure of the German states to unite increasingly led to feelings of frustration and inferiority in relation to France, the oak tree became a convenient, inspiring symbol for an autochthonous, primeval Germanic identity united by culture and history rather than elusive statehood.

Oak trees continued after the Wars of Liberation to play a major role in celebrations organized by students and choral and gymnastic groups, such as the Jenenser Studenten (Students of Jena) and Turner. As part of these celebrations of a newly liberated *Heimat* and *Volk*, local citizens planted and decorated oaks with colorful ribbons.[80] After the long-awaited German unification in 1871, crowns woven of oak leaves honored significant artistic, physical, and military achievement. Oaks also became the tree of choice for honoring fallen soldiers and decorating coins and stamps; years later, a wreath of oak leaves would appear surrounding a swastika and clutched in the talons of the *Reichsadler* (imperial eagle) in a National Socialist emblem.[81]

One particular, very special oak tree bears mention in this context because of its extraordinary history and symbolism. The Goethe Oak, as it was called by Buchenwald concentration camp prisoners, formerly called simply "*dicke Eiche*" (fat oak), once stood in a beech forest on the Ettersberg, a hill not far from Weimar, the city of Goethe and Schiller. Building a concentration camp close to the German city symbolic of cosmopolitan, humanistic values was no ironic accident. As James E. Young explains, the SS chose the Ettersberg for the site of a concentration camp not despite but rather "precisely because it already had a mythological past in the German mind. When Himmler cynically designated Goethe's oak as the center of the camp . . . , he hoped to neutralize the memory of Goethe even as he invoked the philosopher's cultural authority. What better way to commemorate the obliteration of Weimar culture than to seal it in barbed wire, to turn it into its own prison?"[82]

When SS built the Buchenwald concentration camp (for a brief time known as the Ettersberg concentration camp)[83] on the north slope of the Ettersberg and began cutting down trees to make space for camp buildings, they left standing the protected Goethe Oak—a glorious oak said to have been favored by Goethe and Frau Charlotte von Stein during their walks on the Ettersberg. Indeed, the Ettersberg woods are believed to be the site where Goethe composed his famous poem "Wanderers Nachtlied" and were beloved by other Weimar intellectuals as well.

For prisoners of the camp, the great oak remained associated with Goethe and the enlightened, humanist tradition he represented to them. After the oak was destroyed, many Buchenwald prisoners wished to keep remnants of the tree as souvenirs.[84] In his book *Der Totenwald* (1945), Buchenwald political prisoner Ernst Wiechert marvels at the German *Volk* that produced two fully different Germanies, the Germany of Goethe and Weimar and the Germany that produced the concentration camps. The Goethe Oak, he notes, symbolizes the Germany of Goethe. On his last night in Buchenwald, Wiechert stood beneath the oak, where he had stood so many times before. Here, as Bernd Kauffmann explains, we see the stark dichotomy of Weimar—Buchenwald, which has since the end of World War II played a key role in the concept of the *"Januskopfes Deutschland"* (the Janus face of Germany).[85]

On August 24, 1944, the Goethe Oak caught fire, burned, and was ultimately chopped down by the SS after the armament factory of the Deutsche Ausrüstungswerke was struck by Allied bombs. Two traces of the oak remain: the last remnants of the burned oak and its roots, said to "represent the self-empowerment of the inmates and their memories of a better world," and a remarkable artwork from 1944 by political prisoner and Buchenwald inmate Bruno Apitz. Apitz carved his artwork, titled *Das Letzte Gesicht* (*The Last Face*), on a piece of wood that he secretly removed from the damaged Goethe Oak. The carving depicts the suffering face of a dying inmate, his eyes closed and lips slightly parted. Here we see an example of an oak that conjures associations not with nationalism and ur-Germanic myths but rather with humanism and resistance to National Socialism thanks to its evocation of a great figure of German Enlightenment values and the "other" Germany.

Lindens (Tilia)

Like oaks, lindens (of the genus *Tilia*, also known as lime trees), have a long and rich tradition in Germanic cultural history as a *Volksbaum* (tree of the people).[86] Lindens may live for an astounding number of years; in the words of an old folk saying, the linden emerges for three hundred years, stands for three hundred years, and dies for three hundred years.[87] In pre-Christian Germanic mythology, the linden tree was sacred. Associated with Freya, wife of the god Wotan and goddess of fortune, fertility, love, and truth, the linden was venerated as the guardian of life and was believed to be impervious to lightning.[88] Lindens appear in the *Nibelungenlied* in Kriemhild's magical, paradisiacal rose garden as part of a sacred grove, and are linked to the fate of the hero Siegfried.[89]

Beyond the mythological world, lindens also possessed profound symbolic meaning, standing for centuries at the heart of communal German life. The thirteenth-century *Minnesänger*[90] Neidhart von Reuental lamented the winter that drove reluctant villagers from beneath the wide, sheltering village linden back into their narrow rooms, while religious reformer Martin

Luther described the linden as a "*Friede- und Freudebaum*" (tree of peace and joy) beneath which Germans sang, drank, danced, and made merry.[91]

Lindens were also revered as trees of justice. The phrase *Gegeben unter der Linde* (given or decreed under a linden) may be found on ancient Germanic documents and records, testifying to the fact that in Germanic tribal practice, reconciliations between warring parties were staged and tribal judgments issued beneath the linden's dense foliage. In later years, beneath the *Gerichtslinde* (court linden) of the Middle Ages, assemblies and judicial courts met to take and announce their decisions, and beneath lindens oaths were taken and contracts ratified. In some Germanic regions, verdicts continued to be given under lindens (*sub Tilia*) even after Christianization. The linden was uniquely suited for such legal functions: folk wisdom declared that in the shadow of the linden's branches truth came to light and within the orbit of the tree's presence the innocent were exonerated and the guilty punished. Colorful legends tell tales of lindens suddenly and violently shedding their leaves to expose and protest unjust judgement or magically emerging from the ground where an upside-down linden branch had been stuck.[92]

Lindens were believed to divine not only the hidden truths of misdeeds and crimes, guilt and innocence, but also the hidden truths of hearts. According to legend, if a couple swore eternal love beneath a linden, their words would be rendered true. Lindens thus possessed a romantic aura as the sacred trees of lovers, promising fertility and prosperity. The folk symbolism of the linden appears in a number of early songs, including those of the late twelfth- and early thirteenth-century poet Walter von der Vogelweide, whose verses of "Unter der Linden," for example, depict the trees as symbols of love.

Lindens have also been long venerated as *Schutzbäume* (guardian trees), symbolizing home and security, and possessing the power to protect villagers against evil forces and figures like the demons and witches who emerged on Walpurgisnacht.[93] As guardian trees, lindens were treasured fixtures of village and domestic life. The traditional *Dorflinde* (village linden) and *Tanzlinde* (dance linden) were beloved trees around and beneath which villagers danced, met friends and family, fell in love, and married. Extraordinary lindens whose branches had been carefully cultivated even offered dancing platforms high above the ground in lush crowns, permitting villagers to dance not only beneath but within and on top of lindens. In the town of Limmersdorf in Bavaria grows a *Tanzlinde* with dancing platform; this tree is reported to have stood for over three hundred years. Lindens, finally, served as sacred sites of domestic wish fulfillment, with women desperate for children making offerings to the gods beneath linden trees.[94] Even long after Christianity had supplanted pagan religions, lindens were often planted near churches and graveyards to lend the sites their enduring sacred aura.[95]

Although such practices were more typical of medieval and early modern life—in some cases lasting, however, into the early nineteenth century—traces of a close connection between German communities and oaks and lindens endure. With the advent of newly emerging nature protection movements motivated by the fear of *Waldsterben* (forest death) in the late 1970s and 1980s, many German communities and artists began encouraging a reintegration of human and plant life.[96] In 1985, the environmental authority in Hamburg began planting a *Hochzeitswald* (wedding forest) to revitalize an old custom according to which couples planted trees to celebrate weddings or the baptism of a child.[97]

Indeed, folklore scholar Albrecht Lehmann argues, the extreme emotional reaction of many Germans to the news of potential *Waldsterben* cannot be understood without considering the way that folk literature, fairytales, songs, and Romantic poetry have long shaped the relationship of Germans to their woods. As Lehmann further points out, many newspaper articles and other popular publications concerning *Waldsterben* during the 1980s drew on folklore and Romantic literature to illustrate their apocalyptic scenarios.[98] Activism focused on saving German forests thrives in the twenty-first century; recently, thousands of protestors fought to save the last two hundred hectares of Hambach Forest, a twelve-thousand-year-old forest near the city of Aachen, North Rhine–Westphalia.

The rich, centuries-old history of lindens has served many political agendas. During the late nineteenth century, lindens offered an alternative symbolism to the oak, which, having been largely adopted by the political right, had come to exude an aggressive and defiant nationalism with its "massive, craggy, and solid" exterior evoking "the exterior nation, the *Vaterland*, Germany ready for battle."[99] The linden, in contrast, offered a symbol of national identity at once gentler and more peaceful: a graceful tree, the linden became a symbol of the "interior nation, the *Heimat*, Germany at home."[100]

GEDENKBÄUME (MEMORIAL TREES) FOR NOTABLE FIGURES

Not only wars and other momentous events but notable personalities and historical figures as well have been memorialized with trees. *Gedenkbäume* (memorial trees) are oaks and lindens dedicated to extraordinary persons such as Kaiser Wilhelm I and Kaiser Wilhelm II; the trees planted to honor them are called, appropriately, *Kaisereichen* (Kaiser oaks) and *Kaiserlinden* (Kaiser lindens). Typical is the Kaiser-Wilhelm-Eiche in the historic center of Ratekau, Schleswig-Holstein, planted in 1897 to mark the centennial birthday of Kaiser Wilhelm I.

A bevy of other notable Germans figures have been honored with oak or linden trees as well. The four-hundred-year-old "Eva linden," living at the edge of the Harz mountain range in Seesen, Lower Saxony, memorializes the lonely life of Eva von Trott (1505–1567), mistress of Herzog Heinrich the Younger (Henry V, Duke of Brunswick-Lüneburg). The duke, due to familial pressure to end his relationship with Eva, faked his lover's death and kept her hidden away in an isolated castle. Memorial trees also mark extraordinary achievement; the Friedrich Schiller oak in Gittelde, Lower Saxony, and the Martin Luther elm (the *Lutherbaum*) in Worms-Pfiffligheim, Rhineland-Palatinate, are only two of countless examples. Often, legends accompany notable memorial trees. According to one legend concerning the Luther tree in Worms-Pfiffligheim, a detractor of Luther's stuck her walking stick into the ground during an argument with her companion and declared that if Luther were right, the cane would grow into a tree. Sure enough, the stick took root in Tannhäuserian[101] fashion and grew into a magnificent *Lutherbaum*, proving Luther's truthfulness. This tree, now protected as a nature monument, is described in *Die Gartenlaube* (volume 28, 1883) as a sacred tree and the *Schicksalsbaum* (tree of destiny) of Protestantism.

Tree memorials, particularly oaks (like those planted in *Heldenhaine*), also honor soldiers who sacrificed themselves for their fatherland. Among many examples are a gnarled and knobby tree trunk memorial in Wilfersdorf, Austria, that honors German soldiers who died during the 1866 Austro-Prussian War and a memorial in the form of an elaborately twisted tree trunk in Frücht, Rhineland-Palatinate, memorializing fallen German soldiers of World War I and World War II.

In addition to Kaiser Wilhelm I and II, other political figures of significance are also honored with tree memorials. Two notable examples are

Bismarckeichen (Bismarck oaks) and *Hitlereichen* (Hitler oaks). To celebrate Hitler's ascension to power, *Hitlereichen* (and *Hitlerlinden*) were enthusiastically planted in thousands of communities across Germany.[102] The Hitler oak of Gittelde, Lower Saxony, planted in 1933, is typical. Although oaks often live hundreds—and in extraordinary cases, even so long as a thousand—years, this oak survived, fittingly, only as long as Hitler's "Thousand-Year" Reich itself, dying at the youthful age of twelve. Like Hitler oaks but on a megalomanic scale were the *Waldhakenkreuze* or *Hakenkreuzwälder* (forest swastikas) planted in Germany—for example, in Asterode, Hesse. In contrast to Hitler oaks, forest swastikas were relatively rare due to the imposing scale of the project and difficulty of their undertaking.[103]

EINHEITSBÄUME (UNIFICATION TREES)

The newest *Lebensmal* to join the German landscape is the *Einheitsbaum* (unification tree), planted to celebrate and honor Germany's reunification in 1990 after forty-five years of postwar division. Unification trees are memorials that by nature of their very essence—their status as living, growing beings nourished by German sunlight, soil, and showers—resonate with the idea they seek to embody: a healthy, whole, restored Germany that is already present in its core (what Hermann Hesse described as a tree's hidden "kernel, a spark, a thought") but also ever-emerging as the young trees flourish, thrive, and strengthen through time.

As of December 2020, more than 280 German towns and communities had either planted or committed to planting unification trees, including the former German capital city of Bonn, where a unification tree was planted by chancellor Angela Merkel on October 31, 2014. The plan for unification trees is simple: each community, town, or city across Germany will plant three trees in the form of a triangle, each side of which will measure ten meters. The three trees are to include a beech, symbolizing West Germany, a pine, symbolizing East Germany, and an oak, symbolizing reunified Germany.[104] The oak is the natural choice to represent Germany in its ideal and perfect (unified) state, consummate and integral after the long curse of division. It is, in the words of German Jewish philosopher Theodor Lessing, the tree that symbolizes the essence of the German landscape and has accompanied countless generations of Germans from cradle to coffin.[105]

The growth of Germany's unification trees should model the path of Germany itself: as each of the three trees grows in height and breadth through the years, the three crowns will eventually meet and merge with each other, symbolically illustrating the growth and merging of a once divided country.[106] In some towns, for example, Bad König in Hesse, a fourth tree is added to the three initial unification trees, transforming the triangle into a rhombus. This fourth tree, a linden tree, stands for Europe, thereby suggesting that Germany now transcends nationalism and its associated aggression and militarism by embracing a *European* identity. With its heart-shaped leaves, fragrant blossoms, smooth bark, and pyramid crowns, the graceful linden embodies peace, freedom, and community—an ideal constellation to illustrate the values of a post–World War II Germany thriving in brotherhood and harmony with other European nations.

The concept of the unification tree was created by Werner Erhardt of Wunsiedel, Bavaria. Wunsiedel, intriguingly, was once the burial site of Nazi leader Rudolf Hess before Hess's body was exhumed and his grave destroyed in 2011. In 2014, local inhabitants of Wunsiedel, having grown weary of yearly neo-Nazi pilgrimages to their small town, concocted an ingenious plan to transform the neo-Nazi march into an involuntary charity walk to raise funds to fight neo-Nazis: for each meter the neo-Nazis walked, citizens donated ten Euros to the organization EXIT-Deutschland, a group dedicated to helping neo-Nazis and other radicals escape right-wing extremism and begin new lives.[107]

Now, Wunsiedel is home to the mind behind unification trees. Erhardt shared his proposal during a 2011–12 online citizens dialogue led by Chancellor Merkel and conducted alongside a dialogue with experts on the topic "Menschlich und Erfolgreich. Dialog über Deutschlands Zukunft" ("Human and Successful: A Dialog on Germany's Future"). Three questions framed these dialogues: First, how do we want to live together in the future? Second, how do we want to earn a living? And third, how do we want to learn?

Erhardt's proposal was one of over eleven thousand proposals submitted. On the strength of his idea, he was invited to Berlin to present his concept to Chancellor Merkel. Merkel embraced the project enthusiastically, assuming patronage over the project in association with the Schutzgemeinschaft Deutscher Wald (Association for the Protection of the German Forest). If Erhardt's concept is one day fully realized, thirty-three thousand unification trees will bloom throughout Germany. At the heart of his proposal, Erhardt explains, is the belief that unification trees should be visible to all citizens, in contrast to memorials that are available only to inhabitants of major German cities.[108] Planting unification trees in communities across Germany means that Germans everywhere may enjoy the fruits of an inspired memorial project and a true collaborative undertaking of the German people. Three hundred unification tree memorials have already been planted and dedicated across Germany,[109] as well as a similarly conceived *Freundschaftsdenkmal* (friendship memorial) in France, consisting of three different species of tree. A second *Freundschaftsdenkmal* will be dedicated in Ostrov, Czech Republic. The planting and dedicating of unification tree memorials are celebratory occasions, sometimes attended by prominent individuals. The first German cosmonaut Sigmund Jähn and his Russian co-cosmonaut Sergej Saljotin helped to plant the unification memorial in Morgenröthe-Rautenkranz, Saxony, for example.[110]

This vision of a single landscape of memory embracing and uniting all Germans across the nation might have a familiar ring: Lange envisioned exactly such a landscape in the early twentieth century with his proposal for a nationwide network of *Heldenhaine*. Of course, with his formulation that *Heldenhaine* would one day reach across all lands "everywhere the German language is spoken," Lange injected into his memorial project an ominously expansionist note conspicuously absent in the project of unification trees—the values of which, indeed, are radically different from those of the *Heldenhaine*. Nevertheless, we see a familiar motif—a coherent, integrated memory landscape for a coherent, integrated *Volk*.

A grander imagining of a unification tree, fantastically monumental and not-to-be-realized,[111] is the twenty-meter-high semiabstract concrete tree monument proposed by German architects Axel Schultes and Charlotte Frank for the open, international competition for Berlin's new Monument to Freedom and Unity (Freiheits- und Einheitsdenkmal) of 2009 / 2010. Schultes and Frank are perhaps best known for winning first prize in the Berlin urban planning competition of 1992–94, which resulted in the erection of the Federal Chancellery (Bundeskanzleramt) according to their design and completed in 2001.

On November 7, 2007, the German federal parliament decreed that a Monument to Freedom and Unity would be erected at the Schloßfreiheit square on Museum Island, in front of the Berlin Palace in former East

Berlin. This monument would honor the peaceful revolution in East Germany in 1989 and resulting reunification of Germany in 1990. The new memorial should also recall the peaceful movements and efforts at unification of earlier centuries, in accordance with the wishes of most, but not all, political parties represented in parliament.

Schultes and Frank's submission features a larger-than-life tree lit from within, its crown extending into a prodigious overhang to provide shelter and a sheath of light to citizens below. In a description of the design, Schultes and Frank begin with an evocation of Martin Luther's well-known words: "If I knew that tomorrow the world would end, I would plant an apple tree today." This message of sustainability is part of a larger meaning constellation rooted in the multilayered symbolism of the tree in German cultural history. In their description, the architects contrast their tree as symbol for the new German nation to the eagle, a bird of prey, that resided over the plenum of the former parliament. In contrast to this predator, they propose a symbol of peace and environmental renewal: "And is there a more peaceful being under the sun than a tree?" they ask, while acknowledging that the German people has cast its own capacity for peacefulness in doubt. In closing, Schultes and Frank quote Turkish poet Nazim Hikmet (1902–1963): "Leben wie ein Baum, einzeln und frei / doch brüderlich wie ein Wald" ("Live like a tree, alone and free / like a forest in brotherhood").[112] With their design, Schultes and Frank imagine a new monument for a new German people, characterized by environmentalism and peaceful behavior that assure it a place among a brotherhood of nations.

CONCLUSION

Traditional memorials stake their claims to immortality with sturdy limbs of stone, concrete, metal, and glass. They do not live and thus cannot die; they defy the limits to which human mortality and memory are subject. The *Lebensmal*, however, offers a radically different vision of eternity, one rooted not in an inability to die but rather in the promise of new life with reassuring rhythms of cyclical renewal. From peace lindens and *Heldenhaine* to Hitler oaks and unification trees, the tree memorials discussed in this chapter create a resonant memory steeped in the German cultural history of trees and forests. Trees—particularly oak trees—possess auratic power as totemic embodiments of Germanic identity and community. This ability of the tree to serve as a potent symbol of Germanic ethnic, social, and cultural being infuses the *Lebensmal* with a vital force.

In his 1915 novel *Tycho Brahes Weg zu Gott* (*Tycho Brahe's Path to God*), Max Brod's eponymous hero exclaims: "Aren't these forests quite black with the thick, overflowing sap of life, with the green sap which moves sluggishly in them like a dark blood, awaiting the coming of spring, to burst forth again . . . to bestow upon these dead fields the colour of life? In these forests, life is stored up to supply the whole of nature." This passage, while suggesting the renewal and new life of spring, also notes the "thick sap" that flows like "dark blood" through trees, recalling ancient legends of blood pouring forth from oak trees when struck with an axe.[113] The sap of life animating the *Lebensmal* derives its unique power from a rich source, that is, from centuries of art and literature, myth and folklore, that imagine the Germanic forest and its trees as the original wellspring of Germanic being.

CHAPTER FOUR
From Giants' Graves, Stone Dances, and Devils' Stones to the Twenty-First Century
Findlinge in German Memorialization

INTRODUCTION: THE STONE DANCES OF BOITIN

Deep within a forest of beech trees near the village of Boitin (near Bützow), Mecklenburg-Vorpommern, in a series of clearings spotted with ferns and moss, stand the ancient Boitiner Steintänze (Stone Dances of Boitin):[1] a series of four circles of tall, free-standing, stele-like *Findlinge* (glacial erratics) from the Iron Age (approximately 1200 BCE). Three of the circles—one large and two smaller, with between seven and nine stones apiece—stand close to one another; a fourth stone circle stands approximately five hundred feet southeast from the others. The three northern stone circles form an isosceles triangle; the fourth adheres to the geometric pattern of the first and third by way of an invisible line drawn from their midpoints. One of the stones in the second circle, nicknamed the "Brautlade" (Bride's Chest), bears a vertical line of thirteen holes.

A colorful legend accounts for the Boitin stone circles: long ago, the inhabitants of the nearby village of Dreetz celebrated a lavish wedding. The intoxicated villagers indulged in a dissipated game of bowling with sausages, bread, and cakes. A spirit in the shape of an old man suddenly appeared and warned the guests to stop their wicked behavior, but the revelers only mocked him. The spirit then punished the guests by transforming them into the stones that still stand today in the large stone circle. Nearby, a shepherd with his flock of sheep and dog had observed, but not participated in, the game. The spirit ordered the shepherd to flee and—invoking the classic warning of both Greek mythology and the book of Genesis—warned him not to look back. The shepherd fled but, overcome by curiosity, bent over and peeked back between his legs—technically avoiding, he believed, the forbidden act of looking back.

The Boitin shepherd did not turn to salt like Lot's wife, nor did he lose his beloved like Orpheus, but he, his sheep, and his dog were instantly transformed into stones. Their petrified forms stand in the small stone circle at a distance from the others. The legend concludes with a postscript: a red string sticks out of the Brautlade stone on Saint John's Eve, the night before the feast day of Saint John the Baptist on June 24. If one were to pull on this string at midnight, one would not only free the party guests, shepherd, dog, and flock of sheep from their stone prisons but would also inherit the treasures hidden within the Brautlade. The legend of the Boitiner Steintänze reveals several motifs pertinent to a discussion of German memorials and monuments today: the curious mixture of the pagan and the Christian, the admonishing function of memorials, and the role of community in German memory culture.

In this chapter, we turn to German memorials and monuments inspired by some of the earliest monumental forms of Europe, including tomb architecture and other monumental forms of the Neolithic period as well as the later Bronze and Iron Ages and medieval period—times often romanticized in our industrialized age as idyllic periods of Germanic history. As David Lowenthal famously quipped, "If the past is a foreign country, nostalgia has made it 'the foreign country with the healthiest tourist trade of all.'"[2] For "mobile modern man" living in an "alien present," nostalgia is an ailment without a cure—a sickness rooted in estrangement and characterized by longing for a lost, remote past.[3]

We begin this chapter by considering the role of nostalgia for the remote past and for the imagined lost origins of Germanic culture in German memorialization, particularly in relation to memorials based on two forms: the *Findling* (glacial erratic) and the *Hünengrab* (dolmen). In this context we look at the concept of the "ethnie," as theorized by Anthony Smith, as well as the earliest Germanic monuments from the Neolithic period. The chapter then turns to the object of its focus—the *Findling*—and its early functions in German history. After discussing these early uses of *Findlinge*, we turn to *Findlinge* serving as memorials in modern Germany—their arrangements and aesthetics, their rhetorical functions and symbolism. We will then consider a range of *Findling*-themed memorials, including those erected to honor expellees from the East as well as martyrs and heroes, *Findlinge* featured in cemeteries, and *Findlinge* celebrating the reunification of Germany. The chapter closes with a look at *Hünengrab*-inspired memorials in the twentieth and twenty-first centuries. This chapter argues that an enduring reliance on *Findling* and *Hünengrab*-inspired memorial forms illustrates that nostalgic visions of imagined origins have long shaped and continue to shape German memorial culture.

THE LONGING FOR ORIGINS AND MEMORIALIZATION

Nostalgia for a remote past is also nostalgia for prehistorical beginnings and primordial origins, for a time of "supposed innocence and purity."[4] For some, the remote past is "stored not in memory but in the material cosmos" of objects[5] such as *Findlinge*, *Hünengräber*[6] (dolmens, literally "giants' graves"—single chamber megalithic tombs constructed of two or more vertical megaliths with large, flat, horizontal, table-like capstones creating open, boxlike chambers), and *Steinsetzungen* (stone settings). These objects "store" the remote past; as traces of a lost world, they direct the nostalgic gaze of the modern subject back to an idealized pagan history.

An obsession with origins echoes throughout much of German memorial culture. From Bismarck towers[7] to *Findling*- and *Hünengrab*-themed memorials, ancient forms irrepressibly resurface in modern German memorialization. To understand the resurrection of these ancient forms we must consider how monuments and memorials address collective social needs. Why do we, as a species, build and maintain monuments and memorials? Archaeology scholar Richard Bradley points out that this question actually consists of two: the question of what a monument means to those who construct it, and the question of what a monument means to those who inherit and maintain what Christopher Evans has called the "afterlife" of monuments.[8] Monuments and memorials may serve a variety of needs: they may seek to integrate discrete segments of society during periods of drastic change, establish a common ideology among differing factions, legitimate existing power structures, restore stability during times of upheaval, obscure the truth of power by treating it as natural and permanent, or offer a response to other monuments and memorials that exhibit competing ideologies.[9]

Memorials and monuments that resurrect primordial monumental forms, while fulfilling one or more of these functions, also refer to a long-distant past as a source of still-legitimate authority, creating a link between contemporary peoples and remote times and traditions. By referencing a past perceived as frozen—fixed and unchanging—such monuments partake of ritual time rooted in an idealized, static past.[10] Such monuments, furthermore, contribute to the deep social needs of the individual to belong to a greater social collective, rooted in a particular myth of origin, and to the individual's desire to survive through that collective beyond the narrow confines of his or her own life. In a discussion of the notion of immortality, Émile Durkheim has written that "souls are said to be immortal only to the extent that this immortality is useful in making the continuity of collective life intelligible."[11] Monuments and memorials that recall a people's origins, like the idea of the eternal soul, offer individuals the possibility of a collective life that endures the passage of centuries and provides a sense of social cohesion and shared identity.

The German Ethnie

Where, then, lies the longed-for origin to which *Findlinge* and *Hünengräber*, their like and imitators, nostalgically point? The idealized, original state evoked by prehistoric forms, as discussed in chapter 1, is mythic—a romanticized *Volksgemeinschaft* shrouded in amorphous visions of ethnic and cultural purity. Discussions concerning ideas of ethnic community rely on Anthony Smith's seminal work *The Ethnic Origins of Nations* (1986): Smith's "ethnie"—a largely mythic, symbolic, and durable ethnic community residing in a "quartet of myths, memories, values, and symbols"—is transmitted through very slowly changing forms and genres of artifacts and activities over generations and even centuries.[12] In addition to a collective name, shared history, distinctive shared culture, and association with a specific territory—that is, a homeland with a symbolic geographical center, and sense of solidarity—Smith also identifies a common myth of descent and origin as essential to an ethnie.[13]

The nostalgia, according to Smith, with which the modern, alienated individual gazes back at a common myth of origin is the nostalgia for kinship and nostalgia for territory—two types of nostalgia exacerbated by modern conditions. Feelings of estrangement, alienation, homelessness, and anomie drive a desire to connect with one's distant ancestors, while the rapid pace of modern capitalist, bureaucratic society leads to a longing to control the scope of social change. At the core of these desires is the yearning to be reintegrated into and rooted in a lasting social framework with boundaries in time and space, and to achieve immortality through a link to "a community of history and destiny."[14] Landscape, too, plays a central role in nostalgic myths of community, with a remote and inaccessible ancestral terrain—a poetic topography anchored in primordial time—looming large as an inherently mysterious space of origin.[15] In the context of memorialization, durable objects of material culture like granite *Findlinge* and *Hünengräber* act as mnemonic devices, transmitting and sustaining the concept of an ethnic-based community and identity among new generations of Germans.

As discussed in chapter 1, the legend of the Roman soldier Arminius, who led the ancient Germanic tribes in a victorious uprising against the Roman legions in Teutoburg Forest in 9 CE, plays a central role in the myth of an autochthonous Germanic ethnie rooted in Germany's primordial forests. According to legend, Arminius preserved the unique Germanic ethnie and secured the future German nation by preventing the Romanization of the Germanic tribes. The legend of the Battle of the Teutoburg Forest has endured for centuries because it is essentially a creation myth combining elements of heroism, liberation, and the birth of the collective consciousness of the Germanic *Volk* as nation at the site of its mythic origin—the primeval forest.

Expressions of nostalgia for the primordial Germanic ethnic community have long appeared in the writings of *völkisch* writers, Romantic poets, and members of or sympathizers with right-wing extremist groups. Such nostalgia also characterizes the work of individuals who have exercised considerable influence over Germany's memorial culture, such as landscape architect Willy Lange, creator of the modern *Heldenhain* (heroes' grove) memorial in the early twentieth century. As discussed in the previous chapter, Lange's *Heldenhaine* were designed to inspire Germans to return to what he identified as the country's authentic roots: a rural, unified community based on love of homeland and a return to nature—specifically, the forest grove, which Tacitus famously baptized "the cradle of the [Germanic] race."[16] Lange describes the early ancestors of modern Germans (the "*Germanen*") as settlers of the woods and fields, utterly unlike the nomadic, urban creatures who prefer *civilization* (inauthentic city life) over *culture* (authentic, autochthonous German tradition and customs). The German soul, Lange argues, is a forest soul (*Waldesseele*), free from the noise and chaos of the modern city environment.[17]

Lange's *Heldenhaine* express a longing for the mythic, original Teutonic past imagined in "old-Germania"; the heroes' groves themselves were designed to help modern Germans trace an unbroken national tradition from that origin in Germanic prehistory to the present day.[18] Key to this idealized past is the vision of the unified Germanic ethnie. "The myth of a lost unity holds sway over modern German history as a whole," declares Robert Pogue Harrison, who identifies throughout much of German history a "prolonged attempt at cultural, natural, social, spiritual, or racial reunification." The nostalgia for this imagined, unified Germanic ethnic community, Harrison concludes, is "pervaded by the trauma of division or severance."[19] In this chapter, we shall see how *Findlinge* and *Hünengräber*-themed monuments may evoke this imagined primordial, unified ethnic community that predates the trauma of division and may also, in other contexts, celebrate the overcoming of such trauma.

Objects of Nostalgia: The Earliest Monuments

Although the burial rites of our species (namely, the practice of burying our dead in nondomestic, clearly defined areas) may be traced back almost one hundred thousand years, such practice became widespread only during the last six thousand years or so.[20] Monumental architecture remained unknown before the transition from the Paleolithic to the Neolithic period around twelve thousand years ago, when human beings began transitioning from a nomadic, hunter-gatherer lifestyle to a settled lifestyle with farming, villages, and possessions. Thousands of years after the first monumental structures appeared, monumental tomb architecture began cropping up in Neolithic Europe.[21] The earliest monuments from the Neolithic period were monuments to the dead, consisting of earthworks, mounds, and cairns, as well as enclosures (earthworks with ditches and banks).[22] Enclosures typically held deposits of artifacts as well as human and animal remains.[23]

While the earliest monumental graves were simple earthen long barrows or wooden constructions, eventually stone formations and megalithic tombs also emerged. During the Middle Neolithic A period (around 3400 BCE), collective megalithic tombs like large passage graves, reused for centuries, began appearing, to be followed by new collective tombs and graves in rows, clusters, or low mounds during the Middle Neolithic B and Late Neolithic periods. Finally, monumental structures requiring several phases of construction were built to serve multiple, consecutive burials. Erected at communal locations, these burial monuments exhibit similarities to the monumental graves, monuments, and memorials we still see today.[24]

The unifying, cohering social function of these later, communally located, collective burial monuments resonates with the functions of twenty-first-century memorials and monuments. Specifically, Europe's earliest monuments reveal values and beliefs essential to the creation of community and perform the important work of setting boundaries: Neolithic enclosures in northwestern Europe, for example, were increasingly placed at the margins of settled landscapes—perhaps offering protection against attack while also playing a role in ritual activities and rites of passage. As such, these enclosures functioned as the symbolic center of the community, establishing a "new sense of place and new kind of sacred geography."[25] But these early monuments also served an additional function: the continued construction of enclosures in traditional forms despite the passage of time suggests that enclosures were built to reference settlements of the past, recalling (and idealizing) earlier communities that had lived in the same location, and thus revealing attachment to place (territory) and ancestors (kinship).[26]

Many memorials and monuments in modern Germany do much the same work as these early forms: they help create unity and coherence; reveal values and beliefs essential to the creation and preservation of community; mark the (symbolic) boundaries between the homeland and neighboring countries and between the native and the stranger; offer symbolic centers for communities; and, in the case of *Findlinge-* and *Hünengrab*-themed memorials, perform the rhetorical work of nostalgically referencing and recalling remote ancestors and communities.[27]

FINDLINGE (GLACIAL ERRATICS)

> The Greeks have a culture of marble; the Germans should have a culture of granite. Granite is a Nordic and a Germanic stone.
>
> —Julius Langbehn, art historian and philosopher (1851–1907)

The most common memorial object referencing prehistoric Germanic communities is the *Findling* (glacial erratic; from the German *finden* [to find]: a glacially deposited rock that has "wandered" [*errare*] from its original site).[28] *Findlinge* are stones, usually granite, brought to the northern

German lowlands from Scandinavia by glaciers during the Ice Age. Aside from serving as memorials and monuments, many *Findlinge* play central roles in local German cultural traditions and folklore. Some are the focal points of colorful rural legends explaining their locations, markings, and histories. One such legend explains the appearance of the Teufelsstein (Devil's Stone),[29] a sixteen-square-foot granite *Findling* marking the meeting point of three villages—Trebatsch, Mittweide, and Zaue—on the Schwielochsee (Schwieloch Lake) in eastern Brandenburg. This *Findling* bears the imprints of three crosses and what appears to be a handprint beneath them with *Näpfchen* (depressions resembling little cups).

According to the Teufelsstein legend, there once lived in the town of Goyatz on Schwieloch Lake a wealthy vineyard owner, who made a deal with the devil. The vineyard owner promised the devil his beautiful daughter if the latter would build for him a wall around his vineyard between midnight and cock crow of the following morning. The devil agreed and began speedily collecting the largest stones from surrounding fields to build his wall. The peasants of the village of Zaue heard rumors of the agreement and decided to protect the greatest stone of their region by marking it with three crosses to ward off the devil. When the devil, eager to complete his work and having already gathered all the other stones of the region, arrived at the largest stone of Zaue and saw the crosses, he flew into a rage. Before rushing off to find replacement stones, he stamped his foot and struck the stone with his hand, leaving behind the depressions. Meanwhile, the vineyard owner, seeing the almost-completed wall, regretted the deal he had struck. His rooster had yet to crow, and the devil had time to complete his task. On the advice of his grandmother, the vineyard owner struck his leather apron three times, and his rooster instantly crowed. Just at that moment, the devil was fetching a boulder from a mountain in the village of Ressen for his capstone. Hearing the cock crow, the devil knew he had been robbed of his due; he flung the stone in fury at the home of the vineyard owner but missed his target and fled. As is common, the legend accounts for the unusual markings on the *Findling* and offers a moral lesson.

Although predominantly used in memorialization, *Findlinge* and *Hünengräber* were also beloved motifs in early Romantic art. Emblematic are two famous paintings by German Romantic landscape painter Caspar David Friedrich (1774–1840)—*Hünengrab im Schnee* (*Giant's Grave in the Snow*, 1807), mentioned in chapter 2, and *Hünengrab im Herbst* (*Dolmen in Autumn*, 1820), as well as a *Hünengrab* etching by Christoph Nathe (1753–1806) and other works. *Findlinge* and *Hünengräber* have inspired many works of literature and poetry as well, including the poem "Das Hünengrab" ("The Giants' Grave") by Wilhelm Müller (1794–1827).

EARLY FUNCTIONS OF FINDLINGE IN GERMANIC HISTORY

Many tens of thousands of *Findling* memorials and monuments dot the German landscape, especially in the villages and small towns of northern Germany. *Findlinge* appear in heroes' and honor groves dedicated to the fallen of World War I, and hundreds of *Findlinge* memorialize German and ethnic German expellees from Germany's former eastern territories. *Findlinge* also memorialize manifold other historical events and individuals, including prisoners of war and fallen soldiers; figures of national importance or those cast as national heroes or martyrs, such as Albert Leo Schlageter,[30] Horst Wessel, and Hans Mallon; victims of Stalinism;[31] *Heimatdichter* (regional writers) such as the novelist, poet, and fallen soldier Hermann Löns and the poet Robert Haaß;[32] the division of Germany; and Germany's reunification. *Findlinge* dominate, finally, *Ahnenstätten*—small, non-Christian cemeteries.

In addition to acting as memorials, *Findlinge* have served a number of other purposes as well in Germanic history. Achim Timmermann demonstrates that ancient Germanic tribes probably used large standing stones such as *Findlinge* as *Grenzsteine* (boundary stones) to mark the edges of their power spheres.[33] Medieval boundary stones frequently bore emblems and inscriptions and were used not only to keep people out of certain regions and spaces but also to keep people safely within by marking the boundaries of spaces offering sanction in the form of asylum.[34] The placement of boundary stones was so crucial to early Germanic communities that small, imperishable objects called *geheime Zeugen* (secret witnesses), such as pottery shards, glass, or coal, were placed near boundary stones to provide evidence that they hadn't been disturbed or shifted.

In Timmermann's words, the laying of boundary stones was a "quasi-sacred ritual" carried out by specially appointed persons called *Steinsetzer* or *Feldschieder* (stone setters or placers / field separators). Given the significance of placement and the integrity of boundary stones, it is logical that moving such stones was a forbidden, sacrilegious act, punished with fines or corporeal punishment. Local wayside cross legends tell of men beheaded for the crime of shifting boundary stones. Boundaries, indeed, were so sacred that communities staged rituals called "beating of the bounds" to discourage *Grenzfrevel* (boundary sacrilege). During these rituals, children and adolescents were brought to the sites of monuments marking boundaries to have their ears tweaked or boxed, or to be thrashed over the boundary stones, so that "place [was] literally inscribed onto their bodies."[35] The sacred power to mark and thus control space ascribed to *Findlinge* as boundary stones makes them a resonant choice for memorializing the homelands of Germans and ethnic Germans in territories east of the Oder and Neisse Rivers, lost to Germany after World War II and now part of Poland or the Czech Republic. Here, *Findlinge*—the very forms that once proclaimed the boundaries of the homeland—now mark the absence of and longing for the lost *Heimat*.

Additional functions of *Findlinge* in the Germanic past bear mention: in addition to marking boundaries and graves, *Findlinge* were also the most common markers of pagan sites. Relatively immobile due to their size and weight, *Findlinge* embodied place and stability, and were thus ideal for marking the center and focus of sacred spaces. *Findlinge* were imbued with the perceived power of religious sites and served as the precursor to altars, just as statues are formalizations of pillars, which were in turn inspired by stones or trees.[36] As primordial altars, *Findlinge* served various roles in legal contexts: individuals swearing oaths and accused persons standing trial stood on *Findlinge*—practices, according to James George Frazer, that reflect the belief that the stones' "general magical efficacy," strength, and stability would be magically extended to the speech acts taking place upon them.[37]

Findlinge also served as *Gerichtssteine* (judgment stones) during the Middle Ages, marking the boundaries of jurisdictions, serving in executions (for example, as the stones against which the backs of condemned persons were broken);[38] forming the steps on which judgments were pronounced,[39] marking places where condemned persons were consecrated for death,[40] and delineating locations of local *Rügengerichte*. At *Rügengerichte* (public courts held at particular times of the year), locals from villages of the municipality gathered and could, before an assembly of members of the court from various villages, "*rügen*"—that is, reprimand and blame one another for all kinds of legal infractions, including border disputes, water damages, theft, and brawls.[41] Each of these functions of *Gerichtssteine* is based on the perception of *Findlinge* as objects of authority and integrity—be they marking the limits of proprietary rights, justice, or human life, their inherent characteristics of strength and immobility lent gravitas, honor, and binding commitment to the activities taking place on them or in their vicinity. Still today, one may visit an authentic medieval *Gerichtsstein* in the town of Bergen on the German island of Rügen in the Baltic Sea. The stone bears traces of an iron wedge once anchored within as well as discolorations due to being partly buried in the earth, following the custom. With a circumference of almost forty feet and weighing about thirty-five tons, the stone was found beneath the foundation of an old prison where court was once held and judgments granted.[42]

Findlinge with special properties, finally, were believed to possess special powers: stones bearing hollows or holes were believed to possess the power to heal particular ailments such as measles or whooping cough; to stimulate healing, parents placed or passed their children in or through the hollows and holes. Finally, given the array of powers and meanings assigned to *Findlinge* in pagan communities, it is not surprising that some were placed in groves or integrated into shrines, anointed with oil, and worshipped.[43]

FINDLINGE IN MODERN GERMAN MEMORIAL CULTURE

The significance of *Findlinge* in German memorial culture is tied to their prehistoric and ancient histories, including their use in *Hünengräber*, *Hünenbetten* (giants' beds—long barrows or cairns), and Neolithic burial sites. Thanks to these histories, *Findlinge* have long acted as projection screens for political purposes throughout the nineteenth and twentieth centuries, as well as still today.[44] As alleged witnesses to a mythic past occupied by ancient Germanic tribes, *Findlinge* are well-suited to serve as auratic symbols of an emergent German national identity. *Findlinge*, as well as *Hünengräber*, have played starring roles in German memorialization from the early nineteenth century onward, often acting as patriotic symbols of growing national consciousness and a longing for political unity, as well as embodiments of the hope for a strong and independent

German *Volk*. Despite the different purposes they have served, it is safe to say that since the end of the nineteenth century, *Findlinge* have primarily embodied the beliefs of the political right.[45]

Findlinge in Nineteenth-Century Memorialization

In many cases, *Findlinge* have been used to celebrate the victorious Wars of Liberation (1813–14), the Second Schleswig War of 1864, the Franco-Prussian War of 1870–71, and the unification of Germany in 1871.[46] *Findlinge* have also been popular choices for commemorating watershed events years later: the Elsternbusch[47] memorial in Enger, North Rhine–Westphalia, was erected by the Enger community in 1913 on the centennial of the Wars of Liberation. It consists of a large *Findling* perched atop a pyramid of smaller *Findlinge* of varying colors and sizes and engraved with the names of the nine districts of the town of Enger. *Findling* memorials do not only celebrate victory, however: they also mourn division and loss of freedom, including the trauma of defeat in two world wars and the resulting loss of territory, expulsion of Germans and ethnic Germans from eastern territories, and decades of division.

Findlinge in the Twentieth Century

During the first half of the twentieth century, *Findlinge* were often dedicated to Kaiser Wilhelm II, Bismarck, and other important political figures. In Wilhelmine Germany between 1890 and 1918, *Findlinge* became increasingly coopted by *völkisch*, racist ideology and were adopted as symbols for an *ur*-Germanic, autochthonous connection to the land. *Findlinge* imagery emerged as well, however, in other contexts: for example, as a popular motif among adherents of the *Wandervögel* youth movement, where they symbolized a return to nature and rejection of industrialized society.

Since World War I, *Findlinge* (as well as stone circles surrounding them and heroes' groves featuring *Findlinge*) have been primarily associated with the hero worship of warriors and with autochthony; indeed, *Findlinge* were often the most popular choice for expressing revanchist political beliefs during the 1920s and 1930s.[48] Granite *Findlinge* in the post–World War I context symbolized the hardness of German front soldiers and Germany's invincibility (despite losing the war).[49] Karl von Seeger, praising the use of *Findlinge* as war memorials, declares the *Urgestalt* (primordial form) of *Findlinge* ideal for honoring the heroism and heroes' deaths of German soldiers. In his description of a *Hünengrab*, Seeger praises the "monumental beauty" and "primordial power" (*Urkraft*) of the mighty stones and capstone slab: "Their unhewn form resembles the front soldier himself," he writes, "hard and big-boned and colossal, primeval . . . menacing and powerful . . . with defiance and will." Such "primordial forms" (*Urformen*) reveal the spirit of the Germanic ancestors of the Stone Age— both heroes' groves and *Hünengräber*, including the memorial modeled after a *Hünengrab* in Haynau, Silesia (now Chojnów, Poland), express in Seeger's view an "authentic, German, primordial, religious idea."[50]

During and after World War I, many *Heldenhaine* and *Ehrenhaine* (honor groves) incorporated *Findlinge* into their sites: a World War I *Heldenhain* in the town of Meyenburg, Brandenburg, for example, features a great memorial pyramid built of *Findlinge* and crowned with an eagle and Iron Cross; near the pyramid are a series of orderly rows of other *Findlinge* engraved with dedications and the names of the fallen. One *Findling* is engraved with the words "Heldenhain. Du sollst an Deutschlands Zukunft glauben. An deines Volkes auferstehn" ("Heroes' Grove. You should believe in Germany's future. In the resurrection of your people"). A second World War I *Heldenhain* in the village of Nielebock, Saxony-Anhalt, of which only traces remain, featured a stone pyramid with *Findlinge* engraved with the names of the fallen and arranged in a circle. A third *Heldenhain* in the town of Ludwigslust, Mecklenburg-Vorpommern, nestled in a small forest west of town, features one large *Findling* engraved with a dedication to the fallen soldiers of World War I; smaller *Findlinge*, once painted with the names of the fallen, lay scattered about.

Basic *Findling* memorials consist of large, freestanding boulders bearing inscriptions memorializing the fallen of World War I and / or World War II, often near other stones or plaques bearing inscriptions.[51] Many *Findlinge* are crowned with eagles or Iron Crosses[52] and sit atop walls or pedestals of mortared stone.[53] Often, *Findling* memorials feature one large, engraved *Findling* perched atop or surrounded by a number of smaller, supporting *Findlinge*;[54] other memorials feature groupings of *Findlinge* memorializing different victim groups, as in Fissau (Eutin), Schleswig-Holstein, where *Findlinge* commemorate the fallen of World War I and World War II, and expellees from Germany's former eastern territories. It is common for *Findling* memorials to convey the greatness of Germany with their size: a World War I and World War II memorial in Tremsbüttel, Schleswig-Holstein, for instance, stands in the center of a circle surrounded by three oak trees. Three steps lead to a pylon of mortared stones, topped with a *Findling* engraved with the years of both world wars and of such imposing size that it extends past the sides of the pylon.

More elaborate *Findling* memorials, such as a World War I memorial in the village of Ahlum, Saxony-Anhalt, are monumental structures consisting of several large *Findlinge* stacked high, altar-like, atop a flight of steps and surrounded by stones engraved with the names of the fallen. A World War I memorial in the Gilberg cemetery of Eiserfeld (Siegen), North Rhine–Westphalia, features an enormous *Findling* reminiscent of a monolith atop a wall, flanked by two curving stone stairways—a staging that evokes a pagan cult site but for a large church bell on the ground between the two flights of steps.

Occasionally, *Findlinge* are amassed into mounds resembling Neolithic graves and crowned with a single, dominant *Findling*, as in the town of Putlitz, Brandenburg, the hamlet of Markee, Brandenburg, and the villages of Dobberkau and Lostau, Saxony-Anhalt, the latter of which features a large *Findling* engraved with an Iron Cross and the date 1813 (marking the Wars of Liberation) and perched atop a pyramid of mortared *Findlinge* and field stones. Other *Findlinge* boast elaborate reliefs, such as a woman planting an oak tree in the hamlet of Falkenrehde, Brandenburg. Often, *Findlinge* appear in conjunction with round temples[55] or are positioned between two crosses, as in the case of a World War II *Findling* memorial in Schollene, Saxony-Anhalt.

One memorial built in the shape of a *Hünengrab* and featuring many *Findlinge* bears special mention: in the Martin Luther Church cemetery in Trittau, Schleswig-Holstein, stands a World War I memorial designed by Eggert Sommerfeldt, a former pastor in Trittau (dedicated 1926).[56] Each year on Volkstrauertag (Germany's National Day of Mourning), citizens gather at the memorial to remember the fallen of the two world wars. The original memorial is a crypt-like structure consisting of two vertical walls of granite topped with a horizontal capstone in classic *Hünengrab* form. A door bears vertical bronze plates engraved with the names of the fallen, the years of World War I, and a dedication.[57] Two details are worth noting: first, earthworks surround both sides and the back of the structure; against these earthworks are heaped great masses of variously shaped and sized *Findlinge* that evoke the form of a rock-cut tomb—a chamber tomb used for single or collective burial that is cut into solid, natural rock, such as a cliff or sloping rock. Common during the Neolithic and Iron Ages in the Mediterranean region, rock-cut sarcophagi were kept closed with heavy doors and opened only during burial or ceremonies. The second detail is a rising, gold-plated aluminum sun[58] affixed to the back of the capstone. The imagery of a rising sun, evocative of the ancient Germanic sun cult as well as new beginnings and resurrection, is a clear reference to hopes for renewal and rebirth in post–World War I Germany.[59]

Circular Stone Settings

A noteworthy characteristic of many *Findling* memorials in Germany is the use of circular arrangements to mark *Findlinge* themselves, or the spaces the *Findlinge* encircle, as sacred in contrast to profane space. A typical example is a World War I and World War II memorial in Stenum, Lower Saxony: within a clearing surrounded by tall trees stands a circle of six carefully spaced *Findlinge*. Each *Findling* is over six feet tall

FIGURE 4. Memorial in Martin Luther Church cemetery in Trittau. Photo: Marlise Appel, Ev. Akademie der Nordkirche.

and surrounded, in turn, by smaller stones. The circular arrangement of menhir-like *Findlinge* around an empty, central space suggests a ritualistic landscape evocative of pagan practice. A central *Findling* or tower of *Findlinge* are also commonly surrounded with a circle or half circle of field stones or smaller *Findlinge* engraved with the names of the fallen soldiers of World War I, as in Birkenwerder and Rogäsen, both in Brandenburg. An elaborate *Findling* circle arrangement may be found at the memorial site dedicated to the fallen of German wars between 1813 and 1871 in the village of Mechau, Saxony-Anhalt; here, a central, massive *Findling* stands on a hill, crowned with an Iron Cross and encircled by three oak trees and two concentric rings of field stones engraved with dedications and names. The concentric circles emphasize the sacrality of the innermost *Findling*. In three corners lay stones engraved with the dates 1864 (Second Schleswig War), 1866 (Austro-Prussian War), and 1870–71 (Franco-Prussian War).

In their writings on *Heldenhaine*, both Willy Lange, creator of the World War I *Heldenhain* concept, and his collaborator Willy Pastor emphasize the importance of the circular, ringlike arrangement of heroes' groves and stress the significance of the circle to Germanic pagan religions.[60] Pastor focuses on the worship of the sun in Germanic prehistory, arguing that the ancient Germanic tribes' use of circles in their sun shrines as well as graves and burial sites—a shape, he notes, that imitates the path of the sun itself—makes the circles essential to German culture.[61] Lange, in turn, argues that circular stone settings suggest protection of the homeland, noting that rings of walls and ditches should surround heroes' groves in order to create boundaries to protect and defend the groves from attack.[62]

A third perspective is offered by archaeology scholar Richard Bradley, who argues that the predominantly circular shape of prehistoric enclosures, with their multiple entrances facing in different directions, likely emphasized the role of the enclosure as the "centre of a dispersed community" and "mythical settlement" of past generations that linked living communities to ancestral ones.[63] Indeed, the circular structure of early monuments—passage graves and stone circles, for example—reveal a conception of landscape focused on a center, a "complex sacred geography" framing the monuments themselves as the center of the world.[64] All of these possible functions of stone circles—marking the path of the sun in sun worship; delineating protective boundaries; identifying a mythical, dispersed community; or positing a monument at the center of the world—are concerned with the demarcation of space into meaningful categories that define one's place, be it within the path of the sun, the homeland, or the primordial community, or at the center of the world.

In the wake of World War I, stone circles became increasingly popular in German memorialization and inspired several well-known memorials and monuments, including the no-longer-existent Tannenberg Memorial (Johannes and Walter Krüger, dedicated 1924, destroyed 1949), with its octagonal, circular shape and eight massive towers, as well as the large, circular brick colonnade of the Laboe Naval Memorial near Kiel, Schleswig-Holstein (Gustav August Munzer, dedicated 1936). Circular stone settings translated into the pergola form are common as well at German memorial sites. The Meiendorf War Memorial in Hamburg-Rahlstedt, designed by architect Karl Heinz Bouschka (1904–1973),[65] features a round, open-roofed pergola with a *Findling* at its center. Erected in 1933 to honor the fallen of World War I, the memorial was restored and modified to commemorate the fallen of World War II as well in 1963.[66] War memorials in Schwerte-Westhofen, North Rhine–Westphalia, and Perleberg, Brandenburg, also feature pergolas that display at their centers, respectively, a pedestal crowned with a winged Germanic helmet and a statue of a medieval warrior—probably the knight Roland.[67]

A striking example of a circular stone setting translated into architectural form is offered by the Ruhrkämpferehrenmal (Ruhr Warrior Memorial, erected 1934) in Horst (Essen), North Rhine–Westphalia, located near Haus Horst. With a diameter of over sixty-five feet, this open-roofed structure resembles a temple modeled on Stonehenge. The circle consists of twenty-four four-sided, approximately ten-foot-high masoned stone monolith-like pillars; within the structure lies a second stone circle, at the center of which once stood a memorial to the fallen *Ruhrkämpfer* (Ruhr combatants)—members of the Freikorps and army who brutally crushed the insurgency of revolutionary workers in the Ruhr region in 1918–20. In 1985, the memorial was rededicated as a *Mahnmal* (a memorial warning against violence). The memorial's new plaques explaining the history of the memorial have been repeatedly vandalized and stolen.

The Rhetorical Function of Findlinge

In addition to their symbolic function, *Findlinge* also demonstrate a rhetorical function by engaging in conversation with other *Findling* memorials in their vicinity. Echoing Bradley's discussion of the continuity of enclosure styles through time, Cornelius Holtorf explains that graves and monuments "did not fill empty and untouched spaces, but were fitted into a landscape of ancient sites which were still meaningful"; newly built monuments thus took earlier monuments or their traces as "reference points for messages about continuity or change of social identity."[68] We see this rhetorical function in the modern German memorial landscape when new *Findling* memorials are erected in the proximity of older *Findling* memorials commemorating previous wars. World War II memorials, for example, are often erected near World War I memorials, as in Usingen, Hesse, or in the case of the *Heldenhain* of the Holmer Beliebung,[69] in the district of Holm (Schleswig) in Schleswig-Holstein. In the latter example, an original World War I *Heldenhain* with *Findling* memorial was erected in 1920. A second *Findling* memorial for the fallen of World War II, consisting of a large *Findling* engraved with an Iron Cross and dedication along with smaller *Findlinge* engraved with the names of the fallen, was later added to the original site. Other memorial sites, as in Laaber, Bavaria, offer similar groupings of *Findling* memorials dedicated to the fallen of 1870–71, World War I, and World War II.

This layering of *Findling* memorials in space creates a compelling sense of continuity by suggesting a common German fate linking successive generations. In essence, the layered narrative created by echoing memorial forms binds a soldier who fell in World War I or World War II to his ancestral brother who died in the Franco-Prussian War of 1870–71. Such continuity across generations and even centuries lies at the heart of Willy Lange's World War I *Heldenhain* concept as well: in his design of oak and linden trees planted in careful configurations, engraved *Findlinge*, and circular arrangements of ditches and walls we see Lange's preferred narrative of the German nation: one in which Germany achieves sovereignty, unity, and world recognition through a series of wars. In Lange's words, "Old Germania as origin—1813 Germany as longing—1870/71 Germany as fulfilment—1914 Germany as self-assertion on the world stage."[70] In Lange's vision, each war plays an essential role in the unfolding of Germany's destiny, and no soldier has fallen in vain, for each contributes in his way to the master narrative.

The practice of memorializing different groups of German soldiers from different historical periods and wars in proximity to one another can lead to friction. During a Bundeswehr (Federal Republic of Germany armed forces) memorial ceremony on Volkstrauertag in 2012, a scandal unfolded in an honor grove (erected 1961) for the fallen soldiers of the Bundeswehr and Wehrmacht (the armed forces of Nazi Germany), located on the property of the Munster Panzertruppenschule, a training facility for tank forces of the Bundeswehr in Lower Saxony. The honor grove consists of two circles of fifty *Findlinge* bearing the names and symbols of diverse Panzer units with a rock spire in the middle and Iron Crosses engraved on all sides.

During the memorial ceremony, Bundeswehr soldiers lay wreaths not only for other Bundeswehr soldiers but also for Wehrmacht soldiers, including notorious elite units such as Panzergrenadier Division "Großdeutschland," a German Panzer corps that fought on the Eastern Front in World War II and committed racially motivated atrocities against captured African French army soldiers by separating the black soldiers from the white and summarily executing them, as well as the Panzergrenadier Division FHH (Feldhernnhalle), which included soldiers from the SA (Sturmabteilung / Storm Troopers, also known as Brownshirts). Veterans of both the Wehrmacht and SS, furthermore, attended the memorial activities. One elderly man laid a bouquet of flowers on a memorial stone for Waffen-SS units ("PzAbt 101/501" and "Interessenkreis 1.PzKorps"), played the "Treuelied" ("Song of Faithfulness") of the Waffen-SS on his harmonica, and recited part of the song while young Bundeswehr soldiers stood helplessly by at attention. Reporters of the RBB (Rundfunk Berlin-Brandenburg) in attendance later released a video reporting on the incident.[71]

In twenty-first-century Germany, even a spontaneous and unofficial suggestion of an unbroken continuity linking German soldiers of notorious Wehrmacht units and the Bundeswehr is anathema to most.[72] Since this incident, actions have been taken to eliminate the direct link between the Bundeswehr and Wehrmacht by physically separating the memorial site of the former from the *Findlinge* memorials of the latter. This occurrence testifies to how powerful and disruptive the rhetorical function of *Findlinge* may be in certain contexts.

Circular stone settings and stone enclosures surrounding burial sites may exhibit rhetorical functions similar to those of *Findlinge*; such stone settings and enclosures surrounded not only megalithic mounds but also monumental sites throughout the Bronze Age, the pre-Roman Iron Age, and the Slavic Period, thus spanning thousands of years.[73] *Steintänze* (stone dances) of the pre-Roman Iron Age, like those in Boitin described at the beginning of this chapter, or the stone circle of large, irregularly shaped *Findlinge* surrounding a *Hünengrab* in the landscape park of Burg Schlitz (Castle Schlitz) in Mecklenburg-Vorpommern, offer typical examples.

During the period of National Socialism, *Findlinge* and stone circles maintained their popularity as memorials and monuments and were often combined with heroic warrior figures, although they were also criticized by architects and artists for various aesthetic and ideological reasons and were even discouraged for a time during the second half of the 1930s.[74] In the radical political climate of National Socialism, both *Findlinge* and *Hünengräber* were generally venerated as forms depicting the cultural and racial superiority of the German *Volk*—a race whose roots, according to Nazi ideologues, lay in the ancient Germanic peoples of the Neolithic period. The racist tenor of such beliefs manifests in statements by persons such as Dr. Hermann Gauch, who in 1933 declared the ancient Germanic persons whose bones, he claimed, lay beneath *Hünengräber* to be Nordic men with long, light blond hair, blue eyes, noble facial features, and imposing stature; such descriptions recall the mythic figure of Siegfried, a beloved motif in Nazi memorialization.[75]

During the radio broadcast of a 1933 Easter celebration at the Sieben Steinhäuser (Seven Stone Houses), a group of massive *Hünengräber* on Lüneburg heath in Lower Saxony, the *Hünengräber* were described as the memorials of Germany's ancestors, emerging from the secret of the *Urzeit* (primordial time) and bearing with them the "old spirit" of the ancient Germanic peoples. It is as if, the narration claimed, the old spirit would reawaken in the "bearers of the German future"—the members of Hitler Youth and the SA—and the old Germanic peoples would be fighting alongside their modern descendants for a better future.[76] In the same year, Ludwig Damm, head of the Hannover planning authority, declared *Findlinge* to be symbols of Germany's *Urgeschichte* (primordial history), offering contemporary Germans a direct connection to their ancestors and evoking the strength, dignity, and other virtues of the Germans.[77] During the 1950s, postwar West Germany saw a resurgence of *Findlinge* as war memorials, especially those funded by soldier and veteran associations. A second wave of *Findlinge* memorials, often sponsored by community beautification groups, followed during the 1970s.[78]

FINDLING MEMORIALS
Memorials to the Expellees and Germany's Lost Homelands

As previously mentioned, *Findlinge* have long served as symbols of the integrity and unity of an imagined, *ur*-Germanic ethnic community; as such, they emerged as popular memorial forms for mourning division and the loss of German territory or German-speaking populations. This is especially true in the case of post–World War II memorials dedicated to the memory of the over twelve million expellees from Germany's former eastern territories. The *Heimatvertriebene* (those expelled from their homes)—a word implying that the expulsions were unjust—are the Germans and ethnic Germans who fled or were expelled from former German territory east of the Oder River and other areas in central and eastern Europe that had substantial ethnic German populations. Two-thirds of the expellees settled in West Germany, where they began forming, in the late 1940s, homeland societies to unite former residents of specific territories, including Silesia, Pomerania, East Prussia, and the Sudetenland.[79] The remaining one-third of expellees who settled in East Germany (bearing in the East the innocuous moniker *Umsiedler* [resettlers]) were forbidden for political reasons and fear of revanchism to found homeland societies or erect memorials or museums. Most expellee memorials are thus located in the West, where the expulsions played a central role in official Cold War memory culture and politics, and were used as a means of propaganda against the Soviet bloc.[80]

According to a catalogue of memorials to the expellees published by the Bund der Vertriebenen (Federation of Expellees),[81] an umbrella organization for homeland societies (established 1957), over fifteen hundred memorials dedicated to the expellees and lost territories have been erected as of 2008.[82] A significant percentage of these memorials were erected during the 1950s (about 30 percent) by homeland societies,[83] and many express the revanchist goal of seeking to restore the lost territories to Germany.[84] After reunification in 1990, communities in the former East began erecting their own memorials to the expellees—a result not only of their new opportunity to do so but also of a phenomenon that Stephen Scholz identifies as a new postunification German victim discourse in competition with the collective memory of victims of Nazi persecution.[85] The growing preoccupation with German suffering during World War II and promotion of competitive victimhood during the last few decades of the twentieth and early twenty-first centuries encompasses both former East and West Germany.[86]

One indicator of this new discourse of victimhood is the boom in new expellee memorials that started already during the 1980s. A second indicator is the troubling language used on some German memorials and in memorial dedications when referring to the suffering of Germans during and after World War II, including the word *Völkermord* (genocide) to describe the expulsions—a blatant attempt to equate the suffering of expelled Germans / ethnic Germans with the suffering of the victims of Nazi persecution.[87] A memorial to the expellees in Schwabhausen, Bavaria (erected 2002, initiated by the SRK (Soldaten- und Reservistenkameradschaft Schwabhausen 1920), exhibits this tendency. The original plaque affixed to the memorial reads, "Heimatrecht ist Menschenrecht—Vertreibung ist Unrecht" ("The right to one's homeland is a human right—expulsions are unjust"). A provocative new plaque (dedicated on September 14, 2003), proclaims: "Vertreibungsverbrechen und Völkermord kennen kein Vergessen" ("Crimes of expulsion and genocide are never forgotten"). At the dedication of the completed memorial on Tag der Heimat (Homeland Day), September 5, 2004, Albert Winkler, chairman of the SRK, declared that the new dedication refers to the "genocide committed against the German people" as well as the "genocide committed by the German National Socialist Regime."[88] Such claims are highly problematic: they trivialize the Holocaust and seek to neutralize German guilt by touting German suffering.

According to an article in the Bavarian daily *Münchner Merkur*, Winkler also stated that for almost sixty years, Germans have been forced to confront, and have been "almost daily" blamed, for the Holocaust, both within and outside Germany, whereas, Winkler claims, the "crime of expulsion" perpetrated against "at least 16.5 million Germans"[89] is "rarely discussed" or "acknowledged in history books."[90] The dedication on the Schwabhausen memorial, as well as Winkler's problematic remarks, illustrate how national suffering may be instrumentalized to create a (false) equivalency between

Germany (the perpetrator nation) and its victims—a tactic used to mitigate German culpability.[91]

The first memorial in Germany dedicated to the expellees was a simple memorial stone erected in 1945.[92] An emblematic memorial in Birkenfeld, Baden-Württemberg, bears a plaque with a popular inscription: "Der Heimat die Treue, den Opfern der ostdeutschen Heimat" ("Loyalty to the homeland, to the victims from the East German homeland"). Exceedingly popular are *Findlinge* engraved with the names of lost territories. In Goldenstedt-Ambergen, Lower Saxony, stands a memorial site dedicated on the Tag der Heimat 1996, consisting of a group of seven *Findlinge*. The central *Findling* bears the words "Deutsche Heimat im Osten" ("German Homeland in the East"); the other six stones display the names "Brandenburg," "Pomerania," "West Prussia," "East Prussia," "Silesia," and "Sudetenland." The site was expanded in 1983 with the addition of eleven smaller, individually sponsored *Findlinge* dedicated to cities and regions such as Prökuls-Memel (Prikule, Lithuania) and, in Poland, Gröditzberg (Gordziec), Liegnitz (Legnica), and Breslau (Wrocław).

Equally popular are the many dozens of *Findling* memorials engraved with the coats of arms and / or maps of lost territories, as in Coburg, Bavaria (1991), and Eutin, Schleswig-Holstein (1975/1978). Many memorials to expellees and lost territories also display an intriguing mixture of the pagan and the Christian: *Findling* memorials in Murrhardt, Baden-Württemberg, (1949), Piding, Bavaria, and Cham, Bavaria (1955), display crosses in conjunction with *Findlinge*. Occasionally, *Findling* memorials bear overtly revanchist inscriptions: a *Findling* memorial in Marbach am Neckar, Baden-Württemberg, bears the inscription "This stone contains earth from Germany's East. Ancestral German diligence once developed this earth, love and loyalty created a garden homeland. Blind hate robbed this earth of her fathers and sons. In commemoration of the dead, left to rest there, may the grandchildren one day plough this earth."

Although already rich in autochthonous imagery, *Findlinge* memorials sometimes incorporate wells and springs to suggest that the right of a people to its homeland is as natural and inalienable as a water source from the depths of the earth. At the site of the *Egerquelle* (Eger River spring) in Weißenstadt, Bavaria (1923), stand twelve unhewn granite stones surrounding the mouth of a spring. The largest stone bears the name Eger (Egerland, Czech Republic; from 1938 to 1945 part of the Sudetenland) and a coat of arms; the other stones bear names of towns that helped finance the site, including Postelberg (Postoloprty, Czech Republic), Karlsbad (Karlovy Vary, Czech Republic), and Königsberg (Kaliningrad, Russia). Behind the spring is a large *Findling* atop two smaller stones, in the style of a *Hünengrab*, engraved with a poem. A memorial stone nearby, dedicated on Egerlandtag (Egerland Homeland Day, 1955), bears the inscription "Die Welle weiss, wohin sie geht" ("The wave knows where it is going"), a quote from ethnic German Erwin Guido Kolbenheyer (1878–1962)—a right-wing, pro-Hitler, Nazi-supported writer.

A final *Findling* memorial to the expellees bears mention as a unique case: as discussed earlier, *Heldenhaine* and *Ehrenhaine* (heroes' and honor groves) dedicated to the fallen soldiers of World War I offered nostalgic, reactionary memorial spaces. Although less common, honor groves have also been erected and dedicated to the expellees and lost territories, including the Ehrenhain der Vertriebenen (Honor Grove of the Expellees) in Rendsburg, Schleswig-Holstein.[93] The center piece of the grove—a large *Findling* with a cast relief of a map of divided Germany on its front side—stands on a platform atop a flight of stairs within a parklike setting surrounded by trees. Included on this map are West Prussia, Posen, and the Sudetenland.[94] The inscription reads, "Deutschland. Das ganze Deutschland unvergessen. Das gesamte deutsche Volk bleibt aufgefordert, in freier Selbstbestimmung die Einheit und Freiheit Deutschlands zu vollenden" ("Germany. Germany entire, unforgotten. The whole of the German *Volk* remains called upon to achieve the unity and freedom of Germany in free self-determination"). Six smaller *Findlinge*, arranged in a circle around the base of the platform, bear the names and coats of arms of eight former German territories—a design that echoes the labeling and placement of *Findlinge* in Willy Lange's *Heldenhaine*. The act of engraving *Findlinge*, be it with the names of fallen soldiers or former German territories, immortalizes those persons and places now lost but to memory. But engraved *Findlinge* also evoke a sense of immortality in a deeper sense by binding modern Germans in the wake of war to a mythical primordial community, integrating the painful reality of recent losses into an epic narrative unfolding through time.

Findling Memorials for Martyrs and Heroes

As mentioned earlier, *Findlinge* were popular choices for commemorating martyrs or heroes of the Nazi movement, including nationalistic, right-wing *Freikorpskämpfer* (free or volunteer corps—private paramilitary groups in

Germany that appeared in the wake of World War I) and individuals who died (or allegedly died) fighting for the Nazi cause. A prime example is the no-longer-existent memorial dedicated to Hans Mallon, Nazi martyr and former head of the Hitler Youth of Bergen (1914–31), located near Bergen on the Baltic Sea island of Rügen. Designed by Robert Tischler, chief architect of the Volksbund Deutsche Kriegsgräberfürsorge (German War Graves Commission) and designer of Totenburgen (Fortresses of the Dead),[95] the memorial to Mallon sought to combine the functions of an ancient Germanic cult temple and the Nazi *Thingstätte* or *Thingplatz*. *Thingstätten* and *Thingplätze*, such as the Heidelberg *Thingstätte* or the Herchen *Thingplatz*, are large, outdoor amphitheaters built to accommodate *Thingspiele*—multidisciplinary, propagandist theatrical performances.[96]

Photographs of the Hans Mallon memorial reveal a structure resembling a homegrown farmhouse with low stone walls and a steeply pitched, thatched roof. Above the entryway appear words quoted from the *Edda*, popular on war memorials and printed in letters stylized to resemble runes: "Ewig ist der Toten Tatenruhm" ("The fame of a dead man's deeds lives forever"). Depicted on the door are a sun and stars—references to the ancient Germanic sun cult. In the center of the memorial, over the grave of Mallon, stands a great granite *Findling* and in front of the memorial a large open space designed as a *Thingplatz*. Here began each year on Reichsparteitag (the day of the yearly Nuremberg Rally) the march of the Pomeranian Hitler Youth.[97]

Findlinge were also chosen to memorialize a second Nazi martyr: Horst Wessel (1907–1930), a young member of the SA who died from blood poisoning after being shot during a street fight in Berlin against members of the Communist Party. Although the Horst-Wessel cult presented Wessel as a hero and martyr, the truth of his death was significantly more banal: Wessel was the casualty of a mundane brawl in Berlin's red-light district. To the Communists who shot him, Wessel was no symbol of the Nazi movement but rather a mere panderer involved with a prostitute. A marching song written by Wessel for the SA, originally known by the title "Die Fahne hoch" ("Raise the Flag") and then renamed after Wessel himself, was adopted as an official anthem of the Nazi Party.[98]

The memorial to Wessel (known as the Horst-Wessel Stein) was erected on October 8, 1933, in Bielefeld, North Rhine–Westphalia, the town of Wessel's birth, in a large clearing in Teutoburg Forest. The giant sandstone *Findling*, perched atop a heap of several other large *Findlinge*, was engraved with Wessel's name and surrounded by a wide circle of smaller *Findlinge*. In photographs, the tower of *Findlinge*, which reportedly weighed a massive twenty tons, resembles a pagan cult site. The space around the memorial was designed to resemble a *Thingplatz*, much like the space in front of the Hans Mallon memorial; on days of observance, Hitler Youth members stood watch. The Horst-Wessel Stein no longer exists, having been detonated by the British during the last week of April in 1946—the final, obliterating blow to a cult that had, in fact, already faded into insignificance years before. Only the "Horst-Wessel-Höhe"—as the mountain on which the memorial once stood was consecrated—still stands.[99]

Findlinge in Cemeteries

Findlinge serve, finally, as gravestones in *Ahnenstätten* (literally "ancestral sites"), private cemeteries where the departed may rest peacefully without the burden of unwanted Christian symbolism. *Ahnenstätten* tend to bear the burden of right-wing histories and fascist connections, and are some of the places in modern Germany where the ancient meanings of *Findlinge* still survive intact.[100] Recent articles in the German press address controversies concerning the problematic histories of *Ahnenstätten* as well as efforts of communities to rehabilitate the sites. An *Ahnenstätte* in Conneforde, a district of Wiefelstede near Oldenburg, Lower Saxony, for example, has long struggled with its tainted history.[101] Its graves are marked with *Findlinge*, as required by the bylaws, and are engraved with the "life rune" known as *Elhaz* and the "death rune" (symbols popular in Nazi Germany as well as still today among neo-Nazis and neo-Pagans[102]). The word *Sippe* (tribe or clan) appears on graves instead of *Familie* (family) in the Gothic black-letter calligraphic script known as "*Frakturschrift*"—a typeface associated with German nationalism, viewed as the "Nazi font," and preferred by neo-Nazi groups.

Some rather notorious figures lie buried in the Conneforde *Ahnenstätte*, including Nazi millionaire Wilhelm Tietjen, known for his fanatical ideas on racial purity and namesake for the right-wing extremist Wilhelm Tietjen Foundation for Fertilization; Alfred Thoß, former SS member and National Socialist writer; and Gertrud Herr, leader of the *Bund deutscher Mädel* (League of German Girls—the girls' wing of the Hitler Youth), supporter of fugitive, condemned SS men through the Stille Hilfe für Kriegsgefangene und Internierte organization (Silent Assistance for Prisoners of

War and Interned Persons, founded 1951), and a relentless and remorseless Holocaust denier until her death.[103] Both the *Ahnenstätte* in Conneforde as well as a second *Ahnenstätte* in the area, *Ahnenstätte* Hilligenloh in Hude, were founded by Nazi supporters and sympathizers: the former in 1958 by a group led by aristocrat Marie Adelheid Reuß-zur-Lippe, known as "*die braune Prinzessin*" ("the brown princess") due to her *völkisch* convictions and friendship with Richard Walther Darré, chief of the SS Race and Settlement Main Office; and the latter in 1933 by "Deutschvolk," a group influenced by Mathilde Ludendorff—wife of Erich Ludendorff, German general and participant in the 1920 Kapp Putsch and 1923 Beer Hall Putsch. The Deutschvolk is today known as the *Bund für Gotterkenntnis* (League for God-Cognition), an extreme right-wing, antisemitic group, according to the German federal government.

Findlinge and German Reunification

As we have seen, *Findlinge* both celebrate victory and mourn defeat and loss. In recent years, *Findlinge* have served as popular choices for memorials lamenting the division of post–World War II Germany. *Findlinge* engraved and dedicated to the memory of unified Germany, often referred to as *Erinnerungssteine* (memory stones), have been initiated by various groups, including local communities, Landsmannschaften,[104] or the Kuratorium Unteilbares Deutschland (National Curatorium for an Undivided Germany), an organization founded in West Germany in 1954 (dissolved in 1992) and dedicated to keeping the memory of unified Germany alive as well as working for reunification.

In the wake of Germany's reunification, *Findlinge* were also chosen to celebrate the overcoming of division. In Baden-Baden, Baden-Württemburg, for example, a *Findling* monument next to the Festspielhaus (an opera and concert hall), dedicated in 1990, depicts two groups of figures separated by a line marking the border between East and West. The inscription, one that appears on many similar memorials across Germany, reads, "Deutschland ist unteilbar / 1945–1990" ("Germany is indivisible / 1945–1990").

A similar *Findling* monument titled the Grenzdenkmal Elend (Border Monument at Elend) or the Bremke-Begegnungsstätte (Bremke Meeting Place) was erected in 1996 along the former internal German border along the Bremke River, by today's border between Lower Saxony and Saxony-Anhalt. The monument consists of two halves of a granite *Findling* leaning

FIGURE 5. Reunification monument in Baden-Baden.

against each other at an angle and joined at their apexes, their arrangement emphasizing the gap between the two halves. A half circle of bordered paving stones lies before the monument and an inscribed plaque spanning the two halves reads, "Deutchland / 1989 / wieder vereint" ("Germany / 1989 / reunified"). A sign explains that the granite stone signifies *"Spaltung und Wiedervereinigung"* ("Division and Reunification"). Fifteen oak leaves decorate the monument's plaque beneath the dedication: ten leaves on the left and five on the right, separated by a piece of barbed wire, symbolize the formerly separated ten West German and the five East German states.[105] Oaks planted beside the monument are spaced so that in time, their crowns will meet and grow together. An additional *Findling* is engraved with the date on which the border was opened: November 12, 1989.

Occasionally, a *Findling* memorial originally erected to commemorate the unification of Germany in 1871 is modified to celebrate Germany's reunification in 1990. A massive *Findling* memorial in Beetzendorf, Saxony-Anhalt, for example, was first dedicated in 1911 to commemorate the Franco-Prussian War and subsequent unification of Germany. Surrounded by numerous smaller but still substantial *Findlinge*, the central *Findling* bears a round bronze plaque with an image of Kaiser Wilhelm I in profile and is crowned with a bronze eagle with extended wings. The dedication reads, "In Erinnerung an Deutschlands Einigung 1871 / Errichtet 1911 / Erneute Einigung 1990" ("In memory of Germany's unification 1871 / Erected 1911 / Unified once again 1990"). The Beetzendorf memorial thus integrates the recent overcoming of division into a longer historical German narrative of national severance and unification, trauma and healing.

Hünengräber (Dolmens)

Like *Findlinge*, *Hünengräber* have a long and rich history in German memorialization. In the wake of World War I, memorials designed to imitate the ancient forms (such as the memorial in Trittau, discussed earlier) became increasingly popular; some were later modified to commemorate the fallen of World War II as well. Karl Heicke, director of gardens and cemeteries in Frankfurt am Main, suggested in 1918 that the *Hünengrab* should become the general model for soldiers' graves because it captured both simply and objectively the essential purposes of a soldier's grave and thus discouraged any kind of vandalism by the enemy.[106]

Many authentic *Hünengräber* exist still today in northern Germany, including about four hundred dating from between 3500 and 2000 BCE, according to estimates, in Mecklenburg-Vorpommern alone.[107] Holtorf maintains that there are almost twelve hundred megaliths of varying architectural type in Mecklenburg-Vorpommern, all originally associated with the Neolithic Funnel Beaker culture of north-central Europe.[108] On the island of Rügen in the Baltic Sea, about fifty-five *Hünengräber* still exist. The rest were dismantled, their stones plundered for construction material and street paving, the vessel shards and bones thrown away, and diverse grave goods—work tools, clay vessels, and amber beads—pilfered for private collections, occasionally ending up in museum depots.[109]

Questions abound as to the original purpose of *Hünengräber*. Long assumed to be ancient grave sites as well as remnants of pagan religious practice, some scholars suggest they might also have served as boundary markers, demarcating territorial limits and distinguishing neighboring clans from one another.[110] Some of the earliest monumental forms created by the Neolithic north-central Europeans were thus designed to delineate boundaries of identity by drawing boundaries in space—a function shared by many of the great nationalist memorials of the nineteenth and early twentieth centuries in Germany, including the Hermann Monument (Ernst von Bandel, 1875), the Niederwald Monument (Johannes Schilling and Karl Weißbach, 1883), the Kyffhäuser (Barbarossa) Monument (Bruno Schmitz, 1896), the Monument to the Battle of Nations (Bruno Schmitz, 1913), and the ubiquitous Bismarck towers (early twentieth century).

Local folklore offers more colorful explanations for *Hünengräber*: legends report that giants lifted the enormous stones to construct grave sites so that they might secure for themselves luxurious sites of rest in golden coffins.[111] Other legends explain the presence of specific *Hünengräber*: one legend tells the story of a no-longer-existent *Hünengrab* known as *Teufelssteine* (devils' stones) near the town of Laer (now Bad Laer) in the Teutoburg Forest, Lower Saxony.[112] According to legend, a peasant, weary of the long, difficult walk to church, made a contract with the devil: the devil would build for the peasant a nearby church by the following morning's cock crow. In return, the devil would gain the peasant's soul. Before daybreak, just before the devil finished his construction, the peasant imitated the cock's crow and tricked his own rooster into crowing in response. Enflamed with fury, the devil flung the *Schlußstein* (capstone) of the church he was building at the home of his adversary but missed his target. The *Teufelssteine* in this legend are the stones of the unfinished church, carried and arranged by the devil before the peasant's deception.

Ancient monuments like *Hünengräber* possess unique symbolic power. As relics of long-lost ages and ancestors, these monuments act as "time-marks" in the landscape, inviting communities of later ages to "rediscover, reinterpret and reuse" the structures, thereby granting them "new meanings in subsequent history cultures and cultural memories."[113] The evolution of ancient monuments—the ways in which they are interpreted through time by changing communities—reveals the process by which communities learn about the world and successive generations establish "a sense of place and time in relation to the living and the dead."[114]

Hünengräber in the Twentieth Century

In modern Germany, megalithic monuments have assumed a variety of new lives. Some *Hünengräber* and other megalithic forms have been dismantled and used for constructing buildings and roads; in other cases, the stones of *Hünengräber* become the building blocks of new memorials. Such was the fate of two megalithic tombs in Mecklenburg-Vorpommern, including a *Hünengrab* from Quitzerow, which were dismantled and plundered for the construction of an elaborate World War I *Ulanendenkmal* (Uhlan memorial) in Demmin, Mecklenburg-Vorpommern, dedicated to the 2nd Pomeranian Uhlan Regiment Number 9 in 1924.

Designed in the style of a monumental Germanic cult site by sculptor Fritz Richter-Elsner, the Demmin memorial displays the original stones from the ancient grave sites, now embellished with runes and stacked into new formations. A statue of a medieval knight was erected on the elevated upper end of the memorial site and a chain laid at the entrance to the memorial, symbolizing the shackling of post–World War I Germany through the Treaty of Versailles. A stone entry gate modeled on a *Hünengrab* bears an inscription on either side admonishing visitors to bring Germany's subjugation to an end: "Deutscher / denke daran / wenn du / schreitest / über diese /Ketten // Es gilt des / Vaterlandes / Ehre und Freiheit / zu retten" ("German man, remember when you step over these chains / The honor and freedom of Germany must be rescued"). After Hitler proclaimed general military conscription in Germany with the Military Service Law (Gesetz über den Aufbau der Wehrmacht, March 16, 1935), which effectively violated and denounced the terms of the Treaty of Versailles, Uhlan veterans together with local Nazis publicly demolished the chain and affixed the remains to either side of the entrance as a symbol of Germany's liberation.[115]

Memorials and monuments that reference the past, like the Uhlan Memorial with its imitation of the *Hünengrab*, reveal distinct political and social motivations. Richard Bradley suggests that such practice may reveal the attempt of political elites to legitimize their power by lending it "the authority of the past,"[116] while Stefan Goebel argues, in the specific case of the "medievalising" of memory in World War I memorialization, that such referencing of the past is an attempt to "heal the fractures" of the first global, mass-industrialized war "by asserting historical continuity through memorials."[117]

Monuments referencing the past may also help strengthen collective identity. "Awareness of history," writes David Lowenthal, "enhances communal and national identity, legitimating a people in their own eyes," while identifying with a national past "serves as an assurance of worth against subjugation or bolsters a new sovereignty."[118] In times of acute national crisis involving subjugation or loss of sovereignty, monuments referencing ancient forms like *Hünengräber* recall a place and time of origin, unity, and autonomy in the cultural imagination—a place and time beyond the chaos and deprivation of the present.

It comes as no surprise, then, that *Hünengräber* were particularly popular in the wake of World War I and during the years of National Socialism—at least until the beginning of World War II—and in smaller towns, villages, and rural areas, where conservative values dominated.[119] An article printed in 1935 in the official newspaper of the SS, *Das Schwarze Korps* (*The Black Corps*) describes the "Nordic" spirit of a World War I *Hünengrab*-inspired memorial as mirroring "German fate" and "German history" with its cracked, fissured, and fractured façade. The visitor to this memorial, declares the article, comes face to face with a primal form that seems to emerge from the "legendary twilight" of the "depths of Germanic prehistory." Departing from this site, the visitor carries with him till the ends of the earth "the blood and lifeforce" of his ancestors, strong in the conviction that he will once again be "proud and confident" in his race.[120] The *Hünengrab* form, in short, possessed the power to remind Germans in crisis of a collective (racial) identity ready to bolster them in times of need.

A few examples of memorials designed to imitate *Hünengräber* offer a sense of the aesthetics and cultural symbolism of *Hünengräber* in the modern context. Authentic *Hünengräber*, like *Findlinge*, were often surrounded by circular stone settings; these arrangements created a sacred space, at the center of which stood, altar-like, the *Hünengrab*. A direct imitation of a *Hünengrab* without any twentieth-century touches—a facsimile of the ancient form—stands in the military cemetery "Am großen Berg" in Broich (Mülheim), North-Rhine Westphalia, erected in 1932 to honor the fallen of the Lothringen Infantry Regiment 144 in World War I and moved to its current site in 1980. The memorial is built of four massive *Findlinge* and a large, horizontal capstone. It stands on an elevated grassy mound encircled by *Findlinge*. The dedication reads, "Wir werden erst sterben wenn ihr uns vergesst" ("We will die only when you have forgotten us"). A similar memorial once stood in an honor grove dedicated to the fallen soldiers of World War I in Groß Behnitz, Brandenburg. It now consists of a great *Findling* engraved with the years 1914–18 and encircled with smaller field stones engraved with the names of the fallen of Groß and Klein Behnitz. Originally, the large, central *Findling* perched on three smaller *Findlinge* in one of the classic *Hünengrab* styles; the structure was dismantled after 1945 and the wooden remembrance crosses listing the names of the fallen from World War II removed.

A modern adaptation of a *Hünengrab* may be found within the Lehmkuhlen honor grove in the district of Marienwarder (Lehmkuhlen), Schleswig-Holstein. This memorial stands on a circular, cobblestone surface on an elevation encircled by trees at the end of a long cobblestone path, tucked away in its parklike setting from the eyes of any but those who actively seek it. Designed by Albert Ulbrich and erected in 1930, the memorial consists of three stones topped with a large, engraved *Findling* capstone. Three additional oval-shaped stones of varying sizes with polished flat surfaces, added in 1958, flank the *Hünengrab*. The largest stone to the left bears the inscription "Die Gefallenen" ("The fallen") followed by the names of the fallen soldiers of World War II. Its smaller neighbor stone also bears the names of fallen soldiers, while the third stone, to the right of the *Hünengrab*, is engraved with the names of "Die Vermissten" ("The missing") and those who died during the expulsions, with the simple words "Auf der Flucht und Vertreibung starben" ("Died during expulsion and flight"). The capstone of the *Hünengrab* has a smooth, polished surface and bears a long inscription in tiny script dedicating the memorial to the World War I soldiers of Lehmkuhlen, who fell "für Heimat und Vaterland" (home and homeland), followed by the names of the forty fallen soldiers, their military ranks, dates of death, and a final admonishment: "Unsere Dankbarkeit und die Erinnerung an sie sollen nie erlöschen" ("Our gratitude and remembrance of them should never die"). The polished, flat-surfaced stones lend the memorial a contemporary appearance and identify it as a *Hünengrab* adapted to the twentieth century.

A World War II Hünengrab

An intriguing deviation from typical *Hünengrab*-styled memorials stands in a World War II military cemetery—the Ehrenfriedhof am Haddebyer Noor, also known as the Kriegsgräberstätte Karberg—located between Haddeby and Fahrdorf in Schleswig-Holstein. On top of Karberg Hill, overlooking the Haddebyer Noor Lake and surrounded by a dense cluster of green, stands a concrete *Gedenkhalle* (memorial hall) of striking design and imposing size, created by sculptor Robert Müller-Warnke (1915–1990). Bushes, flowers, and trees tightly encircle the open, stone-paved space on which stand four enormous raw concrete pillars of varying shape with jarringly irregular, slanting sides marred by sharp, crisscrossing ridges and lines that create surprising geometric patterns. The pillars support a thirty-three-by-fifty-nine-foot horizontal, irregular star-shaped capstone with sharp points, rough edges, and ridged sides.

Particularly striking is the large triangular gash cut into the capstone of the memorial. With its frayed-looking edges, the gash resembles a massive puncture wound, as if a meteor or bomb had flown through the capstone and plunged into the earth below. There is no hole in the ground beneath the gash, however—only a smooth, gray brick surface adorned with the diagram of a compass against a lighter stone background within a square frame, complete with cardinal and intercardinal points and letters marking north, south, east, and west.

The iconic *Hünengrab* structure shines through the modern accents—the irregularly shaped supporting stones, the scarred, ridged and lined surfaces, and, above all, the punctured capstone. Like other artists who

FIGURE 6. Karberg Memorial Hall, Ehrenfriedhof am Haddebyer Noor. Photo: Wikipedia Commons.

have deconstructed the form of dolmens in their work, including American sculptor and painter Alexander Calder (*Dolmens*, gouache and ink on paper, 1971) and Hungarian artist Laszlo Sallay (*Dolmen*, oil on canvas, 2011), Müller-Warnke interrogates the *Hünengrab* as structure and as concept. Here, recent experiences of trauma and loss among the German people (the expulsions from former German territories and Allied bombings of World War II) are depicted through the puncture wound in the capstone. This depiction disrupts and undermines the impression of formidable strength and endurance through time inherent to the *Hünengrab* form and central to more traditional, romantic depictions of the form (as seen in the paintings of Caspar David Friedrich). The traditional German *Vaterland* and *Heimat*, symbolized by the ancient Germanic *Hünengrab*, has been irrevocably damaged; its scars are now its defining feature.

Konstantin Henkel, managing director of the War Graves Commission (Volksbund Kriegsgräberfürsorge) in Schleswig-Flensburg, denies that the structure recalls a prehistoric megalithic tomb, arguing that it merely represents a house with a destroyed roof, serving as a symbol of vulnerability and the suffering of displacement and expulsion.[121] The website of the War Graves Commission,[122] although agreeing with this assessment, describes the burial (and, presumably, memorialization) of the war dead on a hill as adopting a form of burial that goes back to the pre-Christian times and was favored until Christianization in Schleswig-Holstein.[123] The memorial, of course, can be and perhaps is both: a *Hünengrab* and a bombed-out house—a prehistoric megalithic tomb seen through the perspective of modern annihilation. The *Hünengrab* memorial form, to quote Pierre Nora's description of a *lieu de mémoire*, emerges as an object mise-en-abîme—one with the "capacity for metamorphosis, an endless recycling of [its] meaning" for successive generations.[124]

A striking example of how *Findlinge* may undergo semantic metamorphosis and "endless recycling" is the decision of post–World War II communities to use *Findlinge* as memorials for victims of Nazi persecution, including Jewish victims. The Sudenburg, Saxony-Anhalt, Todesmarschdenkmal (Death March Memorial), located at the Karl-Liebknecht-Platz, for example, consists of a large *Findling* mounted on a rectangular base and bearing a blue-and-white striped square with an inverted red triangle at its center—the badge worn by political prisoners in Germany's concentration camps. This memorial stone was erected in 1946 or 1947 to memorialize the concentration camp victims who died during a death march in April 1945.[125] Here, the massive size and weight and the solidity of the *Findling* promise eternal remembrance of the victims—a promise to withstand time and the natural, inevitable process of forgetting.

A second example stands in the Jewish cemetery of Deidesheim, Rhineland-Palatinate; this *Findling* is adorned with a bronze plaque engraved with a menorah. Beneath the menorah appears an inscription, first in Hebrew and then German, "In lasting memory." Beneath the inscription are listed the names of four Jewish victims—former residents of Deidesheim who were persecuted and murdered by the Nazis—and the dates of their births and deaths.[126] The regional daily newspaper *Die Rheinpfalz* reported on August 1, 2022, that the concept of *Heimat* stood at the heart of the dedication speech of Franz-Josef Ratter, member of the *Arbeitsgemeinschaft jüdisches Leben* (Committee on Jewish Life) in Deidesheim. The four victims of the Shoah being remembered here, Ratter explained, were denied the right to be buried in the soil of their home, but the memorial offers them a symbolic resting place. With these words Ratter rehabilitates the concept of *Heimat*, wrenching it from "blood and soil" ideologies that corrupted the concepts of "home" and "homeland" into a justification for persecution and murder. City mayor Manfred Dörr, also in attendance at the dedication, noted that visible markers of memory like the new Deidesheim memorial play an important role in fighting racism and antisemitism. The Deidesheim *Findling*, like the *Findling* in Sudenburg, reveals how memorial forms may be reimagined and invested with new meanings that not only depart from but may actually contradict their original, prevalent meanings.[127]

CONCLUSION

Although their *völkisch* symbolism has eroded to a large extent since the second half of the twentieth century, *Findlinge* are still popular for the diffuse *Heimatgefühl* (feeling of home) that they evoke among certain populations, especially in small towns, villages, and hamlets, where they are favored forms for marking village commemorations and anniversaries as well as memorializing German and ethnic German expellees. In April 2018, a large granite *Findling* was dedicated as a Memorial to the Expellees in Vogelherd (Schwabach), Bavaria—an initiative led by members of the state legislature and dedicated to the approximately fifty-five thousand expellees from Czechoslovakia, Hungary, and East Prussia who found refuge in Vogelherd's expellee reception camp between 1945 and 1946. Affixed to the *Findling* is a plaque reminding Germans today of the injustice of the expulsions. Two apple trees grafted from branches in the Sudetenland and the Danube River valley frame the *Findling*, symbolizing the roots that expellees have managed to put down in their new homeland.

The most striking indicator, perhaps, of the enduring symbolic cachet of *Findlinge* memorials is the recent erection of seven honor groves (*Ehrenhaine*) featuring *Findlinge* dedicated to fallen members of the German armed forces who died while deployed overseas. These honor groves are part of the Forest of Remembrance (Wald der Erinnerung), a vast memorial site of over 48,000 square feet. Initiated by bereaved family members and designed by the architectural firm SSP Rüthnick in Berlin, the memorial site at the Joint Operations Command at the Henning-von-Tresckow-Kaserne in Schwielowsee, near Potsdam, Brandenburg, was dedicated in November 2014.

The seven *Ehrenhaine* were originally erected overseas by German soldiers for their fallen comrades. After being dismantled and brought home to Germany, the honor groves were reconstructed according to their original designs and embedded in natural clearings surrounded by trees along either side of the Path of Remembrance (Der Weg der Erinnerung), at the heart of the Forest of Remembrance.[128] Several *Ehrenhaine* feature *Findlinge* as centerpieces, including those dedicated to soldiers fallen in Kunduz, Afghanistan; Feyzabad, Afghanistan; Rajlovac / Sarajevo, Bosnia-Herzegovina; and Prizren, Kosovo.[129] The memorial wall within the *Ehrenhain* for Kunduz, shown here, bears the dedication "Unseren Kameraden zum Gedenken" ("In memory of our comrades"); smaller plaques bear the names of the dead.

By bringing the *Ehrenhaine* home, Germany has symbolically returned the fallen soldiers to their homeland while extending the obligation to remember to all Germans. The choice to display *Findlinge* as centerpieces

FIGURE 7. Honor Grove Kunduz, Forest of Remembrance in Schwielowsee. Photo: Wikipedia Commons.

in several of the *Ehrenhaine* reveals an additional dimension: an attempt to repair the trauma of separation (in its latest manifestation) through the primordial form of the *Findling*.

Findlinge are incredibly versatile memorial forms. They have served as the building blocks of giants' graves, stone dances, and *Teufelssteine*, of some of Europe's earliest Neolithic monuments, and of memorials dedicated to Germany's nineteenth- and twentieth-century fallen soldiers, Nazi martyrs and heroes, and expellees from the former eastern territories. They have celebrated the reunification of Germany, mourned the dead of World War II, and honored the fallen of twenty-first-century wars. *Findlinge* are protean memorial forms, but they are also mnemonic devices and nostalgic symbols. Above all, they offer an enduring presence across the German memorial landscape, binding the memories of new generations to those of centuries past and offering a vision of continuity and unity in place of division and estrangement.

CHAPTER FIVE

To Perish on a Hill of Sacrifice
Meaningful Death, Self-Transcendence, and Violence

> We sacrifice our lives / On the altar of the fatherland.
> —Carl Heinrich Schnauffer, Es leb' die Republik (1815)

INTRODUCTION: SACRIFICE FROM ANCIENT TO MODERN TIMES

In the year 405 CE, on the cusp of the European medieval period, the nomadic, Germanic people known as the Goths fulfilled a bloody promise to their gods to sacrifice each and every Roman soldier they captured in battle. According to Roman historian Paulus Orosius, the Goths not only hung their sacrificial victims from trees with ropes but also drowned the Romans' horses in river pools and threw the soldiers' gold, silver, and other valuables into the river.[1] Sacrificial offerings of human and animal life as well as war booty during battles were not uncommon among ancient Germanic tribes; historians describe similar acts committed by the Semnones, the Cimbi, and the Teutones.[2] The Semnones notoriously sacrificed human victims at their tribal assembly (called das Ding—the Thing) to reenact Indo-European myths of cosmic creation through the dismemberment of a sacrificial victim.

Many centuries and wars later, in modern, enlightened twentieth-century Europe, thousands of memorials across Germany would be erected to honor the sacrifices of the generation of 1914—those young German men who rushed to the colors at the start of the Great War to give their lives for their country. The word "sacrifice" (from the Latin *sacrificium*, to make something sacred)—*Opfer* in German—describes two seemingly incongruent acts of giving described above: in the first, one sacrifices something other than oneself—a captured enemy, a horse, a piece of silver, a burnt offering—to a god or other divine being. In the second act of sacrifice, one offers up what is most precious—one's own life—for higher principles such as the fatherland or the redemption and renewal of the nation. The quotation cited at the start of this chapter encapsulates the second meaning of self-transcending sacrifice: a soldier sacrifices his life on the "altar of the fatherland" and thus suffers not a vain, trivial, meaningless death but rather a triumphant one.

This chapter and the next explore the idea of sacrifice as a powerful, often dangerous topos in German memorialization. The iconography and language of sacrifice dominate the German memorial landscape, revealing enduring cultural beliefs about suffering, death, and personal and national renewal, as well as virtues such as courage, vigor, and virility. From the triumphant memorials of Germany's nineteenth-century wars, dedicated to those who died for *"Kaiser, Fürst, und Vaterland"* ("Kaiser, prince, and fatherland"), to the memorials of World War I,[3] with their pathos of Christian imagery and worship of warrior ideals, and, finally, the regretful, mournful *Mahnmale*[4] of World War II, the core concept of sacrifice as a force of renewal and resurrection endures even as the vernacular of its expression changes. Sacrificial imagery encourages violence: this dangerous potential emerges from its tendency to sanctify and recruit support for unjust causes, to aid in the reversal of the roles of aggressor and victim, and to bind future generations to flawed concepts and values by holding them captive to the sacrifices of their forefathers.

We begin with a consideration of theories of sacrifice, self-sacrifice, and victimhood, particularly in the context of war. This chapter then examines sacrificial rituals among the early Germanic tribes and sacrifice depicted in myth before discussing hunting and war as sacrificial rituals, drawing on the works of German scholar Walter Burkert and the German-born American scholar George Mosse. Finally, we turn to languages of heroism and sacrifice during the post–World War I period and under National Socialism, focusing on the connection between self-sacrifice and violence and on narratives of renewal and rebirth.

CHAPTER FIVE

THEORIES OF SACRIFICE

Sacrifice in the Form of an Offering

The first type of sacrifice we shall consider is sacrifice in the form of an offering to higher beings. Philosopher Moshe Halbertal offers a penetrating analysis of sacrifice and violence rooted in a reading of Torah with a focus on three paradigmatic examples of sacrifice: Cain and Abel, Nadav and Avihu, and the Akedah (the binding of Isaac by Abraham in Genesis 22). A portion of Halbertal's analysis focuses on sacrificial ritual as a protocol for approach and successful transfer, designed to protect the individual offering a sacrifice to God from the risk of his offering being rejected (as illustrated in the biblical tale of Cain's rejected offering, his trauma, and subsequent violence against Abel (Genesis 4:3–8).[5] As Halbertal demonstrates with the tale of Nadav and Avihu (Leviticus 10:1–2), a flawed procedure of approach—here, the offering of alien or strange fire—reveals a wrongly presumed intimacy between offeror and recipient that results in death. The successful transfer of an offering, however, produces a cycle of gift exchange[6] and the reassurance of a stable future for the offeror. The normal obligation of the gift cycle, based on receiving and returning, cannot be assumed when an offering is made within a hierarchical context; in the act of making an offering, therefore, a "dangerous gap between giving and receiving is opened up, creating a potential for rejection and trauma."[7] A prescribed approach "erases the individuation of the one who is approaching," thereby eliminating the anxiety and trauma of rejection (as Cain experienced) and protecting the offeror "under the canopy of the secure and recognizable."[8] Halbertal's analysis illuminates Tacitus's description of the Semnones' intricate procedure for entering a sacred grove, to be discussed soon.

Self-Sacrifice

As noted above, an *Opfer* (sacrifice) designates an object, animal, or person offered up to a god or gods for the purpose of seeking favor or atonement.[9] One who engages in self-sacrifice (*Selbstopfer*) becomes, in the religious context, a martyr who emulates Christ and dies for his or her beliefs by offering him- or herself to god—an act that carries a purifying and atoning power. The martyr thus embodies the shift from "sacrificing to" to "sacrificing for," with the sacrificial offeror and sacrificial offering merging into one.[10]

Important for our purposes is the phenomenon whereby the martyrological notion of self-sacrifice is extended from the religious to the ethical and political realms, particularly during times of war.[11] The self-sacrificing martyr in a religious framework becomes, in the context of war, the self-sacrificing soldier and hero. In the context of war memorialization, the self-sacrifice of the soldier for land and countrymen is presented as analogous to Jesus's self-sacrifice for all of mankind, and the celebration of war memorials may resemble a religious service. An inscription on a memorial in Hundisburg, Saxony-Anhalt, illustrates this dynamic: it quotes a line from a folk song called "Fern im Osten gähnt ein Grab" ("Faraway in the east a grave gapes open") with clear religious undertones: "Sie gaben ihr Alles, ihr Leben, ihr Blut, sie gaben es hin mit heiligem Mut für uns, 1914–18" ("They gave everything, their lives, their blood, they sacrificed with sacred courage for us").[12]

Historically, the concept of the self-sacrificing soldier became essential to German culture as volunteer or conscripted soldiers began replacing mercenary soldiers and the motif of the self-sacrificing soldier emerged as the dominant paradigm during the early nineteenth-century Wars of Liberation and persisted during World War I (and, to a lesser degree, World War II).[13] Indeed, as Meinhold Lurz demonstrates, the concept of the fatherland (semantically bound to the concept of *Heimat* (home or homeland), with its connotations of nostalgia and autochthony, has played the decisive role in retroactively assigning meaning to the death of fallen soldiers since the Wars of Liberation. The concept came to the forefront in German war memorialization with the collapse of the monarchy at the end of World War I and assumed the integrative function once performed by the monarchy itself. *Vaterland* and *Heimat* thus became the new source of identification for the German populace, integrating notions of nature, history, population, and territory.[14]

Memorial inscriptions praising soldiers' sacrifice for the *Heimat* abound: a few emblematic selections include a commemorative plaque on a church in Hessigheim / Ludwigsburg declaring that fallen soldiers gave their lives "Zum Schutze der Heimat" (To protect their homeland"), a plaque on the lookout tower "auf dem Weißen Stein" near Heidelberg that gratefully remembers the fallen soldiers who sacrificed their lives "Für Heimat und Herd" ("For home and hearth"); and a World War I memorial in Lühnde-Bledeln, Lower Saxony, that displays an inscription (also found in an *Ehrenhalle* (hall of honor) in a cemetery in Borgeln,

North Rhine–Westphalia) dedicating the memorial to the fallen sons of "die Heimat." Finally, a plaque in a cemetery in Königsbach-Stein, Baden-Württemberg, declares the sacrifice of fallen soldiers who gave their lives "*für Heimat und Herd*" ("for home and hearth") to be a lasting obligation for following generations: "Sind wir es wert?—Herr! Erneue die Treue!" ("Are we worthy of this?—Sir! Renew your loyalty!")[15]

Inscriptions like this last example, which emphasize that gratitude is not merely justified but rather owed, are extremely common. The earliest World War I memorial in Düsseldorf at the Kaiserpfalz ruins in Kaiserswerth, erected 1922 and modified to memorialize civilians who died in World War II as well, is typical: "Helden gleich weihtet dem Vaterland Ihr Euer Leben. / Dauernd Euer gedenkend, weiß Euch das Vaterland Dank / Die Stadt Kaiserswerth ihren im Weltkriege 1914–1918 gefallenen Söhnen / Und den Opfern des Weltkrieges 1939–1945 / Es starben den *Heldentod fürs Vaterland*" ("As heroes you dedicated your lives to the fatherland. / In abiding memory, the fatherland is indebted to you / Dedicated to the fallen sons of the city of Kaiserswerth in World War 1914–1918 / and to the victims of the World War 1939–1945 / They died heroes' deaths for the fatherland").[16] Here, sacrifice and heroes' deaths for the fatherland are twin concepts dictating abiding memory and eternal gratitude as "debts" to be repaid to the dead.

Sacrifice and Victimhood

Sacrifice (*Opfer*), as it appears in the inscription in Kaiserswerth and on thousands of other war memorials, is a semantically rich word in German: in addition to its primary meaning, it also possesses the secondary meaning of "victim" and is used to refer to victims of crime or violence outside of the ritual, sacrificial context, including casualties of war and other violence (*Todesopfer*) as well as victims of murder (*Mordopfer*) and rape (*Vergewaltigungsopfer*). The semantic extension of *Opfer* to refer to victims is rooted in the notion of victimhood as a state of innocence or purity that both a sacrificial animal or person and a victim of crime ideally share.[17] In the context of sacrificial ritual, only a pure (flawless) animal may function as a symbolic substitute for the self or group; once chosen, it carries the burden of sin transferred to it from the offending self or group and may be sacrificed to the gods or, as a scapegoat, banished. The deserved, retributive punishment that would otherwise be directed at the sinning subject is thus transferred to the substitute—the sacrificial victim.[18]

Like the flawless animal, only an innocent (morally pure) person may be viewed as a sacrificial victim. Flawed animals or fallen soldiers of a criminal organization (for example, the Waffen-SS, the military branch of the SS) cannot be imagined as sacrificial victims due to their lack of purity or innocence; their compromised status makes them unworthy of being a suitable sacrificial substitute.[19] It is important to note that in religious literature dealing with sacrifices, sacrificial animals are not designated as victims; rather, they are regarded as willingly volunteering to serve as sacrificial offerings. Victims, in contrast, are subjected to violence against their will, while fallen soldiers are commonly not described as victims at all but rather as heroes who willingly offered up their lives for a greater purpose or ideal. Memorials mourning fallen soldiers as victims of war rather than celebrating their heroism create an ambiguous category of *Opfer* combining self-sacrifice and victimhood.

The dramatic response of the American public to the Bitburg incident of May 1985 reveals the assumption that sacrificial victims may not be flawed (or, in this context, perpetrators). The Bitburg incident began when president Ronald Reagan visited the Kolmeshöhe military cemetery in Bitburg, West Germany, where members of the Waffen-SS were buried among other German soldiers. Neither Reagan's impromptu, reconciliatory gesture of visiting Bergen-Belsen concentration camp nor his explanation that he sees "nothing wrong with visiting that cemetery, where those young men are victims of Nazism also, even though they were fighting in German uniform, drafted into service to carry out the hateful wishes of the Nazis," appeased his critics. Indeed, interred at Bitburg are the remains of soldiers who belonged to the "most brutal fighting units in Nazi Germany," including the First SS Panzer Division Leibstandarte Adolf Hitler (Hitler's Bodyguard or Hitler's Own). which fought in the surprise attack in the Battle of the Bulge (December 1944–January 1945) and the Second SS Panzer Division, Das Reich, responsible for the slaughter of 642 people, including women and children, in the French village of Oradour-sur-Glane on June 10, 1944.[20]

Due to the moral calculus according to which the imagery and language of sacrificial victimhood implies innocence, memorials built exclusively for World War II fallen soldiers tend to avoid the exalted, heroic sacrificial imagery emblematic of World War I memorials. The end of World War II was radically different from the end of World War I—not only was Germany defeated, but the entire German war effort was discredited and "most Germans, even those who had fought in the war, in the midst of total ruin could salvage little honor or glory."[21] Unlike the romanticized cultural and psychological engagement with World War I, which George Mosse has analyzed with his theory of the "Myth of the War Experience" and the "cult of the fallen soldier," the experience of World War II permitted little mythologizing. Indeed, in the defeat of Nazi Germany we may see the moment in which the "Myth of the War Experience flickered and died"[22] and a new language for mourning the loss of German lives became necessary.

TRIBAL SACRIFICE IN GERMANIC SOCIETY

Rituals of Sacrificial Killing

To understand the salience of sacrificial imagery and language in German memorialization, it helps to be cognizant of the rich history of sacrificial ritual and its lingering potency in Germanic culture. Sacrificial ritual is, naturally, not specific to the German-speaking lands: According to some scholars, rituals of sacrificial killing are the most primary forms of ritual[23] and the source of the basic experience of the sacred in human history.[24] Indeed, animal sacrifice was omnipresent in the ancient world. *Homo religiosus*, writes renowned religion scholar Walter Burkert, "acts and attains self-awareness as *homo necans*."[25] Sacrificial violence and killing are thus not tangential but rather fundamental to the very existence of religious consciousness and experience. The most common types of sacrifices involved offerings of animals, objects, and human beings. Besides human sacrifices, horse sacrifices were the most meaningful in Germanic societies; due to the fact, moreover, that humans and horses were often perceived as homologous, horses served in certain contexts as substitutions for human victims.[26]

Tribal Germanic peoples also offered war booty sacrifices–the entire equipment of an invading army, for instance—to demonstrate their thanks to the gods who had shown them favor; peat bogs containing such offerings have been found in Thuringia and Schleswig-Holstein.[27] Other types of sacrifices, including public, private, annual, and seasonal sacrifices, also took place in bogs; earthenware containers that once held food, hemp, wool, weapons, and jewelry have been discovered in bogs, and the bones of ritually sacrificed animals have been discovered in sacrificial deposits in Soest, North Rhine–Westphalia, and Donnstetten, Baden-Württemberg.[28]

Sacrificial Killing and War

In Germanic tribal history, the waging of wars was the most often cited occasion for ritual human sacrifice. Ancient Germanic tribes understood the essence of warfare itself to be sacrifice and believed that battle granted immortality to the warrior who offered up his life in sacrifice.[29] This belief has survived the centuries and is often found on twentieth-century German war memorials. Such sacrifice, however extraordinary in itself, was nevertheless expected: Germanic tribal warriors who deserted from battle were judged as having cheated the gods of their obligation—the duty to offer their lives—and thus, along with traitors, suffered hanging from trees.[30]

The destruction of human life at the hands of the Germanic peoples within the ritual context of sacrifice is legendary. Germanic tribes are said to have dedicated the armies of their enemies before battles to the Germanic god Wodan (Wotan / Odin) or Tiwaz by throwing a spear over the enemy army. The Hermunduri, according to Tacitus's *Annals*, slaughtered both horses and men after conquering the Chatti, killing every tenth prisoner of war through drowning or crucifixion as thank offerings. Other tribes, such as the Saxons and the Cimbri, also sacrificed soldiers of enemy armies, in the case of the latter sacrificing soldiers of the armies of Caepio and Mallius in the year 105 BCE.[31] The most common form of dedicating a sacrifice (to Wodan, for example) was to hang the offering from a tree or from a substitute tree (gallows, for example).[32] Germanic tribes viewed human sacrifice, finally, as a way of unloading impurity: the Saxons, for example, selected sacrificial victims by lot before sailing to ensure safe passage.[33]

One of the best-known tales of human sacrifice in battle is the infamous sacrifice of Roman soldiers from Publius Quinctilius Varus's army in 9 CE by the former Roman officer and chieftain Arminius and his Cherusci warriors in the Battle of the Teutoburg Forest, as discussed in chapter 1. The Roman general Germanicus, who discovered the evidence of the carnage from this disastrous battle (known as the "Varian disaster") six years later, witnessed with his own eyes the gruesome traces of atrocities committed against the Romans, including horse heads nailed to tree trunks, altars where Varus's men had been ritually slaughtered and sacrificed, gallows, and burial pits.

THE ROLE OF SACRIFICE IN GERMANIC MYTH

Manu and Yemo

Sacrifice, the most prominent of all Indo-European rituals in the words of religion scholar Bruce Lincoln, is as essential to Germanic mythology as it was to the ancient Germanic world itself.[34] For our purposes, the role of sacrifice in seminal, cosmological Indo-European myths is particularly important because such myths are the source of Germanic origin myths. According to Indo-European myth, the world emerged from the primordial sacrificial act and, with it, order emerged from chaos: At the beginning of time, two men—a priest (Manu) and his twin brother (Yemo)—were traveling together with an ox. In order to create the world, the priest Manu enacted the first ritual sacrifice by killing his two companions. Manu then dismembered the bodies of ox and brother, generating from their pieces the universe and all of human society.[35] The primordial act of sacrifice and dismemberment was a profoundly creative act—one that forged a cardinal link between killing, sacrifice, and creation (and, in its reiteration, divine renewal). Later rituals of sacrifice and dismemberment would echo and reenact this primal act of sacrifice and creation. Sacrifice, to quote Lincoln, emerges as the "repetition of cosmogonic action."[36]

Ritual Sacrifice, Creation, and Renewal

Ritual human sacrifices of the Germanic tribes, timed in accordance with the waxing and waning of the moon, reenacted this mythical act of creation, thereby renewing time, order, and law through sacrificial ritual.[37] Such rituals were often staged at the tribal assembly known as das Ding (the Thing). The Thing was a festival and meeting of tribal legations taking place every nine years within a sacred grove according to the lunar calendar. Tiwaz was most likely the supreme Germanic god worshipped at the Thing.[38] Common to all Germanic peoples since prehistoric times, this gathering created a sense of nationhood among otherwise scattered peoples while tribal representatives enacted the global reintegration of society.³⁹ The human sacrifice itself took place in a sacred grove, which, because of its religious sanction, granted authority to any actions and decisions taking place within its boundaries.⁴⁰ Many Germanic tribes, including the Nahanarvali (or Naharvali), worshipped their gods (for the Nahanarvali, the god Alcis) in sacred groves, and the presence of putrefying sacrificial remains not only didn't detract from but actually increased the sacrality of the grove.⁴¹

The best source for a description of ritual sacrifice comes to us from the legendary text *Germania*, written around 98 CE by Roman historian and politician Tacitus. In what follows, Tacitus provides a description of sacrifice and sacred grove protocol at the Thing of the Semnones, where legations from one hundred villages met and began their proceedings with a human sacrifice ritually reenacting their creation myth.⁴² His account is remarkable for drawing directly on Germanic informants; it is thus "one of the rarest and most precious items encountered within ancient ethnography . . . [and] the earliest and most thorough description of pre-Christian Germanic sacrifice to be found anywhere."⁴³ Tacitus describes the sacrifice of the Semnones in chapter 39 of *Germania* as follows:

> At a stated time of the year, all the several people descended from the same stock, assemble by their deputies in a wood; consecrated by the idolatries of their forefathers, and by superstitious awe in times of old. There by publicly sacrificing a man, they begin the horrible solemnity of their barbarous worship. To this grove another sort of reverence is also paid. No one enters it otherwise than bound with ligatures, thence professing his subordination and meanness, and the power of the Deity there. If he fall down, he is not permitted to rise or be raised, but grovels along upon the ground. And of all their superstition, this is the drift and tendency; that from this place the nation drew their original, that here God, the supreme Governor of the world, resides, and that all things else whatsoever are subject to him and bound to obey him."⁴⁴

Tacitus's language is severe; he is shocked at the "horrible" and "barbarous" nature of the sacrifice. Bruce Lincoln notes that the word "sacrifice" in the third line of the text is a translation of *caeso*, meaning "dismemberment," recalling the ritual dismemberment of the sacrificial victim that repeats and renews the original act of creation. Lincoln also suggests a sociopolitical interpretation, arguing that the killing and dismemberment celebrate "sociopolitical solidarity and segmentation, in which large . . . tribal aggregations are assembled, reminded of their common bonds, and then dispersed into their constituent subunits."[45] A parallel thus emerges between the sacrificial victim—a whole, integrated entity dismembered into discrete parts—and the tribal peoples themselves, who share a single origin but have dispersed into separate, discrete peoples.

The remaining part of Tacitus's description—the intriguing restrictions and rules for one seeking to enter the sacred grove—enacts the helplessness of men before their gods. The scene recalls the myth of Tiwaz (also known as Tyr), a one-handed Germanic god of war, who bound a wolf named Fenrir and, in the process, sacrificed his arm to the animal's mighty jaws.[46] Here, the willing surrender of one's physical power and mobility signify passivity and subservience in the presence of the divine.

The creation myths of Germanic tribes reveal clear parallels to the Indo-European creation myth described earlier but also introduce unique elements. According to Tacitus, as mentioned in chapter 1, the Germanic tribes worshipped Tuisto, a God sprung from the earth and ancestor of the entire universe and all of humanity, and Mannus, his son, ancestor of the Germans. The names of these primordial ancestors (Tuisto—the "doubled one" or "twin" and Mannus—"man") exhibit similarities to the names commonly given to the main actors in Indo-European myths of creation, according to which the "twin" (Tuisto / Yemo) is the first sacrificial victim and "man" (Mannus / Manu) performs the first offering.[47]

A Myth of Self-Sacrifice

The myth of the Germanic god Wodan or Wotan (also known as Odin), like the myths related above, tells a tale of sacrifice, dismemberment, and creation but also introduces the motif of self-sacrifice.[48] In Norse mythology, chaos reigned at the beginning of time. From this chaos quickened the first living creature—a primal cow. The cow licked Buri, progenitor of the gods, and her milk nourished Ymir, the primal giant, from whose feet were born the frost-giants. From Ymir's limbs also grew the various giant clans, including the clan of Mimir and his sister Bestla, and so Wodan was born, son of Bestla and grandson of Buri. Ambitious to rule but alone unable to destroy the frost-giants, the offspring of chaos, Wodan climbed Yggdrasil, the great tree bearing in its branches all worlds. For nine nights Wodan persevered in Yggdrasil without food or drink; finally, praying for power, Wodan pierced himself with a spear, in effect committing the neat trick of sacrificing himself to himself. In return, Wodan received power from Mimir in form of powerful songs and a drink from the well of creation (located at the roots of the trees of Uror and Mimir). With his new powers, Wodan and his brothers slew Ymir and the frost-giants. The flesh of Ymir was ground in the world-mill into fertile soil; the heavens were created from Ymir's skull and the mountains from his bones. Wodan also committed a second self-sacrifice in order to solve a riddle and discover the fate of the world. The answer to the riddle lay in the well of wisdom, into which Wodan threw one of his plucked-out eyes that it might peer into the future.[49]

Unlike Yemo, who was sacrificed and dismembered by his brother Manu, Wodan is at once subject and object, actor and victim: his two acts of self-sacrifice empower him to acquire that which other gods could not—the power and knowledge (literally, sight) needed to triumph over chaos and create the heavens, universe, and human race. The myth of Wodan, therefore, is special: it illustrates in one narrative the leap from sacrificing (something or someone) to (a god or gods) to sacrificing (oneself) for (something more important than oneself)—an act characteristic, in the religious context, of the martyr. At the heart of the myths of Tuisto, Mannus, and Wodan is the ritual act of sacrifice or self-sacrifice as the impetus for the creation of the universe, humanity, and the Germanic peoples. Sacrifice, as we shall see, defines to a large extent the interpretation of the loss of life in wars in Germany, from the nineteenth-century Wars of Liberation to World War I and, to a lesser but still significant extent, World War II.

HUNTING AND WAR AS SACRED RITUAL

The Language of Ritual

In the previous sections, we discussed sacrificial ritual among Germanic tribes as well as in Germanic mythology—in both history and narrative, sacrificial rituals reveal values and beliefs that illuminate the inner lives of early Germanic peoples. Rituals of sacrifice may be as semantically rich, varied, and complex as language itself. Indeed, such rituals are older than linguistic communication. The language of ritual dramatizes the very order of life, while myths—like those described above—clarify the order of life, explaining and justifying social orders and establishments, and are thereby related to ritual.[50] As the ever-growing body of scholarship on ritual demonstrates, ritual sacrifices of pagan societies fulfilled social, political, and psychological as well as religious needs. Ken Dowden, for example, describes how the death of an animal at the climax of a pagan ritual played a key role in society by helping channel aggression and disperse guilt.[51]

Similarly, regular sacrificial rituals among Germanic tribes at the site where Tuisto allegedly burst from the earth, lived, and finally died served social and political functions by reminding tribal members—by means of reenactment—of their common origins. Memories of these common origins, in turn, helped participating subjects, separated by geography, to perceive their common kinship; in effect, the rituals created a "fictive kinship" among tribals based on a mythic genealogy and belief in shared blood.[52] Choreographed rituals of sacrifice among Germanic tribes at the Thing also strengthened the internal hierarchical structure of the tribes, reinforcing the superiority of the Semnones as the "head" of the Suebi—a phrasing, Lincoln notes, that might be more than mere metaphor in indicating the Semnones' share of the offering.[53]

The Ritual of Hunting and Community

The concept of "fictive kinship" is itself part of a larger phenomenon at the heart of sacrificial ritual—the power of ritual sacrifice to reinforce community, communal identity, and social bonding through killing followed by a special, shared feast. In his seminal work *Homo Necans*, Walter Burkert presents an evolutionary theory of sacrificial ritual based on the similarities between hunting and sacrificial customs.[54] As Burkert demonstrates, the development of hunting during the Paleolithic era depended on the ability of men to work together. The practice of hunting necessitated a new social structure—the *Männerbund* (male community)—a novel social group with an identity and communal bond based on collective killing and eating. Within the context of hunting, the hunted animal became the sacrificial victim and substitute for man himself: an animal resembles man most, Burkert notes, in death.[55]

Hunting, in essence, created community defined as "participation in the bloody work of men."[56] Essential to life within such a community was the willingness to sacrifice part of one's freedom for the sake of the community; these sacrifices, in turn, helped establish the social rules and social identity of the community. Myths and rituals, key to the process, reinforced this sense of sacrifice by reminding the community of sacrifices made by prior community members. Sacrifice thus "forms the basis of culture" and allows for human survival.[57] Being accepted as a member of the *Männerbund* in hunting societies, in essence, meant being initiated into manhood as defined by the community: that is, by confronting and overcoming death.[58] This paradigm will be important to keep in mind later when we consider the virtues assigned to German soldiers and the initiation of young men into the patriotic community.

According to studies of sacrificial rituals in hunting societies, hunters suffered from guilt over slaughtering animals as well as from "anxiety about the continuation of life in the face of death." Hunting rituals such as gathering bones, raising skulls, or stretching skins constituted attempts at reparation—that is, attempts to restore and resurrect the slaughtered animal—as well as attempts to gain forgiveness and reassure that "sources of nourishment will continue to exist."[59] Even after such communal hunting ended and killing was no longer necessary for life, established ritual practices continued because the ritual power to kill created and affirmed social interaction, binding communities together.[60] Sacrifices accompanied the signing of agreements and contracts as well as the forging of alliances in the ancient world, with the object of violence that was "struck" and "cut" becoming "virtually identical with the covenant itself."[61]

Essential to the sacrificial ritual is the creation of an "inside" and an "outside," an "us" and a "them"—a dynamic crucial to communal hunting. Hunters, Burkert explains, released shared aggression against outsiders during the hunt, bonding with each other in the process.[62] Through sacrificial ritual, too, participants became segregated from an external world and bonded with each other. The sacrificial community itself became a model of society, organized and divided by rank and function.[63] The social structure of the community was thus strengthened and preserved over generations.[64]

At the heart of *Männerbund* hunting and sacrificial rituals stands the metaphysical tension between destruction and resurrection, between barriers broken (through killing) and order restored (through postkilling ritual and communal eating). "In the experience of killing" within the ritual context, "one perceives the sacredness of life; it is nourished and perpetuated by death." Life is justified and affirmed through killing; the sacredness of life is revealed through death. That which survives will be all the stronger for having passed through death—the sacrifice, in Burkert's words, "opens and reseals the abyss of annihilation," creating a new order of life.[65] Sacrificial death is thus merely half of the ritual narrative—the other half is resurrection and rebirth as death, overcome and transformed, leads to renewal. To return to the creation myth discussed earlier: the sacrifice of the primordial twin enables the creation of the universe and humanity. In the language of World War I memorials, as we shall see, soldiers sacrifice themselves for the renewal and rebirth of the German nation. This notion would be effectively exploited by National Socialists a few short years later to promote their vision of Germany's *Neuordnung* (New Order)—a vision for a racial state, territorial expansion, colonization, and annihilation of populations perceived unworthy of life.

The Ritual of War in Modern Germany

As we may recall, ancient Germanic tribes viewed warfare as sacrifice. In the ancient world, "hunting, sacrifice, and war were symbolically interchangeable"; war itself was a "ritual, a self-portrayal and self-affirmation of male society"[66]—a definition that will be useful as we shift from ancient Germanic tribes to modern German culture. In their longing for adventure and willingness to confront and defy death, the young German men who made up World War I's generation of 1914 eagerly embraced a male community and concept of a "new man" in which values of virility, camaraderie, courage, patriotism, energy, and physical prowess were venerated above all else. These values, as George Mosse has argued, were the defining values of a new physical, aesthetic, and moral ideal of manliness—a model of "militant masculinity"—that emerged in the years immediately before World War I as part of a general cultural mood venerating youth, speed, uncertainty, and change in contrast to the perceived hypocrisy and complacency of bourgeois society.[67] This embrace of a new cultural mission, a new society, and image of a "new man" would become an essential part of what Mosse calls the "Myth of the War Experience."[68]

The new warrior values, as Mosse demonstrates, exerted an inspiring power over the young men of the generation of 1914. The personal regeneration implied in the vision of the "new man" of vigor, energy, and enthusiasm was also a vision of national regeneration based on an intoxicating sense of national unity and the conviction that the new man would redeem the nation and abolish class structure. As Mosse points out, the ideals of unity and camaraderie would find their apotheosis in the communal experience of the trenches.[69] Within the "Myth of the War Experience," the suffering and death of the soldier was envisioned as a purifying act of sacrifice and resurrection, and war itself as a sacred experience.[70] After World War I, the "cult of the fallen soldier" shaped memorialization by sacralizing fallen soldiers as saints and martyrs who sacrificed themselves for the fatherland.[71] Here, the sacrifice of young German lives enabled the rebirth of the German nation. Meinhold Lurz, considering thousands of war memorials across Germany's war-torn landscape, identified the willingness to sacrifice oneself for the fatherland and thus transcend individual self-interest as the highest *Mannestugend* (masculine virtue) of modern German culture, earning the soldier *Ehrfurcht und Anerkennung* (reverence and recognition).[72]

Although not restricted to Germany during the post–World War I years, the "cult of the fallen soldier" was especially powerful in nations such as Germany, which had not only suffered defeat but also struggled unsuccessfully to transition from war to peace. In the face of devastating loss and social instability, the "Myth of the War Experience" with its "cult of the fallen soldier" was desperately needed to help survivors and citizens find meaning in loss and to mask and transcend the unprecedented extent of mass death experienced for the first time in World War I, a war shaped by modern technology, mass communication, and the horrors of the trenches.[73] The nation, too, for which so many young men had fought and died, required sacralization to enable a new "civic religion" that could justify these mass deaths. The "cult of the fallen soldier" thus became a "centerpiece in the religion of nationalism." During the postwar years, national commissions played a key role in war commemoration, seeking to express through cemeteries, memorials, and monuments the glory of war for the fatherland, its "purposefulness rather than its tragedy," and the "meaningfulness of the fighting and sacrifice."[74] These values, enshrined on memorials and monuments, would serve as an example to future generations. Warrior values were further supported by a body of literature—war prose and poetry written by war volunteers and read in schools and fraternities, and often set to music—that contributed to the "Myth of the War Experience" and cast soldiers as selfless heroes, bound to one another in brotherly camaraderie and sacrificing all for their country.[75]

LANGUAGES OF HEROISM AND SELF-SACRIFICE

The sacralizing language of heroism and sacrifice of this period was not confined to poetry, prose, art, and music—it also characterized nonfiction and academic works of the post–World War I period. In his book *Das Denkmal des Weltkriegs* (1930) (*The Memorial of the World War*), Dr. Karl von Seeger presents a volume of 220 photographs of World War I memorials that epitomize, in his view, the values of heroism, selfless sacrifice, and courage, and that depict the death of soldiers as sacred. In an introductory essay, the author describes in hyperbolic language heroic sacrifice. The opening pages speak of *Heldenehrung* (honoring of heroes), *Heldenmut* (heroic courage), and *Heldenuntergang* (the demise of heroes), of the selfless *Opfer* (sacrifice) of soldiers who, by dying, perfected their heroism and demonstrated to the living the highest fulfillment of duty and loyalty to fatherland—a lesson to be imitated by future generations.[76] Tellingly, Seeger connects the memorialization of World War I soldiers to the memorials of a primordial Germanic past, beginning his essay with a description of modern Germans standing in awe before the massive, ancient giants' graves of the *Urzeit* (prehistoric times), which murmur mysteriously to their visitors from another world of victory and conquest.

Otto Binswanger

Contributing to the portrait of the social and cultural forces that created the "new man" of the 1914 generation is the work of psychiatrist and neurologist Otto Binswanger (1852–1929). In his pamphlet *Die seelischen Wirkungen des Krieges* (*The Psychic Effects of the War*), Binswanger analyzes the outbreak of selfless sacrifice for the fatherland among German World War I soldiers and describes treating a number of young men in his clinic for depression as a result of their being declared unfit for service at the beginning of the war.[77] Intriguing is Binswanger's depiction of the healing effects of war on young men afflicted with nervous conditions. As World War I began, Binswanger writes, he happened to be treating a number of young men suffering from neurasthenia; with the outbreak of war, however, their sickness fell from them at a single blow, and they volunteered for duty. Even in the case of such sickly and frail natures, Binswanger concludes, war—the great purifier—did its work.[78]

Although Binswanger describes patriotism as the highest and most ethical stage of community feeling because it forces the individual to subordinate himself to the (ethnic) community (*Volksgemeinschaft*), he also warns of a morbid intensification and distortion of patriotic feelings whereby the sublime enthusiasm, sense of self-sacrifice, and heroic courage emergent from love of country and devotion to one's people degenerates into cruel hatred, vindictiveness, and desire for utter destruction of the enemy.[79] Such a phenomenon, Binswanger writes, is evident in the present war (World War I), causing him to lament, "Where is our so highly lauded culture heading?"[80]

Self-Sacrifice and Violence

What forces are powerful and insidious enough to distort praiseworthy values such as enthusiasm, self-transcendence, love of country, and courage into the destructive phenomena of hatred, cruelty, and vengefulness? The connections between heroic self-sacrifice (as the ultimate manifestation of self-transcendence) and violence (in the form of war), as Moshe Halbertal argues, are not coincidental but rather intrinsic: the enthusiasm for war is itself strengthened and motivated by risk and sacrifice.[81] Several influential theories posit a connection between sacrifice and violence: Georges Bataille argues that sacrifice is an act through which an excess of life energy, underlying all human action, may be released, while René Girard suggests that the sacrifice of a single innocent victim—the scapegoat or surrogate—serves as the focus of all violence, functioning as an outlet for the natural human tendency toward aggression and violence. Culture and social stability are preserved through sacrifice because it offers a means to channel—and thus limit—human violence in a way that doesn't destroy human society, making ritual sacrifice the basis of culture.[82] Aggression and violence are thus natural and innate to the human race, and culture a precarious balancing act enabled by a controlled release of aggression toward a chosen object.

As our discussion shifts from sacrificial offerings among ancient Germanic tribes to modern acts of self-sacrifice during war, it is helpful to consider the potential pitfalls of ideologies venerating sacrifice and self-sacrifice. The act of self-sacrifice, as immortalized on countless war memorials, is portrayed as an expression of loyalty and love for country—the ultimate selfless gift and transcendence of self-interest. But the very dynamic that makes self-sacrifice such a powerful, ennobling form of giving also makes it potentially dangerous. One source of this danger is the binding effect of sacrifice on later generations. States as well as political and religious communities often rely on the heroic sacrifices of earlier generations to bind, obligate, and essentially hold captive future generations; to refuse loyalty to the principles of those who sacrificed themselves—for a community, people, or country—would amount to betrayal.[83] How many war memorials proclaim that fallen soldiers died "for us"? How many extort us to never forget our debt to them? Although most memorial expressions of debt are dedicated to fallen soldiers, some memorials express debt to those who died fighting for other causes: a memorial dedicated to antifascist resistance fighters executed in the Brandenburg-Görden penitentiary bears an inscription declaring: "Ihr Kampf ist uns Verpflichtung" ("Your struggle is our obligation").

When the modern state presents itself as a vehicle for self-transcendence—for example, through self-sacrifice for the fatherland—it assumes a "quasireligious function." Within this quasi-religious modern state, it is the act of confronting and ultimately overcoming—rather than avoiding—violent death that offers individuals the chance to endow their lives with a meaning that surpasses the limits of their own life spans.[84] This is a seductively persuasive narrative. In the words of Arthur Schopenhauer, a man who dies for his fatherland "has freed himself from the illusion which limits a man's existence to his own person . . . in his widened, enlightened nature he embraces all his countrymen, and in them lives on and on . . . [and] merges himself in the generations yet unborn, for whom he works."[85]

Halbertal identifies three ways in which violence may emerge from the context of self-sacrifice (sacrificing [oneself] for): first, self-sacrifice may appear to sanction an unjust cause through faulty reasoning and a reversal in causal order, based on the assumption that because one has sacrificed oneself for a cause, the cause itself must therefore be worthy of self-sacrifice. Second, self-sacrifice may serve as a "lethal reversal of aggressor and victim" whereby the aggressor, because he has sacrificed himself, perceives himself to be the "true victim." Third, self-sacrifice may become the "impetus for widespread destruction" when exploited for an immoral cause.[86]

Self-Sacrifice and the Third Reich

The most strikingly visible occurrence of how the language of self-sacrifice enables violence may be found in the propaganda and language of the Third Reich. Indeed, one of the primary goals of the vast Nazi propaganda machine was to "grant meaning to the otherwise senseless deaths" of German World War I soldiers by linking "the world of the living to the world of dead heroes by using their example as the model for future sacrifices to be made for the sake of the nation and the Nazi movement."[87] In Nazi ideology, the ability to sacrifice oneself for one's community was a biological gift—the mark of a higher, idealistic, noble racial being. According to such reasoning, so-called inferior, materialistic racial groups (such as Jews) existentially lacked the ability to sacrifice and were thus not only "condemned to an inferior status akin to an animal existence" but also viewed as a threat to the nation.[88]

The ability to sacrifice oneself for one's community thus acted in Nazi ideology as a litmus test of humanity and was used to hold future generations hostage. As Halbertal explains, "A past sacrifice can be a genuine motivating force for a political purpose; it can serve manipulative and dangerous functions . . . the source of its danger lies in the sacrifice sanctifying something that is unworthy and then holding future generations captive to its lingering onus. A primordial sacrifice . . . might become the strongest glue adhering individuals to a political project."[89] As demonstrated in a 1934 speech to the Hitler Youth in which Hitler recalls the Great War's millions who "did not make their sacrifice for Germany in vain," the sacrifice of World War I soldiers was mobilized by the Nazis as a symbolic act to inspire commitment among the populace to Nazi goals.[90]

Memorials, too, demonstrate the power that a primordial sacrifice may play in a nation's founding narrative. Germany's Hermannsdenkmal (Hermann Monument, 1875) in Detmold, North Rhine–Westphalia, featuring Arminius (Hermann), illustrates the staying power of an origin narrative based on a primordial sacrifice. Here, the myth of a battle that allegedly prevented the Romanization of the Germanic tribes and protected the primordial Germanic ethnic community has persisted for centuries as a cultural leitmotif in German art, literature, politics, and memorialization.

Beyond exploiting the deaths of World War I soldiers, Nazi functionaries also drew on the notion of sacrifice to extort particular behaviors from the populace. One notable example is Joseph Goebbels's infamous Sportpalast (Total War) speech of February 18, 1943, given before a select audience in Berlin and broadcast by radio to millions of other Germans. A second example is Heinrich Himmler's "Posen Speech" of October 4, 1943, addressed to SS officers in Poland. In the former, given in the wake of the battle of Stalingrad—a disastrous defeat for the German army and turning point on the Eastern front—Goebbels made ample use of the words *Opfer* (sacrifice), *Heldenopfer* (heroic sacrifice), and *Aufopferung* (self-sacrifice) in an attempt to reinvigorate the German war effort and justify recent austerity measures. In a rousing call to arms, Goebbels exhorted the German people to embrace the sacrifices required for "total war" and the victory that, he proclaimed, still lay within reach if all Germans would follow their duty and subordinate all other aspects of their lives to the war effort. In his "Posen Speech," Himmler frankly addressed the planned evacuation and extermination of the Jews and called on the SS to rise to the challenge while warning them not to violate the "moral" code of their mission through personal enrichment. Relevant here are the following lines:

> Most of you men know what it is like to see 100 corpses side by side, or 500 or 1,000. To have stood fast through this—and except for cases of human weakness—to have stayed decent, that has made us hard. This is an unwritten and never-to-be-written page of glory in our history.... We had the moral right, we had the duty towards our people, to destroy this people that wanted to destroy us.... All in all, however, we can say that we have carried out this most difficult of tasks in a spirit of love for our people. And we have suffered no harm to our inner being, our soul, our character.[91]

In these lines we witness the brazen reversal of victim and aggressor of which Halbertal warns—it is the SS officer, in Himmler's reasoning, who must make the sacrifice and bear the burden of "standing fast" through the trial of accumulating corpses while remaining "decent" and "carrying out this most difficult of tasks"—that is, annihilating the Jews for love of the German people.

Indeed, the language of sacrifice permeated the overall ideology of National Socialism. In the years before becoming chancellor, Hitler spoke of the *Opfer der Kriege und Arbeit* (victims of war and work) and argued that these soldiers and workers deserved better, in terms of both material and social capital, in return for their sacrifices. As Greg Eghigian points out, the language used for the promotion of Germany's annual Winterhilfswerk des Deutschen Volkes (Winter Relief Drive of the German People) from 1933 onward reveals to what extent the notions of sacrifice and victimization shaped the Nazi world view and drove Nazi welfare policy, framing sacrifice and self-sacrifice as necessary acts to enable moral renewal and social redemption.[92] Supporting the Winter Relief Drive—a program under the control of propaganda minister Joseph Goebbels—was framed as a "sacred duty" and a "daily education in sacrifice" through which volunteers could contribute to the *Volksgemeinschaft*, according to program commissioner Erich Hilgenfeldt. A few examples of the language of sacrifice used by promoters and organizers of the relief drive include "*Opferbereitschaft*" (readiness to sacrifice); "*Opferfreudigkeit*" (joy in sacrifice); "*ein Opfern bringen*" (to bring an offering); "*aufopferungsvolle Tätigkeit*" (self-sacrificing activity); and "*opferwilliges Eintreten*" (self-sacrificing support). Collection tins for the relief drive bore the imperative "*Opfert!*" and an *Opfersäule* (sacrificial pillar) was erected in Hamburg to advertise the Winter Relief Drive.[93]

Ominous in the Nazi language of sacrifice is the link between sacrifice and "struggle and battle readiness," as evident in Hilgenfeldt's militaristic phrasing that *Einsatzbereitschaft und Opferfreudigkeit* (readiness for military action and joy in sacrifice) characterize those committed to the Winter Relief Drive.[94] Ultimately, in the Nazi vision, a national community possessing a *Schicksalsgemeinschaft* (common fate) would transform Germans from (passive, powerless) victims into (active, powerful) citizens ready to sacrifice.[95]

Narratives of New Beginnings

Sacrifice, finally, has played a decisive role in the cult of new beginnings and of cultural, spiritual, and national renewal through German history. Narratives of nations overcoming their pasts and beginning anew with a national rebirth have been central since the French Revolution. Key to the founding myths of such national narratives is the idea of breaking with the past as a necessity for beginning a new era. In the cult of new beginnings, the dead are necessary casualties for renewal. Because they died for future generations, their sacrifices impose a responsibility and obligation on the living. Such narratives have resurfaced repeatedly in Germany, emerging as interpretative paradigms through which national upheavals such as the Wars of Liberation, the Franco-Prussian War, World War I, the Beer Hall Putsch, and World War II are made palatable.[96] The metaphor of renewal through death transforms violence and loss into healing and salvation, sacralizing killing and transforming the dead into sacrificial victims to inaugurate a new Germany. At the heart of such myths is the virtue of overcoming—be it the overcoming of Napoleon, lost wars, or the Nazi past.[97]

Today, the German nation—united, peaceful, enlightened, and tolerant—presents a successful model of such overcoming, having emerged like a phoenix from the ashes of a terrible history.[98] In the fall of 1990, political scientist Hans-Peter Schwarz declared that the reunification of Germany offered the new nation "the chance to finally overcome its identity-neurosis, fixated on the past, and to become a normal nation state." In Schwarz's words, "After a long odyssey, the country [Germany] has returned to itself."[99]

As we have seen, ritual sacrifice plays a key role in both Germanic tribal history and mythic Germanic narratives of creation, resurrection, and renewal, while helping to create community, strengthen social and political identity, and preserve social structure. Concepts of sacrifice, including themes of self-transcendence, self-sacrifice, and the transcendence of death and suffering through sacrifice, have served twentieth-century wars and ideologies well. Russian writer, Soviet dissident, and former political prisoner Aleksandr Solzhenitsyn (1918–2008) writes that it is "thanks to *ideology*" that the "twentieth century was fated to experience evildoing on a scale calculated in the millions," for it is ideology that "gives evildoing its long-sought *justification*."[100] Moshe Halbertal agrees: those who view self-transcendence—the overcoming of self-interest—as the basis for morality perceive sacrifice as a core component of moral life. The more absolute, the weightier the obligation, the greater the sacrifice that is justified—with the ultimate sacrifice being one's own life.[101] This ultimate sacrifice possesses a deep internal connection to violence and killing: if one is willing to sacrifice one's own life, then one is justified in taking another's.[102]

CONCLUSION

The loss of human life in the course of the twentieth century's two world wars is staggering: during World War I alone, some thirteen million men died—more than twice as many as had been killed in all major wars between 1790 and 1914.[103] While there are no definitive numbers available for the loss of human life due to World War II and the Holocaust, estimates including both soldiers and civilians range from thirty-five to sixty million. The US Holocaust Memorial Museum estimates fifty-five million deaths worldwide, including six million Jews, over five million Soviet civilians, and approximately three million Soviet prisoners of war. The challenge involved in memorializing losses of such dizzying magnitude has resulted in the need for increasingly evocative, creative, often abstract or negative memorial forms (what *Spiegel* reporters in an interview with Reinhart Koselleck fittingly called "built" or "constructed metaphors"[104]). Such memorials eschew images or inscriptions invoking heroism, nationalism, and patriotism as was common to pre–World War II German memorials; instead, they often depict tortured human forms convulsed in extreme suffering[105] or thematize ultimately unrepresentable absence, loss, and meaninglessness through gaps, fissures, fractures, inaccessible spaces, fields or groupings of (broken) stelae, or voids.

The distrust of monumental structures beloved by totalitarian regimes and the reluctance to follow in the footsteps of earlier memorial trends whose militaristic messages played a role in inciting World War II have led to the phenomenon of inventive memorials that James Young calls "counter-monuments" and defines as "memorial spaces conceived to challenge the very premise of the monument."[106] Countermonuments share certain qualities such as antimilitarism with Alfred Hrdlicka's well-known *Gegendenkmal* (opposition or countermemorial) of 1983 and 1986 at Dammtordamm, Hamburg, which Hrdlicka designed in opposition to the war-glorifying 76er Denkmal (Memorial to the Seventy-Sixth Infantry Regiment, 1936). In recent years, a new type of memorial integrating memorial, archival and exhibition elements—what Bill Niven calls the "combimemorial"—has emerged.[107]

The vast majority of Germany's thousands of war memorials do not exhibit the qualities of the countermonument; rather, they overwhelmingly rely on conservative cultural iconography to interpret the meaning of death and sacrifice, favoring above all Christian themes but also nature or classical imagery, including memorial forms such as *Ehrenhaine* (honor groves), stone circles, and *Findlinge* (glacial erratics), the latter of which exhibit the iconography of German nationalism, as discussed in chapter 4.

From among the thousands of inscriptions engraved on war memorials—many gleaned from biblical verses or the lines of German poets—the most common are those extolling the sacrifices made by fallen soldiers "*für Volk und Vaterland, für Herd und Heimat*" ("for the German people and fatherland, for hearth and home"). The theme of "sacrificing for" and self-transcendence through sacrifice—with all its promises and pitfalls, seductive romanticism and poison—lies at the very heart of German war memorialization.[108] The following lines from Friedrich Hölderlin's poem "Der Tod fürs Vaterland" capture perfectly the sentiment that self-sacrifice is not merely a duty but a longed-for privilege and path to meaningful existence: "O take me, let me join that circle, / so that I will not die a common death! / I do not want to die in vain; but / I would love to perish on a hill of sacrifice."

CHAPTER SIX

Für Herd und Heimat (For Hearth and Home)

Memorializing Sacrifice in the Fatherland

> Den toten Brüdern halten wir Treu- in Leid und Trauer stark. Es schmieden einst ihr Schwert sich neu... Dankbar ehren wir die ihr Leben ließen für Volk und Vaterland, für Herd und Heimat (We remain loyal to our dead brothers, strong in suffering and sorrow. Their swords will one day be forged anew.... With gratitude we honor those who gave their lives for the German people and fatherland, for hearth and home).
>
> —Inscription on a World War I memorial in Mieste, Saxony-Anhalt

> Wer mutig für sein Vaterland gefallen, Der baut sich selbst ein ewig Monument im Herzen seiner Landesbrüder und dies Gebäude stürzt kein Sturmwind nieder (He who courageously dies for his fatherland builds himself an eternal monument in the hearts of his fellow countrymen that no tempest can demolish).
>
> —Inscription on a World War I memorial in Stenden, North Rhine–Westphalia

INTRODUCTION: "JOYFUL, SELF-SACRIFICING DEVOTION"

"The young men, who perhaps never returned, were ablaze with the flames of joyful, self-sacrificing devotion ... their death song was the song of Germany and the roaring hymns of the Rhine ... he [the German soldier] takes his fate seriously, indeed he loves it, and is most proud when it destroys him."[1] So writes Karl von Seeger, author of a book on German war memorials from 1930, describing the joy of self-sacrifice experienced by young Germans marching off to war in 1914. Two inscriptions inscribed on World War I memorials, quoted above, use similar language to praise the men who died for the German *Volk und Vaterland* (people and fatherland), *Herd und Heimat* (hearth and home), securing for themselves eternal glory and an indelible place in national memory. Such romantic sentiments mask the cruel reality of war and suggest a dangerous alchemy in which death is the base metal transformed into the gold of national renewal.

German war memorials, especially those commemorating fallen World War I soldiers, exhibit a rich variety of iconography framing those who died as heroes and sacrificed themselves for *Herd und Heimat*. Although unusual, some memorials explicitly frame soldiers as sacrificial offerings. A memorial in Büdelsdorf, Schleswig-Holstein, created by Alfred Ehlers (1885–1955) and dedicated on December 10, 1930, features four muscular warriors, naked from the waist up and clad in steel helmets, kneeling on a rounded plinth. Their short swords are propped up between their thighs with the hilts resting against their groins. The warriors hold above their heads a great, antique *Opferschale* (an offering bowl used to hold ritual offerings to gods). On the underside of the turned work are engraved the 206 names of local soldiers killed in World War I and (added later) World War II as well as several inscriptions, including one clarifying that the sacrificial offering is actually the 206 fallen soldiers themselves: "Ein Held ist, wer sein Leben Grossem opfert" ("A hero is one who sacrifices his life for greatness").[2] A World War I memorial in Uhlbach, Baden-Württemberg, by Karl August Donndorf (1870–1941) similarly depicts an explicit image of sacrifice: the sculpture of a naked man sprawls across a globe, his arms and legs spilling over the sides. Here, the fallen soldier appears to be a sacrificial object offered up to a god on a cosmic altar.

Occasionally, memorials depict objects used in sacrificial rituals in the vicinity of soldiers to suggest the sacrificial nature of a soldier's death, as in the case of an elaborate World War I and World War II memorial in Großholthausen cemetery (Dortmund), North Rhine–Westphalia (1935, later modified to include World War II soldiers), designed by Fritz Richter Elsner (1884–1970). Atop a plinth at the center of a memorial platform stands a tall, erect soldier with spread legs in uniform, overcoat, and helmet; he is alert, gazing straight ahead and standing watch. The butt of his weapon, held in both hands, rests between his feet. Flanking the stairs leading to the memorial stand two large sacrificial fire bowls, waiting to be filled with sacred fire. A depiction of a fire bowl appears on one of the large, engraved panels as well.[3]

Most war memorials, however, draw on subtler strategies and inscriptions to suggest the symbolism of sacrifice. Memorials sites dedicated to fallen soldiers often draw on symbols, inscriptions, and a variety of techniques, such as elevated platforms, stone circles, and groves of oak trees, to present the sites as sacred. Such sites are, in the words of Koselleck, "hallowed

Für Herd und Heimat (For Hearth and Home) 169

FIGURE 8. Memorial in Großholthausen cemetery.

places that are ritualistically cultivated in order that memory of the dead will be rediscovered" by each new generation.[4] A memorial in Niederau, Saxony, for example, located in front of the parish church, features the figure of a naked man with sharply defined muscles lying on a plinth against a tall memorial wall. Inscribed on the wall, beneath three stars and one of the inscriptions that reads "Ehre unseren gefallenen Helden" ("Honor our fallen heroes"), are the names of the fallen. Propped on one elbow, his left hand clenched into a fist, the soldier gazes upward. A second inscription frames suffering as the path to redemption; it reads: "Durch Leid zum Licht" ("Through suffering to the light"), a translation of "Per aspera ad astra."

This chapter continues the trajectory begun in the previous chapter. While chapter 5 focused on theories of sacrifice as well as the history of sacrificial ritual and practice in Germanic culture and myth, chapter 6, a descriptive chapter, engages the rich and inventive iconography of sacrifice displayed on German war memorials. The purpose of this chapter is to delineate the varied motifs of sacrifice across the German memorial landscape, from Pietà scenes and warrior saints to superhuman fighting machines and loyal comrades. The chapter begins with a short discussion of the agents and actors of German remembrance before turning to the common motifs of nineteenth- and twentieth-century German war memorials. As the postwar period advances, the war memorials we examine will become increasingly aggressive, until a new concept of war memorialization emerges in the post–World War II period. The chapter then focuses on sacred depictions of sacrifice through Christian iconography and, in the final section, on secular depictions of sacrifice in the form of soldierly camaraderie.

AGENTS AND ACTORS OF REMEMBRANCE

Before turning to war memorials themselves, we shall briefly consider the agents and actors of German war remembrance. German historian Edgar Wolfrum uses the term *Deutungseliten* (interpretive elites) to describe those persons in society who possess the symbolic capital to shape and define norms and values in the public sphere.[5] Until the middle third of the nineteenth century, the initiative for German memorials and monuments emerged from *Deutungseliten* like kings and princes in conjunction with elected and self-appointed officials, political and military advisers, and artists and architects favored by political elites.

This began to change during the mid-nineteenth century, specifically during the Second Schleswig War (1864) and the Austro-Prussian War (1866), as committees of veterans, choir groups, marksmen guilds, local politicians, and church leaders began assuming leading roles in erecting memorials and monuments. By the time of the Franco-Prussian War (1870–71), after which almost four thousand monuments were erected across Germany, memorials and monuments were increasingly reflecting the will and values of the people. However, kings and princes were still able to shape to a significant extent the memory of wars and the dissemination of their meanings until the collapse of the German Empire at the end of World War I.[6]

With the end of World War I, the memorialization of war in Germany began relying on the work of five major players who worked together via commemorative networks: memorial committees, veterans and veteran associations, families, artists (directly commissioned or selected through competitions), and the state.[7] In cities, associations of former front soldiers exercised a great deal of influence over war memorials—especially those dedicated to specific regiments, which fell completely under the control of former soldiers. In villages, decisions about war memorials were largely left to veteran associations of former front soldiers, reservists, and local church leadership, with little input from the state.[8] In this sense, memorials to fallen World War I soldiers were predominantly a "bottom up" phenomenon, reflecting the will, intellect, and beliefs of the former soldiers, their local religious communities, and engaged citizens. It is also important to note in this context that memorials to fallen soldiers are essentially political and that collective remembrance of the fallen is always a political act. In the words of Reinhart Koselleck, "Commemorating the dead is part of human culture. Commemorating the fallen, those violently killed in battle, civil war, or war, belongs to political culture.... The political cult of the dead is an anthropological precept without which history is unthinkable."[9] In his seminal writings on war memorials and identity formation, Koselleck describes two essential ways in which war memorials create identity: first, they ascribe to the dead particular identities, depicting the fallen as "heroes, victims, martyrs, victors, kinsmen, and, as the case may be, the defeated ... as upholders and bearers of honor, faith, glory, loyalty, and duty; finally, as custodians and protectors of the fatherland, of humanity, justice, freedom, of the proletariat, or of the current constitution." Second, they ascribe identity to the living who dwell among and behold the memorials—an identity that the living are morally obligated to accept (*mortui viventes obligant*). In Koselleck's words, "The war memorial not only commemorates the dead; it demands the recognition of lost life that makes survival and continued life meaningful." Finally, it is crucial to keep in mind that the meaning assigned to the deaths of fallen soldiers is not in any way natural or self-evident but rather assigned by communities of the living to suit current needs and purposes. It is the survivors and then generations to come, in short, who decide what the fallen have presumably died "for"—and these decisions are always political and subject to change through the passage of time.[10]

WAR MEMORIALS: DYING FOR KING, FATHERLAND, AND VOLK

In general, war memorial inscriptions in German-speaking lands have sought to create the illusion of unity against external or (imagined or real) internal enemies, to preserve or create a new a sense of continuity, to minimize discord, and—beginning with the modern era—to legitimize violent death.[11] As Reinhart Koselleck explains, dynastic European practices of memorialization did not traditionally require violent death to legitimize the power of kings, Kaisers, and princes, but the dawn of the modern era witnessed a nationalization of the polis or city-bound or family and dynasty-bound "*Totenkult*" (cult of the dead) and concurrent shift in memorialization practices, whereby violent death became increasingly utilized by political rulers to legitimize power.[12] The new phenomenon of general conscription, too, helped lead to a second major shift and democratizing trend in war memorialization since the French Revolution: "Since the beginning of general conscription, beginning with the levée en masse, the name of every fallen soldier became worthy of remembrance."[13] In short, every fallen soldier who fought for the fatherland now possessed the right to be memorialized as a hero.

A third structural change in memorialization in the modern era is the transference of the promise of eternity from religious (Christian) to secular (political) discourse. The promise of eternal life for the soul of each departed in heaven, in other words, metamorphoses in the modern era into the promise of eternal remembrance of the fallen among the living and each new generation to come. Eternal remembrance guarantees, in short, that no soldier who died in sacrifice for his country died in vain; with this new concept, the realm of eternity shifts from the transcendent beyond to the present and future. A final phenomenon of modern memorialization is the democratic expectation that all soldiers, including the unknown, the unidentifiable, and the missing, should be rescued from oblivion and remembered as heroes, and that symbolic graves, or cenotaphs, be erected for those deprived of their own graves. In the post–World War I period, as a result of the anonymous mass death suffered by soldiers and the inability to identify and memorialize each victim, memorials and / or symbolic graves and tombs for all unknown, fallen, or missing soldiers were erected in Paris, London, Warsaw, and many other European capitals (except for Berlin). Koselleck describes this development as one of the most important in twentieth-century memorialization and calls it the "last station in the democratization of death," with the unknown soldier standing symbolically for his nation or people.[14]

Common Motifs on Nineteenth-Century and World War I Memorials

Depictions of the self-sacrificing soldier are not new to World War I and World War II memorials. Monuments commemorating nineteenth-century wars against the French (the Wars of Liberation, 1813–14, and the Franco-Prussian War, 1870–71) declare fallen soldiers to have sacrificed themselves not only for *König und Vaterland* (king and fatherland) but also, increasingly, for German unity and freedom, for patriotism, national identity, and the German *Volk*—a shift indicating the transference of loyalty from dynasty to fatherland.[15] These inscriptions helped create a bond between the German *Volk* and the new territories of the German Confederation—a loose political association of thirty-nine states with mighty Prussia at its heart.[16]

Monuments such as Karl Friedrich Schinkel's Prussian National Monument for the Liberation Wars (1821) on Kreuzberg Hill in Berlin bear inscriptions praising soldiers who sacrificed their lives, offering "Gut und Blut dem Vaterlande" ("Wealth and blood for the fatherland").[17] Such inscriptions frame the deaths of soldiers as offerings made on the altar of Germany's rebirth. Other war memorials, like an intriguing memorial in Erfelden, Hessen, that stands within the garden of a Protestant church, seeks to tie recent wars to ancient Germanic history. This bronze sculpture by Hans Dammann (1867–1942) is dedicated to the fallen heroes of World War I and features a soldier atop a broad plinth.

The soldier wears a *pteruges* (a defensive skirt of leather or fabric) worn by Greek and Roman soldiers, and a *Stahlhelm*, and holds a short sword in one hand. He kneels in prayer by a sarcophagus, his hands resting on the stone, his head bowed. The inscription reads, "Fürs Vaterland / Ihren Helden Die Dankbare Gemeinde / Erfelden" (1914–18) ("For the fatherland / dedicated to your heroes / from the grateful community of Erfelden").

FIGURE 9. Memorial in Erfelden.

By clothing this soldier in an iconic Greco-Roman garment, Dammann embeds a twentieth-century soldier into a mythic narrative of heroic warriors that stretches back to antiquity. As part of a continuum of valor, the fallen soldier is only the latest incarnation of the eternal courageous warrior who dies for a great civilization and lives on in legend. Dammann thus creates a symbolic tie between antiquity and modern Germany, investing the death of the German soldier with the grandeur and timelessness of ancient Greece and Rome.

Honor and Rebirth

Unlike nineteenth-century wars, World War I resulted in neither victory nor national renewal but rather a desperate need to discover a sense of meaning in war. The values of patriotism and self-sacrifice for *Volk und Vaterland* as well as comrades in arms filled the abyss, and thousands of memorials extolling these virtues were erected across Germany. The German soldiers' self-sacrifice is presented as willingly undertaken and rewarded with eternal honor and gratitude. Many World War I memorial inscriptions support the imagery of sacrifice by linking the death of soldiers to the rebirth of the German nation. A memorial in Neukloster, Mecklenburg-Vorpommern, bears an inscription proclaiming, "Aus unserem Sterben erblühte dem Vaterlande neues Leben" ("From our death blossoms new life for the fatherland"), while a memorial located on the north side of the Protestant church in Bielefeld / Schildesche by Wilhelm Heilig and Otto Schulz (July 1924) draws on the metaphor of cyclical renewal: "Deutsches Volk, wie ehrst du die Helden, die mit dem Opfer ihres Lebens deine Heimat schützen? Soll die Blut- und Tränensaat der Jahre 1914 bis 18 dir Frucht tragen, so lasse Gottesfurcht deinen schönsten Schmuck, Freiheit dein höchstes Gut und Hingabe ans Vaterland deine heiligste Pflicht sein. Euch, die ihr starbet für uns, ein Mal dankbaren Erinnerns erbaut in schwerer Zeit 1923 bis 24" ("German people, how do you honor the heroes, who protect your home with the sacrifice of their lives? If the seeds of the blood and tears of the years 1914–1918 should bear fruit for you, then let piety be your loveliest jewel, freedom your highest good, and devotion to fatherland your most sacred duty. For you, who died for us, this mark of thankful remembrance, erected in the difficult year of 1923–24"). On a second panel, fallen soldiers are praised as going to battle to defend "home and hearth."[18]

Betrayed

Less common are memorials depicting the fallen soldier's sacrifice being repaid with betrayal due to internal enemies. A World War I memorial by Heinrich Möller in the Alt-Mariendorf cemetery in Berlin (1923), features a nearly naked warrior with bowed head; he crouches, facing west toward France, on a cubic block with sword and shield. The inscription reads, "Unterlegen nicht besiegt" ("Bested but not defeated")[19]—a veiled reference to the *Dolchstoßlegende* (stab in the back) conspiracy theory of post–World War I Germany, according to which the Imperial German Army was never defeated on the battlefield but rather betrayed by civilians—namely, Jews and Socialists—back home. A second example is a World War I memorial in Mainbernheim, Bavaria, designed by Franconian sculptor Richard Rother (1927) and dedicated to the town's fifty-two fallen soldiers.[20] The limestone statue depicts a German soldier in an iconic *Stahlhelm*, standing on a plinth with legs spread, determined, downturned mouth, and arm poised to throw a grenade. Behind his left leg crouches a skeleton—its skull, with open eyes and teeth, peeks out from behind the soldier's thigh, gripping a dagger and preparing to stab the soldier, literally, in the back. The skeleton's reverse side reveals a caricature of a Jewish face with hook nose, as if taken directly from the pages of Julius Streicher's antisemitic smear-sheet *Der Stürmer*. This memorial was removed in 1945 by American troops, erected again in 1982 at the *Rathausplatz* (town hall square), moved to its current location behind the Saint Johannis Church in 1997, and finally supplemented with a new plaque and rededicated in 2010. The memorial's inscription reads, "Der Tod fürs Vaterland ist ewiger Verehrung wert" ("Death for the fatherland is worthy of eternal veneration").

Enchanted Sleep

The sacrifice of fallen World War I soldiers, particularly in the early postwar years, was often depicted as rewarded with repose: in return for their sacrifice, these stone warriors are granted the enchanted sleep of unscathed death. They slumber peacefully on their concrete slabs, their broken and punished bodies restored to wholeness through death. Twentieth-century war memorials name death as such but they also recast it, transforming the brutality of war into images that make death comprehensible and acceptable.²¹ The soldier who rotted in the trenches, maimed and mangled by gunfire and grenades, emerges on the other side of death magically restored to his original, perfect form. This peacefully slumbering soldier presents the ultimate euphemism of war while also revealing what George Mosse identifies as an Enlightenment-inspired change in the perception of death as one in which the "image of the grim reaper was replaced by the image of death as eternal sleep."²²

By depicting fallen soldiers in this idealistic form, memorials not only "regenerate" the disfigured and dismembered soldier but also prepare him for his reawakening and eternal life to come by restoring to him the physical wholeness necessary for such resurrection. The memorial stages, in effect, "a literal and metaphorical replacement for the absent and incomplete bodies of the war dead."²³ The soldier's "deep and joyous" sleep appears as an enchanted intermediate stage between the departure and the return of the dead²⁴—a trope, Stefan Goebel explains, inspired by national mythologies²⁵ and folk tales combined with the Christian idea of resurrection.²⁶ The concept of the dead being restored and continuing to exist after death—and the practice of rituals of departure to ensure the success of this process—preceded Christianity, characterizing both primal religions (for example, in ancient Egypt) and Judaism during the pre-Hellenistic period in the form of beliefs concerning the resurrection of the body and immortality of the soul. Such beliefs are especially important in Christianity, due to its central doctrine of the resurrection of Christ;²⁷ the expectation of resurrection appears in canonical writings, including the Hebrew Bible in the books of Ezekiel and Daniel as well as in the four gospels and letters of the Apostle Paul of the New Testament.

Memorial soldiers depicted lying in tombs in peaceful states of repose often mimic, furthermore, medieval statuary, with their poses and tombs mirroring those of medieval knights and princes in Gothic cathedrals.²⁸ A prime example of such a memorial appears among the picturesque ruins of the medieval Hohensyburg castle in Syburg (a neighborhood of Hörde, in the city of Dortmund), North Rhine–Westphalia. This memorial of 1930 was sculpted by Friedrich Bagdons (1878–1937)—a sculptor known for his monumental granite statue of Paul von Hindenburg, which once stood at the no-longer-existent Tannenberg Memorial. The medieval stone ruins offer an elegiac setting for the Memorial to the Fallen German Soldiers, which commemorates the fallen of the Franco-Prussian War, World War I, and (added later) World War II. Framed by the remains

FIGURE 10. Hohensyburg Castle Memorial.

FIGURE 11. Hohensyburg Castle Memorial (alternate view).

of stone ramparts, the fallen soldier rests on his catafalque on a two-tiered base, still clad in steel helmet and uniform, his head resting on a shroud. At his feet perches a giant eagle—a symbol of Germany—its head erect and facing straight ahead, its enormous wings spread in a protective gesture around the lower half of the soldier's body, its talons resting on the edge of the catafalque. Inscribed on plaques affixed to the stone walls around the statue are dedications to the fallen and lists of their names.

Loretana de Libero persuasively demonstrates that soldiers depicted as if they were lying in state, as in the case of a memorial in Rheingönheim, Rhineland-Palatinate (1931), recalls images preceding even the medieval period, namely, images of warriors laid out for viewing and worship in a Germanic heroes' grove,[29] complete with weeping willow and torch.[30]

Perhaps Germany's most iconic fallen soldier in repose is the World War I memorial located in the Hofgarten (Court Garden) in Munich, directly in front of the Bavarian State Chancellery, designed by sculptor Karl Knappe and architects Thomas Wechs and Eberhard Finsterwalder and dedicated to the fallen soldiers of Munich in 1924. The outer walls of the memorial are decorated with reliefs of marching soldiers and a burial ground, marked with crosses. The aboveground portion of the memorial bears two inscriptions, "Unseren Gefallenen" ("For our fallen") and "Sie werden auferstehen" ("They will rise again"), as well as a series of reliefs of abstract human figures. To enter the memorial, the visitor descends a series of stairs into a rectangular pit coated in limestone. Within the pit stands an open crypt; on a red marble base lies a larger-than-life bronze sculpture of a fallen soldier. He wears his uniform, overcoat, boots, and helmet, and clasps his gun in both hands, but his head rests on a pillow and his eyes are closed. The original memorial statue, now kept in the Bavarian Army Museum in Ingolstadt, was sculpted in red marble by Bernhard Bleeker (1881–1968).

After Bleeker's original sculpture was damaged in World War II, it was replaced with a bronze replica created by Thomas Wimmer in 1972. A dedication, added later, extends commemoration to the victims of World War II from the city of Munich, including fallen soldiers, the missing, and casualties of bombings. The inscriptions cited above make explicit the sacrality hinted at through the unblemished form of the soldier, who lies peacefully, waiting for the moment when he will be reunited with those he left behind. In this underground chamber, death is but a temporary phase that leads to a higher state of being: resurrection and eternal life. For Karl von Seeger,

Für Herd und Heimat (For Hearth and Home)   179

FIGURE 12. Hofgarten Memorial, Munich.

the sleeping warrior who sacrifices himself for country and countrymen inspires feelings of indebtedness[31]—a transactional framing of sacrifice that binds future generations to the past via shackles of obligation.

Challenging the Cliché

Some memorials erected during the post–World War II era in Germany challenge the motif of the fallen soldier lying peacefully in enchanted slumber. One example, designed by architect Manfred Lehmbruck (1913–1992), was erected in the cemetery of Dußlingen (Tübingen), Baden-Württemberg (1965). It lies within a rectangular depression, suggesting a grave. In the center of the depression lies a cast-in-lead sculpture of a supine male figure. Merging with and absorbing the man's body is a massive, solid clamp-like slab of stone. Rigid and evoking a coffin, the mass of stone appears to be in the process of consuming the figure, so that the man's neck, most of his left leg, his left arm, his abdomen, his right thigh, and part of his right arm and ankles have already been swallowed by the stone.

This memorial undermines depictions of fallen soldiers that suggest sleep rather than death; it offers the viewer a snapshot of the inexorable process by which death claims a body, transforming a once-living being

FIGURE 13. Memorial in Dußlingen.

into inanimate matter, and warm flesh into cold stone. A trace of the dead figure's humanity—a handprint, palm up and partially concealed—peeks out from the blank expanse of stone, reminding us of the figure's individuality in the very moment in which he is devoured by death.

A second example of a memorial that challenges the enchanted sleep motif was erected in 1964 on a hill outside the town of Sigmaringen, Baden-Württemberg, and dedicated to the fallen German soldiers of four wars: the Austro-Prussian War, the Franco-Prussian War, and both world wars. The twenty-three-foot-high domed structure of limestone that houses this memorial is a Tholos tomb, also known as a beehive tomb due to its suggestive shape. Tholos tombs were built by late Bronze age Mycenean peoples and contained underground corbelled stone vaults approached via long entrance passages.[32] This tomb contains two openings: a small door and a low rectangular window, both covered with metal grates.

Within the memorial tomb is an austere, stone-walled room, dimly lit through a cross-shaped skylight; in the center of the room, beyond the locked door, lies a red marble sculpture of a fallen soldier by local German sculptor and professor Josef Henselmann (1898–1987). The soldier's facial features are minimalistic and abstract; his helmet, with its sharp contours,

FIGURE 14. Sigmaringen Tholos Tomb (external view).

and his mere hint of a uniform are vague and generic: these could be the remains of any fallen soldier. The lower half of the soldier's body appears to lose its distinct boundaries and melt into the stone slab on which it lies, as if the soldier's limbs were already decaying into detritus and returning to the earth in an act of autochthonous coalescence.

Highly unusual is the absence of any inscription or dedication to the fallen. A small sign beside the memorial offers basic information about the creation and function of the memorial, but there is no trace of the conventional language of German war commemoration: no references to sacrifice or heroism, and no expressions of gratitude, debt, or loyalty. Henselmann's fallen soldier in repose deconstructs the very motif of which it partakes: it is not enchanted sleep that claims this soldier but rather death and erasure. The Sigmaringen memorial, it is worth noting, is not a memorial on which a casual passerby might stumble. To reach it, one follows a gravel path past a sunlit field of poppies bordered by trees to a modest clearing; no sign directs the visitor or even announces the presence of a memorial in the vicinity, and GPS offers no guidance. Only a helpful nun from the nearby Erzbischöfliches Kinderheim Haus Nazareth (a children's home) permitted this visitor to locate the memorial on a hilltop overlooking the town.

FIGURE 15. Sigmaringen Memorial (internal view).

The Protector

Less common but still plentiful are World War I memorials depicting the soldier's sacrifice in the form of protecting one's family from danger. A memorial in Oberhaching, Bavaria, commemorating the fallen of three wars—the Franco-Prussian War of 1870–71, World War I, and World War II—depicts a soldier standing atop a tall plinth, gun in hand, legs spread, one arm held back to protectively shield the cowering figures of a woman and child. The woman gazes up at her protector, but he stares straight ahead in the direction of danger. The inscription reads, "Gedenket der Opfer beider Weltkriege" ("Remember the victims of both world wars"), followed by names of the fallen on the front and sides of the plinth. Here, the soldier's sacrifice for his nation is conflated with his sacrifice for his family: this soldier protects *Herd und Heimat*, irrevocably bound together with the iconography of a vulnerable woman and child. Such memorials grant impunity to soldiers and their actions in war by sanctioning those actions as honorably motivated by love and the desire to protect the vulnerable—a problematic assertion, to say the least, when World War II soldiers are subsumed under the memorial's message.

FIGURE 16. Memorial in Oberhaching.

Fists of Defiance: Increasing Aggression Depicted on World War I Memorials

In contrast to the motifs depicted on the memorials already mentioned, many memorials erected during the early postwar years exhibit aggressive, even revanchist characteristics. During the second half of the 1920s such memorials increasingly depicted German soldiers in warlike poses. A comparison of two memorials illustrates this shift: the first memorial is a bronze statue dedicated to the more than four thousand fallen soldiers of the 5th Guards Grenadier Regiment in Berlin, Spandau (1922), by August Schreitmüller. The memorial soldier sits leisurely on a pedestal of limestone atop a granite slab, naked from the waist up and with a loincloth draped across his waist and legs. His right arm drapes over his knee, and a short sword rests by his left hand. Still clad in his helmet, the soldier gazes straight ahead; an eagle, depicted in profile, sits beside him.

The second memorial is Daniel Stocker's (1865–1957)[33] memorial to the fallen soldiers of World War I in the *Ehrenhalle* (hall of honor) of the cemetery of Stuttgart-Feuerbach (1929), titled Ohnmacht und Wille (Impotence and Will). In the center of a memorial portico, flanked by metal panels engraved with the names of the fallen, stands a statue of two naked warriors. The first stands tall and straight with muscular chest and arms, extending forth two raised fists and gazing forward with slightly upward-tilted head: he is vengeful and defiant, modeling will and spirit. The second warrior kneels at the feet of the first, leaning against his companion's legs; his head and neck are bent over in a cowed posture. One hand is clutched to his chest and the other holds a short sword. His posture suggests submission and defeat; he models impotence.

The defiant, upright warrior refuses to accept the consequences of defeat; he is proudly belligerent and embodies the warrior of the future. His clenched fist is an example of the *Trotz-Faust* (fist of defiance)—a gesture commonly depicted on World War I memorials to demonstrate frustration and resistance in response to the lost war and the Treaty of Versailles.[34] The concept of resentment (*Ressentiment*) as "an habitual ubiquitous emotional reaction to some perceived attack or injury, expressed in the form of an impotent desire for revenge," as developed by philosophers Friedrich Nietzsche and Max Scheler, offers a framework for understanding the *Trotz-Faust*. As Greg Eghigian argues, it was the "perceived failure of national sacrifice as theodician ritual in the wake of World War I" that was the "chief source of the German political culture of resentment."[35] In the wake of World War I, it became clear that sacrifice

Für Herd und Heimat (For Hearth and Home) 185

for the homeland had led not to national rebirth and regeneration but rather to a lost war, a ruined economy, and a chaotic political situation. The *Trotz-Faust* embodies the frustration of *Ressentiment*; it refuses to accept the "dishonorable" peace of Versailles and vows vengeance.

Rising

During the 1930s, Germany's stone and bronze soldiers began preparing for war; they no longer lie or sit; rather, they rise from lying or kneeling positions to stand upright or stride forward, often facing south or west, their weapons within easy reach or already in hand.[36] A typical example is a memorial erected in 1931 in the old cemetery of Neu-Isenburg, Hesse, funded through voluntary donations from the community and dedicated to "Den gefallenen Söhnen unserer Stadt" ("The fallen sons of our city").

The statue depicts a naked warrior perched on one knee and holding his sword with both hands, the tip of its blade resting on the ground. He is poised to rise and gazes steadily forward. The inscription reads, "Ob kalt und stumm sie leben doch, die wir ins stille Grab gesenkt, so lang ein Herz auf Erden noch, in Liebe ihrer treu gedenkt" ("Though cold and mute, those we buried in their silent graves live still, as long as a single heart on

FIGURE 17. Memorial in Neu-Isenburg.

earth remembers them with love and loyalty"). Similarly, a memorial by Hermann Hosaeus called Liegender Krieger (Lying Warrior, 1934), erected in Wanne-Eickel, North Rhine–Westphalia, features a warrior half-lying, half- sitting, clad in steel helmet and overcoat, propped up on his arm and ready to fight.

The inscription, now faded, proclaims: "Des Feindes Erde in fester Hand / So schützen wir Volk einst und Vaterland / Den Tapferen zur Ehre / und unsern Gefallenen zum / Gedenken" ("The earth of the enemy firmly in hand / so did we protect our nation and fatherland / in honor of the courageous / and in memory of our fallen"). In 1995 the city of Wanne-Eickel decided not to restore the memorial and instead allow it to deteriorate—a clear rejection of the militaristic and patriotic sentiments that the memorial expresses.

A third example—a World War I and World War II memorial in the town of Gießen, Hesse—was erected in 1925 and later modified to include the fallen of World War II. The memorial was initiated by a veterans' association and designed by Wilhelm Heidwolf Arnold (1897–1984). Dedicated to the members of the Infantry Regiment "Kaiser Wilhelm" (2nd Grand Ducal Hessian) No. 116, the memorial depicts a soldier half-crouching, half-kneeling, naked but for a cloth draped across his lap. His right hand, resting on his knee, is clenched in a *Trotz-Faust* as he gazes off to one side. His helmet rests on the ground beside him, but the tips of the fingers of his left hand are already touching it, and the muscles in his left arm are taut. The inscription reads, "*Aufwärts*" ("Upwards").

FIGURE 18. Memorial in Wanne-Eickel.

FIGURE 19. Memorial in Gießen.

Awakening

An interesting anecdote concerning the World War I memorial in Lüdenscheid, North Rhine–Westphalia, illustrates well the shift toward increasing aggression in German memorialization. In 1922, the veterans' association of Lüdenscheid began planning a memorial for their city park terrace. The winning design of the 1927 competition was titled "Pro Patria" by sculptor Jakob Wilhelm (Willy) Meller (1887–1974) and architect Fritz Fuss (1889–1945). Meller would later become a member of the Nazi Party and be known for his statue "German Nike" at the Olympic stadium in Berlin, as well as for his collaboration with Nazi architect Clemens Klotz on high-profile projects such as the Nazi estate Ordensburg Vogelsang and the Nazi educational center Ordensburg Crössinsee.

According to the original design, a sculpture of a naked, fallen soldier (*Gefallener*), depicted lying on the ground with his face turned upward and struggling to raise himself, would stand at the center of the memorial. The soldier appears defeated, perhaps wounded by an enemy towering over him. Although this design inspired resistance from the moment of its proposal, it wasn't until 1931, in response to protests by local citizens and veteran associations (which desired a warrior depicted in full armor) that a compromise was reached: the new design would feature an awakening soldier

FIGURE 20. Lüdenscheid Memorial model.

(*Erwachender*), exhibiting strength, courage, and readiness to wage battle. Donations increased dramatically once the new design was adopted, and on March 17, 1935, the memorial was dedicated—one day after Hitler proclaimed general military conscription in Germany with the Military Service Law. Speeches held at the memorial's dedication drew clear connections between the memorial and Germany's new political and military goals.

Erwachender depicts a muscular man naked but for a loincloth; he lies propped on one hand on a wide stone plinth, his other arm raised and bent at the elbow behind his head, one hand clenched in a *Trotz-Faust*. He gazes straight ahead with parted lips; his curly hair recalls ancient Greek statuary. Behind the sculpture stand a series of irregular concave pentagon stone blocks engraved with the names of the fallen. By transforming a figure of defeat into one of awakening, the Lüdenscheid community turned from passive mourning to active aggression. A postscript completes the story: in 1956, a plaque was added to the memorial that glossed over the causes of World War II and ignored the differences between victims and perpetrators among the dead—the deaths of Germans were mourned, but victims of the Nazi regime were excluded. In 1997, a tree of peace (*Friedensbaum*) and a new inscription were added, acknowledging the victims of Nazi persecution in Lüdenscheid. A sign beside the sculpture, erected in 2011 and labeled "*Ein umstrittenes Denkmal*" ("A controversial memorial"), details the history of the memorial.

Für Herd und Heimat (For Hearth and Home) 189

FIGURE 21. Memorial in Lüdenscheid.

Often, World War I memorials depicting soldiers transitioning from passivity to action bear inscriptions that emphasize the importance of the soldiers' sacrifice for generations to come. A World War I memorial by Josef "Sepp" Mages (1895–1977), dedicated in June 1931 to the fallen soldiers of the 23rd Royal Bavarian Infantry Regiment in Kaiserslautern, Rhineland-Palatinate, features seven soldiers in uniform with steel helmets and armed with grenades. They stride forward in close order formation, their faces grim and fists clenched. The foot of the foremost soldier extends slightly beyond the edge of the plinth. The inscription reads, "Ehret die Toten—sie sind nicht vergeblich gefallen. Das Licht ihrer Tat kundet den Enkeln das Heil" ("Honor the dead—they have not fallen in vain. The light of their deeds announces to their grandchildren salvation").

On the Move
Although many memorials erected after 1933 are more intensely aggressive in their heroic iconography and depict the Nazi aesthetics of "redemption and monumentality," certain strains of thought and value motifs, such as a new manliness infused with purity, echo through both Weimar Republic and Nazi monuments.[37] Monuments and memorials

erected during the twelve years of Hitler's Third Reich tended to depict the fallen of World War I in the familiar though often intensified vernacular of World War I imagery. After 1933, memorial soldiers are not only increasingly aggressive but also on the move: a World War I memorial in Odenheim (Östringen), Baden-Württemberg, by Karl Wahl, erected in 1937 and dedicated by the "thankful community" to the 124 comrades who fell, features a soldier with his arm raised high in warning, his mouth frozen open in a cry, weapon slung across his shoulder and one leg striding forward. As de Libero points out, the soldier is about to march over a French helmet (*below left*).[38]

A limestone World War I and World War II memorial in Weinheim, Baden-Württemberg (erected in 1936, modified later to commemorate

FIGURE 22. Memorial in Odenheim.

Für Herd und Heimat (For Hearth and Home) 191

FIGURE 23. Memorial in Weinheim.

fallen soldiers of World War II as well), by sculptor and ceramicist Wilhelm Kollmar (1871–1948), depicts not one lone soldier but rather three identical fighting machines with backpacks, marching forward in lockstep; two of the soldiers carry guns on their shoulders and clench their fists, the third plays a drum. A wall fitted with plaques listing the names of the fallen surrounds the half-circle memorial platform. Next to the memorial, a sign explains that the names of five Jewish soldiers who fell in World War I were added to the memorial in 1946; these names had originally been excluded, even though their families had helped finance the building of the memorial. In contrast to this gesture of reconciliation, an attempt to whitewash history was made in 1959 when the town modified the memorial to include the fallen of World War II: while adding the new names, the ranks of twenty-nine SS members commemorated on the memorial were altered to falsely indicate that they were Wehrmacht instead of SS. A memorial dedicated to the victims of violence, war, and persecution—erected in 1999 as a *Gegendenkmal* (countermemorial) within sight of the original memorial—repudiates its neighbor's militarism and nationalism.

192 CHAPTER SIX

Superhuman Fighting Machines

Memorials erected during the years of National Socialism are not only intensely militaristic and aggressive; they also increasingly eschew any trace of human vulnerability or individuality.[39] A memorial in Kley/Oespel (Dortmund), North Rhine–Westphalia (1934–35), is emblematic: it depicts two soldiers—mirror images of one another—standing shoulder to shoulder in overcoats and helmets, left feet forward and hands on swords, ready to strike.

FIGURE 24. Memorial in Kley/Oespel (Dortmund).

This memorial has been the cause of political debate and has been used by neo-Nazis as a meeting place. In 2002, the local chapter of the political party Bündnis 90 / Die Grünen (Alliance 90 / The Greens) called for the memorial to be demolished; instead, two years later a plaque was added, rejecting the memorial's militaristic message.

The World War I memorial dedicated to the Lower Rhine 39th Fusilier Regiment at Reeser Platz in Düsseldorf, North Rhine–Westphalia, exhibits a similar aesthetic on a grander scale. This memorial was erected and dedicated in July 1939, only two months before the start of World War II. Its inscription reads, "Für des Deutschen Volkes Ehre und Freiheit" ("For the German people, honor and freedom"). Engraved on the wall of the memorial are the names of cities that were conquered by the Germans in World War I, rather than the names of fallen soldiers. The Fusilier memorial is also part of a larger National Socialist utopian narrative, having been erected in connection with the *Reichsausstellung* (*Reich Exhibition*) of 1937 in Düsseldorf called Schaffendes Volk (Productive People), designed to valorize the accomplishments of National Socialists in industry, economics, the arts, and city planning. As part of the exhibition, a *"Modellsiedlung"* (model settlement) or *Schlagetersiedlung*[40] was established in Golzheim, a borough of Düsseldorf, with housing units designed to exist in close harmony with nature and the creation of the Nordpark (North Park).

The monumental, vault-like memorial at Reeser Platz was designed by Rudolf Klophaus and Artur Tachill, and features an elaborate high relief by Richard Kuöhl, with layered soldiers marching into battle on either side of a metal gate (Tor der Gruft—Gate to the Crypt) bearing an Iron Cross and, above, the words *"Die 39er."* The soldiers ascend a series of stairs leading from their crypt; risen from the dead, they emerge from their resting place to fight again for Germany. A plaque installed beside the memorial explains the memorial's historical context and disavows its militaristic message and imagery. A project to reimagine and redesign the Reeser Platz and 39th Fusilier Regiment memorial, initiated by the SPD (Social Democratic Party), the Greens, and the Left political parties, failed.

Today, the memorial, which stands under *"Denkmalschutz"* (protection of historical monuments) since 2002, offers a bleak vision. It stands at the edge of the large, neglected Reeser Platz near residential neighborhoods. Weeds flourish in the cracks between cobblestones, and empty

FIGURE 25. Reeser Platz Memorial, Düsseldorf.

beer cans and traces of plastic bags and other trash lay scattered about. The memorial is unpopular with locals as well as with tourists. While staking out the site during peak tourist season, this visitor glimpsed only two other visitors in the space of several hours, namely, a bicycling father with his child, who paused to sit and enjoy a little refreshment while half-heartedly inspecting the marching soldiers. The memorial does remain relevant, however, for one segment of the population: neo-Nazis and other right-wing extremist groups, who have used the memorial as a meeting spot for marches both in the past and still today.[41]

A New Era: Post–World War II

New challenges for memorialization surfaced during the post–World War II era. Whereas memorials to the fallen soldiers of World War I were being erected already in 1918 and thus emerging in response to the first emotional waves of postwar mourning, Germany did not receive permission from the Allies to construct war memorials after World War II until 1952. The struggle to shape remembrance, however, had begun already in 1946 with the Allies' decision to demolish all monuments built by the Nazis, as well as earlier monuments glorifying militarism. These orders were not consistently followed, although inscriptions such as "Deutschland muss leben, und wenn wir sterben müssen" ("Germany must live, even if we must die") were often removed from memorials.[42]

Despite a slow start, thousands of new war memorials—funded publicly or privately, initiated by politicians, artists, families of victims, or local communities—have been erected to commemorate the dead of World War II. Early memorials tended to lump all victims together and ignore the differences between fallen soldiers, casualties of bombings, and victims of Nazi persecution. The first memorial after the end of the war, other than those erected by prisoners and liberators in former concentration camps and the "cadaver memorials" erected by former prisoners of Buchenwald concentration camp in April 1945,[43] was dedicated in Frankfurt in April 1946. Designed by Benno Elkan, it bears a simple inscription: *Den Opfern* ("To the victims"). Similarly, three World War II memorials sculpted by Gerhard Marcks—perhaps the most important German memorial artist since World War II—titled *Todesengel* (*Angel of Death*, 1949, Cologne), *Friedensengel* (*Angel of Peace*, 1952, Mannheim), and *Trauernde Alte* (*The Old Woman in Mourning*, 1955, Bochum), are dedicated to all victims of World War II. In countless cases, however, new memorials were not erected at all; rather, World War I memorials were marginally modified to include the fallen of World War II with the addition of new name plaques and inscriptions.

West German memory culture began changing in the late 1950s and early 1960s thanks to the emerging Jewish Holocaust narrative that rivaled the reconciliation narrative of German suffering, but it was only during the 1980s that the German memorial landscape as we know it today began emerging in full force, with a wide range of creative, evocative memorials focused on commemorating the victims of Nazi persecution across Germany.[44] Often, such memorials were the fruits of local, citizen-driven initiatives rather than institutional or state initiatives, including the now-ubiquitous Stolpersteine (Stumbling Stones) memorial plaques[45] installed throughout Germany and dozens of other countries.[46]

CHRISTIAN ICONOGRAPHY: TRANSCENDING DEATH

The majority of monuments and memorials erected since World War II are dominated by Christian iconography depicting the act of dying in war as one of sacrifice, through which the fallen soldier transcends death and perishes in imitatio Christi. In many churches, for example, in Rostock,

Berlin, Münster, and elsewhere, fallen soldiers as well as civilian casualties were commemorated using Passion, Pietà, and crucifixion imagery in conjunction with biblical quotations, suggesting that World War II soldiers had died not for Hitler but, rather, for Christ—and that national suffering might function as a means for atonement.[47] Many of these memorials were erected in chapels no longer used in church services; these spaces emerged as ideal memorials for honoring fallen soldiers with sacrificial Christian iconography. Pietà and Passion imagery, often used to commemorate civilian victims of Allied bombing attacks or the suffering of ethnic-German expellees from the east, carries the "obvious meaning ... that the Allies sent the German people down the Via Dolorosa, and that the nation, like Jesus Christ, is sinless."[48] The bombing of German cities, loss of civilian life, and loss of territory were thus depicted as constituting atonement for Nazi crimes. In the words of philosopher Moshe Halbertal, suffering has "a cleansing impact; it wipes the stain of sin."[49]

Pietà

The imagery of sacrifice appears in many guises. One of the most popular is the Pietà, sculpted or painted in the styles of classicism, realism, or modernism. Pietà scenes of Mary holding her dead son Jesus in her lap, her face inclined downward to gaze mournfully at him, appear primarily as memorial sculptures but also in paintings, drawings, or etchings serving as memorials. Germany possesses a rich tradition of Pietà imagery that spans the centuries. The country's earliest Pietàs date to approximately 1300; they appeared in German convents and were first described with the word *Vesperbild* in 1298.[50] Pietàs are valued primarily not for their depiction of Mary's grief, as in the case of lamentation imagery, but rather for their illustration of Jesus's "redemptive wounds" and the meditation on suffering and redemption that they inspire—namely, that suffering directly contributes to and makes possible redemption. Because Pietà imagery "grew out of meditative contemplation of Jesus's suffering in his Transfiguration and served to edify the faithful," believers have traditionally ascribed efficacy to Pietà images, venerating certain Pietàs as "wonder-working images in pilgrimage churches."[51]

In the context of war memorials, the Pietà's depiction of an intrinsic, causal relationship between suffering and redemption translates the sacrificial death of fallen soldiers into hope for national rebirth and renewal. World War I memorials employing Pietà imagery transcend the merely elegiac to depict suffering as a precursor for a greater good—the redemption of the fatherland and German *Volk*. Two models of Pietà in war memorials dominate: traditional Pietà scenes featuring Mary and Jesus and Pietà scenes that replace the figure of Jesus with a fallen soldier. In the latter, soldiers usually appear clad in uniform, with or without *Stahlhelm*, and Mary is usually depicted in traditional dress (or, more rarely, in contemporary garb). In variations, the fallen soldier in the pose of Jesus may be naked or holding a sword. Occasionally, Mary is replaced by a soldier as well, as in the case of a war memorial in Monsheim, Rhineland-Palatinate.[52] Across these variations the essential Pietà dynamic—the sacralized contemplation of the lost, beloved innocent—endures, effectively sacralizing the death of fallen soldiers by eliding the soldier's sacrifice (dying for country and countrymen) with Jesus's own (dying for the sins of mankind).

The most famous Pietà memorial in Germany is the enlargement of Käthe Kollwitz's sculpture Mother with her Dead Son (1937–38/39), located in the Neue Wache (New Guard House) in Berlin. This sculpture has served since 1993 as the centerpiece of the Central Memorial of the Federal Republic of Germany for the Victims of War and Tyranny and has excited a great deal of debate and controversy (discussed in more detail in chapter 8). Much of the disapproval this Pietà has inspired is due to the complicated history of the building itself[53] as well as the inscription engraved on the memorial floor in front of Kollwitz's sculpture: "Den Opfern von Krieg und Gewaltherrschaft" ("To the Victims of War and Tyranny")—a dedication that lumps together under the moniker "victims" fallen German World War II soldiers as well as victims of Nazi persecution.[54]

Some, too, have criticized the Pietà as an infelicitous form with which to mourn victims of persecution in general. German art historian Kathrin Hoffmann-Curtius declares: "The pain and doubt of countless women who, over the centuries, have sought and perhaps found solace in the image of the mother of God is here misused to suggest the inescapable necessity of suffering and sacrifice. The purpose of choosing this statue is to use the image of a suffering mother to promote national unity. Perpetrators and victims are gathered into her lap."[55] This Pietà may indeed, then, be the ideal form for furthering not its alleged but rather its *actual* agenda: that of promoting politically motivated meditation on the relationship between suffering (world war and postwar division) and redemption (the reunification of Germany).

In contrast to the Neue Wache memorial, most Pietà war memorials are modest. A small Pietà sculpture in Hümmel, Rhineland-Palatinate, is typical: this simple Pietà nestles in the niche of a stone memorial wall with a rounded gothic top. It depicts Jesus lying in the lap of Mary, who is wrapped in a shawl. Jesus's head falls backward and Mary gazes down at him. Beneath the sculpture hangs a huge Iron Cross. Rectangular plaques flanking the sculpture list the names of residents who died or went missing during both World War I and World War II. A more evocative Pietà in the communal cemetery of Ense-Bremen, North Rhine–Westphalia, memorializes local citizens killed in both world wars. The stone sculpture depicts Mary with bowed head, tenderly cradling a thin Jesus with protruding ribs in her lap. The inscription reads, "Gross wie das Meer ist dein Schmerz" ("For thy breach is great like the sea"), a quotation from the book of Lamentations 2:13 (King James Version).

Occasionally, a single accent transforms an otherwise quotidian Pietà into an aesthetically evocative one. The war memorial at the parish church in Eckfeld, Rhineland-Palatinate, by Johann Baptist Lenz (1922–2007), erected in West Germany in 1962, consists of five engraved memorial stones in a courtyard space; on the central memorial stone sits a gray stone Pietà. The Jesus figure draped across Mary's lap is strikingly thin and angular; his legs and right arm are exaggeratedly long and spindly, emphasizing his vulnerability and, by extension, the fragility of the fallen soldier.

The Pietà of the Memorial for the Victims of the World Wars in Algermissen, Lower Saxony, in West Germany, erected in the 1970s and created by Hanns Joachim Klug (1928–2013), deviates from most Pietà memorials with its nearly aniconic image of Mary and Jesus. The smooth, rounded forms of the gray sculpture feature a heavily shrouded Mary, with Jesus suspended, perfectly straight, across her lap; his skull protrudes dramatically, emphasizing the vulnerability of his slim neck and shoulders. The pair sits atop a tall four-sided tapered white plinth engraved with an angel. This Pietà depicts the *idea* of the Pietà rather than the Pietà itself—a mediation on the representation of mourning and loss.

Many Pietàs serve as war memorials within churches: the gray stone Pietà dedicated to the victims of both world wars by Andreas Bindl (1928–2010) at the modern Mariä Himmelfahrt parish church in Memmingen, Bavaria, a town whose origins go back to the Roman Empire, projects from a wall of the ground floor of the tower. Mary sits perfectly straight, in contrast to her usual bowing posture, and Jesus lies, stiffly erect, on his side. His torso, head, and neck are held perfectly straight even when extending past Mary's lap, bending only at the knees, so that their figures together visually evoke the form of a cross. Engraved on the wall behind the Pietà is a long dedication beginning with the words "Maria, Queen of Peace, grant us peace" and concluding with a quote from Matthew 6:12: "Lord, forgive us our debts, as we forgive our debtors." Between the two pleas for peace and forgiveness appears a dedication to all victims of World War I and World War II and a list of the names of the countries involved in both world wars.

One of the inscriptions, engraved on the console, reads "Quo vadis?" ("Where are you going?"). These legendary words, according to Catholic tradition, were posed by Saint Peter to the risen Christ, whom he met on the Appian Way. Christ answered Peter that he was going to Rome to be crucified anew, which inspired Peter, who was fleeing Rome, to muster his courage and return to suffer crucifixion on order of the Roman emperor Nero. Per his request, Peter was crucified upside down in acknowledgment of his unworthiness to die in the same manner as Christ. The Memmingen church tower is crowned with the Petrine (Petrus) Cross (the inverted Latin cross). In this context, "Quo vadis?"

FIGURE 26. Memorial in Memmingen at the Mariä Himmelfahrt Church.

frames German soldiers as martyrs who willingly sacrificed their lives for their nation, just as Saint Peter freely submitted to martyrdom by returning to Rome.

As mentioned, Pietà memorials often depict Jesus as a fallen soldier. A well-known Pietà sculpture (1987/88) of this type stands in the Saint Johannis Monastery courtyard in the former East German town of Stralsund, Mecklenburg-Vorpommern. This bronze-coated plaster-cast statue by Hans-Peter Jaeger is a copy of a bronze model originally created in 1932 by Ernst Barlach, an artist whose works were judged "degenerate" (*entartet*) by the Nazis. Barlach submitted his design of a Pietà to Stralsund but, due to objections raised by the Stahlhelm (a World War I veterans' group) and the Kyffhäuserbund (an umbrella organization for war veterans' associations) as well as subsequent delays, withdrew his proposal. Barlach's Pietà is riveting in the still melancholy of its form and its revelation of Mary's sorrow as she sits straight with closed eyes and grimly closed lips, her shawl partly covering her dead son. Here, Jesus and the fallen German soldier for whom he stands have morphed into one form—a young man still clad in *Stahlhelm*, lying with crossed hands across his lap. Mary's hands span the entire length of the soldier's body, which is rigid and perfectly straight. On the plinth is a quote from Barlach: "I reproduce that which is: the real and the true."[56]

A colorful sixteenth-century Pietà and wooden gothic top that serves as a memorial at the Saint Dionysius Catholic Church for members of the parish killed in both world wars in Gondenbrett, Rhineland-Palatinate, is unique for its inscription, which explicitly condemns war as a sin. Mary appears clad in blue and gold, clasping a blood-beflecked Jesus in her arms. On either side of the Pietà stand two wooden panels inscribed with the dates of the two world wars, Iron Crosses, and the names of the dead and missing. The inscription reads, "Mutter der sieben Schmerzen, mit deinem toten Sohn auf dem Schoss, mit deinen sieben Schwertern im Herzen, schneide die Menschheit von der Sünde des Krieges los!" ("Mother of the seven sorrows, with your dead son in your lap, with your seven swords piercing your heart, release mankind from the sin of war!")[57]

Sacred Companions

Beyond the Pietà, a variety of other memorial motifs illustrate that God accepts the lives of fallen soldiers as sacred, sacrificial gifts. As discussed in chapter 5, the act of offering a sacrifice to God is fraught with the anxiety of rejection; sacrificial ritual, with its prescribed protocol, protects the individual offeror from his individuation and thus from the rejection that Cain, Nadav, and Avihu suffered. War memorials depicting the sacrificial offering of soldiers' lives do not illustrate the ritual of offering itself but rather skip directly to God's acceptance and embrace of their sacrificial offerings. The most common form of illustrating such acceptance is the depiction of fallen soldiers in the sacred presence of angels, Jesus, or Mary.

In the town of Pang (Rosenheim), Bavaria, in front of the parish church stands an evocative stone sculpture dedicated in "eternal gratitude" to the "fallen heroes" of World War I and World War II (erected 1922, later modified to include World War II soldiers). The sculpture depicts a kneeling soldier, his head lolling to one side and his eyes closed. The soldier, held in the arms of an angel, still wears his iconic German *Stahlhelm*, and his lifeless, dangling hand clasps a short sword. The angel gazes down at the soldier somberly, his hands resting on the soldier's waist. The angel's presence testifies that the soldier's sacrifice has been accepted by God.

FIGURE 27. Memorial in Pang (Rosenheim).

Also common are memorials depicting scenes in which Christ reaches for or lingers by a fallen soldier: in the town of Ludwigshafen, Rhineland-Palatinate (1926), a sculpture by Theodor Joanni depicts Christ standing over a naked, fallen warrior wearing a steel helmet and holding a broken sword, signifying his defeat. Christ's hands are extended over the dead soldier in blessing. The inscription reads, "Sei getreu bis in den Tod" ("Be true until death"). Other memorials imply rather than explicitly depict divinity by depicting praying soldiers. A memorial chapel (erected in 1931) in Bischofswiesen, Bavaria, features a wooden carved altar with vivid gold background by Anton Stöckl (1901–1946). The haloed Jesus sits, bedecked in robes, next to a kneeling soldier; he holds the soldier's left hand and lays his other arm around the man's shoulders. This scene is framed by two other scenes; to the left, a woman takes leave of two soldiers holding guns and already striding away, and to the right, three soldiers are depicted in action—one is slumped and dying, the second is throwing a grenade, and the third crouches with his gun in hand. Jesus's presence, like that of the angel, signals acceptance.

The Warrior Saint as Martyr: Saint George

One form of Christian iconography that emerged as a particularly popular choice for war memorials is the warrior saint as martyr. The most frequently depicted warrior saint is Saint George, the valiant knight venerated for defeating a wicked dragon and saving not merely the lives but also the souls of pagans by persuading them to convert to Christianity. Saint George has been depicted in the visual arts astride a horse since the twelfth century. The first great bronze cast memorial to feature Saint George together with horse and dragon was erected in Prague in 1373, with the warrior saint depicted as a medieval knight.[58]

According to legend,[59] the courageous knight who would become Saint George hailed from Cappadocia, a province of the Roman Empire in Anatolia. Arriving in the city of Silene (Libya), Saint George learned of a dangerous dragon whose breath was poisoning the people of the land. To appease the dragon, the city inhabitants fed him every day two sheep. Once they had exhausted their supply of sheep, they began a lottery to select youthful members of the population to feed to the dragon instead. One day, the lot fell on the king's daughter; moments away from being eaten, she was discovered by Saint George. The knight drew his sword, made the sign of the cross, charged toward the dragon on his horse, and succeeded in severely injuring the beast. After the king and his people agreed to submit to baptism in exchange for ridding their city of the dragon scourge, Saint George slew the dragon and cut off his head.

At this time, during the reign of the emperors Diocletian and Maximian and their persecution and martyring of thousands of Christians, some began betraying their Christian faith and sacrificing to pagan idols. Saint George beseeched the pagans to give up their gods, thereby attracting the attentions of the provost Dacian, who, after failing to convert Saint George to his pagan beliefs, resolved to murder him. A horrifying catalogue of tortures ensued: Saint George was beaten with iron rods and poisoned, placed between two wheels mounted with swords, and thrown into a cauldron of molten lead—all to no avail, for Saint George emerged, miraculously unharmed, each time. Finally, in revenge for Saint George calling on the Christian God to destroy the pagan temple, idols, and priests, and in rage over the conversion of his own wife to Christianity, Dacian had Saint George beheaded in the year 303. In retribution for Saint George's martyrdom, the provost and his servants were consumed by the fires of heaven.

In subsequent years, the power of the martyr Saint George allegedly survived him: with his white armor and red cross, Saint George led the Christians to victory in their siege of Jerusalem; his tomb, meanwhile, was said to possess healing properties—according to legend, if a mad person placed his head into a hole inside the tomb where Saint George's body (but not his head) lay buried, his sanity would return. As a martyr warrior, Saint George symbolizes courage and righteousness, piety and loyalty; above all, Saint George exemplifies the merit of sacrifice—namely, "sacrificing (oneself) for," a value essential to both sacred martyr and modern German warrior. As Moshe Halbertal explains, "Once the martyr's death was construed as an offering, a new horizon in the understanding of sacrifice emerged . . . sacrifice began to designate not only *giving to* but also *giving up* (for the sake of). The concept of sacrifice can thus be expanded from the religious realm . . . to the ethical and political realm."[60] The self-sacrificing martyr within a religious framework thus transforms, in the context of war, into the self-sacrificing hero who dies for country and countrymen.

Adorning World War I memorials with the figure of Saint George transformed the common soldier into a warrior martyr, uniting love for God with love for fatherland. Within this model of love and sacrifice, a soldier's service and loyalty to king and army doubled as a form of service and loyalty to God. Saint George, once a mere mortal who killed a dragon and saved thousands of bodies and souls, symbolizes the determination to continue fighting against insurmountable odds. On German World War I memorials, Saint George has been used to disguise revanchist intentions and legitimize vengeful, militaristic intentions through Christian imagery.[61]

Saint George–themed war memorials employ a range of aesthetic techniques, including realistic representations as well as modernized, secularized versions. Reinhart Koselleck demonstrates that the figure of Saint George has undergone many changes in European memorial culture, metamorphosing "from sacred helper and rescuer to a ruler and finally, to a soldier." Without losing his sacred character, Saint George has thus been democratized in his depictions on Europe's war memorials.[62] The first Saint George–themed war memorial we will consider stands in the district of Deusen in Dortmund, North Rhine–Westphalia, dedicated and erected by the local veterans' association (*Krieger- und Landwehrverein*) to "Our heroes" of World War I. Saint George, clad in the helmet and armor of a medieval knight, is depicted here in the moment of triumph as he plunges his sword into the dragon's open mouth. The dragon cowering at his feet is already vanquished; Saint George appears calm and fearless, certain of his victory over his archetypal enemy.

A second Saint George war memorial worthy of mention was erected in 1923 to honor the fallen soldiers of the Kaiser Wilhelm I Infantry Regiment No. 124 in the baroque Catholic cathedral in Weingarten, Baden-Württemberg. This small sculpture by sculptor Franz Xaver Eberhard (1867–1937) stood within an arched recess and depicted Saint George with muscular chest and abdomen, gazing to the side with downturned mouth. His sword, steadied with his right hand, lay across his shoulders, and a small shield hung from his left hand; he was clad in an iconic German steel helmet, a chest plate, and pteruges that fluttered open at one side. A mantle draped his shoulders. The German soldier depicted as Saint George stood erect but not primed for battle—his hand draped in a relaxed pose over the handle of his sword, and a conquered dragon with distorted mouth slumped at his feet, the tip of its tail curling out from behind the mantle beside Saint George's foot. The overall impression is one of a classical Greek statue bedecked with twentieth-century accoutrements—a twentieth-century Saint George resurrected to fight Germany's battles against a modern enemy.

FIGURE 28. Memorial in Deusen (Dortmund).

Engraved on the wall on both sides of the statue appeared the dates of the battles and wars in which soldiers of Regiment No. 124 have fought throughout the centuries, including the eighteenth-century War of the Spanish Succession, the nineteenth-century Napoleonic Wars and Franco-Prussian War, and finally World War I. An inscription reads, "12404 Tapfere haben ihr Blut vergossen, davon 149 Offiziere u. Stellvertreter, 428 Unteroffiziere, 3112 Mannschaften ihre Treue mit dem Tod besiegelt. Erfülle dein Herz mit Ehrfurcht!" ("12,404 courageous men shed their blood... and sealed their vows of loyalty with their deaths. Let your heart be filled with awe!") Above the sculpture, among elaborate flourishes and ornamentation, was engraved the following dedication: "Den Gefallenen zum Gedächtnis / den Lebenden zur Mahnung / errichtet in Zeiten der Schmach am Sedantag 1923" ("In memory of the fallen / and a reminder to the living / erected during these times of disgrace on Sedantag 1923"). This original memorial would later be replaced with a modest bronze plaque to honor Regiment 124, and Saint George would be exchanged for a relief of archangel Michael by Fritz von Graevenitz (1892–1959), himself a veteran of the regiment.

A third example of a Saint George memorial sculpture perches above the Saint George fountain in the town of Speyer, Rhineland-Palatinate. Above the stone basin fountain is a large metal bowl from which ascends an obelisk crowned by a Saint George statue. Built in 1930 by architect Karl Latteyer and sculptor Wilhelm F. C. Ohly to honor the 515 local soldiers who fell in World War I, this black statue of Saint George stands in golden armor and black pteruges with a golden wreath adorning his head and golden sword extended, ready for battle. He holds a gold-ornamented shield in his hands and perches, midstride, atop a brilliant gold dragon whose corpse sprawls across a black globe, his tongue extended. The dedication reads, "Unseren Gefallenen zum Gedächtnis und uns selbst als stete Mahnung" ("In memory of our fallen and a constant reminder to us / 1914-1918"). Of the three remaining inscriptions, one reads, "Ich hatt einen Kameraden, einen Bessern findst du nit" ("I had a comrade, A better one you cannot find"). The second inscription reads, "Deutsche Frauen, Deutsche Treue" ("German women, German loyalty")—a line from August Heinrich Hoffmann von Fallersleben's 1841 "Das Lied der Deutschen" ("The Song of the Germans"), part of which still serves today as Germany's national anthem. The third inscription, a popular choice, quotes Heinrich Lersch's 1914 poem "Soldatenabschied" ("Soldiers' Farewell"): "Deutschland muss leben, auch wenn wir sterben müssen" ("Germany must live, even if we must die").

Dramatically different is its aesthetics is the sandstone Saint George statue serving as a World War I memorial in Markt Schwaben, Bavaria, erected shortly after World War I. This memorial depicts Saint George as a handsome young man in boots and pteruges with drawn sword and shield, poised over a rather endearing, cartoon-like dragon that might have been drawn by Maurice Sendak, with bulbous form, perky ears, heavy-lidded eyes, and open mouth.

On the memorial's plinth are engraved the years of World War I, an Iron Cross, and a dedication in "grateful memory to the courageous warriors of Markt Schwaben."[63] The memorial stands tucked away, occupying an inconspicuous spot at the far edge of a small, neglected cobblestone square beset by weeds, next to a large brown receptacle and a traditional checkered blue-and-white Bavarian *Maibaum* (maypole) with colorful signs and figures as well as the town's coat of arms (a falcon with outspread wings).

Occasionally, a Saint George–themed memorial attracts contemporary attention. In Lappersdorf, Bavaria, a statue depicts Saint George sitting astride his horse with his lance lodged in the throat of the dragon. Erected in front of the church, this memorial is dedicated to the fallen soldiers of Lappersdorf of World War I and World War II as well as soldiers from the Franco-Prussian War. In a witty reenactment of medieval myth, the Lappersdorf Saint George was subjected to decapitation, suffering beheading in July 2020. Local papers asked, "Wo ist der Kopf von Saint Georg?" ("Where is Saint George's head?"), and local veteran Christian Notzon offered five hundred Euro to anyone who might bring forth evidence leading to the identification of Dacian's successor.[64]

Although most Saint George–themed memorials were erected in the wake of World War I and then modified to include the fallen of World War II as well, memorials from the post–World War I period were occasionally integrated into new memorials, as was the case in 1979 in the town of Oberdolling, Bavaria. Here, the local veterans' association chose a design submitted by sculptor Franz Maurer (1938–1993)—the most expensive design from among the three designs submitted—which consisted of integrating a Saint George figure from an old memorial into a

FIGURE 29. Memorial in Markt Schwaben.

new one.⁶⁵ More common, however, was the practice of erecting new Saint George memorials to commemorate the fallen soldiers of both world wars. A memorial in Harsewinkel (district of Marienfeld), North Rhine-Westphalia, located in the historic spring house of the former Cistercian Marienfeld Abbey, honors the fallen soldiers of World War I and World War II. Dedicated on November 16, 1955, this somber stone statue depicts Saint George with large eyes, sharp cheekbones, and stoic mien. Described in a local paper as an extraordinarily disciplined knight after a successful battle, Saint George holds in his hands the grip of his sword, its point resting on a simple, coiled dragon on which he stands. On the pedestal are engraved a *Stahlhelm* flanked by sprigs of leaves, the years of both world wars, and the simple inscription: "*Unvergessen*" ("Unforgotten").

A Saint George memorial in Griethausen, North Rhine-Westphalia, is unusual in exclusively commemorating fallen soldiers of World War II. The elaborate white stone statue against a white pentagon backdrop depicts Saint George frozen in motion, captured in the moment of slaying the dragon.⁶⁶ Saint George is naked except for his *Stahlhelm*; his legs are spread, his left foot planted on the ground and encircled by the coiled tail of the dragon, his right foot astride the neck of the dragon, his knee jutting forward, the muscles in his arms and legs sharply delineated. His groin is covered by one of the dragon's wings. In his left hand he holds a shield, and with his right he thrusts his lance into the dragon's mouth. The statue stands atop a memorial structure with a large alcove in which are mounted plaques with the names of the fallen. Engraved on either side are the dates 1939-45.

Although such unequivocally heroic memorials built to honor the soldiers of World War II were uncommon, Saint George continued to appear on war memorials in Germany during the post-World War II years. Scenes depicting Saint George conquering the dragon, particularly in Catholic communities, could still embody soldierly values in demilitarized, postwar Germany.⁶⁷ In the cloister of the abbey church of Öhringen, Baden-Württemberg, stands a small, simple statue of Saint George and the dragon, mounted in a shallow alcove (erected 1959). Saint George stands on a petite, defeated dragon, one hand lifted to the heavens, accompanied by an inscription praising the sacrifice of the fallen soldiers: "Alle die gefallen im weiten Land sind / gefallen in Gottes Hand / aus unserm Tod lernt für euer Leben / aufopfernd für die Andern / hinzugeben und unser Sterben wird / gesegnet sein" ("All who fell across this vast land have fallen into God's hands. From our deaths learn to sacrifice for others and our deaths will be blessed"). Other Saint George memorials erected in the post–World War II period may be found in Koblenz-Arzheim, Rhineland-Palatinate, and in Darmstadt-Waldkolonie, Hesse, where a relief by sculptor Fritz Schwarzbeck (1902–1989) depicts a kneeling Saint George beside a vanquished dragon in the Paul-Gerhardt church.

One might question the decision to erect Saint George–themed war memorials in the wake of World War II. Sculptures of Saint George vanquishing the dragon allegorize the victory of good over evil. Who embodies the forces of good and evil in such a tableau—the German army and the Allies, respectively? With the German army not only defeated but also disgraced, and the German war effort discredited, it becomes difficult to justify such iconography. World War II permits in hindsight little mythologizing—whence, then, such memorials?

In closing, we might consider an inscription ornamenting a memorial in the military cemetery of Barmen-Elberfeld, North Rhine–Westphalia. This 1922 memorial consists of ten pillars in a half circle that once supported an open roof; the centerpiece is a proudly erect lion on a plinth, his head held high, by sculptor Paul Wynand (1879–1956). Built to honor the fallen of World War I, the memorial now also honors World War II soldiers through an additional plaque. The inscription was selected from the writings of Willi Vesper (1882–1962), a writer, native of Barmen, and member of the Nazi Party who not only gave a ceremonial speech at the 1933 book burning in Dresden but was also one of the eighty-eight authors who signed the Gelöbnis treuester Gefolgschaft (Vow of the Loyal Followers) for Hitler in 1933. Small wonder, then, that Thomas Mann condemned Vesper as "one of the worst of the nationalist idiots."[68] The memorial inscription encapsulates the motif of sacrifice and redemption in the form of national renewal: "Hier schweige ein jeder von seinem Leid / Und noch so großer Not. Sind wir nicht / Alle zum Opfer bereit und zu dem Tod, / Eines steht groß in den Himmel gebrannt: / Alles darf untergehen / Deutschland, unser Kinder und Vaterland, / Deutschland muß bestehen" ("Here, each man keeps silent his suffering / and even greater hardship. Are we not / all ready to sacrifice and to die / One [truth] blazes across the heavens: / Everything may perish / But Germany, the land of our fathers and children / Germany must endure").

CAMARADERIE

A particularly beloved motif of World War I memorials, and one that endured even after World War II, is the motif of soldierly camaraderie—a moral behavior rooted in loyalty. Depictions of camaraderie among soldiers transcend the difficult ethics of commemorating World War II soldiers who fought for Germany under the Nazi regime. The glorification of soldierly camaraderie became a safe, noncontroversial choice emphasizing the honorable values of devotion and fidelity while avoiding depictions of more contentious values, such as patriotism. In the words of George Mosse, "The idea of self-sacrifice motivated by a feeling of solidarity moved to the foreground: loyalty to individual fellow soldiers rather than to any overriding purpose."[69] Self-sacrifice in the form of camaraderie embodies the principle of "sacrificing for," as explained in chapter 5, whereby the sacrificial offeror and sacrificial offering merge into one as the martyr offers up his own life as a gift to God. In this context, however, the soldier as martyr offers his life for his comrades rather than his country.

Memorials depicting camaraderie reflect the principles of an idealized community of men based on shared values. In chapter 5, rituals of sacrifice were shown to play a key role in reinforcing community, communal identity, and social bonding. Male community (the *Männerbund*), as Walter Burkert demonstrates, emerged hand in hand with the development of hunting; shared aggression directed outward during the hunt as well as during war allowed for the creation of close personal community between men. Essential to this community was the willingness to sacrifice oneself for one another and the community. Inherent to the *Männerbund* was thus a fundamental dichotomy of "us" and "them"—be it the "them" of the hunted animals or enemy soldiers.

Faithful until Death

After World War I, the ideal of camaraderie in the trenches, of soldiers protecting and remaining loyal to each other even beyond death, became a favorite theme for war memorials: hundreds of memorials across Germany depict soldiers caring for, supporting, rescuing, mourning, or praying over comrades. A classic motif depicts two soldiers together: one is depicted in a lying or kneeling pose, often succumbing to his wounds, and presented without helmet to emphasize his vulnerability. The second soldier stands by his wounded comrade's side, protective and defiantly alive. The symbolism suggests a wounded but still living and breathing Germany.

Such an example may be found at the mid-thirteenth-century Saint Urbanus Church in Huckarde (Dortmund), North Rhine–Westphalia (erected 1933). It features a bronze sculpture of two soldiers atop a limestone pedestal embedded in a stone wall. One soldier is clad in uniform and *Stahlhelm*, an ammunition pouch on his belt; he stands upright, his chest extended and an unfurled flag in his hand. His face is stoic, his head turned to the right as he surveys the horizon. His arm lies protectively around the shoulders of a second soldier, who crouches, bare-headed and vulnerable, at his feet. The latter clasps one hand to his heart and gazes up at his unwounded comrade. The statue bears a common inscription "Ich hatt einen Kameraden" ("I had a comrade"). These words are gleaned from the traditional lament of the German armed forces called "Der gute Kamerad" ("The Good Comrade"), composed as a poem by Ludwig Uhland in 1809 and set to music by Friedrich Silcher in 1825. This patriotic anthem mourns the loss of a comrade; the complete line from which the inscription was taken reads, "Ich hatt' einen Kameraden, / einen bessern findst du nit" ("I had a comrade, a better one you cannot find"). The song concludes with the words "Bleib du im ew'gen Leben / Mein guter Kamerad!" ("Stay in eternal life / my good comrade!")

A second example stands in the city park of Oppenau, Baden-Württemberg. Commissioned by the Oppenau veterans' association and designed by sculptor Hugo Knittel (1888–1958), the memorial was erected in June 1934. It was briefly removed and restored in 2014–15, and then reerected in a different spot within the city park.[70] Atop a wide, square pedestal stands a statue of two soldiers, dedicated to the fallen of both world wars.[71] One soldier is unscathed and strong, the other wounded and dying. The inscription reads, "Wenn Tausend einen Mann erschlagen: Das ist nicht Sieg, nicht Ruhm noch Ehr! Und heißen wird's in späten Tagen: Gesiegt hat doch das deutsche Heer" ("When a thousand men slay one: that is neither victory, fame nor honor! And so it will signify in later days: the German army has nevertheless prevailed"). The unwounded soldier stands erect in his uniform with *Stahlhelm* and with clenched fists, his right knee thrust forward, a *Stielhandgranate*—a grenade with wooden handle used by the German army during World War

I and World War II—clutched in his hand. Between his legs and leaning against him slumps his fallen comrade, bareheaded, with one hand pressed to his chest. The fallen soldier's shirt is slightly open, his neck exposed, and his eyes are closed; his other arm lies between his legs, a grenade dangling from his fingers. The names of the fallen World War I soldiers of Oppenau are engraved on the memorial; two columns, added after 1945, bear the names of the 190 fallen World War II soldiers.

The Strong Supporting the Weak

Depictions of soldiers holding or propping up the body of a wounded or fallen comrade are especially common. A war memorial in the town of Langenberg, North Rhine–Westphalia, features a statue of a helmeted soldier sitting upright and holding in his lap a fallen comrade, whose head falls lifelessly to the side. The plinth on which they sit is engraved with an Iron Cross and a single word: *Kameraden* (Comrades). Behind the monument stands a wall of panels engraved with the names of the fallen from 1866, 1870–71, World War I and, added later, World War II. The inscription reads, "Sie starben / für uns" ("They died / for us").[72]

A striking example stands in Opherdicke, North Rhine–Westphalia, created by sculptor Fritz Richter-Elsner (1884–1970) and dedicated in 1928 to the fallen soldiers of World War I. The memorial features two soldiers: one is taller and older—a veteran of a previous war; he is bearded, wears a helmet, and has an overcoat draped over his shoulders; an Iron Cross is pinned to his uniform. The second soldier is visibly younger, his face boyish and smooth; he leans against the older man, his head bare and bowed, one arm pressed to his body, the other holding a belt with a dagger. The older man supports the younger, holding his arm and looking down at him with solicitude. Implied is the continuity of warrior values from one generation to the next.

A final example worthy of mention is the Memorial to the 116th Panzer Division of the Wehrmacht, the Windhund-Division (Greyhound Division)—a memorial that has sparked contention between local citizens. The Windhund memorial stands next to the Vossenack cemetery in North Rhine–Westphalia, erected 1966 by the local veteran association. It features a bronze statue[73] atop a stone wall of a slim, youthful soldier standing erect, naked but for his helmet, and holding in his arms a dying comrade. Beneath the statue is a plaque reading, "Tote Soldaten sind niemals allein denn immer werden treue Kameraden bei ihnen sein" ("Dead soldiers are never alone, because loyal comrades will always be beside them"). The 116th Panzer Division waged battle, as an additional plaque informs us, in the battles of Hürtgen Forest—the fiercest battles fought on German soil—against American troops during the winter of 1944–45. The plaque reads, "Mahnmal / Der Windhund-Division. Tritt ein mit Ehrfurcht vor dem Opfertod der Soldaten aller Nationen, die im Hürtgenwald starben" ("Memorial / The Greyhound-Division. Enter with reverence for the sacrificial deaths of the soldiers of all nations, who died in Hürtgen forest"). A second plaque states that the memorial admonishes the world to strive for peace.[74] Despite this admonishment, the local veteran's association of the Hürtgen Forest region is known to have cultivated over the years and even to this very day the legend that the Wehrmacht was in no way implicated in the crimes of National Socialism,[75] a myth debunked by, among other historical studies and investigations, the 1995–99 traveling exhibition *War of Annihilation: Crimes of the Wehrmacht, 1941–1944*.

For years, the Windhund memorial served as a meeting place for right-wing extremists. Ingo Haller, a former NPD (Germany's far-right National Democratic Party) politician who was expelled from the NPD due to his neo-Nazi leanings, once joined the yearly commemoration of Windhund heroes. In objection to the memorial, Andrea Volk, a local SPD (Germany's center-left Social Democratic Party) representative and history teacher, published a letter in the local paper. In response, Volk received an angry missive from the chairman of the *Familienverbandes der Windhunde* (family association of former Windhund members and relatives) accusing her of defiling the honor of the fallen soldiers—in short, of being a *"Nestbeschmutzer,"* one who denigrates one's family or country and thus "soils one's nest." In addition to the letter, Volk also received a second retort in her mailbox: a clump of dog feces bound with a Windhund association emblem.[76]

"I Had a Comrade": Bearing the Remains

The next motif we shall consider is that of soldiers literally bearing the burden of their fallen comrades by carrying their remains on their shoulders or biers. The World War I memorial to the fallen students, faculty, and university officials of the Georg-August-University Göttingen, Lower

Saxony, designed by Josef Kemmerich and dedicated on Totensonntag (Sunday of the Dead, a religious day of observance for the dead) in 1924, offers an evocative example. Sculpted from dolomite, the memorial stands atop a long, narrow plinth in front of the university auditorium. It features a sculpture of eight young, naked men carrying on their shoulders their dead comrade. The bearers of the corpse stand midstride with bent knees and massive, muscular bodies. Their heads are bowed, bent beneath the weight of their comrade. One soldier gazes backward with mournful glance and downturned mouth for a last glimpse of the site where his comrade fell. On the front of the pedestal are engraved the 748 names of the fallen as well as an inscription: "Den Toten der Georgia Augusta 1914–1918" (Dedicated to the fallen of Georgia August [University] 1914–1918). In April 1957, the dates of World War II (1939–1945) were added.

Similarly, in the town of Kerken, North Rhine–Westphalia, stands a memorial erected to commemorate the fallen soldiers of World War I and World War II. Designed by Theo Akkermann (1907–1982) and dedicated in 1932, the memorial depicts six uniformed soldiers with helmets and weapons striding forward and carrying the coffin of a fallen comrade on their shoulders. The burden carried by the soldiers appears great, as the men use both hands to hold their comrade aloft. Around the base of the monument runs a wide scroll engraved in large block letters with the dates of World War I and the words "Ich hatte einen Kameraden" ("I had a comrade"); "Für Volk Heimat und Vaterland" ("For countrymen, home, and fatherland"); and "Den Helden" ("Dedicated to the heroes"). Loyalty to one's comrades thus blends seamlessly into loyalty to one's country and countrymen.

Loyalty beyond Death

Numerous World War I memorials demonstrate a soldier's sacrifice in the context of camaraderie with depictions of soldiers standing vigil over dead comrades. An elaborate memorial tableau next to a Catholic church in Waldkirch-Kollnau, Baden-Württemberg, created by Erwin Krumm and erected in 1935, features an open-walled memorial pavilion with six life-sized concrete soldiers in full army dress complete with ammunition pouches, weapons, and steel helmets. They stand watch around a seventh, fallen comrade who lies in the center of the memorial space on an elevated, two-tiered slab of stone and surrounded by walls on three sides, still wearing his helmet and uniform and holding his weapon. The soldiers' faces show no expression but reveal slight variations suggesting differences in age and experience; their bodies, however, are identical fighting machines in the typical Nazi memorial aesthetic. Running across the top of the tallest wall are the dates of World War I and the words "Unseren Helden" ("For Our Heroes"). Listed on plaques below are the one hundred names of the fallen. Added in the year 1952 are the dates of World War II and the names of the fallen (both soldiers and victims of bombings) and the names of the missing. The inscription reads, "Kameraden, wir warten auf euch" ("Comrades, we are waiting for you").

Like many memorials erected during Hitler's regime, the Kollnau memorial has been heavily criticized. Historian Marion Bentin has argued that the memorial sought not to mourn the deaths of young men but rather to exploit heroic imagery to prepare a new generation of young men to die in the next war. The soldiers, she notes, are "dehumanized, their bodies appear to be those of machine-made robots. The individual is nothing—the ethnic community [*Volksgemeinschaft*] is everything."[77] In 1998, restorers added two inscriptions to the side of the sarcophagus: "Nie mehr Krieg" ("Never again war") and "Frieden" ("Peace"). A scroll-like

FIGURE 30. Memorial in Waldkirch-Kollnau.

tube crafted from weathering steel and engraved with a verse from the 2 Corinthians 3:3 stands facing the memorial. A pillar beside the memorial bears a plaque recounting the history of the memorial, as well as efforts of the Waldkirch-Kollnau community to confront its National Socialist past. A second pillar is dedicated to Catholic priest Eduard Trabold, an opponent of National Socialism who led the Kollnau church until his death in 1949. Like countless other war memorials in Germany, the Waldkirch-Kollnau memorial has been vandalized: in 2020, the memorial was spray-painted with slogans such as "Fuck Militarism," "Militärkult zerschlagen" ("Annihilate the cult of the military"), and "Nazi Propaganda."

CONCLUSION

"Wer mutig für sein Vaterland gefallen, Der baut sich selbst ein ewig Monument im Herzen seiner Landesbrüder und dies Gebäude stürzt kein Sturmwind nieder" ("He who courageously dies for his fatherland builds himself an eternal monument in the hearts of his fellow countrymen that no tempest can demolish"). This inscription, inscribed on a World War I memorial in Stenden, North Rhine–Westphalia, declares the gratitude that the fallen soldier secures for himself in the hearts of his compatriots to be immutable—a monument that, unlike stone or bronze monuments, transcends the limits of physical matter. And indeed, what is such eternal gratitude within the discourse of German war memorials other than a form of immortality for the soldier who sacrifices himself? Through the act of self-sacrifice, the soldier assumes the role of both offeror and offering, transforming his transient human substance—that "mere chance pile of flesh and bone"[78]—into a sacrificial gift that, unlike Cain's fruits of the soil and the strange fire of Nadav and Avihu, is guaranteed acceptance.

CHAPTER SEVEN

Bitte Gott, Mache die Seele von Pein Wieder Frei

Wayside Memorials of Admonishment, Remembrance, and Atonement

INTRODUCTION: THE PHILANDERING MONK

Tucked into a tower passage in a church in Steinhagen, Mecklenburg-Vorpommern, stands a fifteenth-century *Mordwange* of Gotland limestone known as the Mönchsstein (Monk's Stone, 1492).[1] With a height of over eight feet and weighing over 2,750 pounds, this memorial stone possesses the idiosyncratic *Mordwange* form of a stele topped with a round head piece and engraved with commemorative images and inscriptions. The compound *Mordwange* consists of two words: *Mord* (murder), and *Wange* (the decorated bench end of a choir stall)—the shape of which the *Mordwange* resembles.[2]

The Steinhagen *Mordwange*, like many others of its kind, no longer stands in situ; it originally stood outside, exposed to the elements, in Grün Kordshagen. The headpiece bears an engraving of Jesus as the judge of mankind on the Day of Resurrection; beneath on the shaft appears a full-figure portrait of a praying monk in the act of being fatally stabbed from beneath, a sword puncturing him just above his waistline. A delicate banner of words carved in Carolingian minuscule script—a medieval European calligraphic script—extends from his hands. The words belong to Psalm 51, one of the penitential psalms: "*Misere[re] mei deus*" ("Have mercy on me, oh God"). Beneath the figure of the monk appears, again in Latin minuscule script, the words "In the year of our

Lord 1490, two days after the festival of Incovavit, Brother Detmarus Muurdorp died. Pray for him."[3] At the bottom of the *Mordwange* appears an inscription in Plattdeutsch[4] reading, "Alle de her henne gan ik bidde se en klenasta unde bidde got kortedit make desele pyne qujd" ("To all those who pass by here, I ask you to pause and stand here for a moment, to ask God to render the soul for a short time again free from pain"). The reverse side of the *Mordwange* displays a depiction of the crucifixion on the head piece and a second depiction of the praying monk on the stele.

According to one of two legends concerning the *Mordwange*, Brother Muurdorp, a *Landreiter* (gendarme) of the Cistercian Abbey Campe (later the Neuenkamp / Franzburg Abbey) died a violent, unexpected death due to his secret love affair with a young farmer's wife. The jealous husband allegedly stabbed the monk to death in a fit of rage on catching the couple in flagrante. In penance, the farmer erected the *Mordwange*. A second legend claims that the farmer heard his wife's cries for help and, catching Muurdorp attempting to rape her, stabbed the monk and fled. Since farmers did not normally carry swords, and given the political circumstances at the time, there is good cause to doubt the veracity of this legend. During this period, in the wake of the Reformation, abbeys and monasteries were being suppressed, and church-owned property was flowing into the hands of local aristocrats and land holders, or into the coffers of city treasuries. Rumors of the salacious behavior of monks like Muurdorp helped to justify the confiscation and redistribution of church property.[5]

The claim, however, that Muurdorp's killer erected the *Mordwange* in atonement rings true, for the erection of *Sühnemale*[6] (namely *Sühnesteine* or *Sühnekreuze*—penance stones or crosses) was a standard requirement of medieval *Sühneverträge* (atonement contracts). These contracts negotiated reconciliation between perpetrators and the families of their victims and included both financial reparations and ecclesiastical obligations. Although the offender's acceptance of wrongdoing and responsibility, expression of remorse, and acts of recompense were part of atonement, the reconciliation of relationships between wrongdoers, their victims, and their communities also played a key role. Through reconciliation, furthermore, the wrongdoer was reintegrated into his larger community, restoring not only his own social standing but harmony to the populace as well.

Three primary intentions motivated the erection of the memorials discussed in this chapter: admonishment, remembrance, and atonement. Previous chapters of this book analyze the ways in which the goals of admonishment and remembrance are translated into memorial form. World War I memorials remind new generations to remain grateful for the sacrifices of fallen soldiers and to stay true to traditional, patriotic values, while memorials to the expellees and lost eastern territories in the wake of World War II admonish Germans to hold on to their ancestral roots and resist Germany's subjugation. The concept of atonement as a motivator of memorialization, however, requires a closer look. This chapter begins with a discussion of Jewish and Christian theories of atonement, followed by a brief consideration of secular atonement. With the key principles of Jewish and Christian atonement in mind, we turn to medieval and early postmedieval Germanic atonement in the form of *Wergild* and atonement contracts, respectively. We shall then focus on wayside memorials: their locations, forms, and types as well as their markings, iconography, and the victims they memorialize. The final section of the chapter engages the colorful, often lurid legends explaining the presence of wayside memorials across the German landscape.

THEORIES OF ATONEMENT

Sacred Atonement

In everyday usage, the word "atonement" refers to the reparation of wrongdoing, often by acknowledging guilt, apologizing, and changing one's behavior. The linguistic origins of the word ("at-one-ment"), however, reveal that reconciliation resides at the heart of atonement. In essence, atonement is a two-sided action aiming to unite in harmony parties engaged in strife. Tellingly, the Hebrew root for atonement is *kpr*, which means "to cover" or "wipe away" and appears throughout the Hebrew Bible. The root also appears in the name of the most important and solemn day of the Jewish liturgical calendar—Yom Kippur, the Day of Atonement on the tenth of Tishrei. During this Jewish fast day arriving at the end of the Ten Days of Repentance (Aseret Y'mei Teshuvah), Jews collectively repent for sins committed during the past year. Only sins committed against God are forgiven on Yom Kippur. As stated in the Talmud: "The Day of Atonement atones for sins against God, not for sins against man, unless the injured party has been appeased" (Mishna Yoma 8:9). In the case of murder, however, there can be "no complete repentance, since there is no way to appease the injured party." This is a "distinctively Jewish belief [that] separates most Jewish thinkers from their Christian counterparts."[7]

The practice of rituals of repentance (from the Latin "*paenitere*," "to be sorry, to grieve, to regret")[8] can be found in other religious traditions as well. Broadly speaking, repentance is a "ritual procedure intended to repair a breach in relations between the gods and an individual (or—since ritual and moral pollution are communicable—between the gods and a group)." As a way of eliminating guilt and expressing remorse, repentance is above all a "restorative religious technique."[9] In Jewish as well as Christian traditions, the verbal confession of sin is essential to repentance. Jewish confession, in contrast to Christian confession, however, is communal rather than personal. On Yom Kippur, Jews gather in synagogue to recite a prayer called the *Viddui* (confession). The *Viddui*, together with the *Al Khet* (For Sins [that we have committed]) prayer, includes an alphabetical acrostic of sins composed in the first-person plural, emphasizing the shared, communal nature of responsibility, culpability, and repentance. With each listed transgression, penitents gently beat their chests with their fists, enacting a symbolic form of punishment.

In contemporary Christian usage, atonement is "the process by which reconciliation with God is accomplished through the death of Christ."[10] Christianity inherited its emphasis on repentance primarily from Judaism; its sacrificial language of atonement points back not only to the crucifixion at Calvary but also to the sacrificial ritual of atonement practiced by the Israelites and known to early Christians (Leviticus 17:11: "For the life of the flesh is in the blood: and I have given it to you upon the altar to make an atonement for your souls: for it is the blood that maketh an atonement for the soul") (King James Version).

The Latin sacrament of penance, as reaffirmed by the Council of Trent (1545–63), consists of three parts: contrition, confession, and satisfaction. Contrition demands that the offender accept blame for committing a wrong, reject this wrong, accept responsibility for the consequences of the wrong actions, and commit to better values. Confession, the outward expression of contrition, consists of verbalizing the wrongs one has committed. Satisfaction, finally, must be paid to God, according to *Cur deus homo* (circa 1097), the most influential text on Christian atonement by Anselm, Archbishop of Canterbury. In Anselm's analysis, a sin against God requires punishment or infinite "satisfaction" (Anselm's term for ransom), which mere mortals could never pay. Only the death of Christ—the sinless God-man—possessed the "superfluous merit" to act as adequate satisfaction for the sins of humankind.

Anselm's economic language of ransom and satisfaction may reflect the influence of feudalism and Teutonic blood money customs on his thought. Christ's sacrifice itself may be viewed through the commercial image of a ransom, through which humankind is released from sin. Mark 10:45 declares: "For even the Son of man came not to be ministered unto, but to minister, and to give his life a ransom for many" (King James version).[11] In Christianity, sinners are debtors who discharge their debts to God through repentance. The Reformation, in contrast, turned to Anselm's notion of punishment rather than satisfaction. John Calvin, for example, interpreted Christ's sacrifice as the "vicarious and substitutionary endurance of God's punishment on behalf of humankind or of the elect."[12] Still today, almost a millennium since Anselm penned his *Cur deus homo*, the economic language of guilt and repentance, debt and repayment suffuses our modern vernacular. Expressions such as "to pay our (moral) debts" or "to make amends" (from the Old French *amendes*: pecuniary fines and penalties) reveal the economic, transactional nature of atonement, as does the German word *Schuld* (meaning both "debt"—usually used in the plural form of *Schulden*—and "guilt").

Through repentance and the cathartic experience of confession, guilt is expiated and purified. In Jewish tradition, although atonement can be definitively granted only by God, the moral transformation of the individual plays a key role in the process. Confession serves as the outward expression of *teshuvah* (from the Hebrew root "*shuv*" [turn, turn back])—an internal process of "returning" (re-turning) to / toward God. *Teshuvah* takes place in stages: "The sinner must recognize his sin, feel sincere remorse, undo any damage he has done and pacify the victim of his offense, and resolve never to commit the sin again."[13] It is important to note that the concept of *teshuvah* bears connotations of space and direction: through transformation of the moral self, the penitent turns again toward God, reorienting him- or herself in space to once again face the divine. Human initiative thus paves the way to returning to God, who, in turn, "will respond by completing the process of purification, ultimately leading to the reintegration of the fragmented human self" and restoring the relationship between (and thus reconciling) man and God. In Christian theology as well, including the writings of Karl Barth and Dietrich Bonhoeffer, atonement rectifies the alienation caused by sin and reconciles the sinner with God.

Secular Atonement

The reliance on spatial and directional metaphors for understanding moral states is not unique to religious discourse. In Charles Taylor's phenomenological account of the modern self, identity is ultimately a question of how we position or orient ourselves within certain frameworks and horizons, in relation to the good, the valuable, and the significant. In Taylor's words, "To know who I am is a species of knowing where I stand."[14] Atonement thus reveals itself to be a form of reorientation—a concept important for the next chapter's focus on modern German memorials of atonement.

Just as satisfaction in the Christian context must be paid to God, so must satisfaction in the secular context be paid to wronged individuals or groups in order to discharge moral debts. Here, it is other mortals, not God, granting the wrongdoer redemption and salvation. Secular satisfaction requires that the wrongdoer offer restitution. This may be retributive (a mimetic, imitative form of repayment, whereby a moral debt is discharged through punishment or vengeance) or restitutive (whereby compensation is made for the loss of the victim).[15] Mere restitution, however, does not suffice: following the reconciliation theory of Linda Radzik, atonement fulfills its etymological promise by calling not for one-sided action but rather interaction between the wrongdoer, the victim, and the community.[16] By repairing and restoring human relationships, atonement brings a community beset by discord back into harmony, protecting the offender as well as others from violence and other harmful consequences. Redemption thus takes the form of moral reconciliation—a process that normalizes the status and value of the wrongdoer by permitting him to be recognized once again as a trustworthy member of his moral community.[17]

In the religious context, penitents express regret and remorse through symbolic actions, including donning sackcloth and rags, smearing themselves with ashes or mud, hurting themselves, fasting, abstaining from sex, rending their clothes, strewing earth on their heads, and sitting in ashes. In Job 42:6, the righteous Job enacts penance by retracting his earlier demands to God for an explanation for his suffering and repenting "in dust and ashes." Ahab, King of Samaria, repents for his sins of murder and theft in I Kings 21:27 by rending his clothes, fasting, and putting "sackcloth upon his flesh" (King James Version). In the New Testament (Matthew 11:21), Jesus condemns the towns of Chorazin and Bethsaida for failing to accept him as the Messiah and declares that if the people of Tyre and Sidon had witnessed such miracles, they would have "repented long ago in sackcloth and ashes." As will be discussed, repentance through the medium of atonement contracts, including the erection of atonement memorials, draws on a different system of symbols and rituals, but the purpose—reconciling and restoring fractured relationships—remains the same.

MEDIEVAL GERMANIC ATONEMENT

When one thinks today of German memorials of atonement, the first that spring to mind are memorials dedicated to the victims of Nazi persecution. But already during the High Middle Ages and even earlier,[18] memorials of atonement created a rich tapestry across the German countryside. Although countless of these memorials have disappeared, thousands still survive: they stand beside country roads and footpaths, at the edges of cemeteries and near churches, in town squares and nestled within stone walls, and tucked away in fields and woods. Their misshapen forms, missing limbs, and crumbling stone testify to the passage of centuries; some are sinking slowly into the ground while others are tenaciously intact. They offer us a glimpse into the culture of crime, punishment, and atonement in medieval and early modern Germany; indeed, there once was barely a *Feldmark* (a portion of undeveloped land within a municipal district or estate) without at least one or several memorials of atonement.[19]

The practice of erecting memorials of atonement, including *Sühnesteine* (penance stones), *Sühnekreuze* (penance crosses), *Mordwangen*, and *Mordkreuze* (murder crosses), played a key role in social and communal Germanic life. Before exploring the types, forms, and functions of these memorials, we shall take a brief look at the early medieval Germanic system of *Wergild*, the predecessor to the medieval system of customary laws that dictated compensation for victims and ecclesiastical punishments for perpetrators of crimes.[20]

Medieval Wergild: "Renumeration for a Man"

According to early medieval Germanic law, *Wergild* (or *Wergeld*), literally "renumeration for a man," was the sum of money paid in private settlement by the perpetrator of a homicide to the family of his victim. *Wergild* was part of the composition system of the *leges barbarorum* ("barbarian laws" of continental Europe), which described appropriate compensation for acts of wrongdoing as an alternative to personal vengeance or blood feud. The laws governing *Wergild* could be quite specific: the laws of the Salian Franks, for example, specified the process and timeline by which a perpetrator was expected to secure *Wergild*: an insolvent perpetrator was permitted to foist the responsibility for his debt on his relatives (up to fourth-degree kinship) after surrendering any assets he possessed. If these relatives were also insolvent, the liability returned to the perpetrator. Across four *Dingtage* (public, yearly days of judgment), the perpetrator presented his case before further-removed kin; if none willingly agreed to settle his debt, the perpetrator had to submit to *ius talionis* and pay his debt with the only means left to him: his life.[21]

Wergild essentially offered a means of atonement by compensating the victim's family for loss of life (in accordance with the victim's status) and brokering reconciliation. Paying *Wergild* served not only to pacify the victim's family but also to protect the perpetrator.[22] Acts of homicide predominantly affected the victim's family, of course, but they also breached the general peace (*Friedensbruch*), because vengeance (*Blutrache*) in the form of destructive vendettas or blood feuds was legitimized by custom and viewed as legal recourse.[23] Such feuds caused a cycle of escalating and retaliatory violence, not only against the perpetrator but also against his family, unleashing chaos and fear within the community. The economic reconciliation system of *Wergild*, therefore, compensated the bereft family while also forestalling retaliation and returning the offender "to the protection of the general peace."[24]

Fundamental to both the *Wergild* system and the high and late medieval atonement contracts to be discussed soon is the basic structure of exchange at the heart of early Germanic communal life. In his seminal study *The Gift*, Marcel Mauss notes that Germanic society long existed as an essentially feudal and peasant society without markets. In these societies, reciprocity as a binding force between community members assumed a crucial role. The Germanic system of exchanges in the form of gifts (*dons*)—"voluntarily and forcibly given, received and reciprocated"—was essential for the successful moral and economic functioning of society, allowing clans, tribes, chiefs, and kings beyond the "close confines of the family group" to communicate and form alliances.[25] Those excluded from gift-giving occasions such as baptisms, engagements, and marriages were excluded from the crucial forging and strengthening of relationships. German fairy tales such as "Sleeping Beauty" thematize such exclusion.[26]

In addition to gift giving, pledges also played a crucial role in early Germanic societies as an essential aspect of contracts, including atonement contracts: "The pledge is obligatory . . . every contract, every sale or purchase, loan or deposit, includes the making of a pledge . . . [it] not only obligates and binds, but . . . also commits the honor, authority, and the *mana* [magical, religious, spiritual power] of the one who hands it over."[27] Atonement contracts between perpetrators of homicide and the families of their victims included pledges to secure fulfillment of the terms within; a penalty for breach of contract helped ensure that the perpetrator would do his duty.[28]

Atonement Contracts

The late medieval and early postmedieval periods in Germany, during which the majority of penance crosses and stones were erected, were turbulent and violent ones. Men openly carried swords, daggers, and spears, and communities lacked an effective, organized system of justice.[29] During these years, *Faustrecht* (law of the fist) reigned supreme, contributing—along with increasing population density—to an "accelerating spiral of violence."[30] Homicide, a common occurrence, was treated as a private matter between the family of the victim and the perpetrator; public authorities with the power to punish intervened only when requested.[31] Negotiations between the family of the victim and the perpetrator led to agreement in the form of the *Sühnevertrag* (atonement contract).[32] The practice of negotiating such contracts belonged to everyday medieval culture for about four to five hundred years, with the high point falling between the fourteenth and sixteenth centuries.

According to the provisions of atonement contracts, perpetrators of homicide were responsible for fulfilling both sacred and secular obligations as a part of their *Totschlagsühne*—atonement for homicide. The required obligations were based on Old Germanic folk law, canon law, and, later, Roman law.[33] Many atonement contracts specified the site where the cross was to be erected and stipulated specific financial terms for supporting surviving family members.[34] In addition to compensating the victim's family financially, the perpetrator was expected to cover fees paid to local authorities and to secure provisions for both sides during negotiations.[35] The offender was also required to fulfill sacred obligations, including donations of wax or candles to a local church, paying for masses and vigils for the deceased[36] as well as for attendees for masses, financing additional masses on the anniversary of the death for at least ten but as many as thirty years, and undertaking two to three pilgrimages to holy sites such as Aachen, Einsiedeln, and Rome. Perpetrators were permitted to pay a professional pilgrim—a proxy—to make some or all pilgrimages on his behalf, bringing back a confirmation voucher to prove the pilgrimage requirement had indeed been fulfilled.[37]

Finally, the offender was required to pay for a penance cross for the victim, often produced according to specific configurations dictating material and dimensions. Although the sacred requirements of atonement contracts varied, the erection of a penance cross was almost always included.[38] Specific demands might include carvings of the shield and helmet of the deceased, steps leading up to the cross, a height of seven to ten feet, the depiction of the coat of arms of the family, or even a twelve-foot-high stone pair of scales engraved with a crucifix and name of the deceased. Beginning in the mid-fifteenth century, requirements for penance crosses became increasingly elaborate, calling for chapels outfitted with altars, crucifixes, statuary, and portraits.

Like displays of penance depicted in the Bible, the practice of negotiating an atonement contract possessed symbolic and ritual elements. In northern and western areas of medieval Germany, where the greatest coherence in atonement contract tradition were found, the time for reconciliation was usually set on a Sunday morning or on the day of the *Leichzeichen*—a ritual of displaying a bier or coffin during an anniversary mass for the deceased, arranged and paid for by the perpetrator. After the mass, the two parties to be reconciled visited the open grave of the deceased. Here, the perpetrator asked three times for forgiveness from the family of his victim and recited prayers (the Paternoster and Ave Maria) for the soul of his victim. After prayers, the lead member of the victim's party reached out to the perpetrator from across the grave and handed him "*die todte Hand*" (the dead hand) of the victim, known as the *Leibzeichen*. The perpetrator then dropped the *Leibzeichen* into the grave and extended to the opposite party the first installment of his atonement payment, thereby setting reconciliation in motion. The *Leibzeichen*, it is worth noting, could also be used as evidence in court proceedings. The practice of severing the victim's hand and displaying it in court was described as "*das Leibzeichen nehmen*" (to take the *Leibzeichen*) and "*mit der todten Hand klagen*" (to go before the law / sue / litigate with the dead hand).[39]

As demonstrated, atonement contracts contained both sacred and secular provisions, demanding spiritual as well as financial restitution. By financing masses for the dead and erecting a penance cross—before which passersby might stop and pray for the departed—the perpetrator sought to correct a wrong done to the victim's soul as well as his body. In Christian belief, sudden, unexpected death robbed the victim of the opportunity to confess, atone for sins, and seek God's forgiveness: masses and prayers would help rectify this injustice by securing the victim's redemption. Required pilgrimages, meanwhile, were designed to save the soul of the perpetrator. In the restoration clauses of atonement contracts, we see a continuation of the early medieval *Wergild* system as well as continuity with previous practices described in the Germanic *Volksrechte* (local laws) of the early Middle Ages.[40]

A final aspect of atonement contract-based reconciliation worth noting is the duty of the perpetrator to finance and stage a penitential procession. Dressed in penitential robes and carrying a candle, the perpetrator walked together with priests and acolytes (also in penitential robes and bearing candles) to the grave of the victim and perhaps to the penance cross as well. At the heart of this theater of atonement was the public prostration of the perpetrator: his humbling, self-abasing performance of repentance was rewarded at the end with a solemn display of absolution.[41] To the sacred and the secular elements of medieval atonement, then, we may add the third element of the dramatic—a pageant of penance and contrition reassuring spectators that repentance had been made and order restored.

Composed in polished legalese, atonement contracts were often sealed multiple times and preserved in private homes.[42] The number of atonement contracts still surviving in archives today[43]—considering that atonement contracts were kept as personal possessions and mostly lost—reveals to what extent they were a part of everyday life. Additional documents, such as records of donations made by perpetrators to churches, chronicles of pilgrimages, and records of stone purchased from quarries for fashioning penance crosses, shed light on just how ubiquitous atonement contracts were.[44]

The private process of atonement via contract emerged from a societal order based on strong bonds of kinship and lack of central authority. As these bonds weakened and central authority grew, the practice began dying out.[45] In 1532, the first general German penal code—the *Constitutio Criminalis Carolina* or *Carolina* (*Peinliche Halsgerichtsordnung Karls V*) was ratified. With the *Carolina*—part of a larger effort to unify the legal system of the Holy Roman Empire—the practice of atonement contracts officially ended and was replaced with justice issued by central authorities. The actual shift away from private atonement took time, however, and for many years the two systems coexisted. Atonement contracts from Ingerkingen / Volkesheim (Biberach), Baden-Württemberg, in 1570 and Kardorf (Unterallgäu), Bavaria, in 1556 testify to the continuing reliance on atonement contracts after the ratification of the *Carolina*.[46] Only in the seventeenth century did homicide come to fall exclusively under the control of central authorities and the practice of private atonement for homicide, for over half a century the province of kin, territorial sovereignty, and the church, became forbidden.[47]

WAYSIDE MEMORIALS: AN INTRODUCTION

We now turn to the memorials erected in compliance with atonement contracts as well as other memorials of similar purpose and form not necessarily stipulated by contract. Wayside memorials belong to a class of monuments called *Kleindenkmale* (small memorials) or *Flurdenkmale* (meadow / field memorials). They mark sites where sudden, usually violent deaths occurred and where victims are believed to lie buried.[48] Categories of wayside crosses include accident crosses (*Unfallkreuze*), memorial crosses (*Gedenkkreuze*), and penance crosses (*Sühnekreuze*). The purpose of wayside crosses is to inspire remembrance and urge passerby to offer up prayers for the souls of the deceased.[49] Typically, wayside crosses were erected at or near the sites of death and where they might be seen by ample passersby, along busy public roads, at forks or junctures, on bridges, at crossroads, along paths to churches and cemeteries, on city squares, and by city gates.[50] Many crosses standing in open country today testify to the former existence of well-traveled paths or old traffic and trade routes, while sites marked with clusters of crosses suggest locations once heavily trafficked.[51] Not all memorials discussed in this chapter can be traced to atonement contracts, but all engage in admonishment, remembrance, or atonement. Many wayside memorials, finally, bear names tied to the legends that accompany them: the *Linsenkreuz* (lentil cross) in Großrinderfeld, Baden-Württemberg, is exemplary: it marks the spot where two shepherds allegedly killed each other while eating lentil soup.[52]

Locating and Identifying Wayside Memorials

Wayside crosses often appear clustered in particular areas: many lie along routes that once led to and from taverns or dance venues, for drunkenness is often mentioned in wayside cross legends as a motive for violence. A penance cross standing beside a cemetery wall in Betzigau, Bavaria, is typical in this respect: it was erected in compliance with an atonement contract of 1577 between a perpetrator and the father of his homicide victim, twenty-five-year-old Max Möst. The intoxicated young man, returning home from Kempten to Betzigau one night and behaving poorly, drew the attention of Kempten locals Jörg Frei and his servant, who so injuriously maltreated Möst that he died the next day. The atonement contract stipulated restitution as well as other penalties.[53]

Estimates vary, but it is safe to say that wayside crosses were cropping up in rural areas by the early thirteenth century.[54] One of the oldest known stone crosses is the severely damaged red sandstone cross patteé known as the *Bischofskreuz von Betzenhausen*, located in Freiburg im Breisgau, Baden-Württemberg, in the Saint Albert-Bischofslinde chapel. This cross bears the date of 1299 and the name of the nobleman Konrad von Lichtenberg. A plaque mounted in the wall of the chapel explains that the cross atones for the death of Konrad von Lichtenberg, Bishop of Straßburg, who fell during a battle between the nobility and bourgeoisie at the hand of a local butcher on July 29, 1299.[55] This cross served for many years as a site of pilgrimage for parents of sick children because von Lichtenberg, honored as a saint, allegedly lies buried there.[56]

In many cases, wayside crosses are accompanied by small wooden signs or engraved stone plaques explaining the circumstances of their erection. A wooden sign standing beside a penance cross in Illerbeuren, Bavaria, reads, "An dieser Stelle erschlug im Jahre 1530 Wolfgang Zesenmayer, Schmied in Steinbach, den Joh. Walch daselbst. Zur Sühne mußte der Täter dieses Steinkreuz setzen" ("On this very spot in the year 1530 Wolfgang Zesenmayer, a blacksmith in Steinbach, killed Joh. Walch. To atone, the perpetrator was required to erect this cross").[57] A similar marker in Kardorf, Bavaria, explains that the penance cross was erected in atonement by Thomas Waldvogel, who viciously murdered his neighbor, Georg Biechelin, in 1556.[58] Occasionally, the names of perpetrators and dates of homicides appear on penance crosses themselves; a penance cross in Valwig (Cochem), Rheinland-Pfalz, names Petrus Lentzen as the murderer of Iohannes Humphen in 1612.[59]

Happily, some archived atonement contracts may indeed be matched to surviving penance crosses. A damaged penance cross with rounded edges and broken arms in Obersontheim, Baden-Württemberg, for example, was erected as part of a 1448 atonement contract between Seitz Künlin and the family of his victim, Hans Leydig. In addition to the cross, the killer was obliged to pay the victim's three young daughters 150 gulden, to undertake two pilgrimages, to pay for twelve priests and twelve masses, and to pay for fifty men to visit the grave of the victim while carrying candles.[60]

The *Sühnebildstock* (penance shrine) in Heidingsfeld (Würzburg), Bavaria, also corresponds to a surviving atonement contract. A copy of the original shrine, topped with a *Tafel* (panel) depicting the crucifixion, stands on the Wenzelstraße. The original shrine, now kept in the Saint Laurentius Catholic Church of Heidingsfeld, formerly stood in front of the Gothic late fourteenth- / fifteenth-century Nikolaustor (Nicholas Gate)—the northern opening in the historic city's fortification wall. On the shaft of the shrine in bas-relief appear two images: Saint Laurentius (the patron saint of Heidingsfeld), holding aloft in his right hand the instrument of his martyrdom—a gridiron, on which he was tortured and cooked—and beneath, the kneeling victim with a prayer extending forth from his mouth in a banner of Gothic minuscule script: "*Miserere mei deus.*" At the bottom of the shaft an inscription explains that in 1428 Kunz Rüdiger stabbed Hans Virnkorn to death. Four years later, in 1432, as dictated by the atonement contract, Rüdiger had a stone cross (*eyn steyne crewtz*) erected. He was also required to compensate the victim's family, donate wax to the church, and undertake three pilgrimages.[61]

Unlike elaborately engraved *Mordwangen* and *Bildstöcke* (wayside shrines), most penance and accident crosses are plain and roughly hewn from local stone; they lack imagery and possess neither engravings nor reliefs. Many surviving crosses have been so badly mutilated by time, weather, and vandalism that they are barely recognizable as such. Achim Timmermann aptly refers to wayside crosses as "public 'memory banks'" of the later Middle Ages, offering "information about historical events and persons," providing "proof that certain legal processes had taken their due course," confirming "ancient boundaries," helping the bereaved to mourn, and acting as signposts and exhortations to prayer.[62]

Common Forms of Wayside Memorials

Wayside memorials exhibit a variety of forms. The oldest, most common form is the basic Latin cross, with its right-angled four arms. The so-called Maltese cross—its arms slightly indrawn toward the center and resembling the Iron Cross—is also extremely common, as is the *Tatzenkreuz*—a type of Maltese cross with rounded arms. More unusual are the Antonius cross, lacking the uppermost arm and resembling a "T," and the Gothic cross (with or without an opening in the middle for an eternal light). A range of other types, such as the *Plattenkreuz / Kreuzstein* (plate cross) and *Rundkreuz / Scheibenkreuz* (round / discoidal cross), feature embossed or engraved crosses on traditional arc-shaped slabs or round disc backgrounds.[63] The elaborate *Bildstockkreuz* (*Bildstock* or *Marterl*) (wayside shrine) or *Schöpflöffel* (scooping ladle, so named due to its shape) consist of a supporting shaft or column with an "upper niche-, tabernacle- or cube-shaped top that usually bore a roof or small spire." Within the gable-roofed tabernacle stood a figure or picture of "locally venerated saints as well as Marian and Passion imagery."[64]

Variations include crosses with openwork rings or wheels (the *Radkreuz* or *Ringkreuz*), such as the Gotland limestone *Kleverschusskreuz* from 1436 in Lübeck, Schleswig-Holstein, which served as a signpost for pilgrims seeking the Wilsnack *Wunderblutkirche* pilgrimage site—home to three hosts and a miraculous legend—in the district of Prignitz. According to legend, Hans Klever, a traveling merchant on his way home to Lübeck, fired his gun to comply with regulations against entering the city with a loaded weapon. Klever shot carelessly, however, and accidentally killed his fellow merchant, traveling companion, and friend. He was arrested and held in the Absalom Tower at the Hüxter Gate. To prove his innocence, Klever—an ace shooter—gained permission to shoot his gun at the penance cross erected at the site of his friend's killing. He shot three times into the left arm of the cross and left behind three bullet holes in the shape of a shamrock.[65]

Elaborate penance crosses such as *Mordwangen* memorialize prominent members of the community, including mayors, members of the nobility, pastors, priests, and monks. The imposing, almost nine-foot-tall Monk's Cross (*Mönchskreuz*) or Steiger Cross (*Steigerkreuz*) of 1323, a sandstone cross pattée in the Steigerwald (Steiger Forest) of Erfurt, Thuringia, memorializes the priest of noble family Magister Heinrich von Siebleben, murdered on December 10, 1323, by count Graf Heinrich VII von Schwarzburg. The victim is depicted kneeling in profile, clad in robes and biretta. The Gothic minuscule inscription reads: "Hic est occisus magister henricus de Sybeleybin sacerdos": "Here was murdered the priest Magister Heinrich von Siebleben."

Mordwangen, like the one discussed at the opening of this chapter, often reach imposing heights of seven feet or more and are topped with iconic horseshoe-shaped head pieces and occasionally earlike protuberances. They bear engravings and reliefs depicting a crucifixion scene and depictions of the deceased kneeling, with words of prayer in Gothic minuscule script emerging in a banner from the penitent's mouth: "*Miserere mei deus*." Additional inscriptions offer details of the death and pleas for prayers from passersby. Some *Mordwangen* have been moved to secure locations in churches and museums; others, as in the case of a *Mordwange* near the village of Everstorf (Grevesmühlen), Mecklenburg Vorpommern, which marks the homicide of Ludeke Mozellenburch of Wismar in 1391, remain in situ.

Although *Mordwangen* and other elaborate penance crosses were typically erected for distinguished or eminent persons, there are exceptions. In 1513 in Lappersdorf, Bavaria, for instance, a high cross was erected by Martin Lerch (Reichsmünzmeister zu Regensberg / Master of the Mint of Regensberg) to atone for slaying one of his servants in a rage. The front side of the cross depicts in high relief an image of the crucifixion, and on the reverse side is a second bas-relief crucifixion. On the shaft appears the coat of arms of the Baron Batzendorf. Lerch also had a crucifixion group of four statues erected in front of Saint Emmeram's Abbey in Regensburg (now kept in the Historisches Museum).[66] Although unusual, erecting a penance cross for a servant is not unheard of: a diminutive penance cross in Unterfarrnbach (Fürth), Bavaria, is said to memorialize the death in 1598 of a servant who—suspected of stealing–had been killed by his master, the Count Wolf von Wolfsthal of Burgfarrnbach.[67]

The Departed

Within the hierarchy of homicide victims memorialized with wayside crosses, men of the cloth ranked particularly high. In the legal code issued by Charlemagne (*Capitulatio de Partibus Saxoniae / Capitulary for the Saxon Regions*, c. 785), the killing of a bishop, priest, or deacon was to be without exception punished by death.[68] It is therefore not surprising that many of the grand *Mordwangen* still in existence memorialize the deaths of priests and pastors. The Swedish limestone *Mordwange* in the cemetery of Gustow, on the island of Rügen in Mecklenburg-Vorpommern, bears seven rosette-shaped ears on its headpiece and reaches a height of almost nine feet. It was erected in 1510 to mark the homicide of pastor Thomas Nörenberg, who was killed while trying to reconcile three brawling, drunken farmers. Engraved on the stele of the *Mordwange* is a crucifix with two angels holding aloft the loincloth of Christ; to the left appears the kneeling, murdered pastor, a sword lodged in his head, hands raised in prayer, and his plea for God to have mercy on him extending forth from his lips. To the right are engraved a chalice and a coat of arms with the family crest. An inscription beneath names the victim, the date of his death, and the circumstances of his slaying. In addition to erecting the penance stone, the killers were also obligated to pay for the construction of a church or chapel.[69]

Although penance crosses were often erected in accordance with atonement contracts, many were erected by members of the victim's own family in remembrance as well, as in the case of the Saunstorf *Mordwange* of Gotland limestone erected for Johannes Steenvord by his brother in 1439. The original *Mordwange* is kept in the City History Museum of Wismar. Similarly, the *Kreuzstein* in Schönberg, Mecklenburg-Vorpommern, at its new location at the Saint Lorenz and Katharina Church since 1895, was erected by Vicke Carlow for his father, the knight Hermann Carlow, in 1410. The Carlows were robber barons embroiled in constant feud with neighbors. On the front side appears a crucifixion scene and praying figure, with a banner proclaiming the usual words of prayer: "*Misere mei deus*."[70]

It is difficult to judge the accuracy of the stories explaining the presence of most penance crosses: most crosses lack inscriptions, perhaps because they were erected during times of widespread illiteracy. Many crosses, too, have been moved to new sites—for example, to a local *Kreuznest* (cross nest), an assembly of crosses gleaned from neighboring areas. Although thousands of wayside crosses still exist, untold numbers have been demolished. Until the 1970s, wayside crosses were destroyed on a vast scale to accommodate expanding villages, new industrial areas, and, above all, new roads; only in rare case were crosses preserved and relocated.[71] The abundance of wayside crosses still today hints at the wealth of crosses that once existed and the meaningful roles they played in rural memory culture.

ADMONISHING, REMINDING, AND ATONING: PURPOSES OF WAYSIDE CROSSES

In rural legends, wayside crosses mark the sites of unnatural deaths ranging from the banal to the mysterious and bizarre. The crosses and their legends remind new generations not only of the hardships of earlier village dwellers but also of collective calamities like war, famine, and plague. Many legends offer moral lessons by depicting the fatal consequences of greed, covetousness, irascibility, impiety, and debauchery. Together, wayside crosses and their legends weave a variegated narrative of the adversities of medieval and early modern rural life, but they also offer insight into the ways that early Germanic rural societies imagined and understood themselves as communities with shared identities, memories, and values.

Marking Identity

The deceased memorialized by wayside crosses are identified by their roles and positions in their communities, namely, by their professions, status, or familial relationships—or, in the case of traveling journeymen, strangers, Jews, or Roma and Sinti (referred to as *Zigeuner* [Gypsies] in legends), by their lack of belonging. The world depicted in wayside cross legends is a violent and rigidly moral one in which blasphemy, infidelity, dishonesty, and intemperance are harshly punished. In legends, the tragic fates of the ubiquitous "shepherd" (*Schäfer*), "maiden or young girl" (*Mädchen, Jungfrau*), and "young man" (*Bursche*) emerge as leitmotifs; the sins and afflictions to which they fall prey, while predictable and repetitive, are often inventive in their unfolding.

Memorial Narratives

Numerous wayside memorial legends resemble gruesome horror stories—they describe victims being buried or immured alive, slaughtered by scythes and pruning hooks, gored to death by oxen, sliced into strips, and hammered full of nails. The sources of these legends are impossible to trace accurately. As living witnesses to events died off, so did direct memory of the circumstances behind the crosses. Over time, the task of memory fell to ever newer generations of village inhabitants, who, drawing on memories of older denizens as well as on the crosses' depicted images or structural details, passed along vivid tales to explain the memorials dotting their landscapes. These narratives drew on common stores of beliefs, ideas, myths, and legends and were embellished with the color and texture of rural, artisanal life.

Wayside cross legends often begin with a characteristically amorphous reference to time using the words "earlier" or "long ago,"[72] resembling the classic opening to German fairy tales: "*Es war einmal . . .*" ("There once was . . ." or "Once upon a time . . ."). Wayside cross legends resemble fairy tales and other folk tales in another crucial way: as oral narratives passed down from generation to generation, fairy tales and folk tales relied on "popular motifs which were thousands of years old"; they were also, however, "generally transformed by the narrator *and* audience in an active manner through improvisation and interchange to produce a version which would relate to the social conditions of the time" in each historical epoch, allowing the tales to connect to the "objective ontological situation" of narrators and their audiences.[73] The communal nature of rural life encouraged and eased the process of transmitting legends to new generations. Tales were passed down within common spaces during everyday activities—during spinning bees, for instance, or while drinking in local taverns. In the case of wayside cross legends, references to three types of traumatic circumstances dominate–plague outbreaks, famines, and war, namely, the Thirty Years' War (1618–48).[74]

In many cases, such historical traumas were integrated into otherwise mundane tales of killing and robbery, explaining or at least contextualizing violent behavior while also revealing the enduring power of collective trauma in the memory of communities and their impact on communal identity. Such crosses often bear nicknames such as *Pestkreuz* (plague cross)[75] or *Schwedenkreuz* (Swedish cross), referring to the Swedish intervention in the Thirty Years' War (1630–35).[76] A fifteenth-century cross in Hellmannshofen (Frankenhardt), Baden-Württemberg, known as the *Mörderklinge* (murderer's blade), for example, is said to memorialize a wealthy farmer who, having gone to bury his money during the Thirty Years' War, was murdered and robbed by his servant on the way home.[77]

In many cases, details of wayside cross legends reflect the structural peculiarities of the memorials, including their nest-like arrangements or mutilated, pockmarked forms. A one-armed cross is said to mark the place where a one-armed person was killed, for example.[78] A nest of badly damaged penance crosses in Wellmitz (Neißemünde), Brandenburg, is explained by an elaborate tale: The four sons of a successful farmer fell into a ferocious quarrel one Sunday and attacked each other with a scythe, a threshing flail, a pitchfork, and an axe. During the melee one brother lost both legs, one his right arm, and another, the unluckiest, his head. The fourth, victorious son inherited their father's property and erected mutilated crosses to reflect the injuries suffered by his brothers: one cross lacks "legs," another an "arm," and the third a "head."[79] The geographical locations of crosses are also often incorporated into legends, so that a cross located along a narrow pass is explained by a tale of two wagon drivers who slaughtered each other over the right of way, as in the case of a fifteenth- / sixteenth-century penance cross that, according to an engraved slab in front of the cross, was erected to atone for the murder of a postilion in Chemnitz, Saxony.[80]

Iconography

Although the majority of wayside crosses are plain, a substantial number bear engravings, reliefs or other markings. Most common are depictions of objects indicative of rural occupations: sickles, spades, knives, swords, hammers, axes, wheels, ploughshares, colters, pitchforks, pruning hooks, weavers' shuttles, and distaffs, among others. Such depictions usually signified the professions of the deceased, but local legends often interpreted the images as depicting the weapons used in the killing.[81] In other cases, the professions of killer and / or victim were directly incorporated into wayside cross legends in the absence of images. The *Schmiedskreuz* (blacksmith's cross) in Schlettach, Bavaria, engraved with a hammer, is said to mark the place where a blacksmith killed his wife with a hammer because of her slovenly ways,[82] and in Wollrode (Guxhagen), Hesse,[83] a gray sandstone cross marks the spot where two tailors allegedly pricked each other to death with needles. Other common markings include coats of arms with family crests and swords symbolizing the judgements of courts and executions.[84]

Occasionally, images engraved on wayside crosses have given rise to various interpretations: a fifteenth-century cross known as the *Wagnerkreuz* (wainwright cross) in Büchenbronn (Pforzheim), Baden-Württemberg,[85] bears illustrations of a seven-spoke wheel and an axe. According to legend, the cross memorializes a wagon driver or miller who died in a deadly confrontation with a butcher.[86] Another version of the legend avers that the signs signify the method of execution suffered by the deceased: namely, being broken on the wheel and then beheaded.

More elaborate crosses like *Hochkreuze* (high crosses) often bear reliefs of the crucifixion or inscriptions stating the name and year of death of the deceased. Many crosses bear nicknames that thematize the deaths of the victims: a cross in Möglingen, Baden-Württemberg,[87] which allegedly marks the spot where a beater was shot to death after having been mistaken by a hunter for a rabbit, is fittingly called *Hasenkreuz* (rabbit's cross).[88] Other nicknames refer to the professions of the deceased, such as the *Pfarrerkreuz* (pastor's cross) in Brettheim (Rot am See), Baden-Württemberg.[89] Other examples include a *Spinnmädchenkreuz* (spinner maid's cross), *Glockengießerkreuz* (bell founder's cross),[90] and *Eselskreuz* (donkey's cross, named for a deceased donkey driver).[91]

LEGENDS OF MURDER, MAYHEM, AND OTHER UNNATURAL DEATHS

Legends explaining the presence of wayside crosses offer a glimpse into the precarious, often savage nature of medieval rural life. In addition to ubiquitous references to war, famine, and plague epidemics, mundane motives for homicide abound as well, including excessive drinking, quick tempers, unrestrained competitions of strength and speed, carelessness, sexual rivalry, distrust of strangers, cupidity, vengeance, and jealousy. Death—unpredictable and merciless—is the great leveler in the curious and cruel world depicted in these legends, striking down one and all from the poor farm hand to the pious monk or wealthy nobleman.

Homicide

Most wayside cross legends describe cases of homicide. Some crosses are engraved with details of the killings; others, like the wayside cross of 1822 in Bebenhausen (Tübingen), Baden-Württemberg, display only the word *Mord* (murder)[92] or are accompanied by vague legends that "someone was killed here,"[93] as in the case of a cross on the road to Engelhardshausen in Hilgartshausen (Rot am See), Baden-Württemberg.[94] The act of killing itself is usually stated in general terms using the words *erschlagen* or *umgebracht* (killed), but occasionally with more detailed words such as *gemordet* (murdered), *erschossen* (shot), or *erstochen* (stabbed).

Simultaneous Homicide
The most prevalent type of homicide legend tells of two people killing each other simultaneously. Victims and perpetrators are often described in simple terms as men, women, or children, or identified by familial relationships: they are daughters, sisters, mothers, fathers, and, especially, brothers. Most often, perpetrators and victims of homicide are, as previously mentioned, identified by their occupations: prevalent are butchers, shepherds, tailors, stonebreakers, servants, farmers, soldiers, bakers, grass mowers, musicians, apprentices, spinners, traveling journeymen, and seamstresses. Exceedingly common are bare-bone legends of two shepherds, or a shepherd and a girl, killing each other without further detail.[95]

The surprising preponderance of legends describing simultaneous killings has inspired various explanations, including the history of dueling in German-speaking lands. Bernhard Losch offers a persuasive theory: as we have seen, penance crosses were erected as one of the requirements of *Totschlagsühne*—atonement for homicide. The contractual dynamic at the heart of such reconciliation, however, was too intricate to accommodate popular memory and survive oral transmission, and thus disappeared from local legends. The crucial dynamic of the atonement contract process itself, however—a symmetrical, two-sided action—could be easily retained in the form of legends that reimagined and translated reciprocity from an act of rapprochement into one of violence.[96] Tales of homicide atoned through reconciliation contracts thus morphed into gruesomely embellished tales of simultaneous homicide, preserving—if nothing else—the reciprocal dynamic of the original event. Legends tell of simultaneous killings of butchers, wagon drivers (fighting over the right of way),[97] shepherds (fighting over pasture borders), reapers,[98] and peddlers;[99] of women and girls slaying each other with sickles, distaffs, and spades;[100] and, in the bizarre case of the *Schlüsselkreuz* (keys' cross) in Mellrichstadt, Bavaria, of the two female cooks of a clergyman who slew each other with bundles of keys—a case clarified by the helpful detail that their actions were due to the interference of the devil.[101]

Simple Homicide

The second most common type of legend describes a single homicide. A penance cross standing across from the church in Stimpfach, Baden-Württemberg, for example, is said to mark the place where a lord killed his servant for the sin of delivering him too late to church.[102] Tales of travelers, tramps, or migrants killed while pursuing peripatetic lives are also bountiful, both reflecting and reinforcing prejudice against strangers.[103] Legends of homicide committed against family members are especially frequent: most common are legends of *Brudermord* (fratricide). Two wayside crosses in Hüffenhardt, Baden-Württemberg,[104] known by the name *Russenkreuz* (Russian's cross), mark the spot where, according to one legend, a Russian is buried, and, according to a second legend, where two brothers, one a soldier on the French side and the other a soldier on the German side, killed each other during an unnamed war.[105] A cluster of three crosses embedded in a brick wall in Zerbst, Saxony-Anhalt, purportedly memorializes three brothers who, while bowling with beans, fell into an argument so savage that they all stabbed each other.[106]

Other legends of fratricide offer a surprising twist, as in the case of a cross in Dilsberg (Neckargemünd), Baden-Württemberg, which, according to legend, marks the spot where a disheveled thief, lying in wait for a passerby to waylay and rob, failed to recognize his brother after the latter's absence of many years as a traveling journeyman and robbed and killed him. Finding his brother's papers on the corpse and tormented by guilt, the killer lingered by the site until he, too, died.[107] Other legends tell of parents accidentally or intentionally killing their children, especially unwed mothers killing their babies to avoid shame, as in Frischborn (Lauterbach), Hesse, and Rötlein (Fichtenau), Baden-Württemberg.[108]

Robbery and Poaching
Two particularly popular motives for homicide according to legend are robbery and poaching, suggesting the ubiquity of such crimes. Sundry legends describe men and women being shot by poachers[109] or robbed because they were mistakenly believed to be carrying valuable goods or money: the clanging nails in a victim's pockets are mistaken for coins,[110] for example, or a farmer, returning from the market, is killed and robbed of a large sack that turns out to merely hold fresh butter.[111] Other crosses have been erected for victims killed during land or water disputes; especially common are legends of shepherds killing each other over access to grazing land or springs.[112] Oxen, as particularly valuable possessions, often play a key role in legends involving theft: the *Bürkleskreuz* in Singen (Remchingen), Baden-Württemberg, allegedly marks the death of a man named Bürkle from Schwann who was robbed and killed for the money he carried on his way home from successfully selling oxen in Bretten.[113] A slight variation on this motif appears in the legend of a wayside cross in Ringelbach (Oberkirch), Baden-Württemberg, said to commemorate the death of a woman gruesomely slaughtered for money she was believed to be—but in fact was not—carrying after a sale of oxen by her husband. The legend features a macabre epilogue: the killer was captured, condemned, and torn apart alive by oxen on the very spot where the cross stands.[114]

A notable example of a wayside cross erected for a victim of robbery is the *Mordwange* of Sülsdorf, Mecklenburg-Vorpommern. Built of Gotland limestone and featuring the iconic horseshoe-shaped headpiece, this *Mordwange* presents the typical relief of a crucifixion scene and praying man, his face tilted upward toward Jesus. Emerging from his hands, folded in prayer, are the usual words of prayer in minuscule script: "*Misere mei deus.*" At the foot of the *Mordwange* appears a plea for prayers for the victim, Marquard Börtzow, who died in 1398. A unique detail—the depiction of a purse hanging from the belt of the praying figure—points to the cause of Börtzow's death: the victim was a merchant from Lübeck who was killed by two robbers while traveling toward Dassow. Ten years later, according to legend, a girl overheard two men reminiscing at the site of the crime about the robbery and killing. She reported the nostalgic killers, and the men were executed.[115] Other legends incorporate motifs of lies and truth telling: the *Hebenkreuz* (midwife's cross) of Diedesheim (Mosbach), Baden-Württemberg, marks the spot where a midwife, returning home from delivering an insolvent farmer's baby, was killed by a thief who did not believe her truthful explanation that she had not been paid her fee.[116]

Crimes of Passion

In addition to robbery and poaching, unrequited love,[117] sexual jealousy, and infidelity count among the more typical motivations for homicide. Such legends detail a rich variety of brutalities, including tales of girls tearing each other to pieces or beheading each other with scythes over a shared love interest,[118] soldiers returning home from war and stabbing faithless lovers to death,[119] and brothers killing each other due to romantic rivalry.[120] Numerous legends tell of multiple men fighting over a single girl, as in the legend of a wayside cross in Herlebach (Obersontheim), Baden-Württemberg, according to which three knights, riding together toward Einkorn, fought over a maiden traveling with them. They wounded each other grievously and later died at three separate sites.[121] A hyperbolic variant on the theme appears in a legend explaining a cross nest of fourteen penance crosses in Reicholzheim (Wertheim), Baden-Württemberg. According to legend, thirteen young men killed each other simultaneously over one apparently exceptional girl with whom they were collectively smitten. The girl's brother, in a fit of rage over the carnage, added to the body count by killing his own sister.[122]

Adding an element of forbidden love to the mix is the legend of a wayside cross in Lobenhausen (Kirchberg an der Jagst), Baden-Württemberg, which recounts the tale of a man who kidnapped a nun and stabbed himself to death out of longing for her after she escaped his clutches.[123] A most surprising legend accounts for a pair of wayside crosses with a tale of two monks from a nearby monastery who killed each other over a girl.[124]

Other legends of murder stand out for the brutal nature of the weapons, such as axes[125] or pruning hooks, as in the case of the legend of the *Blutstein* (blood stone) in Oberschüpf (Boxberg), Baden-Württemberg.[126] A few legends offer stunningly gruesome details—for example, of punishments that include cutting strips of flesh from a killer's body (Schwarzkollm, Saxony).[127]

Wedding days or soon thereafter are particularly dangerous times in wayside cross legends, with multiple tales describing newlyweds murdered by jealous lovers.[128] Two wayside crosses at the Dorfplatz in Milkel, Saxony, mark the place where a young man killed first his unfaithful lover and then himself.[129] A legend explaining the *Frauenkreuz* of Krofdorf-Gleiberg (Wettenberg), Hesse, claims that the shrine was erected by a count for his wife, whom he killed in a fit of rage due to a report of her infidelity that was later revealed to be false. This legend was most likely inspired by the eighth-century tale of Genovefa von Brabant, who, suspected of infidelity by her husband, the *Pfalzgraf* Siegfried, escaped death thanks only to a Snow White–like twist in which the hunters charged with her killing chose instead to abandon her in the woods.[130]

Vengeance and Punishment

Vengeance, though a less common motive than jealousy, is also a familiar motif in homicide legends. An elaborate, openwork Latin-inscribed Gotland limestone Greek cross in Sommersdorf (Randow), Mecklenburg-Vorpommern, was allegedly erected to mark the death of the nobleman Hinrik von Ramin of Wartin in 1423, who was killed by a posse of vigilante farmers in retaliation for the violence he had committed against one of the farmer's wives. Rumors, however, suggested the more radical tale that it was the avenging village women themselves who slaughtered the reprobate.[131] Unusual but not unheard of are legends of servants avenging themselves on abusive masters, as in the case of a penance cross in Hilgartshausen (Rot am See), Baden-Württemberg, or of students killing professors.[132] A final example concerns two wayside crosses that mark the deaths of two shepherds: the first was slain by the second during an argument over grazing land, and the killer was then killed in turn by his victim's loyal and avenging sheepdog.[133]

Punishment, finally, appears as a motif in a handful of legends: a cross in Hermersberg (Niedernhall), Baden-Württemberg, has inspired three different legends, one of which reports that intractable servants and foresters were buried up to their necks at the site in order to ease the procedure of lopping off their obdurate heads.[134] Two legends explaining the presence of a cross in Eichach (Zweiflingen), Baden-Württemberg, also relate tales of beheading as punishment—in the first, of a man who illegally shifted boundary stones and in the second, of a man who stole the blade and colter from a plough in a field. In the latter case, as in the legend of Hermersberg, the thief was first buried in the ground up to his neck before his head, according to the German description, was *abgezackert* (ploughed off—a fitting expression, considering his crime) and buried at the same spot.[135]

Occasionally, wayside cross legends refer to infamous upheavals in a town's history: in Gudensberg, Hesse, a remarkable legend of betrayal, arson, and execution explains the *Kasseler Kreuz*. In the year 1387, the town of Gudensberg was under siege (presumably during the "Town War," a series of interlocking feuds of 1376–89) but holding strong when a citizen made an offer to the enemy to burn down his city in return for generous payment. The traitor started the fire as promised, and the city was conquered by the enemy. When his betrayal was discovered, the traitor fled but was captured on the *Kasseler Strecke* (route); his fellow citizens tore his tongue from his throat and buried him alive. The *Kasseler Kreuz* is said to mark the spot where he died.[136]

Although legends of homicide account for the majority of wayside crosses, death as a form of retribution for blasphemy or religious fanaticism are also plentiful. Bolts of lighting by the hand of an avenging God strike down a cobbler disturbing church goers on Sunday with his hammering and laughter,[137] a blaspheming servant named Martin Weber in 1602,[138] and a farmer who shook his pitchfork at the sky in rage over a storm.[139] Zealotry may also lead to untimely death, as in the case of the legend of the *Hirtenstein* in Lampenhain (*Heiligkreuzsteinach*), Baden-Württemberg, said to mark the spot where two shepherds—a Catholic and a Protestant—slew each other during a dispute over the superiority of their faiths.[140]

Other wayside crosses mark sites where those who consorted with the devil are reported to lie—the *Spinnjungfernkreuz* of Morlesau (Hammelburg), Bavaria, recalls the death of a spinner maiden who made a pact with the devil[141]—or where tempters of the devil incurred his wrath, as in the case of a cross in Nordenberg (Windelsbach), Bavaria. On this spot, according to legend, a young spinner foolishly boasted of her fearlessness before the devil and was later discovered without a head (or with her head turned about).¹⁴² A wayside cross in Thanheim (Ensdorf), Bavaria, according to an amusing legend, marks the place where a maiden, refusing to pray on the eve of a holy day, boldly declared her behavior to be no more sinful than it was likely that her sickle could hang by itself, suspended in the air. The audacious girl then flung her sickle aloft, watched in shock as it hung suspended above her, and turned into stone on the spot.¹⁴³ Acts of hubris before god also fall into this category; in the case of a cross in Saerbeck (Middendorf), North Rhine–Westphalia, a shepherd is said to have cracked his whip to drown out the sound of thunder during a storm, brazenly asserting to the heavens that he could do better. A fatal flash of lightning was his answer.¹⁴⁴

Hunger

Hunger—particularly during times of famine and war—appears in scores of wayside cross legends. Many describe killings (usually simultaneous) over food—in most cases, over a small piece of bread, a roll (*Brötchen*, *Semmel*, or *Wecken*), or a loaf of bread.¹⁴⁵ The chronicler of penance crosses Bernhard Losch and his coauthors aptly titled their collection of penance crosses in Baden-Württemberg "*. . . und erschlugen sich um ein Stücklein Brot*" (*. . . and killed each other over a morsel of bread*)—a reflection of the preponderance of such tales. Numerous legends illustrate extreme food scarcity with hyperbolic tales of men slaying each other over the paltry meal of single mouse. According to the legend of the *Mausstein* (mouse stone) *Bildstock* (1462) in Greith (Halblech), Bavaria, one shepherd stabbed another over such repast.¹⁴⁶ A cross in Unter-Abtsteinach (Abtsteinach), Hesse, marks the spot where two soldiers returning home during the Thirty Years' War are said to have killed each other over a mouse (a common legend from this period due to the catastrophic famine of the war years),¹⁴⁷ while a *Bildstock* in Stallenkandel (Wald-Michelbach), Hesse, of 1708 marks the site where two knights allegedly killed each other over a mouse.¹⁴⁸

Additional legends follow the same leitmotif, varying predominantly in the type of food motivating the killing and the identities of the perpetrators and victims. A wayside cross in Nankenhof, Bavaria, bearing an engraving resembling a pitchfork, marks the spot where three siblings, while spreading manure, reportedly killed each other over *Kartoffelbrei* (potato puree).¹⁴⁹ Legends of hunger-motivated homicides are often conspicuously brutal, demonstrating the desperation of the starving: one legend, explaining the presence of the *Kässtein* (cheese stone) cross in Ortenberg, Hesse, tells of two brothers massacring each other with sickles over *Händkäse*, a type of sour milk cheese;[150] another legend, in reference to a *Tatzenkreuz* (cross pattée), claims that a wandering beggar was slaughtered and eaten in Boragk (now Altenau [Mühlberg]), Brandenburg.[151] One extreme example explains a cross nest of once seven (now six) crosses in Neunstetten (Herrieden), Bavaria, with the tale of a vicious knife battle among seven wagon drivers who massacred each other over a single loaf of bread.[152]

Variations on the theme of hunger in wayside cross legends are inexhaustible. Crosses often bear nicknames that refer to the type of food fought over or otherwise playing a role in the deaths of the victims: the *Pfannkuchenstein* (pancake stone) in Bad Salzschlirf, Hesse, for example, marks the spot where two woodsmen are said to have killed each other over *Pfannkuchen* (the name may also stem from the round disc engraved at the base of the depicted cross on the stone).[153] *Kreppel* and *Krapfen*—pastry cream jam doughnuts—were highly desirable and clearly worth killing over: among sundry examples, the *Kreppelstein* in Lengers (Heringen), Hesse, and the *Kreppelstein* in Stockhausen, Hesse, mark sites of homicides motivated by *Kreppel* greed: the former tells a tale of two women who killed each other over a *Kreppel*, and the latter of a pastor who killed a beggar over a *Kreppel*.[154]

A few singularly grotesque legends report deaths caused not by starvation but rather by its opposite—gluttony and unbridled consumption of voluntary or involuntary nature. One legend explains the existence of a cross pattée, called the *Käsestein* in Dahlowitz, Saxony, with the gruesome tale of a coachman who exploded while gorging himself on an entire wheel of cheese.[155] The Saulboum cross in Petersbuch, Bavaria (1629), a rectangular stone with a cross pattée relief and topped with an orb, is said to memorialize the death of a worker in a tavern who was forced-fed sausages to death by a sadistic merchant.[156]

Natural Disasters, Animals, and Accidental Death

Second in occurrence to legends of homicide are legends describing death due to natural disasters and animals. These include tales of victims killed by lightning bolts,[157] dying in vehicle accidents[158] (mail coaches, horse-drawn carts, wagons, and ploughs, often caused by shying horses and runaway oxen), suddenly collapsing cemetery walls,[159] freezing weather,[160] and wild or rabid animals, including wildcats, wolves, and bulls. Such crosses often bear descriptive names such as *Katzenstein* (cat stone) or *Wolfskreuz* (wolf cross).

Two such legends offer cautionary tales about feeding wild animals. The first explains the presence of a sandstone memorial with a cross relief located in Ebenhards, Thuringia, within a forest called *Katzenholz* (cats' wood). According to legend, a girl traveling between Hildburghausen and Ebenhards each day laid out a daily roll on a stone for a large wildcat. One day she neglected the ritual and was torn to pieces by the hungry cat.[161] The second legend accounts for a remarkable *Bildstock* known as *Das eiserne Händl* (the little iron hand) in Neustadt an der Donau, Bavaria, about a third of a mile north of the village of Hienheim. A unique detail explains the memorial's name: a small iron hand with outstretched fingers extends from the apex of the roof above a niche holding the figure of Saint George.

Although probably serving as a *Wegweiser* (signpost), legend has it that a seamstress, passing each day on her way to work in Haderfleck, often met a wolf and fed him pieces of bread. One day, the seamstress—having failed to bring the wolf his snack—became the meal herself. The wolf graciously left her right hand—the hand with which she had habitually fed him—untouched.[163]

A handful of wayside cross legends tell of bizarre accidents. In the municipality of Saerbeck, North Rhine–Westphalia, a modest sandstone cross marks the site where, more than a century ago, a boy allegedly died while he and other boys from his village were playing *Floitepiepen* (small hand-carved wooden recorders): the unlucky flautist drew a breath so deep that the flute slipped into his throat and suffocated him to death.[164] Myriad crosses memorialize children who died while playing a game called *Hängerles* (from "*hängen*," "to hang"), *Henkerles* (from "*Henker*," "executioner"), or, simply, *Mörder* (murderer). Children playing this macabre game hanged to death when their playmates, after staging a hanging scene, became distracted and ran off to chase rabbits, leaving their companions to die. Two examples include a sandstone fifteenth- / sixteenth-century cross called *Dreifuß* (tripod—referring to the three-footed rabbit that distracted the boys playing the roles of executioner) in Tiefensall (Zweiflingen)[165] and the *Knabenkreuz* (boy's cross) in Illingen, Baden-Württemberg.[166]

FIGURE 31. Original glass plate photograph (taken between 1900 and 1910) of Das Eiserne Händl, Neustadt a.d. Donau. Photo: Stadtarchiv Abensberg.

Other wayside cross legends relate archaic forms of death: in Tremmen, Brandenburg,[167] an engraved *Mordkreuz* (murder cross) on the brick side of a church tower marks the site where a murderer is said to have suffered a death sentence of live entombment, while in Zerbst, Sachsen-Anhalt,[168] three crosses set into a brick town wall mark the place where three children were allegedly immured after throwing bread at one other—a clear condemnation of wasting food in a time of famine. Other strange deaths include two cases of death during running competitions[169] and men shot to death because they were mistaken by hunters for rabbits or wild boars (memorialized by crosses known as the *Hasenkreuz* [rabbit's cross][170] and *Jägerkreuz* [hunter's cross]).[171]

A startling number of wayside crosses are explained by legends of death by tickling. The victims allegedly tickled to death are predominantly children but occasionally adults (knights or blacksmiths) and, in the surprising case of a sandstone *Kitzelstein* (tickle stone) in Warle, Niedersachsen,[172] a clergyman. In many cases, the deceased are said to have tickled each other to death simultaneously, as in the case of the *Kitzelkreuz* (tickle cross) in Mittelhembach, (Schwanstetten), Bavaria.[173] Particularly memorable is the legend accompanying the *Kettelkreuz* (Plattdeutsch for *Kitzelkreuz*) in Mechtshausen (Seesen), Lower Saxony. According to legend, in the year 1626, during the Thirty Years' War, a girl betrayed her shepherd bridegroom to mercenaries, who then coated the soles of the unhappy groom's feet with salt and tortured him to death by the means of the tickling tongue of a goat.[174]

Legends of tickling to death recall claims of tickling as a form of torture during the Middle Ages. The use of salt and goats as a form of tickle torture, meanwhile, was allegedly practiced during Roman times.[175] References to tickling as a form of violence and torture appear in stories such as the Czech fairy tale "Die Waldfrau" ("The Woman of the Woods"), translated into German by Josef Wenzig (1807–1876), and the word *kitzeln* appears in German phrases such as "*mit dem Degen (zwischen den Rippen) kitzeln*" (to tickle someone with a sword between the ribs), "*einen mit dem Stocke kitzeln*" (to tickle someone with a cane), and, of course, "*zu Tode kitzeln*" (to tickle someone to death).[176]

Markers of Prejudice and Guilt

Wayside crosses also offer insight into prejudice against strangers or those marked as different and "other"—usually, Jews[177] or Roma and Sinti. In several cases, legends reproduce classic stereotypes and prejudices. A wayside memorial in Hesse, for example, marks the spot where a Jew allegedly killed a clergyman,[178] and a cross in Münzesheim (Kraichtal), Baden-Württemberg, memorializes a Jew and Christian who allegedly beheaded each other over money owed by the latter to the former—a nod to the prejudicial association of Jews with usury.[179] Many wayside crosses are accompanied by legends concerning "Gypsies." According to one legend concerning a memorial in Sandebeck, North Rhine-Westphalia, a "Gypsy" woman was killed by young townsmen (she was believed to have ensnared one of them in her power and to have cursed the town).[180] A second, reflecting the prejudicial belief that Roma and Sinti are thieves, tells of a "Gypsy" woman killed by a farmer who caught her stealing from his field. The woman, according to legend, had read the farmer's palm and warned him of his irascibility earlier in the day. To atone for his evil deed, the farmer undertook a pilgrimage to Rome, sold his field, and erected the penance cross.[181]

Other examples include legends of a family killed in 1705 by itinerant "Gypsies"[182] and a cross in Gersdorf, Saxony, etched with the image of a long knife and said to mark the spot where a gang of "Gypsies" stabbed a child to death.[183] A second wayside cross identifies the site where a "Gypsy" woman is believed to have buried her child alive; according to legend, lamenting cries may be heard every seven years at the identical time and spot. The cross is thus referred to as the "*Auwehchen*" (a cry of pain).[184]

In two instances, wayside crosses are believed to have revealed hidden guilt: in Wechterswinkel (Bastheim), Bavaria, once home to a Cistercian abbey, a cross is said to bear the footprint of a nun who, accused of being pregnant, stamped her foot on the stone and declared that her foot was just as likely to leave a mark as she was to be pregnant. When her foot indeed left a mark, she died of shock on the spot.[185] A second legend, explaining a wayside cross in Lembeck, North Rhine–Westphalia, tells of a cobbler journeyman killed by his companion. A stonemason engraved onto his cross the outlines of the victim's and absconded killer's footprints, copied from prints found on the ground. Years later, the killer returned to the crime scene, laid his foot on the footprint outline on the cross, and was caught in the act and executed. When the cross sinks deeply enough into the ground that its arms one day touch the earth, the killer will at last be absolved of his crime.[186]

Although the above-mentioned legends are the most common, wayside crosses have also been erected for a multitude of other reasons, according to legend, including the following: memorializing victims of dueling, marking the borders of spheres of jurisdiction beyond which criminals could not be pursued, identifying sites of death due to demanding employers, memorializing instances of perjury, marking sites where the condemned rested on their way to the gallows, identifying sites where witches were burned, marking places where deserters were subjected to corporal punishment, identifying sites of executions or mass graves from the Thirty Years' War, and, in one unique case, marking the spot where a donkey died.[187]

In hundreds of cases, wayside crosses are explained by multiple legends offering alternative or overlapping tales ranging from natural disasters to accidents to homicides. The *Hasenkreuz* in Möglingen, for example, bears two legends in addition to the one already mentioned: first, that after a hunt all of the killed rabbits were laid out by the cross, and second, that a man named Jäcklin Rohrbach was arrested and executed in 1525 at the site of the cross.[188] Three legends, similarly, explain the *Kreppelstein* (jam doughnut stone) cross in Stockhausen, Hesse: according to one legend, a pastor killed a beggar over a jam doughnut; a second legend reports that two brothers, while reaping crops, became entangled in a brawl so brutal over a remaining doughnut from breakfast that it ended in homicide; and a third legend, utterly different, tells of a secret underground passage connecting a monastery in Stockhausen with a convent in Blankenau. A monk, who used this passage to meet his nun paramour, encountered the devil, who had already killed his lover along the way. In rage, the monk committed suicide beside his murdered love.[189]

The Negative Sacred

Testifying to the salience of wayside crosses in medieval and early modern rural German culture are folk beliefs that the crosses possessed special powers. In these beliefs, wayside crosses demonstrate the power of what Émile Durkheim calls the negative sacred. Similar to the sacred in form but qualitatively different, the negative sacred distinguishes certain spaces, objects, and experiences as fundamentally other and of a different order than that of the ordinary, everyday, or mundane. Before the negative sacred, one experiences fear and awe; the negative sacred is associated with dangerous, frightening forces and instills in the observer a reverential quality[190] and respect "founded on aversion and fear."[191]

According to superstition, the dust of wayside crosses marking sites of suffering and death can both heal and ward off sickness. This belief reflects the core healing principle of homeopathy—"like cures like"—developed in Germany over two hundred years ago. Many penance crosses, such as the cross in Tiefensall (Zweiflingen), Baden-Württemberg, bear small grooves and furrows or little indentations called *Näpfchen*, marking the spots whence villagers collected stone dust.[192] Shepherds used this dust to protect cows from illness, and even in modern times, shepherds in Wasungen, Thuringia, engaged in this practice to treat goiter. Villagers and farmers, meanwhile, sharpened knives, sickles, and other tools on wayside crosses to gain strength and secure good harvests. Crosses marking sites of homicide were also believed to possess the power to lift curses: after walking three times counterclockwise around the cross, a cursed person need only break off a piece of stone and throw it into running water while reciting: "Ich wirf Dich in diesen Fluß, damit alle Zauberei und Unglück hinwegfließe" ("I throw you into this river, so that all sorcery and bad fortune flow away"). This practice helps account for the fact that many surviving crosses are chipped and mutilated.[193]

At nighttime, tales of haunting at wayside crosses motivate locals to choose longer routes home to avoid fright and harm. In dozens of legends, cats and dogs with fiery eyes haunt wayside crosses during the *Geisterstunde* (witching hour).[194] Although cats and dogs—often black—dominate such tales, other animals, such as spectral calves, billy goats, and rabbits, appear in legends as well. Also common are tales of bright lights shining in the dark,[195] sounds of wailing or ghostly feet running,[196] resounding face slaps,[197] and blows to the head.[198] Other legends report witches or ghosts jumping on the backs of passersby,[199] headless horsemen,[200] or little gray men and talking fish.[201] Some tales are fantastically elaborate, describing a *Feuerrad* (a straw-entwined cart wheel set aflame) rolling through a herd of sheep;[202] a ghost of a young, unwed mother washing the diapers of her murdered child in a creek;[203] a sheepdog haunting the grave of his murdered master.[204] One famous legend reports sightings of the *Sarlachbäbele*—the ghost of murdered twenty-two-year-old Barbara vom Sarlach-Bauernhof (1488)—sitting on a cross and leading wanderers and farmers astray, or demanding to be carried to a second cross, located a half hour away.[205] Other legends tell of wayside crosses causing grievous bodily harm to passersby, as in the case of a cross in Langensall (Neuenstein), Baden-Württemberg, said to mark the site where a saddler died and to still possess the power to strike unconscious anyone who jumps around the cross three times.

Although the practice of erecting penance crosses has died out, new *Gedenkkreuze* (memorial crosses)[206] and *Unfallkreuze* (accident crosses) still appear across the German landscape. The most popular form of wayside crosses today is the *Unfallkreuz*, which, like many of its predecessors, marks sites of deaths due to traffic accidents. Although no longer recalling fatalities caused by shying horses or overturned wagons, twentieth- and twenty-first-century *Unfallkreuze* offer the contemporary traveler a glimpse of a trace of a tradition that has endured over eight hundred years.

CONCLUSION

Wayside memorials fulfilled three vital functions in medieval and early modern Germanic communities: admonishment, remembrance, and atonement. Modern German monuments and memorials demonstrate the functions of admonishment and remembrance in a variety of ways and thus carry on, albeit in different forms, the traditional memory work of wayside crosses. The practice of erecting penance memorials, specifically designed to atone, did not, however, resume in modern Germany on a grand scale until the last several decades of the twentieth century in the wake of World War II and the Holocaust.

As noted, abundant legends report haunting around wayside crosses—often described in legends with the simple words *"es geistert dort"* ("ghosts walk there"). The word *wewwern* in Hessian dialect, meaning to incessantly move about in an agitated state, captures the disquietude of ghosts lingering beside wayside crosses, as in the case of the *"steinerne Hacke"* (stone pickaxe) penance cross marking the site of a homicide in Heddesbach, Baden-Württemberg.[207] Past this cross, where ghosts *wewwern*, draft animals refuse to walk and wheels fail to turn.[208] In many legends, it is crosses that had been struck down, vandalized, walled up, or moved that are reported to be haunted. Only once the crosses have been restored to their original conditions or sites were the haunting spirits finally quieted.[209]

In such legends, haunting emerges in response to interrupted or truncated atonement. As symbolized through the seemingly immutable stone of penance crosses, atonement is an eternally binding commitment—in both religious and secular language, it is a debt never to be discharged. The mere passage of time cannot grant absolution. By betraying the promise of atonement, the living conjure restless ghosts. The concept of atonement as an enduring commitment—indeed, as a project to be borne by entire communities and across generations—is the bridge that carries us to our next and final chapter on German memorials of communal atonement.

CHAPTER EIGHT

From Medieval Blood Feuds to Modern Genocide and Refugees
Memorials of Collective Atonement, Reconciliation, and Reorientation

INTRODUCTION: MEMORIALS AND THE WORK OF "TURNING"

After exploring medieval and early modern wayside memorials erected to admonish, recall, and atone in the previous chapter, we shall now turn to memorials engaged in collective atonement, reconciliation, and reorientation. The early, sacred memorials discussed in this chapter perform their moral work through Christian repentance and reorientation: a "turning" again toward God and away from sin. This notion of reorientation originates in Judaism with the concept of *teshuvah* (returning [returning] to / toward God) but appears in the theodicy of Saint Augustine as well. For Augustine, human beings commit evil actions and sin when they turn away from God and thus from "an immutable good to a mutable good," abandoning the "better things."[1]

The sacred and secular memorials of the twentieth and twenty-first centuries perform a different kind of moral work: they also depict an act of turning, but their reorientation is primarily directed not toward God but rather toward enlightened values such as democracy, multiculturalism, tolerance, and charity toward strangers. In the case of Germany, moral reorientation is part of a larger project of recasting the country as a rehabilitated nation with a morally enlightened citizenry and a deserved place among the democratic Western nations. Chapter 8 begins with a discussion of biblical and classical conceptions of collective guilt and punishment before turning to a few examples of memorials of collective atonement from the late Middle Ages and early postmedieval period. We then leap forward to the twentieth century, to consider, first, the possibility of assigning collective guilt to a nation-state, and then, second, the question of collective guilt and atonement in post–World War II Germany. The remainder of the chapter focuses on both sacred and secular memorials of reconciliation and reorientation. Memorials of reorientation, as we shall see, strive for and achieve something very different from those post–World War II German memorials focusing primarily on identifying with or mourning the victims of the Holocaust and World War II.[2]

COLLECTIVE GUILT AND PUNISHMENT

The Doctrine of Original Sin

If we are to consider German memorials as capable of expressing collective German atonement for the sins of the past, we must, as noted above, interrogate the notions of collective atonement and guilt as they may apply to a nation. The ideas of collective guilt, punishment, and atonement that still shape notions of guilt today are rooted in a common Western heritage of biblical and classical sources. The Christian doctrine of original sin is the most influential notion in the West of dispositional guilt imposed on a collective and transmitted from generation to generation. This doctrine, central to Catholicism and many branches of Protestantism (but not Judaism or Islam), holds that each new generation of mankind is born tainted by the sin committed by Adam in the Garden of Eden—the eating of the fruit of the tree of knowledge. This act condemned Adam and Eve and all future generations of human beings to mortality (Genesis 2:17: "But of the tree of the knowledge of good and evil, thou shalt not eat of it: for in the day that thou eatest thereof thou shalt surely die"). Saint Paul addresses the transmission of original sin through the generations in Romans 5:12: "Wherefore, as by one man sin entered into the world, and death by sin; and so death passed upon all men, for that all have sinned."

According to Saint Augustine's interpretation, original sin is an "infection which propagates itself from father to son through the act of generation." The stigma of original sin is thus impressed on the body and soul of each new human being, marking humankind, in Augustine's most pessimistic and anti-Pelagian interpretation, as "massa peccati, massa luti, massa damnationis, massa damnata."[3] As an inherited condition and disposition, original sin condemns humankind to dispossession from a perfect environment, susceptibility to physical ailments, bodily disorders such as sexual lust, and death.[4] Even the largely secular societies of the West cannot free themselves from the cultural impact of this enduring idea of objective, transmissible guilt, with the result that the "biblical understanding of objective guilt as a stain on the entire people still shapes our intuitions."[5]

Guilt without Intention or Blame

Original sin is not the only instance of collective guilt and punishment in biblical literature. The Hebrew Bible offers several descriptions of collective guilt in which intention and blameworthiness are incidental. Genesis contains tales of Pharaoh and Abimelech being deceived into believing that Sarai (Sarah) and Rebekah were the sisters rather than the wives of Abraham and Isaac. Although Abraham and Isaac are "guilty" in our modern sense of the word because they lied, it is Pharaoh and Abimelech—and their houses and kingdoms—who and which are punished or threatened with punishment for the sin of adultery (Genesis 12:17: "And the LORD plagued Pharaoh and his house with great plagues because of Sarai Abram's wife"; Genesis 20:18: "For the LORD had fast closed up all the wombs of the house of Abimelech, because of Sarah Abraham's wife"). Abimelech chastises Abraham and Isaac for their deceptions, emphasizing the collective nature of their transgressions: "What hast thou done unto us? and what have I offended thee, that thou hast brought on me and on my kingdom a great sin?" (Genesis 20:9); and again, "What *is* this thou hast done unto us? One of the people might lightly have lien with thy wife, and thou shouldest have brought guiltiness upon us" (Genesis 26:10).

The transmission of sin and guilt is likewise not restricted to the doctrine of original sin. Exodus 20:5 declares that God will visit "iniquity of the fathers upon the children unto the third and fourth *generation* of them that hate me," while Deuteronomy 23:2 states that a "bastard shall not enter into the congregation of the LORD; even to his tenth generation shall he not enter into the congregation of the LORD." Ezekiel 18:2–3 and 18:20, however, condemn the transmission of sin and guilt in explicit terms: the former states, "What mean ye, that ye use this proverb concerning the land of Israel, saying, The fathers have eaten sour grapes, and the children's teeth are set on edge? *As* I live, saith the Lord GOD, ye shall not have *occasion* any more to use this proverb in Israel," and the latter, "The soul that sinneth, it shall die. The son shall not bear the iniquity of the father, neither shall the father bear the iniquity of the son."

Similar to the punishing plagues and infertility of biblical literature is the plague that descends on Thebes in Sophocles's Athenian tragedy *Oedipus the King* in response to Oedipus's (unintentional) patricide and incest. Once again, guilt is not a personal, subjective state but rather dispositional and imposed on one due to unintentional sins. Tragedy is the most fitting genre for the depiction of dispositional guilt, explains sociologist John Carroll, because dispositional guilt does not allow for the possibility of remission. Oedipus ends up "banished, blinded, to end his days wandering in miserable and lonely guilt on the slopes of Cithaeron, where he should have died as a baby." At the heart of this world, Carroll concludes, is the "haunting guilt" of one who is not culpable.[6]

In the Hebrew Bible, the atonement of collective guilt is accomplished through sacrifices including burnt offerings and scapegoating rituals: "Aaron shall lay both his hands upon the head of the live goat, and confess over him all the iniquities of the children of Israel, and all their transgressions in all their sins, putting them upon the head of the goat, and shall send *him* away by the hand of a fit man into the wilderness: And the goat shall bear upon him all their iniquities unto a land not inhabited: and he shall let go the goat in the wilderness" (Leviticus 16: 21–22).

Not only animals but human beings as well may serve as scapegoats. In his study of mimetic desire and generative violence, René Girard explains the scapegoat mechanism as a means for restoring cohesion to a community at risk due to the triangulation of desire. A single, surrogate victim is selected to serve as the scapegoat and to bear the sole responsibility for the disorder and discord in a community; his sacrifice banishes the disorder threatening to destroy the cohesion of the group.[7] Girard describes Oedipus of Thebes as the "prime example of the human scapegoat" who, like the *pharmakoi* of Athens, kept on hand for calamities like plagues, famines, invasions, or internal conflicts, becomes the "repository of all the community's ills."[8] With the cathartic expulsion or sacrifice of the *pharmakos*, order is restored to the community and reciprocal violence avoided.

Concepts of collective guilt continued into the High Middle Ages with interdicts—sanctions issued against entire communities and nations as the result of one or more members of the community (usually the ruler) sinning against the church.⁹ Interdicts deprived community members of the spiritual benefits of membership in the church but were limited to punishment on earth—as *pena temporalis*, they did not condemn one to damnation after death as did anathema. An interdict had a twofold purpose: it punished a ruler's subjects for failing to restrain their ruler from sin and sought to turn the ruler's subjects against him, thereby compelling him to reform. At the heart of the former purpose is the Augustinian notion that one who does not resist another's sin in effect consents to that sin.[10]

EARLY MEMORIALS OF COLLECTIVE ATONEMENT

We shall now look at a few memorials from the late Middle Ages and early postmedieval period. These memorials were erected to atone for homicides or murders possessing a collective dimension, having been carried out by lynch mobs or resulting in violent feuds.

The Lynching of a Provost

The first memorial we shall consider concerns a fourteenth-century murder committed in the midst of a power struggle between a Kaiser and a pope. On August 16, 1324, the provost Nikolaus von Bernau was lynched by a crowd of angry citizens of the *Doppelstadt* (twin city) of old Berlin and Cölln. The crisis began in 1323, when Kaiser Ludwig IV of the House of Wittelsbach granted his son, still a minor, the principality of Brandenburg after the Brandenburg branch of the House of Ascania died out. This act profoundly displeased Pope John XXII of Avignon, who supported Rudolf von Sachsen-Wittenberg of the Ascania dynasty for the position of Markgraf von Brandenburg. The power struggle climaxed with the excommunication of Ludwig IV and his supporters in 1324. Nikolas von Bernau, a supporter of the pope, gave the citizens of the twin city on the fateful day a proper tongue-lashing from the pulpit of the Marienkirche (St. Mary's Church). Von Bernau was later dragged from the home of a colleague and lynched by an angry mob; his corpse was burned, and a second fire was lit to reduce any lingering bones to ash.

One year later, the pope issued an interdict against Berlin-Cölln, banning the city's citizens from the church: sacraments were forbidden, churches closed, and priests no longer attended burials. The twenty-year interdict had negative consequences that expanded beyond the spiritual realm as trading partners withdrew and the city suffered economically. After ten years, the citizens atoned and fulfilled the conditions of penance but were still forced to wait an additional decade before Pope Clemens VI lifted the interdict in 1345. In penance, the citizens paid an enormous *Geldbuße* (fine) of 850 Brandenburg silver marks and financed the erection of a new alter for the Marienkirche as well as a penance cross with an eternal light at the site of the lynching (the memorial was moved to a new location in 1727). The simple, crudely sculpted limestone penance cross on a pyramid-shaped pedestal stands today to the left of the tower entrance of the Marienkirche in Berlin-Mitte. It reaches a modest height of just over three feet and bears a series of holes where a crucifix probably once hung.[11]

The Mordwange of Rostock

A second penance memorial, the *Mordwange* of Rostock, Mecklenburg-Vorpommern (1494), also atones for the lynching of a religious figure—in this case, Thomas Rode, the Rostock provost murdered in 1487 by local citizens during the Rostock Cathedral Feud (1487–91). The obligation to erect the *Mordwange*, now kept in the Rostock Cultural History Museum, along with other punitive damages was imposed on the city of Rostock. The two sides of the *Mordwange* depict the kneeling victim, complete with escutcheon and chalice, praying to the crucified Jesus. The words of the deceased's prayer are inscribed on a banner extending from his lips: "*Miserere mei deus.*"[12]

A Nine-Year Blood Feud

The story of the *Staffeler Kreuz*, a massive ten-foot-high cross of basalt that stood in the district of Sayn, Rhineland-Palatinate, for hundreds of years before vanishing, offers an example of communal repentance dictated by an atonement contract. This story begins in the fourteenth century with Dittrich von Staffel, a man living in a state of enmity with nobleman Henn Bretten von Heiresbach, a mercenary soldier and captain from the nearby town of Limburg (Limburg an der Lahn, Hesse). In 1371, while riding his horse to a wedding, von Staffel spotted his enemy riding to the same destination and pursued him. Realizing that von Staffel had caught up to him, von Heiresbach drew his sword and thrust backward, stabbing von Staffel in the eye and killing him. The homicide led to a nine-year blood feud between von Staffel's supporters and the city of Limburg. In

1380, the feud reached its climax when knights from neighboring areas—allies of von Staffel—plundered and set Limburg aflame.

The attack on Limburg drew the attention of the Archbishop of Trier,[13] who interceded to end the feud. As mediator, the archbishop helped draw up an atonement contract between von Staffel's supporters and the citizens of Limburg, according to which the latter would atone for von Staffel's death with pilgrimages, donations of an eternal flame, a mass, twelve hundred pounds of wax to the church, and the erection of a penance cross—the *Staffeler Kreuz*.[14] Here, although a single man committed homicide, the citizens of the town were obliged to atone for their role in prolonging the discord.

THE NATION AND THE POSSIBILITY OF ATONEMENT

Atonement during the late Middle Ages and early postmedieval period was both sacred and mundane, demanding not only the redeeming of souls but also the recompensing of victims' families, reflecting the "double character of the medieval perspective on life, which ascribed to human beings a mundane as well as transcendent, spiritual existence."[15] In a predominantly secular nation-state like modern Germany, however, the question arises: How does a state express remorse and regret without relying on explicitly religious rituals? Can a modern, secular nation-state be said to bear guilt and to thus be capable of atonement?

When discussing the concept of secular atonement, it is helpful to consider the writings of Charles Taylor on the modern self. For Taylor, the modern self is one that positions and orients itself within moral space, so that knowing *who* one is means knowing *where* one stands in relation to the good, the valuable, and the significant.[16] One defines oneself, Taylor argues, by defining whence one speaks—including from within the "space of moral and spiritual orientation." A self is indeed only a self, Taylor maintains, as it moves "in a certain space of questions" and seeks to find "an orientation to the good."[17] When considering the phenomenon of collective atonement, however, we must first ask to what extent a collective—be it a community, an institution, or a nation-state—is capable of repenting and atoning. Can a collective, like an individual self, repent, atone, and reorient itself toward the good? If we accept the notion that a collective, such as a nation-state, may be viewed as a "single entity abstracted from the individuals who constitute it"; that is, if we ascribe to the idea of the popular will in the associative sense of Jean-Jacques Rousseau (*la volonté generale*) (the general associative will),[18] then we may also accept the nation-state as an actor expressing certain beliefs, values, and principles, which—at least nominally—its citizens embrace. In this case, an argument for the possibility of collective atonement can persuasively be made.

Linda Radzik explains that as long as retribution against individuals is not sought and the injustices committed are collective ones (as in cases of state-sponsored persecution and genocide, for example), states may be viewed as agents holding collective responsibility.[19] Acts of atonement and efforts at reconciliation by a collective like a nation-state, furthermore, may follow the same pattern as in cases of individual wrongdoing. In order to reestablish itself as a "trustworthy member of the moral community," the atoning state must engage in external actions communicating internal moral change, including acknowledging wrongs, admitting responsibility, showing dedication to the dignity and equal moral status of all human beings, and committing to moral norms and just laws in the future. The atoning collective must also commit to repairing the damage done as far as possible and to communicating respectfully with the victims and victim community.[20]

Germany: A Case for Collective Guilt

George P. Fletcher, scholar of comparative and international criminal law, presents a persuasive argument for collective guilt in Germany. According to the International Criminal Court statute of 1998, only individuals committing crimes "in the name of the groups they represent" and "pursuant to or in furtherance of a state organizational policy" may be charged with crimes against humanity. Arguing forward from this basic principle and considering the influential theories of Hannah Arendt and Karl Jaspers as well as details of current German law,[21] Fletcher makes the case that Germany may indeed be said to bear collective guilt.[22] Fletcher is careful, however, to describe this guilt as "nontransitive associative guilt": that is, guilt that "remains in the nation but . . . bears no relationship to individual guilt," thereby avoiding the "baleful and pernicious" idea of the transmission of guilt from generation to generation.

A crucial point in Fletcher's argument concerns "moral degeneracy." Fletcher explains that those persons "who generate a climate of moral degeneracy bear some of the guilt for the criminal actions that are thereby endorsed. These circumstances of criminal action ... require teachers, religious leaders, politicians, policies of the state, and a network of supportive laws. Identifying the agent responsible for the climate of hate is not so easy. Sometimes we should call it the 'society.' Sometimes it is a political party of the government. Sometimes it is the people or the nation as a whole ... where evil has become banal, the people constituting the society bear some of the guilt."[23] According to this line of reasoning, collective guilt may be borne by those who, while not technically committing criminal acts, contribute in some way to the moral corruption of a group, institution, or nation-state.

It was, moreover, in the words of Dan Diner, the "abstractness of the extermination" of the Holocaust, "that is, the functional participation of German society as a whole in industrial mass murder organized through a division of labor, [that] renders everyone, with the exception of active resistance fighters, a part of the killing process." Despite the trials and (inadequate) punishment of some Nazi criminals after the war, "a critical mass of guilt remains which cannot be attributed to any particular person."[24]

If, under circumstances such as these, a nation is willing to accept responsibility for the past and acknowledge its guilt, this acknowledgement serves a vital purpose: it "provides a bridge for the victims and those who identify with the victims to enter into normal social relations"[25] and enables victims to regain dignity. The offending nation's recognition of guilt acts as a "symbolic bow, an act of self-deprecation, in order to acknowledge the relative dignity of those who once suffered."[26] It is helpful in this context to consider the work of theologian Katharina von Kellenbach, who argues that acts of modern genocide, which "exceed human possibilities of justice," especially demand such acknowledgment. In her work on collective guilt within the context of genocide, Kellenbach draws on the work of philosopher Arne Vetlesen to explain that genocidal agents claim to act on the behalf of their community. When an individual believes to be acting on the behalf of his group, he becomes capable of committing and sanctioning acts of evil he might otherwise be incapable of. "Collective evil," declares Vetlesen, "obliterates personal conscience and replaces it with a powerful collective cohesion and corporate identity. Ideology supplants personal moral agency and blocks the perception of the humanity, value, and personal identity of victims."[27] Actions rooted in collective evil are the result of the "deliberate abdication of personal responsibility" and the denial of personal moral agency.[28] Collective atonement is therefore the appropriate moral response to collectively evil actions.

Steps toward Atonement

There are many avenues open to nation-states seeking atonement, including official apologies; reparations and other forms of compensation; declarations of guilt, responsibility, and the commitment to not repeat the wrong; and staging trials for perpetrators. Organizations and commissions such as Germany's Aktion Sühnezeichen Friedensdienste (Action Reconciliation Service for Peace),[29] the Claims Conference (Conference on Jewish Material Claims Against Germany), and the Truth and Reconciliation Commission of South Africa may be established. Finally, states may institute ritual forms of atonement, organizing days of remembrance or erecting memorials.

In post–World War II Germany, memorials of atonement for the Holocaust serve as a form of ritual compensation to survivors and their descendants by seeking to restore communal peace and repair the damaged relationship between the German nation and its victims. Many also demonstrate remorse, disavow the past, and publicly declare commitment to a future based on the sanctity of human rights. They thereby testify to the moral transformation of Germany and its reorientation toward morality and "the good," justifying its reintegration into the community of Western nations. Such memorials are a form of communication between the wrongdoer (the offending nation), the victims and survivors, and the larger community.[30] Although Germany is the most widely recognized atoning nation, the growing phenomenon of nation-states apologizing for past crimes has led Roy Brooks to declare our age the "age of apology," characterized by a "matrix of guilt and mourning, atonement and national revival." For Brooks, such remorse is a useful tool that both "improves the national spirit and health" and "raises the moral threshold of a society."[31]

POSTWAR GERMANY: THE GOLD STANDARD OF ATONEMENT

West German Repentance

Today, Germany is often lauded as the gold standard of national atonement.[32] During the early postwar years, West Germany created a compensation and restitution program to support Holocaust victims in negotiation with the new state of Israel and the Claims Conference, founded in 1951 to support Israel's claims and to help Jews living outside Israel submit individual claims for compensation. After six months of negotiations, on September 10, 1952, an agreement on reparations was reached and signed in Luxembourg by Moshe Sharett, Israel's foreign minister, and West German chancellor Konrad Adenauer. The agreement included a total of 845 million dollars, with 110 million earmarked for allocation by the Claims Conference and the rest reserved for Israel.[33] Over the years, additional allocations have been approved; to this day, the German government has paid out approximately ninety billion dollars.

It is worth noting, however, that West Germany embraced reparations only after David Ben-Gurion, Israel's first prime minister, called for compensation of 1.5 billion dollars in September 1951 and received political support by the Allied High Command of the four occupying powers. Adenauer's first governmental declaration of September 20, 1949, ignored the plight of the Jews, instead focusing on "the German 'victims' of war," namely, expellees from the East, survivors of bombings, and war widows and orphans. As Stefan Engert concludes, "It is questionable indeed whether Germany would have paid reparations at all if the Israeli government had not been insistent." At the time, German support of reparations to Israel and the Jewish people was very low—about 11 percent—but Adenauer was aware that reparations were required "if Germany wanted to be rehabilitated into international society."[34]

In addition to financial indemnification, Germany today possesses a rich Holocaust memory culture, including a day of remembrance (International Holocaust Memorial Day, January 27), copious Holocaust museums, exhibits, and memorials, ongoing efforts to preserve former concentration camps, and numerous networks, centers, and institutes to support historical research into the period of the Holocaust and World War II.[35] In 2017, Germany established its first Holocaust studies professorship at the Goethe University Frankfurt, supplementing an already robust academic engagement with the Holocaust and Jewish history in Germany conducted at centers of research such as Munich's Center for Holocaust Studies (at the Institute for Contemporary History), Leipzig's Simon Dubnow Institute for Jewish History and Culture, and Berlin-Brandenburg's Selma Stern Center for Jewish Studies.

One method of interpreting Germany's early postwar atonement, as demonstrated by Engert, is through the sacrament of penance. Within this model, West Germany acted as a repentant sinner by fulfilling the three aspects of penance: a true display of remorse (*contritio cordis*), a confession of guilt (*confessio oris*), and satisfaction of deeds (*satisfactio operis*). Three watershed events in postwar German history correspond to these three stages: Willy Brandt's spontaneous demonstration of remorse by kneeling before the Warsaw Ghetto Monument on December 7, 1970, in Warsaw; German president Richard von Weizsäcker's speech on May 8, 1985—the fortieth anniversary of Victory in Europe Day—before the Bundestag, in which he named the sins and admitted the guilt of Germany for the Holocaust and World War II; and Adenauer's satisfaction of deeds by signing into effect West Germany's law of reparations in 1952.[36]

Official versus Private Memory Culture

Demonstrating resonance between the official memory culture of Germany and individual memory in the minds of actual German citizens is much more difficult. A study led by Harald Welzer[37] and published in 2005 under the name *Grandpa Wasn't a Nazi! The Holocaust in German Family Remembrance*[38] reveals a profound discrepancy between official and private cultures of remembrance.[39] This study explores the way that stories and histories of the Holocaust and National Socialism are passed on within families. Based on individual interviews as well as group conversations with forty volunteer families spanning three generations (cohorts of the Nazi period, their children, and grandchildren), the study's findings reveal that the children and grandchildren adopt a strategy of "ignoring perpetrator stories" that "occurs accidentally, as if on automatic—the tape recorder records the stories, but the family's memory does not." Over time, family members increasingly heroize their parents and grandparents, dismissing dissonant information and granting their relatives moral integrity while also viewing them as victims.[40] According to familial memories, within the families of both former West and East Germany—despite other differences due to the divergent memory cultures of the two postwar German states—there were no Nazis to be found, merely "misused idealists."[41]

A larger survey conducted in 2002 on the roles, attitudes, and behavior of the surveyed persons' relatives during the Third Reich revealed that "anti-Semites and perpetrators appear to be practically nonexistent in German families." Only 6 percent of those questioned reported that their relatives had held positive attitudes toward Nazism, 3 percent admitted their relatives had been anti-Jewish, and a mere 1 percent believed it was possible that their relatives had been directly involved in crimes. Of the highly educated, 30 percent believed that their relatives had helped victims of persecution and 71 percent stated that their relatives had suffered greatly during the war.[42] This narrative recalls the special role of German suffering in German collective memory during the first postwar decades as well as since reunification.[43]

From Welzer's findings, a few key insights emerge: First, that Germany's "public culture of commemoration differs greatly from private recollections." Second, that "a civil religion of confession and responsibility, the historical and political elements are disappearing from German historical consciousness of National Socialism. What is becoming lost is the awareness that it was possible, in a civilized twentieth-century society, with the active participation of the overwhelming majority of a well-educated population, to exclude a part of this same population from the 'universe of obligations,' to see them as harmful and worthless, to look on at their deportation and to accept their extermination."[44] And third, that "whoever was guilty of the Holocaust, whoever committed the crimes in the extermination camps, the forced labor system, and the camps—one thing is clear to all German citizens: Grandpa wasn't it!"[45]

MEMORIALS OF RECONCILIATION AND REORIENTATION

Victim-Centered Memory

Although Germany's postwar memorial landscape has attracted a great deal of well-deserved praise and appreciation, it has also attracted legitimate critique. In an interview with *Spiegel*, historian Ulrike Jureit argues that Germany's Holocaust memory culture has "hardened into ritual" and is too heavily focused on identifying with the victims rather than grappling with the perpetrators and the structures in society that allowed the Holocaust to happen.[46] Both personal identification with the victims as well as the institutionalization of victim-centered memory in Germany reveal a wish to belong to the nonguilty and to avoid deeper, more troubling questions.[47] While identifying with victims promotes empathy, its domination in the politics of commemoration[48] facilitates a view of the perpetrators from the victim perspective, allowing perpetrators to appear "other" and outside the community, rendering them and their deeds anonymous.[49]

A fixation on remembering and identifying with victims as the cardinal method of dealing with the Nazi past is also problematic because of the implicit promise accompanying such remembrance in German memorial discourse. During his speech of May 8, 1985, mentioned earlier, Richard von Weizsäcker quoted the Ba'al Shem Tov's words that "memory is the secret to redemption."[50] This quote has in the decades since "conquered Germany's political culture" and become a "magic incantation" known to almost every German child.[51] The quote has been interpreted within a Christian framework to mean that remembrance of the Jewish victims is the prerequisite for and path to reconciliation, forgiveness, and redemption. When applied to the secular work of coming to terms with the past, this fundamental misunderstanding of the Jewish concept of remembrance offers a promise of redemption that cannot be fulfilled and leads to a "frantic standstill" at the heart of Germany's memory culture.[52]

One expression of this standstill, Jureit explains, is the sense that, for many Germans, a saturation point has been reached. Since the 1980s, every opportunity has been seized as an opportunity to remember the Holocaust. The excess of sentimentality typical of such memorial events has led to exhaustion, boredom, and general unease.[53] Jureit's claim is confirmed by a poll conducted by the Bertelsmann Stiftung in 2021[54] revealing that about half of all Germans polled (49 percent) agree with the statement that after almost eighty years, Germans should no longer talk so much about the persecution of the Jews and finally "draw a line under the past."[55]

Germany's preeminent Holocaust memorial—Peter Eisenman's two-hundred-thousand-square-foot Memorial to the Murdered Jews of Europe in Berlin (2005)—demonstrates the political and aesthetic trend of identifying with victims, especially for the second generation.[56] The memorial stands as a monument of Germany's regret and atonement—or disgrace and shame, according to some critics[57]—in the center of Berlin near the Brandenburg Gate. In an interview of 1998, Eisenman stated that the memorial should rob visitors for a moment of their sense of orientation, making them feel the terror of being abandoned, destabilized, isolated, and perhaps, even forced into a gas chamber. Such a vision of memorial work reveals "the potential for trivialization and denial inherent in Germany's victim-identified memory culture."[58]

Seeking Reconciliation

A majority of German Holocaust memorials engage in the victim-centered memory of which Jureit warns us. A few select German memorials, however, move beyond victim identification to seek reconciliation through committing to moral transformation and a new, enlightened, tolerant future.[59] Some draw on images like clasping hands or embraces to symbolize the overcoming of division and reparation of relationships. The Adenauer-de-Gaulle Memorial in Berlin, for example, dedicated on January 22, 2003, marks the fortieth anniversary of the signing of the Élysée Treaty, the West German–French treaty of friendship signed by chancellor Konrad Adenauer and president Charles de Gaulle in Paris in 1963. Designed by artist Chantal de la Chauvinière-Riant, the memorial consists of two bronze plaques mounted on a concrete stele. The upper plaque features a high relief of Adenauer and de Gaulle facing each other and clasping both of each other's hands in rapprochement after centuries of enmity between the nations. Also relying on the symbolism of clasping hands to depict unity and the overcoming of division is the almost thirty-foot-tall sculpture by Josep Castell (1952–2001) depicting two enormous, clasped hands. Titled La voûte des mains (Clasping or Vaulted Hands) and dedicated on German Unity Day (October 3) 1995, the sculpture stands along the former internal border of Germany near Helmstedt and commemorates the reunification of Germany.

A third memorial displaying imagery of reconciliation is the Reconciliation sculpture (1999) at the Berlin Wall Memorial, located near the Church of Reconciliation on Bernauer Straße.[60] The bronze sculpture by Josefina de Vasconcellos (1904–2005) depicts a man and woman kneeling and embracing. Between the two figures lies a Bible bound by barbed wire. The materials of the plinth—ground-up seashells from Ireland mounted in concrete from the Berlin Wall and pieces of rubble from Hiroshima, Nagasaki, and Dresden—symbolize the desire to overcome the violent past and find peace. "Reconciliation," Vasconcellos explains, represents "not only the union between two people but . . . a reunion of nations." The sculpture was inspired by the story of a woman who walked across Europe searching for, and finally finding, the husband she had lost during World War II.[61]

Würzburg's Memorial of Reconciliation

Reconciliation memorials also draw on Christian symbols and language to frame their messages in sacred terms. Würzburg's Denkmal der

Versöhnung (Memorial of Reconciliation), designed by sculptor Thomas Reuter and dedicated on May 9, 2002, stands at the Wilhelm-Schwinn-Platz in front of the Saint Stephan Lutheran Church.[62] The Ecumenical Community of the Cross of Nails in Würzburg, supported by the City of Würzburg, the Lutheran and Catholic Deans' Offices, and the "Road to Peace" initiative, conceived the idea for this memorial in 2001. The memorial is built from blocks of stone originally intended for the construction of National Socialist buildings and consists of three stations symbolizing the path to reconciliation.

The first station, called "The Stone Blocks in Formation" (Der Aufmarsch der Blöcke) features blocks of stone arranged in a ramp formation of increasing height. These stones, according to a plaque at the site, symbolize how the guilt of Germany's violent past breaks forth and comes to light, demanding confrontation. The second station, "The Dawn of a New Era" (Der Aufbruch des Neuen), is an arrangement of stone blocks representing a flower bud not yet fully blooming but bursting forth from the earth. This bloom symbolizes the "hope of reconciliation," lighting the way to a new path where "intolerance and hatred will be transformed into the realization of reconciliation."[63] The third station, "The Redemptive Word" (Das erlösende Wort) consists of a series of stone tablets of different shapes installed in the stone surface of the ground. The title "the redemptive word" firmly situates the memorial's quest for reconciliation within a Christian narrative of atonement and forgiveness.[64] The tablets bear mosaics of the word "reconciliation" in different colors and languages, including German, Hebrew, Sinte Romani, Russian, French, Czech, Arabic, and English; additional stone tablets will be added in the future. A plaque explains: "Versöhnung ist die Brücke in eine lebenswerte Zukunft und wächst auch auf diesem Platz" ("Reconciliation is the bridge to a livable future; it grows, here, too"). The ceremonial installations of the tablets are preceded by dialogues that bring together people of different nations and religions, so that the very act of memorializing is rooted in and bound to the work of sharing and engaging in open exchange. The Würzburg memorial thus not only depicts but also stages the elements of Christian penance: contrition, confession of guilt, commitment to moral transformation, and the resolution to make amends through dialogue, acknowledgment of suffering, and working for a better, shared future.

The Protestant Church of Reconciliation at Dachau

A better-known example of a reconciliation memorial is the Protestant Church of Reconciliation at the former concentration camp Dachau. The foundation stone of this church was laid on May 8, 1965, and the completed church consecrated on April 30, 1967. Pastor Martin Niemöller, founder of the Confessing Church and former prisoner of Dachau, gave the first sermon, clearly marking the church as an expression of National Socialist resistance. The Church of Reconciliation is dedicated to all victims of National Socialism and offers religious services, concerts, talks by Holocaust survivors, presentations, seminars, discussions, and exhibits; the church leadership displays a deep commitment to a better, more tolerant future, furthermore, by committing to interfaith dialogue and working together with representatives of Jewish and Muslim communities as well as with Christians of other confessions and secular partners.

The founding of the Dachau church was not uncontroversial. In the wake of World War II, the inhabitants of the town of Dachau opposed the creation of a memorial site.[65] The initiative for the site and church came from Dutch survivors of Dachau (notably, Dirk A. E. de Loos, a Dutch resistance fighter) with the support of the Conference of European Churches.[66] The name of the church (Versöhnungskirche–Church of Reconciliation) was chosen to communicate the idea that all human beings are in need of the reconciliation that can only be granted by God.[67] The president of the EKD (Evangelische Kirche in Deutschland/ Protestant Church in Germany) Council, Kurt Scharf, appealed for donations for the church in 1964, declaring that the intention of the new church would be to testify to the bond between the Protestant church and all victims of Nazi tyranny, to urge repentance, to summon solidarity with the persecuted, and to create a path to reconciliation and peace among peoples.[68]

Architect Helmut Striffler designed the Reconciliation Church—a large, exposed-concrete structure—as a counterpoint to the former concentration camp Dachau itself. The church's two main rooms, the *Gesprächsraum* (meeting room) and the *Gottesdienstraum* (religious services room), are visible from an inner courtyard through high glass walls. The rooms were designed to avoid right angles, which Striffler viewed as symbolic of the murderous system of National Socialism itself: floors and ceilings are thus crooked and walls are irregular, defying the tyranny of order, control, and uniformity that defined the prisoners' existence within the camp. The church as a whole creates an impression of fluidity with its sloping, curving lines. To enter the church, the visitor descends a large, wide outdoor flight of stairs that grows increasingly narrow and leads to a covered passageway. The structure of the stairs recalls "opened arms," with one arm reaching out toward the camp memorial site and the other turning toward the Catholic "Todesangst-Christi-Kapelle" (Mortal Agony of Christ Chapel) and the Jewish memorial, suggesting that "here, all are welcome."[69]

According to a brochure written by Pastor Christian Reger, long active in the Dachau church, the architecture of the church should affect visitors on a visceral level and be experienced as a sanctuary or refuge (*Zufluchtsort*). After experiencing the depressing desolation of the former camp, he writes, visitors would experience relief to reach the stairs to the church—a feeling akin to that on arriving at a place of refuge, much as a desperate prisoner would feel who, exhausted from longing for rescue, turns to God.[70] Other notable details include two reliefs by Hubertus von Pilgrim depicting two prostrate human forms—a mere suggestion of the tens of thousands of deaths at Dachau—and a pivoting steel gate leading to the inner courtyard, designed by Fritz Kühn and engraved in Polish, French, Dutch, and German with words from Psalm 57: "In the shadow of thy wings will I make my refuge."

Repentance and moral transformation stand at the heart of the church's sense of purpose. The church defines reconciliation as following the example of Jesus and "breaking the cycle of violence, acknowledging one's own guilt, and standing up for those threatened by danger"[71]—a mixture of self-reflection and activism. It openly acknowledges the failure of most Protestants and Protestant churches to protect the persecuted and resist Nazism,[72] and the church's activities reveal an ongoing effort to confront the past and forge a more peaceful future. Among other projects, the church's foundation offers two positions for volunteers from the Action Reconciliation Service for Peace, engages in outreach work with survivors of Nazi persecution and other persecuted persons, and critically examines the conduct of the church during the Third Reich. Here, we see once again all the required aspects of atonement: contrition, confession, moral transformation, and a commitment to good deeds. Finally, a hope for forgiveness appears in the lines of the Lord's Prayer quoted at the beginning of the church's brochure: "Forgive us our trespasses, as we forgive them that trespass against us, and lead us not into temptation, but deliver us from evil."[73]

The Neue Wache Memorial in Berlin

A third memorial, mentioned in chapter 6, offers a counterexample. The creation of the Zentrale Gedenkstätte der Bundesrepublik Deutschland für die Opfer der Kriege und der Gewaltherrschaft (Central Memorial of the Federal Republic of Germany to the Victims of War and Tyranny), located in the Neue Wache (New Guard House) in Berlin, was initiated by conservative politician and chancellor Helmut Kohl (CDU, die Christlich Demokratische Union Deutschlands [Christian Democratic Union of Germany]) and dedicated in 1993 as the first memorial built as a central site of remembrance after German reunification. The history of the memorial's founding as well as that of the Neue Wache itself have been thoroughly documented elsewhere.[74] This brief discussion will focus on the problematic nature of the memorial's suggestion of reconciliation between Germany and its victims via a depiction of shared suffering.

At the heart of the Neue Wache memorial stands a sculpture at the center of the bare, cavernous space and lit by an open skylight. The almost five-foot-tall statue by Käthe Kollwitz depicts a mother in mourning, holding in her lap her dead son. The sculpture is an enlarged casting of the original, thirty-seven-centimeter-high bronze sculpture titled Mother with her Dead Son / Mutter mit totem Sohn.[75] The pose of the mourning mother and son clearly evokes a Pietà—the word that Kollwitz herself used when describing her statue. The memorial's dedication, inscribed on the floor in front of the statue, reads, "Den Opfern von Krieg und Gewaltherrschaft" ("To the victims of war and tyranny").

Many critics have noted as problematic the decision to group together all victims of war and tyranny—including fallen soldiers of World War I and World War II, civilian casualties, fallen Waffen-SS soldiers, and victims of Nazi persecution. The dedication has been criticized as an example of "Bitburg history" and accused of using the rhetoric of German victimhood in order to create a new, integrated German identity for the newly reunited nation.[76] After several prominent individuals (including Ignatz Bubis, former head of the Central Jewish Council in Germany) criticized the dedication, Kohl and his administration added two new plaques, placed outside at the entrance to the memorial. One of the plaques names the groups of victims memorialized within, based on a list adapted from Richard von Weizsäcker's May 8, 1985, speech. This plaque itself, however, led to further controversy by changing the order of victims.[77]

Kollwitz's sculpture itself has also attracted copious criticism. Reinhart Koselleck has objected to its Christian imagery and condemned it as "sentimental kitsch,"[78] arguing that it is the task of the church, not the state, to promise salvation. In an article published in the *Frankfurter Allgemeine Zeitung*, Koselleck asks: "For whom and to whom does this sculpture actually speak?" While a mother mourning her fallen soldier son was an appropriate symbol for commemorating the fallen of World War I, Koselleck argues, it fails in the wake of World War II, as it cannot speak for the millions, both male and female, who died not on the battlefield but rather in bombings, concentration camps, mass shootings, and gas chambers.[79] The Christian symbolism of the Pietà, furthermore, as discussed in chapter 6, promises reconciliation and redemption through sacrifice within a specifically *Christian* context: it therefore not only fails to speak for Jewish victims or to their mourners, but, even worse given the "Christian antecedents of the National Socialist mass murders" and the implied accusation of Jewish deicide innate to Pietà symbolism, it tends "inevitably toward an anti-Jewish gesture."[80] Regardless of its intentions, the Neue Wache memorial fails to suggest an authentic reconciliatory gesture by eschewing the self-awareness and effort at moral transformation necessary for a memorial of atonement.[81]

MEMORIALS OF SECULAR REORIENTATION

In the final section of this chapter, we shall consider a few examples of memorials and memorial projects that demonstrate secular moral reorientation. As previously discussed, reorientation in the sacred context means turning away from sin and toward God: in the secular context, reorientation means turning toward the good, the valuable, and the significant. In the case of post–World War II Germany, secular moral reorientation involves rejecting the ideologies and principles of the nation's past and embracing enlightened, democratic values of tolerance and multiculturalism.

In an interview in 1996, German artist Horst Hoheisel argued that the new Holocaust memorial in Berlin should point to the perpetrators rather than (merely) the victims: "One cannot erect a memorial that reminds us of Yad Vashem in the middle of the state capital of the former perpetrators. A memorial in the land of perpetrators must look utterly different; it must reflect the perpetration. Otherwise, Germany slips unnoticed among the ranks of countries victimized by Nazi terror and suddenly, the perpetrators have vanished beneath the memorial and we are all victims of a "'tyranny' that broke over us like a natural disaster."[82] Such memorials lack, in short, the historical specificity and self-awareness (even self-indictment) characteristic of memorials of reorientation. Reinhart Koselleck, with characteristically incisive language, raises the same question: "Perhaps," he muses, in the case of a memorial erected not by survivors but by the nation that produced the mass murderers, "the perpetrators and their crimes should also be presented . . . or should primarily the victims be remembered, the victims whom we ourselves–with masterful terror and consummate bureaucratic skill—produced?"[83]

"The Crushed Brandenburg Gate"

Our first examples of memorials of reorientation are two proposals submitted to the Berlin Holocaust memorial competitions of 1994–95 and

FIGURE 32. Horst Hoheisel, "The Crushed Brandenburg Gate," Proposed Memorial for the murdered Jews of Europe, 1994. © 2024. Photo: Artists Rights Society (ARS), New York / VG Bild-Kunst, Bonn.

1997 by Horst Hoheisel[84] and Jochen Gerz, respectively.[85] Although not selected and thus unrealized, these two proposals present powerful, provocative visions of moral reorientation that would have avoided what Ute Scheub of *taz* (*die tageszeitung*) fittingly calls the "congealed dismay-kitsch" typical of many German Holocaust memorials.[86]

Horst Hoheisel's proposal for the first Berlin Holocaust memorial competition, titled "The Crushed Brandenburg Gate," called for demolishing Berlin's iconic Brandenburg Gate, which stands just one block north of the memorial site in Berlin-Mitte. A diptych photograph (photolithograph with oil crayon and pencil additions) depicts the memorial site.

The left image resembles an old picture postcard with a black-and-white Brandenburg Gate. Carefully spaced in typewriter font in the foreground are the names of Nazi extermination camps in Poland: "Auschwitz Treblinka Majdanek Stutthof Sobibor Kulmhof Belcec." The only

splashes of color are a small, inverted German flag waving in the wind to the right of the gate and a few traces of yellow traffic paint. The second image depicts the empty space where the Brandenburg Gate would have once stood by the Pariser Platz; in the foreground is a description in English and German of the memorial: "The Brandenburger Tor is going to be ground to dust. The dust will be spread on the area of the memorial. The area will be covered with granit [sic] plates. As the memorial two blank voids are created, its double voids—and this is the actual memorial—are hard to stand. But it almost shows the impossibility of expressing the Holocaust by means of art."

The neoclassical Berlin town gate known as the Brandenburger Tor has long symbolized military victory, national pride, and—most recently—the reunified German nation. Built by Carl G. Langhans between 1788 and 1791, the gate was modeled on the Propylaea in Athens and commissioned by Prussian King Frederick William II. During the French occupation of Berlin (1806–08), Napoleon famously stole the Quadriga—the statue of the goddess of victory driving a chariot drawn by four horses—that topped the gate. After Prussian soldiers captured Paris in 1814, the Quadriga was reinstalled atop the gate, but now with an Iron Cross to symbolize Prussian victory. On January 30, 1933, the Brandenburg Gate again played a role in history as a torchlight procession of Stormtroopers and SS strode through the gate to celebrate Hitler's appointment as chancellor. Fifty-six years later, on December 2, 1989, the gate—formerly trapped in the no-man's land between East and West Berlin—became a symbol of reunification as West German chancellor Helmut Kohl and East German premier Hans Modrow together opened the gate, allowing thousands of Germans to rush joyously through the archway. For Hoheisel, the postreunification symbolism of the Brandenburg Gate posits a false ideal—an "unfractured German identity and historical continuity"—that ignores the "rupture in civilisation since Auschwitz."[88]

Hoheisel's proposal asks a provocative question: "Would the nation of perpetrators be ready to sacrifice this national symbol?" The answer was a resounding "No."[89] Hoheisel has acknowledged that he never actually expected his proposal to be accepted; indeed, it was eliminated from consideration during the first round and has been described by tour bus guides in Berlin as the idea of a "crazy artist."[90] But Hoheisel's concept offers us a valuable vision. Many well-known "countermonuments" evoke absence through negative spaces.[91] Micha Ullman's subterranean memorial Empty Library (Bebelplatz, Berlin, 1995), for example, presents a room filled with empty bookshelves in remembrance of the Nazi book burning of May 10, 1933. The two materials of which this memorial was composed are "emptiness and silence."[92] With his proposal, however, Hoheisel takes the evocation of absence one step further: rather than marking and reflecting on absence, Hoheisel seeks to actually *create* absence through creative destruction. The resulting "double void" of the demolished gate—in Hoheisel's words the "national symbol of the nation of the perpetrators"—and an absent Holocaust memorial would have forever tied the destruction of the European Jews to the destructive nature of German nationalism, making it impossible for spectators to contemplate the former without also confronting the latter.[93] Reflecting on his own artistic trajectory, Hoheisel notes the development in his work "from commemorating the victims to confronting the perpetrators. This is the German legacy." Hoheisel's proposal embraces this legacy by refusing to decouple the criminals from the crime.

"Why. Why Did It Happen?"

Jochen Gerz's proposal, titled "Warum. Warum ist es geschehen?" (Why. Why did it happen?), was one of four finalists in the second memorial competition of 1997. Gerz's proposal called for a 14,500-square-meter concrete surface, thirty-nine light poles displaying the word "why" from luminous light-wave conductors in the different languages spoken by European Jews, and a building called "Das Ohr" ("The Ear"). The answers posed to the question of "why" by the visitors to the memorial were to be collected and housed in "The Ear" as well as engraved on the concrete surface of the memorial square until the space was filled.

Gerz's proposal sought to transform visitors into participants who would contribute their own unique and individual answers while also immersing themselves in the answers of others. In Gerz's words, "The history of Germany's most radical—not least cultural—disempowerment (*Entmündigung*)—can only be answered by giving back—and helping the individual again to find—his or her own voice."[94] The essence of Gerz's proposal is democratic: "As in democracy," he explains, "there is in this artistic concept actually no spectator, except as part of the work itself." Gerz envisioned extending the memorial space all the way to the Berlin Tiergarten (an inner-city park), thereby integrating the Ebertstraße with its traffic and daily, unintentional "visitors" into the memorial work as well.[95] The memorial itself would not offer an answer to the question of "why"—no one, Gerz explains, can answer this question for the visitors—no artist, no politician, no award-granting authority. No foreign visitor to the memorial wants to be told by Germans in Berlin what will move them, Gerz declares: "We have in that respect the worst of all possible cards. Therefore, I must keep the space empty and open for the visitor; for this reason, the building is called 'The Ear.' Our position can only be one of humility, of listening, of making space for the contribution of others."[96]

In response to Gerz's proposal, art historian and director of the Liechtenstein National Gallery Friedemann Malsch praised the artist's concept of memory as "the mainspring of human uncertainty and self-questioning." It is only through this uncertainty, Malsch continues, that self-awareness free from self-deception may emerge. For Gerz, Malsch declares, "it is not just a matter of remembering, but above all, one of making memory relevant to the present situation and of gaining insight into its fundamental importance of an ethics for the future."[97]

Both Hoheisel's and Gerz's proposals for the Berlin Holocaust memorial demonstrate moral reorientation by rejecting the Germany of the past: Hoheisel seeks to demolish a potent symbol of values that led to violence and destruction, and Gerz deprives the memorial of the right to dictate a German narrative of Holocaust remembrance. Both proposals embrace a vision of a new future: in the former, a future in which perpetrators are exposed and idols smashed, and in the latter, a future that is democratic, polyvocal, and open to the other.

"EXIT: The Dachau Project"

A second project conceived by Jochen Gerz, an exhibit titled "EXIT: Das Dachau Projekt" ("EXIT: The Dachau Project") (1972/1974), interrogates the very act of memorializing while offering a unique example of self-indictment and moral reorientation. The exhibit consisted of two long rows of wooden tables and chairs dimly lit by exposed light bulbs. A soundtrack played three sets of sounds: a person running and breathing, the rattling sounds of an electric typewriter, and a camera shutter periodically clicking. On the tables lay black albums containing photographs that Gerz took at the Dachau concentration camp memorial site and museum on September 3, 1972.

Rather than photographing the museal objects typically photographed by tourists, Gerz photographed instead the signs and other textual markings throughout the museum concerning the functioning of the museum itself, including regulations and orders according to which the museum visitors were given information, choreographed, and controlled. The photographs depict museum texts of various kinds, including signs listing what is forbidden (smoking, dogs, heavy baggage, unaccompanied children, damaging objects, leaving paths, etc.). Other photographs depict notices of museum hours, ordinances, directories, transportation timetables for visiting the museum, directions, signposts, notices, warnings, and other instructions and labels, including *"Kein Zutritt"* (No Entrance), *"Verwaltung"* (Administration), and, as critics have noted, a macabre sign—given the context—stating *"Ausgang"* (Exit).[98]

As Gerz explains in a brief introduction to his project, "The inscriptions in the concentration camp and reproduced in the museum—but not included here—show that they have the same function in the museum as in the camp. They are the medium which makes both possible. The Dachau Museum is latent in the inscriptions from the camp and the camp in those from the museum."[99] The project essentially seeks to expose the authoritative system of labeling, instructing, ordering, and controlling people and their behavior that is inherent to modern bureaucratic systems of all kinds, including concentration camps as well as their memorial site museums. Such systems are driven by the principles of usefulness and efficiency as they calculate and classify, collect, label, and process—be it works of art, objects, or human beings.

Gerz seeks to show us, finally, not only the parallels between the practices of operating a concentration camp and operating a memorial site museum but also the parallels between life and death in the concentration camp and life and death in modern Western society.[100] "The commensurability of the linguistic organization of that, which is generally seen as an extreme case of restricted existence [life in a concentration camp] and that, which is commonly accepted as life-enriching (museum culture) is in Dachau something palpable" writes Gerz in his "Notizen zum Dachau-Projekt."[101] Here, Gerz takes the project of moral reorientation one step further, indicting not only the German values and ideology of the past but modern bureaucratic organization and functioning in general—a system that processes human beings as information and reduces them to their usefulness or lack thereof, and a system that found its most extreme manifestation in the extermination camps.

Schmuddelkind

Our next example of a memorial of reorientation is a sculpture and art intervention that served for a short time as a *Gegendenkmal*.[102] Christened the "Schmuddelkind" (the term for a grubby, ragamuffin, street urchin-like child), this sculpture was erected by the antifascist group No Excuses at the Heidefriedhof, a cemetery and memorial site in Dresden, on February 6, 2015—one week before the seventieth anniversary of the bombing of Dresden.[103] The almost ninety-pound white sculpture depicts an angry-faced girl child clad in a skirt and hooded sweatshirt, her left foot planted forward to signal an active stance. Her left hand is clenched in a fist by her side (a reimagining of the *Trotz-Faust* discussed in chapter 6) and her right arm extends straight outward as she points accusingly with her index finger at the memorial across from her—Magorzata Chodakowska's Tränenmeer (Sea of Tears) memorial (2010), dedicated to the victims of the bombing of Dresden on February 13, 1945. Sea of Tears features a bronze sculpture of a barefoot young girl standing barefoot at the edge of a granite basin filled with water.[104]

The Schmuddelkind, removed by cemetery management shortly after its installation, presents a defiant counterimage to Chodakowska's mourning girl, who stands demurely with downcast eyes, a tidy braid hanging down her back and her head bowed. Her arms are crossed in front of her chest and extended horizontally, her palms facing upward, so that her figure resembles a crucifix. No Excuses erected their sculpture with a celebratory viewing, including champagne and an audience of thirty to forty people. Before the sculpture was unveiled, representatives of No Excuses gave a speech criticizing the official memory culture of Dresden.[105]

In essence, the speech attacks the Sea of Tears memorial as the latest "attraction in Dresden's victim-circus" by using the figure of a young girl to symbolize the German casualties of the bombing and thereby suggesting that those killed were innocent victims who, like a young girl, were naïve and did not know what they were doing and thus cannot not be held responsible.[106] The crucifix shape of the girl's figure, the speech declares, is also problematic because it evokes forgiveness and absolution

FIGURE 33. Sea of Tears memorial, Dresden. Photo: Wikipedia Commons.

by suggesting an equivalency between the Passion and the suffering of Germans during the bombing of Dresden.[107] For these reasons, the activists of No Excuses decided to erect a new memorial to battle Dresden's "victim cult" with its "historical glorification and revisionism": the Schmuddelkind, a *Nestbeschmutzer*[108] who "points out what no one wants to see": namely, that "Dresden and its population were predominantly not innocents, but rather supporters of the implementation of a criminal idea!"[109] The Schmuddelkind is a girl who "dares to confront the crying victim on the 'Sea of Tears' with contempt and say: 'It was you! You symbolize the entire city population that shuts its eyes to the fact that it was not politically insignificant in Nazi Germany . . . a National Socialist city in National Socialist Germany' . . . it was you, you and your city, you were Nazis, part of a great, functioning human-destroying system. And as such was Dresden bombed.'"[110]

In reaction to No Excuses' art intervention, Chodakowska defended her statue, declaring it to be a symbol of forgiveness and peace.[111] In a statement on February 11, 2015, No Excuses responded, "Forgiveness can only be granted by those who suffered pain and injustice. Should this suffering and injustice, caused solely by Germany, be atoned for with her [Chodakowska's] Christlike sculpture?"[112] Unorthodox in method and outside, perhaps, the usual range of ethically acceptable forms of protest, the Schmuddelkind art intervention nevertheless takes a moral stand by passionately calling for moral reorientation. The sculpture accuses and reprimands, but it also calls for action—for a reorienting of Dresden's memory culture and for self-awareness and rejection of the victimhood narrative among Dresden's citizens.

The Monument for Strangers and Refugees

Our final example of a memorial of reorientation is the Monument for Strangers and Refugees (Das Fremdlinge und Flüchtlinge Monument, Kassel, 2017), created by Olu Oguibe, Nigerian-born American artist and winner of the Arnold Bode prize.[113] Although not erected to address German crimes during the Holocaust or World War II like the other examples we have considered, Oguibe's monument confronts the historical and enduring problem of German xenophobia and thus shares with the other examples the goal of moral transformation. Oguibe created his stunning black concrete monument of over fifty-two feet for the art exhibition *documenta 14*.[114] The monument bears on each of its four sides an inscription of a biblical verse, gilded in gold leaf, in either Arabic, German, English, or Turkish (Kassel's four predominant languages): "I was a stranger and you took me in" (Matthew 25:35). The memorial was originally erected on Kassel's eighteenth-century Königsplatz,[115] the central city square and pedestrian zone that has served as a space for assemblies and protests, including a protest in 2015 concerning refugee living conditions. This initial location assured the memorial a visible presence in the city's political life.

As an artist, Oguibe uses form as a powerful vehicle to draw the spectator's attention; once he holds that attention, he shares his message with his audience.[116] The obelisk, Oguibe explains, is a fitting form for this monument, because although originating in Africa, the obelisk has been used around the world. It is important to note that the obelisk, like the pyramid and triumphal arch, the colonnade, sarcophagus, cenotaph, and chapel, are forms that resurface again and again throughout the history of memorialization.[117] The universal and timeless obelisk form resonates with the monument's twofold principle, also universal and timeless: charity and hospitality toward strangers and gratitude to one's hosts. It is a "natural law," Oguibe says, to show kindness and generosity to other people, but it is also natural to expect gratitude in response, as well as to expect strangers to adapt and help build their new community: "Charity and hospitality in effect deserve reciprocity," Oguibe states. Oguibe explains further that he understands that the decision to open one's country and city to strangers is a risk, and that the host's anxiety is logical and should not be dismissed. The charity of admitting strangers, he stresses, is an act of faith—deserving of the acknowledgement, recognition, and gratitude of the stranger.

Oguibe conceived his monument during the refugee crisis of 2014/2015. He emphasizes, however, that the state of being a stranger is not restricted to the refugees of the recent past; it is, rather, an eternal condition of humanity, for "we are all strangers at some point in need of generosity, kindness, and hospitality." In his poem "Conversations," excerpted here, Oguibe speaks to this universal human condition: "The mirror is a window. / It offers a glimpse / Of where we are from / But cannot return. / We are all travelers / On this endless road / Condemned to roam / Without repose."[118]

Oguibe emphasizes, furthermore, that strangers not only receive the gifts of others; they also contribute positively to their new environments by enriching their new communities with their differences and their experiences. All of these ideas of charity and gratitude, hospitality and expectation, Oguibe maintains, are woven together in the biblical text inscribed on the monument. The reciprocity of the host-stranger relationship lives at the heart of Oguibe's monument: to read the message of the monument as one-sided—as merely about charity and generosity—is to misread the true intention and meaning of his work. Although Oguibe was commissioned to create his monument for *documenta 14*, he stresses that he really created this monument for the people of Kassel. In preparation, Oguibe researched the history of immigrants and refugees in Kassel, which, although complicated, has also included hospitality to strangers, including to the Huguenots who were permitted to settle in Kassel in the late seventeenth century. Oguibe envisions his monument as creating "a space for reflection, contemplation, perhaps even debate around the questions of hospitality and gratitude" at the heart of the city.

The message of Oguibe's monument as well as his personal history as a child survivor of the Biafran War (1967–70) have made the monument not only a place of pilgrimage for pro-migration and democracy activists but also a target for vandals and right-wing extremists, including members of the right-wing, xenophobic, anti-immigration AfD party (Alternative für Deutschland), who opposed Merkel's decision to welcome more than one million refugees into the country.[119] Kassel City councilman and AfD member Thomas Materner, for example, described the obelisk as "ideologically polarizing, deformed art."[120] The words "deformed art" (*entstellte Kunst*) are alarmingly similar to the infamous Nazi term "degenerate art" (*entartete Kunst*) used to describe the art despised by the regime—namely, modern art created by Jews, communists, abstract artists, and Expressionists. Not content to malign the monument itself, Materner also broadly accused migrants and refugees of being terrorists, warning that the AfD would call for demonstrations in front of the monument "after each terrorist attack carried out by an immigrant."

In anticipation of the initial monument loan agreement between Oguibe and Kassel expiring on September 30, 2018, the city of Kassel launched a crowdfunding campaign to raise money to purchase the monument and secure its future on the Königsplatz. Although the fundraising goal was not reached, Oguibe agreed to accept a substantially more modest sum.[121] The Kassel city council, however, demanded that the monument be relocated to a less central spot in the city. Oguibe resisted, having designed his monument to resonate with unique features of the Königsplatz.[122] The council, however, reached a majority vote on September 24 to remove the monument, and dismantling and removal began before dawn on German Reunification Day, October 3, 2018. Oguibe and the city of Kassel soon reached an agreement, however, and the monument was reinstalled in early 2019 on the Treppenstraße pedestrian zone. While the local branch of the AfD bragged on Facebook that "champagne corks are popping" and prophesized a "coming revolution in migration policy," Oguibe remains steadfast in his commitment to create a better community for all, declaring: "As the forces of intolerance resurge and try to reverse the human values and institutions that many have fought so hard to advance and protect, we need the monument and its message ever more urgently."[123] Oguibe's vision is open and inclusive; he looks to a German future shared by residents native-born and newly arrived alike, and his monument seeks to reorient Kassel's citizens to a model of moral goodness rooted in charity, gratitude, and reciprocity—a model that citizens of all countries might follow.

CONCLUSION

Evaluating his own artistic development, Horst Hoheisel notes that "each generation recreates its own past from its present. The past is an endless stratification of many different images. We only retrieve those that fit with our present. Such is the case with memorials too. They always say more about us and our time, our art and style than exposing the past. This is gone and all the images that we make of the past and form into monuments no longer reach it. Everything that I as an artist do regarding monuments is incorrect. I simply have the chance to do it more or less incorrectly. Would the right thing thus be to no longer make any monuments?"[124] Is it possible, without eschewing future monument building, to prevent Germany's memory culture from "ossifying into ritual" through endless reiterations of the incomprehensibility of the past?[125] Memorials of reconciliation and reorientation offer the possibility of a living, relevant memorial landscape and a path forward out of the "frantic standstill" of German memory culture by reorienting Germany and its citizens toward a concept of the moral good rooted in concepts and values of self-awareness, historical responsibility, tolerance, democracy, and dialogue.

In Judaism, the true sign of repentance—according to Moses Maimonides, the great twelfth-century rabbinic scholar, physician, and philosopher—is for one who has previously committed a sin to not commit that same sin again, given the same situation. If, given identical circumstances, one abstains from sinning, then one is a true penitent (Mishneh Torah, "Laws of Teshuvah," 2:1).[126] Given this condition, how are we to judge Germany's moral reorientation? One indication of change may be seen in Germany's embrace, under the leadership of Angela Merkel, of more than 1.2 million refugees fleeing war and persecution during the recent refugee crisis. Merkel's actions were controversial: they led to a well-documented surge in anti-immigrant sentiment and xenophobia, thereby strengthening the AfD, which, previously unrepresented in the German parliament, became the third-largest party in the 2017 Bundestag.[127]

Merkel's course of action resonates with the spirit of Moses Maimonides's words. The thirteenth-century rabbi Jonah Gerondi declared that "the repentant sinner should strive to do good with the same faculties with which he sinned.... With whatever part of the body he sinned, he should now engage in good deeds. If his feet had run to sin, let them now run to the performance of the good. If his mouth has spoken falsehood, let it now be opened in wisdom. Violent hands should now open in charity.... The trouble-maker should now become a peacemaker."[128] And Germany, the country that less than a century ago persecuted and murdered millions of Jews, Roma and Sinti, homosexuals, and others, creating the greatest refugee crisis of the twentieth century, has now greeted with open arms and *Wilkommenskultur*[129] those at risk of persecution and murder, thereby mitigating the largest refugee crisis since World War II and securing a safe haven for generations to come. Green Party politician and theologian Katrin Göring-Eckardt famously declared the Germans to be the "*Weltmeister der Hilfsbereitschaft*" ("world champions of helpfulness") and the welcoming of refugees to Germany a "*September-Märchen*" ("September fairy tale").[130] A better illustration of moral reorientation and a more fitting memorial to Germany's past victims is difficult to imagine.

CONCLUSION

In 2019, reporters for the internet film news portal Bochumschau of the city of Bochum, North Rhine–Westphalia, made an intriguing discovery: nestled among decorative blue glass balls, plants, and stones beside a garden pond in Bochum lay the decapitated stone head of a memorial soldier. The property on which the head was found belongs to one of the persons responsible for the 1987 beheading of the World War I and World War II memorial in Langendreer (a district of Bochum) to which the head belongs.[1]

Commissioned by the local veterans' association, the Langendreer memorial was designed by Hans Dammann (1867–1942) and dedicated on July 28, 1929. The memorial features an erect soldier in relaxed pose, helmet in one hand and weapon in the other. On the front side of the memorial appears a standard inscription dedicating the memorial to the fallen soldiers of World War I, but the reverse side of the memorial bears provocative words: "Einst kommt der Tag da alle Welt euren Ruhm verkünden wird!" (One day all the world will proclaim your glory!) On the south side of the memorial are engraved the years of World War I, and on the north side of the memorial, added in 1968, the years of World War II. In 1987, the Langendreer memorial soldier was beheaded and had to wait seventeen years before finally receiving a new head thanks to the efforts of Bochum's *Ehrenmal-Verein* (memorial association), which declared the Langendreer memorial to be a "Mahnmal für Frieden und Gewaltfreiheit" ("memorial for peace and nonviolence"), erected to honor the "Opfer eines imperialistischen Wahns in Europa" ("victims of imperialistic delusions in Europe")—a claim that doesn't resonate with

FIGURE 34. Memorial in Langendreer (Bochum).

the megalomanic inscription predicting Germany's future worldwide glory.

The story, however, does not end here. On Volkstrauertag (Germany's National Day of Mourning) in 2009, the Bochum NPD (National Democratic Party of Germany), a far-right / neo-Nazi political party, assembled at the Langendreer memorial to commemorate the fallen soldiers of both world wars with torches and black, white, and red *Reichsfahnen* (flags of the German Reich). Shortly before the next National Day of Mourning in 2010 and a likely repetition of NPD activity, the memorial soldier suffered his peculiar fate a second time as unknown persons once again filched and absconded with his head. Due to the high cost of a new head and the likelihood of additional decapitations, Langendreer's memorial soldier remains headless to this day.²

Despite the singular details, the case of the Langendreer memorial is not unique: over the past several decades, the German press has reported many instances of memorial and monument vandalism, from spray painting and mutilation to *Denkmalsturz* (the toppling of memorials). Many of the targeted memorials and monuments exhibit explicit militaristic, war-glorifying, and revanchist imagery and inscriptions. Assailants attacked a World War I memorial in the Bochum city park, for example, in February 1983, sawing two memorial soldiers off at their legs and writing on the wall behind them in spray paint: "50 Jahre sind genug" ("Fifty years are enough"). The sawed-off soldiers have been restored and are now kept in the Bochum Stadtarchiv, the Center for City History. Vandals often target memorials dedicated to the victims of Nazi persecution as well: Berlin's Memorial to Homosexuals Persecuted under Nazism suffered vandalism in 2019, and memorial trees at the former concentration camp Buchenwald were attacked and twice felled within one week in 2022. The Berlin Memorial to the Murdered Jews of Europe, too, has been vandalized: in 2002—only one week after the attacks on Buchenwald's memorial trees—seven of the memorial's steles were desecrated with eleven Nazi swastikas in red and black paint.

More creative acts of resistance seek to draw attention to a continuity of militarism in German culture: on February 5, 2015, performance artist Wolfgang Kastner changed the inscription on a war memorial in Munich[3] by removing select letters from "Sie starben für Deutschlands Ruhm und Ehre," a popular inscription meaning "They died for Germany's glory and honor," to "Sie starben für Deutschlands Unehre" ("They died for Germany's dishonor"). Kastner then mailed the five bronze letters he had removed (R, U, H, M, and D) to minister of defense Ursula von der Leyen in Berlin, to whom Kastner had already written with a request to change the inscription.[4]

Repeated vandalism, *Denkmalsturz*, and creative acts of resistance like Kastner's reveal the ability of even decades-old monuments and memorials to incite anger and action in contemporary German communities. Austrian writer Robert Musil famously quipped that "nothing is more invisible than a monument," but these attacks and actions suggest otherwise. Be it leftist attacks on incendiary, warmongering World War

I memorials or right-wing assaults on memorials commemorating the victims of Nazi persecution, actions against monuments and memorials acknowledge the power of such structures to continue to shape German cultural, collective memory, belying the idea of their irrelevance to later generations.

As this book has shown, monuments and memorials appear in many forms, from magically evocative *Findlinge* (glacial erratics), *Hünengräber* (giants' graves), and *Lebensmale* (living memorials) to the sacralizing contours of war memorials and articulations of atonement on post–World War II memorials. These motifs and themes cross the thresholds of generations, recurring again and again in German memorial history in different guises. As we advance into the twenty-first century, new trends in memorialization emerge alongside traditional motifs and forms. Increasingly popular across the German memorial landscape are "combimemorials," as Bill Niven has christened them—memorial forms that integrate into one Gestalt memorial, archive, and exhibition. Horst Hoheisel's Denksteine (Think Stones) installation (Kassel 1993) is an example of a "combimemorial." For this project, schoolchildren of Kassel researched the lives and deaths of Jewish victims deported from Kassel. They then composed narratives about their chosen persons and wrapped the narratives around cobble stones dedicated to the victims. Finally, the stones and narratives were displayed in archival bins on the rail platform of Kassel's central railway station—the site from which Kassel's Jews were deported.[5]

DAS GRÜNE BAND (THE GERMAN GREEN BELT)

Other memorials and monuments create entirely new concepts of remembrance, blending memorial projects with nature preservation: Das Grüne Band (the German Green Belt), for example, a project of Germany's BUND,[6] is a 1,393-kilometer nature reserve running along the former internal German border. What was once a "death strip" of high walls, watchtowers, and barbed wire has been reborn as a "nature lifeline" and refuge for more than twelve hundred rare and endangered plant and animal species. Two examples are the *Bachneunauge* (brook lamprey or nine-eyed eel, so named for the seven openings along each side of the body in addition to nostrils and eyes) and the endangered *Braunkehlchen* (whinchat), a migratory songbird that flies over five thousand kilometers from beyond the Sahara to breed in Germany. Landscape ecologist Melanie Kreutz describes the German Green Belt as an *Erinnerungslandschaft* (memory landscape), a *Nationales Naturmonument* (national nature monument), and "ein lebendiges Denkmal für einen Wandel zu Freiheit und Demokratie" ("a living monument to a transition to freedom and democracy"). In addition to supporting the Green Belt as a nature preserve, efforts to preserve historic border structures along the belt, together with the erection of memorial sites and plaques commemorating those who died fleeing East Germany, justify Kreutz's description of the Green Belt as a triad of "Nature—Culture—History."[7]

Like the Green Belt, other memorials of the late twentieth and early twenty-first century are breaking the mold of traditional memorialization by seeking to actively engage visitors and passersby. A most exciting, ongoing memorial project is artist Gunter Demnig's Stolpersteine (Stumbling Stones) project. Because it is both geographically and temporally limitless, the potential of Stolpersteine is inexhaustible; it challenges the usual boundaries of time- and site-bound memorials and reimagines the very nature of memorialization.

Stolpersteine (Stumbling Stones)

On May 26, 2023, the one hundred thousandth Stolperstein was laid in Nuremberg for Johann Wild, a German man executed for anti-Nazi resistance activity in 1941 in the Munich Stadelheim prison. Next to Berlin's Memorial to the Murdered Jews of Europe, Stolpersteine—the world's largest decentralized memorial site—is perhaps the most widely known German memorial today. Since 1992, Stolpersteine have been laid at more than eighteen hundred locations across Europe. These ten-by-ten-centimeter brass-plated cuboid concrete memorial blocks are embedded into the pavement in front of the homes where victims (persecuted or murdered victims of National Socialism) last lived voluntarily. They are not to be gathered into centralized spots or laid before prisons, deportation points, or cemeteries. Each stone is inscribed with the victim's name, birth year, year and site of deportation, and fate beneath the words "*Hier wohnte* " ("here lived"). Other inscriptions, such as "*Hier lehrte*" ("here taught"), are also used.

Stolpersteine are the polar opposite of Berlin's Memorial to the Murdered Jews of Europe: where the latter is centralized and anonymous, collectively memorializing Jewish victims of the Holocaust, Stolpersteine mourn the loss of all victims of Nazi persecution but remember each individual *as* an individual, restoring to each victim his or her name, noting the details of each victim's persecution and death, and marking the site where each person's story and victimhood began—in the words of Demnig, at the places "where the terror started"—at home, among friends and neighbors with whom one had previously celebrated holidays and shared one's life.

Much has been written on Stolpersteine, both in the press and in academic publications,[8] so a few observations here will suffice. Stolpersteine, as Demnig explains, change the cityscapes within which they appear: they not only transform a normal street into a site of memory but also enlist passersby in a ritual of remembrance. Stolpersteine appear suddenly, without warning, and interrupt one's passage. They demand engagement: a pause; a physical adjustment to bend over or crouch down; a flinch on reading the words *verhaftet* (arrested), *deportiert* (deported), *ermordet* (murdered), and the familiar names of camps and ghettos: Auschwitz, Majdanek, Treblinka, Lodz; a quick calculation to determine the victim's age at time of death; a glance from the stone to the victim's former home; and a final glance back at the stone. While giving a lecture in Stuttgart, Demnig displayed a photograph of a man bending over sharply to read a Stolperstein's inscription. As passersby bow to read the stones' inscriptions, he explained, they also bow before the victims: their physical posture changes as their bodies engage in memory.

Stolpersteine also create new encounters by bringing together families torn apart by the Holocaust. When one researches the history of a victim of Nazi persecution for a Stolperstein, one is instructed to research that victim's family as well, so that the other family victims or survivors can receive Stolpersteine of their own next to their lost relative, reuniting in stone families ripped apart and scattered about the globe. The Stolpersteine laid for the Freund family in Heidelberg is an example of such a reunited family. In some extraordinary cases, family members are reunited not only symbolically but in person as well when they come together for the laying of Stolpersteine. Such an occurrence happened in Rome: family members who had never known of each other's existence met for the first time, in Demnig's words, *"über die Steine"* ("over the stones").

Finally, Stolpersteine offer survivors a geographical and memorial anchor, tying them to lost loved ones and a lost past. Such was the case for a man who survived the Holocaust thanks to a *Kindertransport*.[9] Visiting the Stolpersteine laid for his mother and grandmother, both murdered at Auschwitz, he declared that the Stolpersteine were, for him, *Schlusssteine*:[10] he could go home now, but could also return to Germany. In this moment, Demnig declared, it was clear to him why he does what he does, and why this project had to originate in Germany.[11]

When queried about the origin of the name "Stolpersteine," Demnig likes to quote a schoolchild who explained that one does not actually stumble and fall over the stones, rather, "one stumbles with the mind and heart."[12] The concept of stumbling is an apt one for describing monuments and memorials that trip us up, seize our attention, and invite us to share in their narratives of mourning and loss, triumph and renewal. These narratives may shock and shame us, but they may also embolden and challenge us—as does Olu Oguibe's Monument for Strangers and Refugees in Kassel—to interrogate our roles as citizens of communities and nations, and to contemplate what we owe to each other.

Notes

INTRODUCTION

1 Folk psychology, as defined by Jerome Bruner, is culture-specific consciousness and psychology—a cognitive system that dictates our most essential beliefs about personhood, communal life, and theory of mind, all of which we tend to take for granted as natural or commonsensical. Folk psychology is one of the "most powerful constitutive instruments" of all cultures—"a set of more or less connected, more or less normative descriptions about how human beings 'tick,' what our own and other minds are like, what are possible modes of life, [and] how one commits oneself to them." Jerome Bruner, *Acts of Meaning* (Cambridge, MA: Harvard University Press, 1990), 34–35.
2 Bruner, *Acts of Meaning*, 45.
3 Bruner, *Acts of Meaning*, 39–40, 43.
4 Richard Bradley, *Altering the Earth: The Origins of Monuments in Britain and Continental Europe* (1991–92 Rhind Lectures) (Edinburgh: Society of Antiquaries of Scotland, 1993), 69.
5 Pierre Nora, "Between Memory and History: Les Lieux de Mémoire," special issue, Memory and Counter-Memory, *Representations* 26 (Spring 1989): 7–9. Nora defines a *lieu de mémoire* as "any significant entity, whether material or non-material in nature, which by dint of human will or the work of time has become a symbolic element of the memorial heritage of any community"; Pierre Nora, "From *Lieux de Mémoire* to *Realms of Memory*," in Pierre Nora, *Realms of Memory: Rethinking the French Past*, vol. 1, *Conflicts and Divisions*, ed. Lawrence D. Kritzman, trans. Arthur Goldhammer (New York: Columbia University Press, 1996), xvii.
6 Ernst Renan, *What Is a Nation?* trans. Wanda Romer Taylor (Toronto: Tapir Press, 1996), 47. Cited in Aleida Assmann, *Shadows of Trauma: Memory and the Politics of Postwar Identity*, trans. Sarah Clift (New York: Fordham University Press, 2016), 24, 27.
7 Walter Benjamin, "Theses on the Philosophy of History," in *Illuminations*, ed. Hannah Arendt, trans. Harry Zohn (New York: Schocken Books, 1968), 256.
8 Christopher Evans, "Tradition and the Cultural Landscape: An Archeology of Place," *Archaeological Review from Cambridge* 4, no. 1 (1985): 85–88.

9 Denkmal für die Gefallenen des niederrheinischen Füsilier-Regiments Nr. 39. An inscription honored the soldiers of the 39th Fusilier Regiment from the Austro-Prussian War and the Franco-Prussian War.
10 Sedantag was a memorial holiday during the German Empire celebrating the 1870 victory of the Prussian army in the Battle of Sedan during the Franco-Prussian War.
11 Both Rübsam's memorial and its replacement, erected 1939, were selected, financed, and erected by an association of former members of the 39th Fusilier Regiment.
12 Jörg-Thomas Alvermann, "Historie: Ein Denkmal für das 39er Regiment," accessed June 12, 2024, www.filmwerkstatt-duesseldorf.de/studio-ar/duesseldorf-augmented/. The inscription reads: "Überrest des von Jupp Rübsam 1927/28 geschaffenen und von den Nationalsozialisten entfernten Denkmals für die Gefallenen des Füsilier-Regiments 39 als Mahnung gegen Terror und Intoleranz an der Stelle des ursprünglichen Denkmals neuaufgestellt 1978."
13 Kunstkommission der Landeshauptstadt Düsseldorf; Filmwerkstatt and Bezirksvertretung 01.
14 "App macht Denkmal 'Innere Festigung' von Jupp Rübsam sichtbar," *Lokal[büro], Düsseldorfer Nachrichten Dienst*, www.lokalbuero.com/2021/06/19/app-macht-denkmal-innere-festigung-von-jupp-ruebsam-sichtbar/.
15 Nora, "Between Memory and History," 19.
16 Nora, "Between Memory and History," 23.
17 Reinhart Koselleck, "Einleitung," in *Der politische Totenkult: Kriegerdenkmäler in der Moderne*, ed. Reinhart Koselleck and Michael Jeismann (Munich: Wilhelm Fink Verlag, 1994), 10. Unless otherwise indicated, all translations are my own.
18 Koselleck, "Einleitung," 9. See also Reinhart Koselleck, "Kriegerdenkmale als Identitätsstiftungen der Überlebenden," in *Geronnene Lava: Texte zu politischem Totenkult und Erinnerung*, ed. Manfred Hettling, Hubert Locher, and Adriana Markantonatos (Berlin: Suhrkamp Verlag, 2023), 27; and Reinhart Koselleck, "Die bildliche Transformation der Gedächtnisstätten in der Neuzeit," in *Geronnene Lava*, 149–50.
19 Michael Rowlands, "The Role of Memory in the Transmission of Culture," special issue, Conceptions of Time and Ancient Society, *World Archaeology* 25, no. 2 (October 1993): 141.
20 Rowlands, "Role of Memory," 144.
21 Rowlands, "Role of Memory," 143.
22 Rowlands, "Role of Memory," 142.
23 Assmann, *Shadows of Trauma*, 21–22. To suggest that "German memory" as such exists would be to ascribe to discredited views of collective or national memory as being passed, like inherited traits, from generation to generation—a form of "racial inheritance." See Jay Winter and Emmanuel Sivan, *War and Remembrance in the Twentieth Century* (Cambridge: Cambridge University Press, 1999) 20, and the book's first chapter, "Setting the Framework" (6–39).
24 Maurice Halbwachs, *On Collective Memory*, ed. and trans. Lewis A. Coser (Chicago: University of Chicago Press, 1992), 38.
25 Winter and Sivan, *War and Remembrance*, 6.
26 Stefan Goebel, "War Memorials (Germany)," in *1914–1918-online: International Encyclopedia of the First World War*, ed. Ute Daniel, et al. (Berlin: Freie Universität Berlin, 2014).

27 Assmann, *Shadows of Trauma*, 19–21.
28 Assmann, *Shadows of Trauma*, 20–21.
29 Assmann, *Shadows of Trauma*, 21.
30 See Rudy Koshar, *From Monuments to Traces: Artifacts of German Memory, 1870–1990* (Berkeley: University of California Press, 2000); Hans A. Pohlsander, *National Monuments and Nationalism in NineteenthCentury Germany*, New German-American Studies 31 (Bern: Peter Lang, 2008).
31 See Insa Eschebach, *Öffentliches Gedenken: Deutsche Erinnerungskulturen seit der Weimarer Republik* (Frankfurt am Main: Campus Verlag, 2005).
32 See Bill Niven and Chloe Paver, ed., *Memorialization in Germany since 1945* (New York: Palgrave Macmillan, 2010); Natasha Goldman, *Memory Passages: Holocaust Memorials in the Holocaust and Germany* (Philadelphia: Temple University Press, 2020).
33 See Anna Saunders, *Memorializing the GDR: Monuments and Memory after 1989* (New York: Berghahn Books, 2018).
34 See Stefan Goebel, *The Great War and Medieval Memory: War, Remembrance, and Medievalism in Britain and Germany, 1914–1940* (New York: Cambridge University Press, 2007); James E. Young, *The Texture of Memory: Holocaust Memorials and Meaning* (New Haven: Yale University Press, 1993); and *The Art of Memory: Holocaust Memorials in History* (Munich: Prestel Verlag, 1994); Stephan Scholz, *Vertriebenendenkmäler: Topographie einer deutschen Erinnerungslandschaft* (Paderborn, Germany: Ferdinand Schöningh, 2015).
35 Brian Ladd, *The Ghosts of Berlin: Confronting German History in the Urban Landscape* (Chicago: University of Chicago Press, 1997); Bernhard Losch, *Sühne und Gedenken: Steinkreuze in Baden-Württemberg: Ein Inventar* (Stuttgart: Theiss Verlag, 1981); and *... und erschlugen sich um ein Stücklein Brot: Sühnekreuze in den Landkreisen Schwäbisch Hall und Hohenlohe* (Schwäbisch Hall, Germany: Hällisch-Fränkenisches Museum, 2001); Hartmut Schmied, *Die schwarzen Führer, Mecklenburg-Vorpommern* (Freiburg: Eulen Verlag, 2001); Heinz Köber, *Die alten Steinkreuze und Sühnesteine Thüringens* (Erfurt, Germany: Stolzenberg, 1960).
36 Meinhold Lurz, *Kriegerdenkmäler in Deutschland*, 6 vols. (Heidelberg: Esprint-Verlag, 1985–87).

CHAPTER ONE

1 Jeffrey K. Wilson argues that the "steadfast oak" came to represent Germany and German national character during the years of the Napoleonic Wars; Wilson, *The German Forest: Nature, Identity, and the Contestation of a National Symbol, 1871–1914*. German and European Studies (Toronto: University of Toronto Press, 2012), 200. The German oak has long embodied "the strength and longevity of the Fatherland" and served as a "nationalist and militarist emblem" that is "coded as conservative" (Wilson, *German Forest*, 201).
2 H. R. Ellis Davidson, *Gods and Myths of the Viking Age* (New York: Bell, 1981), 154.
3 *Der Vertriebene* (newsletter) 7/99 (Thüringen, Germany: Bund der Heimatvertriebenen e. V. Landesverband Thüringen, 1999), 10.
4 Gilad Margalit, *Guilt, Suffering, and Memory: Germany Remembers Its Dead of*

World War II, trans. Haim Watzman (Bloomington: Indiana University Press, 2010), 197.
5 Stephan Scholz, *Vertriebenendenkmäler: Topographie einer deutschen Erinnerungslandschaft* (Paderborn, Germany: Ferdinand Schöningh, 2015), 222.
6 Scholz, *Vertriebenendenkmäler*, 222.
7 Davidson, *Gods and Myths*, 11.
8 Rudolf Simek, "Continental Germanic Religion," in *The Handbook of Religions in Ancient Europe*, ed. Christensen Lisbeth Bredholt, Olav Hammer, and David A. Warburton (Durham, UK: Acumen, 2013), 291.
9 H. R. Ellis Davidson explains that the name "Tuisto" probably stems from the Old Swedish word *twistra* (separate) and refers to a twofold being (Davidson, *Gods and Myths*, 199).
10 Cornelius Tacitus, "Germany," in *Voyages and Travels Ancient and Modern*, The Harvard Classics Series, trans. Thomas Gordon (New York: P. F. Collier & Son, 1910), 93.
11 Tacitus, "Germany," 115, 93–94. The linking of German topography to an "apparently indigenous nature of the race" would be exploited by prominent National Socialists Heinrich Himmler, Alfred Rosenberg, Hermann Wirth, and Richard Walther Darré. Simon Schama, *Landscape and Memory* (New York: Knopf, 1995), 78–81.
12 Tacitus, "Germany," 114–15.
13 Robert Pogue Harrison, *Forests: The Shadow of Civilization* (Chicago: University of Chicago Press, 1992), 176.
14 Schama, *Landscape and Memory*, 83.
15 Brian Vick, "The Origins of the German Volk: Cultural Purity and National Identity in Nineteenth-Century Germany," *German Studies Review* 26, no. 2 (May 2003): 242.
16 Michael Imort, "Forestopia: The Use of the Forest Landscape in Naturalizing National Socialist Ideologies of Volk, Race, and Lebensraum, 1918–1945" (PhD diss., Queen's University, 2000), 7.
17 Imort, "Forestopia," 465.
18 Thomas M. Lekan, *Imagining the Nation in Nature: Landscape Preservation and German Identity, 1885–1945* (Cambridge, MA: Harvard University Press, 2004), 2.
19 Lekan, *Imagining the Nation*, 4.
20 Anthony D. Smith, *The Ethnic Origins of Nations* (Oxford: B. Blackwell, 1988), 15.
21 Smith, *Ethnic Origins*, 22.
22 See Mircea Eliade, *The Sacred and the Profane: The Nature of Religion*, trans. William R. Trask (New York: Harcourt, Brace and World, 1959), for a discussion of the axis mundi.
23 Richard Bradley, *The Significance of Monuments: On the Shaping of Human Experience in Neolithic and Bronze Age Europe* (London: Routledge, 1998), 82, 163.
24 Smith, *Ethnic Origins*, 183.
25 Lekan, *Imagining the Nation*, 9.
26 Harrison, *Forests*, 168.
27 Imort, "Forestopia," 65.
28 Maria Tatar, "Grimms Märchen," in *Deutsche Erinnerungsorte*, vol. 1, ed. Etienne François and Hagen Schulze (Munich: C. H. Beck, 2001), 277.
29 Jack Zipes, "Media-hyping of Fairy Tales," in *The Cambridge Companion to Fairy*

Tales, ed. Maria Tatar (Cambridge: Cambridge University Press, 2015), 206. Other examples of collections in this vein include Ludwig Tieck's *Volksmärchen* (1797), Achim von Arnim and Clemens Brentano's *Des Knaben Wunderhorn* (1805/1808), and Herder's *Stimmen der Völker in Liedern* (1778/1807).

30 Oskar Walzel, *German Romanticism* (New York: Frederick Ungar, 1965), 3.
31 Richard Hayman, *Trees: Woodlands and Western Civilization* (London: Hambledon and London, 2003), 102.
32 Jeffrey K. Wilson criticizes the approaches of George Mosse, Fritz Stern, and Simon Schama for casting the German relationship to the forest in an exaggeratedly negative light in *German Forest*.
33 Rudy Koshar, *From Monuments to Traces: Artifacts of German Memory, 1870–1990* (Berkeley: University of California Press, 2000), 68–69.
34 Lekan, *Imagining the Nation*, 5.
35 Lekan, *Imagining the Nation*, 7, 12.
36 See Robert A. Pois, *National Socialism and the Religion of Nature* (London: Groom Helm, 1986), on the way in which Nazi ideology sought to transform the nation into a *Volksgemeinschaft*.
37 Lekan, *Imagining the Nation*, 3.
38 Schama, *Landscape and Memory*, 119.
39 Lekan, *Imagining the Nation*, 14, 18. The Third Reich passed in 1935 the "world's most comprehensive piece of environmental conservation legislation, known as the Reich Nature Protection Law" (Lekan, *Imagining the Nation*, 12). See Franz-Josef Brüggemeier, Mark Cioc, and Thomas Zeller, eds., *How Green Were the Nazis: Nature, Environment, and Nation in the Third Reich* (Athens: Ohio University Press, 2005).
40 Harrison, *Forests*, 175.
41 Magnus Brechtken, "Leaving the Forest: 'Hermann the German' as Cultural Representation from Nationalism to Post-modern Consumerism," in *Germania Remembered: Commemorating and Inventing a Germanic Past*, ed. Christina Lee and Nicola McLelland (Temple, AZ: ACMRS, 2012), 314.
42 Albrecht Lehmann, "Der Deutsche Wald," in *Deutsche Erinnerungsorte*, vol. 3, ed. Etienne François and Hagen Schulze (Munich: C. H. Beck, 2001), 190.
43 Ken Dowden, *European Paganism: The Realities of Cult from Antiquity to the Middle Ages* (London: Routledge, 2000), 61.
44 Hayman, *Trees*, 2, 4.
45 Carole M. Cusack, *The Sacred Tree: Ancient and Medieval Manifestations* (Newcastle upon Tyne: Cambridge Scholars, 2011), 10.
46 Eliade, *Sacred and Profane*, 26.
47 Dowden, *European Paganism*, 35.
48 Cusack, *Sacred Tree*, 25.
49 Tacitus, "Germany," 98.
50 Schama, *Landscape and Memory*, 86.
51 Dowden, *European Paganism*, 65.
52 Cusack, *Sacred Tree*, 154.
53 Dowden, *European Paganism*, 74, 77.
54 Dowden, *European Paganism*, 34.
55 Cusack, *Sacred Tree*, 1.

56 Harrison, *Forests*, 8.
57 See Werner M. Doyé, "Arminius," in *Deutsche Erinnerungsorte*, for a discussion of earlier, less influential accounts (3:587–602).
58 Martin Winkler, *Arminius the Liberator: Myth and Ideology* (New York: Oxford University Press, 2016), 33.
59 Dieter Timpe suggests that the battle was not actually an uprising of a nascent nation against its oppressors but rather a mutiny of German auxiliary troops, including Cheruscans and led by Arminius, an officer under Varus. The battle seems to actually have not taken place in the Teutoburg Forest; excavations suggest that the real location of the battle was outside Kalkrise near Osnabrück in Lower Saxony (Winkler, *Arminius*, 2–3).
60 Aleida Assmann quotes Renan's book *What Is a Nation* as follows: "More valuable than common customs and frontiers that conform to strategic ideas is to have a shared heritage of glory and regret, a common plan of action for the future, and to have suffered, rejoiced and hoped together." Assmann, *Shadows of Trauma: Memory and the Politics of Postwar Identity*, trans. Sarah Clift (New York: Fordham University Press, 2016), 27.
61 Assmann, *Shadows of Trauma*, 27–28.
62 Winkler, *Arminius*, 303–5.
63 Winkler, *Arminius*, 305.
64 Winkler, *Arminius*, 303–5.
65 Winkler, *Arminius*, 305–6.
66 Winkler, *Arminius*, 306–7.
67 Winkler, *Arminius*, 31.
68 Imort avers that more than seventy-five literary works celebrating Arminius / Hermann were written during the nineteenth century (Imort, "Forestopia," 69).
69 Doyé, "Arminius," 587–88; John L. Flood, "Conrad Celtis (1459–1808), the Pride of the German Humanists," in *Germania Remembered*, 28. See Rachel MagShamhrain, "The Two Faces of a National Hero: Ulrich von Hutten's *Arminius* and Heinrich von Kleist's *Herrmann*," in *Germania Remembered*.
70 Ronald Mellor, *Tacitus' Annals: Oxford Approaches to Classical Literature* (New York: Oxford University Press, 2010), 201.
71 Vick, "Origins of the German Volk," 242.
72 Schama, *Landscape and Memory*, 76–77.
73 Mellor, *Tacitus' Annals*, 51.
74 Hayman, *Trees*, 100.
75 Schama, *Landscape and Memory*, 81.
76 Hayman, *Trees*, 100.
77 Schama, *Landscape and Memory*, 93. See also Rainer Guldin, *Politische Landschaften: Zum Verhältnis von Raum und nationaler Identität* (Bielefeld, Germany: transcript Verlag, 2014), 99, on how Tacitus depicts the German forest as the paradigmatic model of a healthy, uncivilized space in contrast to the corrupt and decadent Roman civilization.
78 Imort, "Forestopia," 60.
79 Doyé, "Arminius," 591.
80 Bedrich Loewenstein, "'Am deutschen Wesen . . .'" in *Deutsche Erinnerungsorte*, 1:292–93.

81 Charlotte Tacke, *Denkmal im sozialen Raum*, Kritische Studien zur Geschichtswissenschaft 108 (Göttingen: Vandenhoeck & Ruprecht, 1995), 31, 39–40.
82 For a detailed analysis of the Hermann Monument, see Klaus Bemmann, *Deutsche Nationaldenkmäler und Symbole im Wandel der Zeiten* (Göttingen: MatrixMedia Verlag, 2007).
83 Bemmann, *Deutsche Nationaldenkmäler*, 104.
84 Doyé, "Arminius," 600.
85 Winkler, *Arminius*, 84–85.
86 Winkler, *Arminius*, 88, 97.
87 Bill Niven, "The Legacy of Second German Empire Memorials after 1945," in Bill Niven and Chloe Paver, eds., *Memorialization in Germany since 1945* (New York: Palgrave Macmillan, 2010), 403.
88 Doyé, "Arminius," 600.
89 Doyé, "Arminius," 600–601.
90 Doyé, "Arminius," 587.
91 Winkler, *Arminius*, 68, 73, 94; Doyé, "Arminius," 592.
92 Loewenstein, "Am deutschen Wesen," 29.
93 Pierre Nora, "Between Memory and History: Les Lieux de Mémoire," special issue, *Memory and Counter-Memory*, *Representations* 26 (Spring 1989): 22, 7, 20.
94 The myth of the Battle of the Teutoburg Forest has been the subject of many works of German literature, including Friedrich Gottlieb Klopstock's drama *Hermanns Schlacht* (1769); Heinrich von Kleist's drama *Die Hermannsschlacht* (1809); Christoph Martin Wieland's epic "Hermann"; and Christian Dietrich Grabbe's drama *Die Hermannsschlacht* (1835–36).
95 Bernd Weyergraf, *Waldungen: Die Deutschen und ihr Wald* (Berlin: Akademie der Künste, 1987), 236.
96 Viktoria Urmersbach, *Im Wald, da sind die Räuber: Eine Kulturgeschichte des Waldes* (Berlin: Vergangenheitsverlag, 2009), 8, 21, 27.
97 The theme of sacrifice is discussed in more detail in chapters 5 and 6. For a discussion of narratives of battle as a form of ritual, see Alf Hiltebeitel, *The Ritual of Battle: Krsna in the Mahabharata* (Delhi: Motilal, 2017).
98 Clifford Geertz, *The Interpretation of Cultures* (New York: Basic Books, 1973), 112–13.
99 Quoted in Mellor, *Tacitus' Annals*, 74.
100 Dowden, *European Paganism*, 182.
101 George Mosse, *Fallen Soldiers: Reshaping the Memory of the World Wars* (New York: Oxford University Press, 1990), 22.
102 Mosse, *Fallen Soldiers*, 4, 7.
103 Mosse, *Fallen Soldiers*, 7.
104 Mosse, *Fallen Soldiers*, 202. The post–World War I *Dolchstoßlegende* (stab-in-the-back myth) held that the German army was never actually defeated on the battlefield but rather betrayed back home by Jews, Socialists, and Bolsheviks.
105 Mosse, *Fallen Soldiers*, 217.
106 See Moshe Halbertal, *On Sacrifice* (Princeton, NJ: Princeton University Press, 2012).
107 Dowden, *European Paganism*, 52.
108 Halbertal, *On Sacrifice*, 15.

109 Dowden, *European Paganism*, 169–70.
110 Dowden, *European Paganism*, 185.
111 Davidson, *Gods and Myths*, 191.
112 Cusack, *Sacred Tree*, 155.
113 Christoph Mick, "The Dead and the Living: War Veterans and Memorial Culture in Interwar Polish Galicia," in *Sacrifice and Rebirth: The Legacy of the Last Habsburg War*, ed. Mark Cornwall and John Paul Newman (New York: Berghahn Books, 2016), 239–40.
114 Hermann Hesse, *Wandering: Notes and Sketches* (London: Triad/Panther, 1985), 49.
115 Dowden, *European Paganism*, 66–67.
116 Wilson, *German Forest*, 37. *Die Gartenlaube—Illustriertes Familienblatt* (*The Garden Arbor—Illustrated Family Journal*) was a widely read, mass-circulated German newspaper from 1853 to 1944. It featured essays on the natural sciences, short stories, poetry, current events, and biographical sketches.
117 Davidson, *Gods and Myths*, 191.
118 Davidson, *Gods and Myths*, 195.
119 Robert G. Lee and Sabine Wilke, "Forest as *Volk*: *Ewiger Wald* and the Religion of Nature in the Third Reich," *Journal of Social and Ecological Boundaries* 1, no. 1 (Spring 2005): 27.
120 Davidson, *Gods and Myths*, 28–29.
121 Davidson, *Gods and Myths*, 34–35.
122 Quoted in Lehmann, "Deutsche Wald," 195.
123 Schama, *Landscape and Memory*, 120.
124 Claus Hecking, "Was wurde eigentlich aus dem Waldsterben?" *Spiegel*, January 3, 2015, www.spiegel.de/wissenschaft/natur/umweltschutz-was-wurde-aus-dem-waldsterben-a-1009580.html.
125 Hayman, *Trees*, 110.
126 Wilson, *German Forest*, 15.
127 Quoted in Imort, "Forestopia," 1.

CHAPTER TWO

1 In 1986, Kurt Allgeier described a fourteen-hundred-year-old oak near Erle, North Rhine-Westphalia, in *Die Heilkraft der Bäume: Alte Weisheiten und neue Erkenntnisse* (Munich: Wilhelm Heyne Verlag, 1986), 146.
2 The category *Nationales Naturdenkmal* was established in March 2010 as part of the Federal Nature Conservation Act (*Gesetz über Naturschutz und Landschaftspflege* (*Bundesnaturschutzgesetz—BNatSchG*), section 24 *Nationalparke, Nationale Naturmonumente*). It reads: "National nature monuments are areas that have been designated in a legally binding manner and that 1. for reasons of science, natural history, cultural history or national heritage, and 2. because of their rarity, special characteristics or beauty are of outstanding importance. National nature monuments are to be protected in the same manner as nature conservation areas."
3 "Die Eichen zu Ivenack," *Die Gartenlaube* 34 (1895): 580.
4 Trees—for example, May trees (or Maypoles), Christmas trees, and birth trees—still

play an important role in many German and European customs. See James Frazer, chapter 10 of *The Golden Bough: A Study in Magic and Religion* (New York: Collier Books, 1963), for a discussion of the relics of tree worship in modern Europe.

5 See Eugen Mogk, *Germanische Religionsgeschichte und Mythologie: Die Götter, Dämonen, Orakel, Zauber- und Totenkulte der Germanen* (Leipzig: Bohmeier, 2010); and Friedrich von der Leyen, *Die Götter der Germanen* (Munich: C. H. Bech'sche Verlagsbuchhandlung, 1938).
6 Albrecht Lehmann, "Einführung," in *Der Wald—Ein deutscher Mythos? Perspektiven eines Kulturthemas*, ed. Albrecht Lehmann and Klaus Schriewer (Berlin: Dietrich Reimer Verlag, 2000), 12.
7 Rainer Guldin, *Politische Landschaften: Zum Verhältnis von Raum und nationaler Identität* (Bielefeld, Germany: transcript Verlag, 2014), 98.
8 Richard Bradley, *The Significance of Monuments: On the Shaping of Human Experience in Neolithic and Bronze Age Europe* (London: Routledge, 1998), 80–81.
9 Johannes Baptista Friedreich, *Die Symbolik und Mythologie der Natur* (Würzburg: Verlag der Stahel'schen Buch- und Kunsthandlung, 1859), 169. Friedreich quotes here the poem "Baum und Bach" from Friedrich von Sallet.
10 Bernd Weyergraf, *Waldungen: Die Deutschen und ihr Wald* (Berlin: Akademie der Künste, 1987), 142.
11 Oswald Spengler, *The Decline of the West*, vol. 1, trans. Charles Francis Atkinson (New York: Knopf, 1926), 396.
12 Simon Schama, *Landscape and Memory* (New York: Knopf, 1995), 83.
13 Walter Benjamin, "The Work of Art in the Age of Mechanical Reproduction," in *Illuminations*, ed. Hannah Arendt, trans. Harry Zohn (New York: Schocken Books, 1968), 220.
14 Benjamin, "Work of Art," 221–23.
15 Benjamin, "Work of Art," 222; Walter Benjamin, "On Some Motifs in Baudelaire," in *Illuminations*, 188.
16 Andrew Benjamin, "The Decline of Art: Benjamin's Aura," *Oxford Art Journal* 9, no. 2 (1986): 33.
17 Émile Durkheim, *The Elementary Forms of Religious Life*, trans. Karen E. Fields (New York: The Free Press, 1995), 237–38.
18 Rudi Beiser, *Baum and Mensch: Heilkraft, Mythen, und Kulturgeschichte unserer Bäume* (Stuttgart: Eugen Ulmer KG, 2017), 164.
19 Durkheim, *Elementary Forms*, 131.
20 Paul Reinhold Wagler, *Die Eiche in alter und neuer Zeit: Ein mythologisch-kulturgeschichtliche Studie*, part 2 (Berlin: Verlag von S. Calvary, 1891), 41.
21 Paul Wagler argues that the early custom of entering the oak grove only with bound hands was the precursor to folding one's hands during Christian prayer (Wagler, *Die Eiche*, 41). This conflicts, of course, with other theories that cite Jewish, Roman, Buddhist, or Hindu customs as a model for Christian practice.
22 Wagler cites both Jakob Grimm's *Weistümer-Sammlung* and Georg Ludwig von Maurer's *Geschichte der Markverfassung*.
23 Frazer, *Golden Bough*, 127.
24 Wagler, *Die Eiche*, 42.
25 Durkheim, *Elementary Forms*, 208.
26 Durkheim, *Elementary Forms*, 208.

27 Durkheim, *Elementary Forms*, 238, 272.
28 Durkheim, *Elementary Forms*, 91.
29 Durkheim, *Elementary Forms*, 231–32.
30 Durkheim, *Elementary Forms*, 230.
31 Albrecht Lehmann, "Der Deutsche Wald," in *Deutsche Erinnerungsorte*, vol. 3, ed. Etienne François and Hagen Schulze (Munich: C. H. Beck, 2001), 191–92.
32 Viktor Rydberg, *Investigations into Germanic Mythology*, vol. 2, part 2, *Germanic Mythology*, trans. William P. Reaves (New York: iUniverse, 2004), 10.
33 Carole M. Cusack, *The Sacred Tree: Ancient and Medieval Manifestations* (Newcastle upon Tyne: Cambridge Scholars, 2011), 12.
34 Cusack, *Sacred Tree*, 13.
35 Bruce Lincoln, *Theorizing Myth: Narrative, Ideology, and Scholarship* (Chicago: University of Chicago Press, 1999), 147.
36 Hermann Hesse, *Bäume: Betrachtungen und Gedichte* (Frankfurt am Main: Insel Taschenbuch, 2020), 19, 23.
37 Cusack, *Sacred Tree*, 151.
38 Cusack, *Sacred Tree*, xv, 1.
39 According to myth, in the Mesopotamian paradise called Dilmun (similar to Eden), the god of wisdom, Enki, planted a Tree of Life, which was protected by the gods Shamash and Tammmuz (Cusack, *Sacred Tree*, 24).
40 E. O. James, "The Tree of Life," *Folklore* 79, no. 4 (Winter 1968): 241.
41 Don Cupitt, *The World to Come* (London: SCM Press, 1982), 29.
42 Ernst Cassirer, *Language and Myth*, trans. Susanne K. Langer (New York: Dover, 1953), 5.
43 Cassirer, *Language and Myth*, 5.
44 Cassierer, *Language and Myth*, 9.
45 Chapter 7, Snorri Sturluson, *The Younger Edda; Also Called Snorre's Edda, or The Prose Edda*, trans. Rasmus Björn Anderson, Project Gutenberg eBook, July 31, 2006 [eBook #18947], www.gutenberg.org/cache/epub/18947/pg18947-images.html.
46 Chapter 12, Sturluson, *Younger Edda*.
47 Chapter 7, Sturluson, *Younger Edda*.
48 The earliest evidence of Germanic pagan practice comes from archeological findings dating from the Iron Age (400 BCE and later); Rudolf Simek, "Continental Germanic Religion," in *The Handbook of Religions in Ancient Europe*, ed. Christensen Lisbeth Bredholt, Olav Hammer, and David A. Warburton (Durham, UK: Acumen, 2013), 291.
49 Cusack, *Sacred Tree*, 19.
50 Scholars argue that the concept of the forest in German thought possesses the characteristics of a myth (Lehmann, "Einführung," 10). Bernd-A. Rusinek focuses on the use of the forest in National Socialism to argue that in German language and culture, the concept of the forest qualifies as a myth; Rusinek, "'Wald und Baum in der arisch-germanischen Geistes- und Kulturgeschichte'—Ein Forschungsprojekt des 'Ahnenerbe' der SS 1937–1945," in *Der Wald—Ein deutscher Mythos? Perspektiven eines Kulturthemas*, ed. Albrecht Lehmann and Klaus Schriewer (Berlin: Dietrich Reimer Verlag, 2000), 267–70.
51 Anthony D. Smith, *The Ethnic Origins of Nations* (Oxford: B. Blackwell, 1988), 183.
52 *Lebensstichwort* may be translated as "catchword" or "life cue." Dean Krouk settles

on "cue to go on living"; Krouk, "Forest Fictions: Thomas Bernhard's *Holzfällen* and Henrik Ibsen's *Vildanden*," *Scandinavian Studies* 86, no. 2 (Summer 2014): 143–44.
53 Schriewer chooses the term "syndrome" in reference to the work of Hans Paul Bahrdt, who uses the phrase "Vorstellungs-, Empfindungs- und Verhaltenssyndrom" to describe a pattern of forest perception typical among Germans; Bahrdt, *Umwelterfahrung: Soziologische Betrachtungen über den Beitrag des Subjekts zur Konstitution von Umwelt* (Munich: Nymphenburger Verlag, 1974), 67.
54 Klaus Schriewer, "Aspekte des Naturbewußtseins. Zur Differenzierung des 'Syndroms Deutscher Wald,'" in Lehmann and Schriewer, *Der Wald* 70–71, 73.
55 Schriewer, "Aspekte des Naturbewußtseins," 79.
56 Weyergraf, *Waldungen*, 244. "Das deutsche Volk ist von Haus aus ein Waldvolk, und immer noch spiegelt sich diese Herkunft im Grundzug seines Wesens ab. Die Baumverehrung der Germanen, der Waldglaube . . . mit einem Worte die Seelenverfassung, die die Umgebung, die Waldmasse prägte, sie lebt im vererbten Blute fort."
57 Albrecht Lehmann, *Von Menschen und Bäumen: Die Deutschen und ihr Wald* (Hamburg: Rowohl Verlag, 1999), 11. The concept of *Waldsterben*, believed to be caused by air pollution and acid rain, became a key political issue in Germany during the early 1980s and received extensive media coverage. See Franz-Josef Brüggemeier, "Waldsterben: The Construction and Deconstruction of an Environmental Problem," in *Nature in German History*, ed. Christof Mauch (New York: Berghahn Books, 2004), 119–31.
58 Lehmann, *Von Menschen und Bäumen*, 101.
59 *Künstlerspende für den deutschen Wald*, organized by the *Gesellschaft zur Förderung der forstlichen Forschung und des forstlichen Hochschulunterrichtes in Mitteldeutschland* (Dresden). The participating painters and graphic artists assembled and donated a portfolio of works titled "Für den deutschen Wald" ("For the German Forest"), the proceeds of which would support the sponsoring society.
60 Weyergraf, *Waldungen*, 291–92.
61 Germany lost 13 percent of its European territory as a result of the 1919 Treaty of Versailles to France, Belgium, Denmark, Poland, Czechoslovakia, and Lithuania.
62 Lehmann, "Deutsche Wald," 189–90.
63 Thomas M. Lekan, *Imagining the Nation in Nature: Landscape Preservation and German Identity, 1885-1945* (Cambridge, MA: Harvard University Press, 2004), 6–7.
64 Wilhelm Heinrich Riehl, *Land und Leute* (Stuttgart: J. G. Cotta, 1854), 34.
65 Riehl, *Land und Leute*, 22. "Ein Volk muss absterben, wenn es nicht mehr zurückgreifen kann, zu den Hintersassen in den Wäldern, um sich bei ihnen neue Kraft des 'natürlichen, rohen Volkstumes zu holen.'" See also Guldin on Riehl and his vision of the *Urwald* as a source of renewal and regeneration for a *Volk* in need of *Lebensenergie* (life energy). Riehl declares that even if the German *Volk* no longer needs the wood of the forest to keep it warm, the Germanic race will rely even more so on the forest: "zur Erwärmung seines inwendigen Menschen" (Guldin, *Politische Landschaften*, 102–3).
66 Conrad Ferdinand Meyer, "Das Heiligtum": "Waldnacht. Urmächt'ge Eichen, unter die / Des Blitzes greller Strahl geleuchtet nie!"
67 Beiser, *Baum and Mensch*, 96.
68 Allgeier, *Heilkraft der Bäume*, 149–53.
69 Beiser, *Baum and Mensch*, 103.

70 Beiser, *Baum and Mensch*, 101–2.
71 Beiser, *Baum and Mensch*, 102.
72 Allgeier, *Heilkraft der Bäume*, 95–96.
73 Beiser, *Baum and Mensch*, 165–67.
74 Beiser, *Baum and Mensch*, 166.
75 Ken Dowden, *European Paganism: The Realities of Cult from Antiquity to the Middle Ages* (London: Routledge, 2000), 37.
76 Beiser, *Baum and Mensch*, 102.
77 In August 1831, seven months before his death at the age of eighty-two, Goethe traveled to Martinroda in Thuringia to say goodbye to an oak tree he had known for almost sixty years. Just two days before, Goethe had introduced the oak to his grandchildren, much as one might introduce one's progeny to valued friends (Lehmann, *Von Menschen und Bäumen*, 98).
78 Johann Wolfgang von Goethe, *Goethe's Botanical Writings*, trans. Bertha Mueller (Honolulu: University of Hawaii Press, 1952), 13, 23.
79 Goethe, *Goethe's Botanical Writings* 25–26.
80 Weyergraf, *Waldungen*, 188.
81 Gerda Gollwitzer, *Bäume: Bilder und Texte aus drei Jahrtausenden* (Herrsching, Germany: Schuler Verlagsgesellschaft, 1980), 15.
82 Margit Stadlober, *Der Wald in Malerei und Graphik des Donaustils* (Vienna: Bohlau, 2006), 107, quoted in Guldin, *Politische Landschaften*, 112.
83 Quoted in Lehmann, "Einführung," 11. See also Jacob Grimm, *Deutsche Mythologie*, vol. 2, 3rd ed. (Göttingen: Dieterichsche Buchhandlung, 1844), 613–60, for a description of trees that bleed and cry when struck.
84 Lehmann, *Von Menschen und Bäumen*, 98.
85 Andrea Wulf, *The Invention of Nature: Alexander von Humboldt's New World* (New York: Vintage, 2016), 2, 5.
86 Alexander von Humboldt, *Views of Nature*, ed. Stephen T. Jackson and Laura Dassow Walls, trans. Mark W. Person (Chicago: University of Chicago Press, 2014), 158.
87 Humboldt, *Views of Nature*, 159.
88 Humboldt, *Views of Nature*, 159–60.
89 Humboldt, *Views of Nature*, 161.
90 Weyergraf, *Waldungen*, 180.
91 Weyergraf, *Waldungen*, 138.
92 Jeffrey K. Wilson, *The German Forest: Nature, Identity, and the Contestation of a National Symbol, 1871–1914*, German and European Studies (Toronto: University of Toronto Press, 2012), 18.
93 Wilson, *German Forest*, 5.
94 Wilson, *German Forest*, 19–20, 47. Wilson argues that the romantic idealization of the German forest was a bourgeois and aristocratic, rather than working-class, phenomenon (Wilson, *German Forest*, 46–47).
95 Dowden, *European Paganism*, 35.
96 Dowden, *European Paganism*, 70.
97 Dowden, *European Paganism*, 118.
98 Cusack, *Sacred Tree*, 139.
99 *Marienlinden* were also sites of pilgrimage for the devout, and sacred statues and altars were often fashioned from the sacred linden wood (known as "*Lignum sanctum*") (Beiser, *Baum and Mensch*, 162–63).

100 Achim Timmermann, *Memory and Redemption: Public Monuments and the Making of Late Medieval Landscape*, Architectura Medii Aevi, 8 (Turnhout, Belgium: Brepols, 2017), 31, 280–82.
101 "Ich trat in einen heilig düstern / Eichwald, da hört ich leis und lind / Ein Bächlein unter Blumen flüstern, / Wie das Gebet von einem Kind. / Und mich ergriff ein süßes Grauen, / Es rauscht der Wald geheimnisvoll, / Als möcht er mir was anvertrauen, / Das noch mein Herz nicht wissen soll; / Als möcht er heimlich mir entdecken, / Was Gottes Liebe sinnt und will: / Doch schien er plötzlich zu erschrecken / Vor Gottes Näh–und wurde still."
102 Johann Gottfried Herder, *Werke. Erster Theil. Gedichte*, ed. Heinrich Düntzer (Berlin: Hempel, 1879), 152–53.
103 Spengler, *Decline of the West*, 396.
104 Spengler, *Decline of the West*, 396.
105 Spengler, *Decline of the West*, 396.
106 Lehmann, *Von Menschen und Bäumen*, 35.
107 *Epigraph*: Lehmann, *Von Menschen und Bäumen*, 35. The German *völkisch* movement was an ethnic, nationalistic, antisemitic, and racist movement that thrived from the late nineteenth century to the end of the Nazi era. Albrecht Lehmann states that mythic, romantic views of the forest (*die Waldromantik*) and the fear of forest atrophy (*Waldsterben*) are inextricably linked (Lehmann, "Einführung," 10). See also Kate Connolly, "German Far-Right Extremists Tap into Green Movement for Support," *Guardian*, April 28, 2012, www.theguardian.com/world/2012/apr/28/germany-far-right-green-movement.
108 Quoted in Konrad H. Jarausch, "Normalisierung oder Re-Nationalisierung? Zur Umdeutung der deutschen Vergangenheit," *Geschichte und Gesellschaft* 21, no. 4 (October–December 1995): 583.
109 Rudolf Düesberg, *Der Wald als Erzieher: Nach den Verhältnissen des preußischen Ostens Geschildert* (Berlin: Verlagsbuchhandlung Paul Parey, 1910), 4.
110 Wilhelm Heinrich, *Die Naturgeschichte des Volkes als Grundlage einer deutschen Sozial-Politik*, vol. 4 (Stuttgart: Cotta, 1907), 55.
111 Michael Imort, "A Sylvan People: Wilhelmine Forestry and the Forest as a Symbol of Germandom," in *Germany's Nature: Cultural Landscapes and Environmental History*, ed. Thomas Lekan and Thomas Zeller (New Brunswick, NJ: Rutgers University Press, 2005), 60.
112 Michael Imort, "Forestopia: The Use of the Forest Landscape in Naturalizing National Socialist Ideologies of Volk, Race, and Lebensraum, 1918–1945" (PhD diss., Queen's University, 2000), 116.
113 Quoted in Imort, "Sylvan People," 60.
114 Weyergraf, *Waldungen*, 244.
115 Quoted in Szilvia Odenwald-Varga, *"Volk" bei Otto van Bismarck: Eine historisch-semantische Analyse anhand von Bedeutungen, Konzepten und Topoi* (Berlin: De Gruyter, 2009) 153.
116 Imort, "Forestopia," 3. Imort demonstrates the role played by foresters in creating and spreading images of and ideas about the forest (including German superiority, resilience, and lost greatness), which were used for political purposes between 1918 and 1945. Foresters created a "Forestopia"—"an organicist blueprint for a new, *völkisch* Germany that was to be modelled on the meta-organism of the forest" (Imort, "Forestopia," 5).

117 See Bernd-A. Rusinek's discussion of the "Wald und Baum" (forest and tree) project, led by Dr. Walther Wüst and conducted by the Nazi research institute "Das Ahnenerbe" (Rusinek, "'Wald und Baum'").
118 Mary Beth Stein, "Wilhelm Heinrich Riehl and the Scientific-Literary Formation of 'Volkskunde,'" *German Studies Review* 24, no. 3 (October 2001): 489.
119 Richard Hayman, *Trees: Woodlands and Western Civilization* (London: Hambledon, 2003), 107.
120 Guldin, *Politische Landschaften*, 101.
121 Translated in Hermann Glaser, *The Cultural Roots of National Socialism* (New York: Routledge, 1978), 91.
122 Weyergraf, *Waldungen*, 280–81.
123 Lehmann, *Von Menschen und Bäumen*, 33.
124 For example, Franz von Mammen's book *Der Wald als Erzieher: Eine volkswirtschaftlich-ethnische Parallele zwischen Baum und Mensch und zwischen Wald und Volk* (1934) and Franz Heske's *German Forestry* (1938).
125 Imort, "Forestopia," 368. The scholarship of Karl Rebel (*Der Wald in der Deutscher Kultur*, 1934) and Julius Kober (*Deutscher Wald—Deutsches Volk*, 1935) are two examples from among many books published in the 1930s promoting *völkisch* views of the forest (Hayman, *Trees*, 108).
126 Guldin, *Politische Landschaften*, 118.
127 Robert G. Lee and Sabine Wilke, "Forest as *Volk: Ewiger Wald* and the Religion of Nature in the Third Reich," *Journal of Social and Ecological Boundaries* 1, no. 1 (Spring 2005): 23.
128 Imort, "Forestopia," 261.
129 Lee and Wilke, "Forest as *Volk*," 38.
130 Eberhard Schmidt, *The Hitler Conspirator: The Story of Kurt Freiherr von Plettenberg and Stauffenberg's Valkyrie Plot to Kill the Führer*, trans. Cordula Weschkun (Barnsley, UK: Frontline Books, 2017), 82.
131 "Wald und Volk in nationalsozialistischer Auffassung haben viel Wesenverwandtes. Auch das Volk ist eine Lebensgemeinschaft, ein großes, organisches ewiges Wesen... Ewiger Wald und ewiges Volk gehören zusammen" (quoted in Lehmann, "Deutsche Wald," 192). See also Guldin, *Politische Landschaften*, 116–18.
132 Elias Canetti, *Crowds and Power*, trans. Carol Stewart (New York: Macmillan, 1984), 173–74.
133 Guldin, *Politische Landschaften*, 114.
134 See Hans Dickel, "Zerstörte Heimat: Wald-Motive in der deutschen Nachkriegskunst," in Lehmann and Schriewer, *Wald*.
135 Publius Quinctilius Varus, 46 BC–9 AD, the Roman general and politician who lost three legions of Roman soldiers against Germanic tribes led by Arminius during the Battle of the Teutoburg Forest (Hermanns-Schlacht). Varus took his own life during the battle.
136 I would like to thank Odilia van Roij for helping me obtain this image.
137 Schama, *Landscape and Memory*, 127–28.
138 Schama points out that *Varus* quotes Caspar David Friedrich's iconic painting *The Chasseur in the Forest*, but with "suicidal trees"—that is, "scraggly, weather-beaten trees"—replacing Friedrich's "sacred fir forest" and the name "Varus" replacing the French soldier (Schama, *Landscape and Memory*, 127).

139 Matthew Rampley, "In Search of Cultural History: Anselm Kiefer and the Ambivalence of Modernism," *Oxford Art Journal* 23, no. 1 (2000), 76.
140 Weyergraf, *Waldungen*, 246–47.
141 See Guldin for a discussion of Prigann's installation *Die Falle* (1987) as a site of ambush and confrontation with German history (Guldin, *Politische Landschaften*, 121).
142 Dieter Appelt, "Abhörung des Waldrandes," accessed November 23, 2023, www.extended-compositions.de/?page_id=913&lang=en_US.
143 Guldin, *Politische Landschaften*, 112.
144 Dieter Borchmeyer, "A Very Special Relationship, Germans and Their Forest." *German Times*, April 2019, www.german-times.com/a-very-special-relationship-germans-and-their-forest/.

CHAPTER THREE

1 "In ihren Wipfeln rauscht die Welt, ihre Wurzeln ruhen im Unendlichen," Hermann Hesse, *Bäume: Betrachtungen und Gedichte* (Frankfurt am Main: Insel Taschenbuch, 2020), 9–11.
2 Heinrich Heine, Über Deutschtland—*Elementargeister und Dämonen* (Hamburg, 1868; Projekt Gutenberg-DE), Band 7, https://www.projekt-gutenberg.org/heine/element1/element1.html.
3 Erich Schmidt, "Theodor Fontane, gehalten bei der Enthüllung des Wieseschen Denkmals in Neuruppin am 8. Juni 1907," *Deutsche Rundschau* 132 (July–September 1907): 189. Another example of the use of *Lebensmal* appears in the phrase "seal of life" in a German rendering of Solomon Gabirol's synagogue hymn "Judge of All the Earth," *A Rabbinic Anthology*, ed. C. G. Montefiore and H. J. M. Loewe (New York: Cambridge University Press, 2012), 308.
4 Cited in Gary Shapiro, "The Meaning of Our Confederate 'Monuments,'" *New York Times*, May 15, 2017, www.nytimes.com/2017/05/15/opinion/the-meaning-of-our-confederate-monuments.html#:~:text=Why%20do%20we%20name%20some,embody%20the%20myths%20of%20beginnings.
5 Ursula K. Heise, *Imagining Extinction: The Cultural Meanings of Endangered Species* (Chicago: University of Chicago Press, 2016), 97.
6 "Der Anblick alter Bäume hat etwas Großartiges, Imponierendes; die Beschädigung dieser Naturdenkmäler wird daher auch in Ländern, denen es an Kunstdenkmälern fehlt, streng bestraft." Alexander von Humboldt, *Reise in die Äquinoktial-Gegenden des Neuen Kontinents*, vol. 1, ed. Ottmar Ette (Frankfurt am Main: Insel, 1991), 623.
7 Thomas M. Lekan, *Imagining the Nation in Nature: Landscape Preservation and German Identity, 1885–1945* (Cambridge, MA: Harvard University Press, 2004), 21.
8 Jeffrey K. Wilson, *The German Forest: Nature, Identity, and the Contestation of a National Symbol, 1871–1914*. German and European Studies (Toronto: University of Toronto Press, 2012), 32.
9 Act on Nature Conservation and Landscape Management (Federal Nature Conservation Act—BNatSchG) of July 29, 2009.
10 *Deutscher Bund Heimatschutz*, the German Association for Homeland Protection, was founded by Ernst Rudorff (1840–1916).

11 Lekan, *Imagining the Nation*, 4.
12 Lekan, *Imagining the Nation*, 4.
13 Dieter Borchmeyer, "A Very Special Relationship, Germans and Their Forest," *German Times*, April 2019, www.german-times.com/a-very-special-relationship-germans-and-their-forest/.
14 Lekan, *Imagining the Nation*, 7.
15 Wilson, *German Forest*, 32–36.
16 See the website of the Deutsches Baumarchiv, www.deutschesbaumarchiv.de/wir-ueber-uns/.
17 Wilson, *German Forest*, 3.
18 Adolf Kröner, ed., "Die Kaditzer Linde," *Die Gartenlaube: Deutschlands Merkwürdige Bäume* 4 (1890): 130.
19 Rudi Beiser, *Baum and Mensch: Heilkraft, Mythen, und Kulturgeschichte unserer Bäume* (Stuttgart: Eugen Ulmer KG, 2017), 164.
20 Ernst Ziel, "Die tausendjährige Linde in Puch bei Fürstenfeld," *Die Gartenlaube: Deutschlands Merkwürdige Bäume* 18 (1883): 300.
21 Hugo Kruskopf, "Die Priorlinde an der Kluse bei Dahl a.d. Volme," *Die Gartenlaube: Deutschlands Merkwürdige Bäume* 19 (1896): 324.
22 Borchmeyer, "Into the Woods."
23 Karl von Seeger, *Das Denkmal des Weltkriegs* (Stuttgart: Hugo Matthaes Verlagsbuchhandlung, 1930), 28.
24 Ken Dowden, *European Paganism: The Realities of Cult from Antiquity to the Middle Ages* (London: Routledge, 2000), 107, 110.
25 Cornelius Tacitus, "Germany," in *Voyages and Travels Ancient and Modern*, The Harvard Classics Series, trans. Thomas Gordon (New York: P. F. Collier & Son, 1910), 98.
26 Bernd Weyergraf, *Waldungen: Die Deutschen und ihr Wald* (Berlin: Akademie der Künste, 1987), 179.
27 Dowden, *European Paganism*, 27.
28 Dowden, *European Paganism*, 96.
29 Mircea Eliade, *The Sacred and the Profane: The Nature of Religion*, trans. William R. Trask (New York: Harcourt, Brace and World, 1959), 10.
30 Dowden, *European Paganism*, 94.
31 Robert Pogue Harrison, *Forests: The Shadow of Civilization* (Chicago: University of Chicago Press, 1992), 6.
32 Harrison, *Forests*, 10–11.
33 Dowden, *European Paganism*, 276–77.
34 Almost four hundred names appear on a list of supporters and benefactors in *Deutsche Heldenhaine*, primarily from the educated middle-classes, including teachers, doctors, professors, pastors, civil servants, mayors, and officers; Gerhard Schneider, "Heldenhaine als Visualisierung der Volksgemeinschaft im Ersten Weltkrieg," in *Die visuelle Dimension des Historischen: Hans-Jürgen Pandel zum 60. Geburtstag*, ed. Gerhard Schneider (Schwalbach am Taunus: Wochenschau Verlag, 2002), 51.
35 Association for Germany's Heroes' Groves
36 Gert Gröning and Uwe Schneider, "Naturmystifizierung und germanische Mythologie—Die Heldenhaine, ein nationalistisches Denkmalskonzept aus dem ersten Weltkrieg," in *Gartenkultur und Nationale Identität: Strategien nationaler*

und regionaler Identitätsstiftung in der deutschen Gartenkultur, ed. Gert Gröning and Uwe Schneider (Worms: Wernersche Verlagsgesellschaft, 2001), 94–95.
37 Gröning and Schneider, "Naturmystifizierung," 95.
38 Willy Lange, "Vorwort," in *Deutsche Heldenhaine*, ed. Willy Lange (Leipzig: J. J. Weber, 1915), 3; Willy Lange, "Der Wert der Heldenhaine für die Siedlungskultur," in *Deutsche Heldenhaine*, 18.
39 Weyergraf, *Waldungen*, 286.
40 Johannes Speck, "Heldenhaine und Jugendpflege," in *Deutsche Heldenhaine*, 27.
41 Willy Pastor, "Die Bedeutung des Ringes im Heldenhain," in *Deutsche Heldenhaine*, 14.
42 Lange, "Der Wert der Heldenhaine," 19; Willy Lange, "Allerlei Einwände und ihre Erwiderung," in *Deutsche Heldenhaine*, 67.
43 Stefan Goebel, *The Great War and Medieval Memory: War, Remembrance, and Medievalism in Britain and Germany, 1914–1940* (New York: Cambridge University Press, 2007), 78–79.
44 Willy Lange, "Die leitenden Gestaltungsgedanken für die Heldenhaine," in *Deutsche Heldenhaine*, 5, 7. "Siegfried" refers to the legendary hero of Germanic and Norse mythology (of the *Niebelungenlied* and *Poetic Edda*).
45 Lange, "Die leitenden Gestaltungsgedanken," 6–7; Lange, "Der Wert der Heldenhaine," 19; Speck, "Heldenhaine," 27.
46 Lange, "Der Wert der Heldenhaine," 19; Speck, "Heldenhaine," 27.
47 Goebel, *Great War and Medieval Memory*, 77.
48 Speck, "Heldenhaine," 20–23, 26.
49 Lange, "Die leitenden Gestaltungsgedanken," 7.
50 Lange, "Die leitenden Gestaltungsgedanken," 9–10.
51 Lange, "Die leitenden Gestaltungsgedanken," 8.
52 Lange, "Allerlei Einwände," 69; Willy Lange, "Heldeneichen und Friedenslinden," in *Deutsche Heldenhaine*, 80. Gert Groening refers to the linden in its honored position in the *Heldenhain* as a "tree of freedom from foreign suppression"; Gert Groening, "Nature Mystification and the Example of the 'Heroes' Groves in Early Twentieth-Century Germany," in *A History of Groves*, ed. Jan Woudstra and Colin Roth (New York: Routledge, 2018), 186.
53 Lange, "Die leitenden Gestaltungsgedanken," 7–8.
54 Lange, "Die leitenden Gestaltungsgedanken," 8.
55 Lange, "Vorwort," 3; Lange, "Der Wert der Heldenhaine," 18; Willy Lange, "Die Herstellung der Heldenhaine," in *Deutsche Heldenhaine*, 47.
56 Lange, "Die Herstellung," 34.
57 Lange, "Die leitenden Gestaltungsgedanken," 8, Pastor, "Die Bedeutung," 15.
58 Lange, "Vorwort," 3.
59 Lange, "Die leitenden Gestaltungsgedanken," 6; Lange, "Allerlei Einwände," 67; Lange, "Heldeneichen," 78, 80.
60 Pastor, "Die Bedeutung," 13.
61 Goebel, *Great War and Medieval Memory*, 77.
62 Goebel, *Great War and Medieval Memory*, 28–29.
63 Alfred Möller, "Forstliche Bemerkungen zur Pflanzung von Eiche und Linde," in *Deutsche Heldenhaine*, 53–54.
64 Lange, "Vorwort," 3.

65 Speck, "Heldenhaine," 26; Felix Freiherr von Stenglin, "Der Widerhall von draußen und daheim," in *Deutsche Heldenhaine*, 81.
66 Paul Reinhold Wagler, *Die Eiche in alter und neuer Zeit: Ein mythologisch-kulturgeschichtliche Studie*, part 2 (Berlin: Verlag von S. Calvary, 1891), 68–69.
67 Stenglin, "Der Widerhall von draußen und daheim," in *Deutsche Heldenhaine*, 82.
68 Schneider, "Heldenhaine, 50–51.
69 Gröning and Schneider, "Naturmystifizierung," 97.
70 Goebel, *Great War and Medieval Memory*, 77.
71 They are too numerous to catalogue here: a few examples include Eberswalde, Nielebock, Meyenburg, Hahn, Stuttgart-Degerloch, Schaafheim, Gross Behnitz, Niederschönhausen-Nordend, Warnau, Hiddesen, Theuma, Melle, Würgau, Lübz, Upleward, Erfurt, and other towns and villages throughout Lower Saxony, Schleswig-Holstein, Bavaria, North Rhine–Westphalia, Brandenburg, and Thuringia.
72 Schneider, "Heldenhaine," 63.
73 See the 2017 article "Heldengedanken in Süddeutschland," Der Dritte Weg, https://der-dritte-weg.info/2017/11/heldengedenken-in-sueddeutschland/.
74 Rolf Ziehm, "Vom Helden- zum Opfergedenken," *sh:z* (Schleswig-Holsteinischer Zeitungsverlag), November 9, 2012, https://www.shz.de/lokales/neumuenster/artikel/vom-helden-zum-opfergedenken-40882284.
75 Émile Durkheim, *The Elementary Forms of Religious Life*, trans. Karen E. Fields (New York: The Free Press, 1995), 91.
76 Lange, "Die leitenden Gestaltungsgedanken," 6. *Reformationsbäume* (trees planted in honor of the Reformation) were also common; Albrecht Lehmann, *Von Menschen und Bäumen: Die Deutschen und ihr Wald* (Hamburg: Rowohl Verlag, 1999), 127.
77 See, for example, "Die Eiche," by Annemarie Hürlimann, in Weyergraf, *Waldungen*, 62–68; Alfred Detering, *Die Bedeutung der Eiche seit der Vorzeit* (Leipzig: Curt Kapitzsch, 1939).
78 H. R. Ellis Davidson, *Gods and Myths of the Viking Age* (New York: Bell, 1981), 191.
79 "Frei und unerschütterlich / wachsen unsere Eichen / Mit dem Schmuck der grünen Blätter / stehn sie fest in Sturm und Wetter / wanken nicht noch weichen. / Wie die Eichen himmelan/ trotz den Stürmen streben / wollen wir auch ihnen Gleichen / frei und fest wie deutsche Eichen / unser Haupt erheben. / Darum sei der Eichenbaum / unser BUNDESZEICHEN / daß in Thaten / und Gedanken / wir nicht schwanken oder wanken / niemals muthlos weichen."
80 Hürlimann, "Die Eiche," 65.
81 Hürlimann, "Die Eiche," 67.
82 James E. Young, *The Texture of Memory. Holocaust Memorials and Meaning* (New Haven: Yale University Press, 1993), 73–74.
83 Klaus Neumann notes that the original name was dropped because "Weimar's literary establishment had protested against the name first chosen 'because Ettersberg is connected with the life of the poet, Goethe'"; Klaus Neumann, "Goethe, Buchenwald, and the New Germany," *German Politics & Society* 17, no. 1 (Spring 1999): 56.
84 Neumann, "Goethe," 57.
85 Theodore Ziolkowski, "Das Treffen in Buchenwald oder Der vergegenwärtigte Goethe," *Modern Language Studies* 3, no. 1 (Spring 2001): 134–35.
86 Beiser, *Baum and Mensch*, 163.

87 Beiser, *Baum and Mensch*, 159.
88 Beiser, *Baum and Mensch*, 165.
89 Beiser, *Baum and Mensch*, 161.
90 *Minnesänger* were German-language poet-musicians of the twelfth and thirteenth centuries.
91 Beiser, *Baum and Mensch*, 164.
92 Beiser, *Baum and Mensch*, 164.
93 Saint Walpurgis Night—eve of the Christian feast day of Saint Walpurga.
94 Beiser, *Baum and Mensch*, 161, 164.
95 Alina M. Tenche-Constantinescu, C. Varan, F. Borlea, E. Madosa, and G. Szekely, "The Symbolism of the Linden Tree," *Journal of Horticulture, Forestry and Biotechnology* 19, no. 2 (2015): 239.
96 See Hans Dickel, "Zerstörte Heimat: Wald-Motive in der deutschen Nachkriegskunst," in *Der Wald—Ein deutscher Mythos? Perspektiven eines Kulturthemas*, ed. Albrecht Lehmann and Klaus Schriewer (Berlin: Dietrich Reimer Verlag, 2000).
97 Lehmann, *Von Menschen und Bäumen*, 99.
98 Lehmann, *Von Menschen und Bäumen*, 269–70.
99 Wilson, *German Forest*, 200.
100 Wilson, *German Forest*, 200–201.
101 According to the legend, Tannhäuser begged pardon for his sin of worshipping the goddess Venus from the Pope, who stuck his staff into the ground and declared that his staff would as soon blossom as Tannhäuser be forgiven. The staff indeed took root and bore leaves and blossoms, which the Pope discovered three days later.
102 Lehmann, *Von Menschen und Bäumen*, 127.
103 Lehmann, *Von Menschen und Bäumen*, 128–29.
104 Matthias Bäumler, "Denkmal für die Einheit," *Frankenpost*, December 2012, 7.
105 Theodor Lessing, "Deutsche Bäume," in *Ich warf eine Flaschenpost ins Eismeer der Geschichte: Essays und Feuilletons*, ed. Rainer Marwedel (Darmstadt: Luchterhand, 1986), 305.
106 Bäumler, "Denkmal für die Einheit," 7.
107 See the EXIT-Deutschland website at www.exit-deutschland.de.
108 Bäumler, "Denkmal für die Einheit," 7. For further information, see the website of the Schutzgemeinschaft Deutscher Wald (Association for the Protection of the German Forest) at www.sdw.de/fuer-den-wald/aktivitaeten-im-wald/einheitsdenkmal/.
109 For a list of memorials, see the website of the Schutzgemeinschaft Deutscher Wald at www.sdw.de/fuer-den-wald/aktivitaeten-im-wald/einheitsdenkmal.
110 Written communication with Werner Erhardt.
111 The winning proposal by Sebastian Letz (Milla & Partner) is a giant, rocking dish—an enormous, kinetic steel wing that will hold up to fourteen hundred people at a time, and requires about twenty participants to set the dish in motion. The bed of the monument will be engraved with the slogans of the 1989 revolution: "Wir sind das Volk" ("We are the People") and "Wir sind ein Volk" ("We are one people"). The Bürger in Bewegung (Citizens in Motion) monument was originally scheduled to be completed in 2013. After a series of delays, a new opening date of 2024 was set, but as reported in the *Berliner Morgenpost* on March 25, 2024, the monument's opening has yet again been delayed due to the bankruptcy of the construction

firm. See Thomas Schubert, "Rückschlag für Einheitswippe: Warum das Projekt stockt," *Berliner Morgenpost*, March 25, 2024, https://www.morgenpost.de/bezirke/mitte/article241969380/Rueckschlag-fuer-Einheitswippe-Warum-das-Projekt-stockt.html.
112 www.schultesfrank.de/portfolio_page/freiheits-und-einheitsdenkmal/.
113 Max Brod, *Tycho Brahe's Path to God*, trans. Felix Warren Crosse (Evanston, IL: Northwestern University Press, 2007), 71.

CHAPTER FOUR

1 *Steintänze* like these, from the pre-Roman Iron Age, were used to surround prehistoric burial mounds, but they also served as references to ancient grave architectural traditions and reveal what could be interpreted as a religious or political statement. Other interpretations suggest the association of such megaliths with "ancestors, the realm of the dead, religious deities, and the stones as creations of nature . . . [and] therefore . . . of great cosmological significance." Stone settings such as these, finally, "could signify the border between the world of the living and that of the dead"; Cornelius J. Holtorf, "The Life-Histories of Megaliths in Mecklenburg-Vorpommern (Germany)," special issue, The Past in the Past: The Reuse of Ancient Monuments, *World Archaeology* 30, no. 1 (June 1998): 31.
2 David Lowenthal, *The Past Is a Foreign Country* (Cambridge: Cambridge University Press, 1985), 4. Lowenthal quotes here L. P. Hartley and Sheridan Morley.
3 David Lowenthal, "Past Time, Present Place: Landscape and Memory," *Geographical Review* 65, no. 1 (January 1975): 2.
4 Lowenthal, *Past*, 55.
5 Lowenthal, *Past*, 19.
6 According to folklore, *Hünengräber* are so named because only giants could transport and stack the enormous stones making up the structures; Christian Fuhrmeister, "Erratische Steine: Die (politische) Bedeutung von Findlingen in den letzten 200 Jahren," Zentralinstitut für Kunstgeschichte, www.zikg.eu/personen/pdf/fuhrmeister-erratische-steine-die-politische-bedeutung-von-findlingen-in-den-letzten-200-jahren, 3.
7 Towers and columns dedicated to Otto von Bismarck during the late nineteenth and early twentieth centuries. The number of Bismarck towers—234, of which 165 still exist—in addition to Bismarck monuments in Berlin (Reinhold Begas, 1901), Hamburg (Hugo Lederer, 1906), and elsewhere testify to a "Bismarck cult" that began before Bismarck's death in 1898; Hans A. Pohlsander, *National Monuments and Nationalism in Nineteenth Century Germany*, New German-American Studies 31 (Bern: Peter Lang, 2008), 217, 226. Approximately 500 to 550 Bismarck monuments were erected in total. After the dissolution of the German Empire, seven additional Bismarck towers and columns were erected (Pohlsander, *National Monuments*, 218).
8 Christopher Evans, "Tradition and the Cultural Landscape: An Archeology of Place," *Archaeological Review from Cambridge* 4, no. 1 (1985): 85–91.
9 Richard Bradley, "Studying Monuments," in *Neolithic Studies: A Review of Some Current Research*, ed. Richard Bradley and J. Gardiner (Oxford: BAR, 1984), 62–63.

10 Bradley, "Studying Monuments," 63.
11 Émile Durkheim, *The Elementary Forms of Religious Life*, trans. Karen E. Fields (New York: The Free Press, 1995), 272.
12 Anthony D. Smith, *The Ethnic Origins of Nations* (Oxford: B. Blackwell, 1988), 15–16.
13 Smith, *Ethnic Origins*, 22.
14 Durkheim, *Elementary Forms*, 175.
15 Durkheim, *Elementary Forms*, 183.
16 Quoted in Robert Pogue Harrison, *Forests: The Shadow of Civilization* (Chicago: University of Chicago Press, 1992), 164.
17 Willy Lange, "Der Wert der Heldenhaine für die Siedlungskultur," in *Deutsche Heldenhaine*, ed. Willy Lange (Leipzig: J. J. Weber, 1915), 18–19.
18 Gert Groening, "Nature Mystification and the Example of the 'Heroes' Groves in Early Twentieth-Century Germany," in *A History of Groves*, ed. Jan Woudstra and Colin Roth (New York: Routledge, 2018), 186.
19 Harrison, *Forests*, 175.
20 Neanderthals also had burial customs but did not distinguish cemeteries from domestic spaces; Lisbeth Bredholt Christensen, Olav Hammer, and David A. Warburton, "Studying Prehistoric Religions," in *The Handbook of Religions in Ancient Europe*, ed. Lisbeth Bredholt Christensen, Olav Hammer, and David A. Warburton (London: Routledge, 2013), 16.
21 Christensen, Hammer, and Warburton, "Studying Prehistoric Religions," 15–16.
22 Richard Bradley, *The Significance of Monuments: On the Shaping of Human Experience in Neolithic and Bronze Age Europe* (London: Routledge, 1998), 10.
23 Bradley, *Significance of Monuments*, 68.
24 Charlotte Damm, "Religious Practices in Northern Europe 4000–2000 BCE," in *Handbook of Religions*, 64–65.
25 Bradley, *Significance of Monuments*, 68, 79–80, 163.
26 Bradley, *Significance of Monuments*, 80.
27 Holtorf, citing Ian Hodder, "The Narrative and Rhetoric of Material Culture Sequences," *World Archaeology* 25, no. 2 (1993), describes earthen (burial) mounds and surrounding stone enclosures as examples of elements "rhetorically referred to" in "material culture narratives"; these narratives are created in landscapes where later monuments refer to earlier (ancient) monuments (Holtorf, "Life-Histories," 31).
28 "Die Griechen haben eine Kultur von Marmor, die Deutschen sollten eine solche von Granit haben. Der Granit ist ein nordischer und germanischer Stein." Quoted in Meinhold Lurz, *Kriegerdenkmäler in Deutschland*, vol. 6, *Bundesrepublik* (Heidelberg: Esprint-Verlag, 1987), 209.
29 "Die Sage vom Teufelsstein," *Literatur Port: Ein Portal des Literarischen Colloquiums Berlin (LCB) und des Brandenburgischen Literaturbüros (BLB)*, accessed October 15, 2024, www.literaturport.de/literaturlandschaft/orte-berlinbrandenburg/text/die-sage-vom-teufelsstein/.
30 Many *Findlinge* have been dedicated to Schlageter, including a large memorial on the Luhberg peak near Peine, erected 1925, consisting of a megalith built of multiple *Findlinge*.
31 For example, the *Findling* dedicated to victims of Stalinism in Berlin by Willy Treichel, 1951.

32 The 1921 memorial to German writer and fallen World War I soldier Hermann Löns (1866–1914) stands on Lüneburg Heath near Müden, Lower Saxony. A *Findling* dedicated to Robert Haaß in 1908 stands in the Beiertheimer Wäldchen in Südweststadt (Karlsruhe), Baden-Württemberg.
33 Achim Timmermann, *Memory and Redemption: Public Monuments and the Making of Late Medieval Landscape*, Architectura Medii Aevi, 8 (Turnhout, Belgium: Brepols, 2017), 200.
34 Timmermann, *Memory and Redemption*, 202.
35 Timmermann, *Memory and Redemption*, 206.
36 Ken Dowden, *European Paganism: The Realities of Cult from Antiquity to the Middle Ages* (London: Routledge, 2000), 36, 61.
37 James Frazer, *The Golden Bough: A Study in Magic and Religion* (New York: Collier Books, 1963) 38.
38 Emmy Sachs, "On 'Steinalt,' 'Stockstill,' and Similar Formations," *Journal of English and Germanic Philology* 62 (1963): 595.
39 Sandy Viek, "Der mittelalterliche Altar als Rechtsstätte," *Mediaevistik* 17 (2004): 142n194.
40 Hans Hochenegg, "Das Zauberbüchlein eines Oberinntaler Bauern aus dem Beginn de Zwanzigsten Jahrhunderts," *Österreichische Zeitschrift für Volkskunde*, Neue Serie 27 (1973): 289.
41 Franz Wilhelm, "Ruhsteine—Dorfsteine—Gerichtssteine," *Zeitschrift für österreichische Volkskunde: Organ des Vereines österreichische Volkskunde in Wien*, ed. Michael Haberlandt (Vienna: Verlag des Vereins für österreichische Volkskunde, 1906), 131–32.
42 Ingrid Schmidt, *Hünengrab und Opferstein: Bodendenkmale auf der Insel Rügen* (Rostock: Hinstorff Verlag, 2001), 46–47.
43 Dowden notes that stones were worshipped by pagans in northern Lithuania as late as 1583 (Dowden, *European Paganism*, 64).
44 Fuhrmeister, "Erratische Steine," 1.
45 Fuhrmeister, "Erratische Steine," 7, 15. Fuhrmeister notes that this interpretation of *Findlinge* has increased their popularity in Germany in the last few decades.
46 Although rarer, *Findlinge* have also been used to memorialize concentration camp victims or, in Landau, Rhineland-Palatinate, German-French friendship. In these cases, the granite is a symbol of indestructibility (Lurz, *Kriegerdenkmäler*, 6:207). Such uses of *Findlinge* recall the polyreferentiality of *lieux de mémoire* included in Pierre Nora's *Les Lieux de Mémoire* (1984); *Realms of Memory: Rethinking the French Past*, vol. 1: *Conflicts and Divisions*, ed. Lawrence D. Kritzman, trans. Arthur Goldhammer (New York: Columbia University Press, 1996). See Lawrence D. Kritzman's forward, x.
47 Elsternbusch was a pleasure wood where, according to legend, the eighth-century leader of the Saxons who waged war against Charlemagne, named Widukind, kept his aviaries. Josef Dettmer, *Der Sachsenführer Widukind nach Geschichte und Sage* (Würzburg: Woerlsche Buch- und kirchl. Kunstverlagshandlung) 1879, 146.
48 Lurz, *Kriegerdenkmäler*, 6:206.
49 Lurz, *Kriegerdenkmäler*, 6:206.
50 Karl von Seeger, *Das Denkmal des Weltkriegs* (Stuttgart: Hugo Matthaes Verlagsbuchhandlung, 1930), 28.

51 For example, in the towns of Garlin (Karstädt) and Helle (Groß Pankow), Brandenburg, and Bad Essen, Lower Saxony.
52 In the village of Brädikow, in Güterfelde (Stahnsdorf), and in the hamlet of Schmolde (Meyenburg), all in Brandenburg; in Rockenthin, Bismarck, and village of Poppau, all in Saxony-Anhalt; and in the cemetery of Hahn (Pfungstadt), Hesse.
53 As in Guhlsdorf (Groß Pankow), Brandenburg.
54 See the *Heldenhaine* in Stade, Lower Saxony; Pessin, Brandenburg; in the hamlet of Genzien (Arendsee); and in the villages of Weißewarthe and Dolchau, Saxony-Anhalt.
55 In Wittstock / Dosse, Brandenburg.
56 My thanks to Marlise Appel, Ev. Akademie der Nordkirche, for sharing with me photographs of this memorial.
57 "Unseren Gefallenen 1914–1918" ("For our fallen soldiers").
58 The original bronze sun was removed for the Metallspende des deutschen Volkes (Metal Donation by the German People) during World War II (the collection and donation of raw materials and metal objects to further the war effort). A replacement sun was erected in 1980 thanks to donations collected by the *Heimatverein* (homeland association). See Stephan Linck, *Denk Mal* (Evangelische Akademie der Nordkirche), accessed October 15, 2024, www.denk-mal-gegen-krieg.de/kriegerdenkmaeler/schleswig-holstein-s-u/.
59 In 1955, a second memorial was added to commemorate the fallen of World War II: this stone cenotaph by Richard Kuöhl lies on an elevated stone plaza in front of the original memorial. The inscription on the cenotaph beneath an Iron Cross enclosed within an oak leaf wreath dedicates the memorial "in honor of the victims of the Second World War" ("Zur Ehre der Opfer des Zweiten Weltkrieges 1939–1945"); an inscription engraved around the sides of the sarcophagus reads, "I had a comrade, a better one you cannot find" (from the 1809 poem and later song, written by Ludwig Uhland).
60 Willy Lange, "Die leitenden Gestaltungsgedanken für die Heldenhaine," in *Deutsche Heldenhaine*, 7–8.
61 Pastor, "Die Bedeutung," 15.
62 Lange, "Die leitenden Gestaltungsgedanken," 8; Willy Lange, "Die Herstellung der Heldenhaine," in *Deutsche Heldenhaine*, 32.
63 Bradley, *Significance of Monuments*, 82.
64 Bradley, *Significance of Monuments*, 163.
65 I would like to thank Tobias Gohlis, Stefan Gierlich, Burkhard Arrenberg, and Georg Rummel for tracking down this information for me.
66 The *Findling* bears an inscription declaring that the memorial honors the dead of the first and second World Wars.
67 The Germanized version of the classical Greek pergola structure—a round, square, or quadratic vaulted structure with pillars and open-roofed, originally used to encase tombs—has been popular in German memorialization since the nineteenth century. Such structures usually feature a central memorial and were assumed to refer to ancient Germanic ancestry. Similar are memorial structures in the style of a monopteros; Meinhold Lurz, *Kriegerdenkmäler in Deutschland*, vol. 4, *Weimarer Republik* (Heidelberg: Esprint-Verlag, 1985), 198–99. See the pergola war memorial in the Kehl World War II cemetery, Baden-Württemberg (1958, Robert Tischler), and

woodcut illustrations of the sepulcher of Adonis's tomb in Italian painter Francesco Colonna's work *Hypnerotomachia Poliphili* (1499) for a classic depiction of the pergola.
68 Holtorf, "Life-Histories," 31.
69 The Holmer Beliebung is a burial society (guild) founded in 1650, after the Thirty Years' War, to help community members bury their dead—particularly during times of catastrophe such as plagues and wars.
70 Willy Lange, "Allerlei Einwände und ihre Erwiderung," in *Deutsche Heldenhaine*, 67. "Alt-Germanien als Ursprung—1813 Deutschland als Sehnsucht—1870/71 Deutsch land als Erfüllung für sich—1914 Deutschland als Behauptung in der Weltgeltung."
71 "Unselige Traditionspflege bei der Bundeswehr," a report for the Berlin magazine *Kontraste*, November 20, 2012, YouTube.
72 In an article titled "Eine Tradition wird entsorgt," published in the right-wing weekly *Junge Freiheit*, Hans-Joachim von Leesen defends the tradition and points out that the "Treuelied" of the Waffen-SS begins with a benign praise of loyalty and was originally used during the Wars of Liberation.
73 Holtorf, "Life-Histories," 31.
74 Lurz, *Kriegerdenkmäler*, 6:206; Meinhold Lurz, *Kriegerdenkmäler in Deutschland*, vol. 5 (Heidelberg: Esprint-Verlag, 1986), 209.
75 Lurz, *Kriegerdenkmäler*, 5:208.
76 Fuhrmeister, "Erratische Steine," 12.
77 Lurz, *Kriegerdenkmäler*, 5:207.
78 Lurz, *Kriegerdenkmäler*, 6:206, 210.
79 Gilad Margalit, *Guilt, Suffering, and Memory: Germany Remembers Its Dead of World War II*, trans. Haim Watzman (Bloomington: Indiana University Press, 2010), 196–97). Homeland societies were grouped under the VOL: Vereinigte Ostdeutsche Landmannsschaften (1949), renamed in 1951 the VdL: Verband der Landsmannschaften.
80 Margalit, *Guilt, Suffering, and Memory*, 186–87.
81 The preface to this catalogue was penned by Erika Steinbach, the controversial, former CDU right-wing politician who served for sixteen years as president of the Bund der Vertriebenen and now supports the radical right, populist Alternative für Deutschland (Alternative for Germany) party.
82 Erika Steinbach, "Vorwort," in *Mahn- und Gedenkstätten der deutschen Heimatvertriebenen* (Bonn: Bund der Vertriebenen—Vereinigte Landsmannschaften und Landesverbände, 2008), 3. Stephan Scholz gives the figure of 1,584; Scholz, *Vertriebenendenkmäler: Topographie einer deutschen Erinnerungslandschaft* (Paderborn, Germany: Ferdinand Schöningh, 2015), 41.
83 Scholz, *Vertriebenendenkmäler*, 42.
84 Lurz, *Kriegerdenkmäler*, 6:377.
85 Scholz, *Vertriebenendenkmäler*, 303.
86 Scholz, *Vertriebenendenkmäler*, 12. For a discussion of issues concerning the expellees and their postwar organizations, including German victim discourse since reunification, see Margalit, *Guilt, Suffering, and Memory*. Margalit discusses victim discourse in relation to former expellees and in relation to victims of Allied bombings.
87 Scholz, *Vertriebenendenkmäler*, 304, 309.
88 "Das beinhaltet den Völkermord am Deutschen Volk und auch den Völkermord, der vom deutschen Regime des Nationalsozialismus begangen worden ist."

89 This is a high estimate: most historians cite between twelve and fourteen million expellees.
90 Simone Wester, "Holocaust überdeckt alles," *Münchner Merkur*, September 17, 2003, www.merkur.de/lokales/regionen/holocaust-ueberdeckt-alles-151474.html.
91 Margalit, *Guilt, Suffering, and Memory*, 72–75. Margalit identifies Dresden, the expellees, and German POWs as the three major symbols of the discourse of German victimhood in postwar Germany's reconciliation narrative (common to both East and West Germany) (250).
92 Scholz, *Vertriebenendenkmäler*, 41. Scholz reports that forty-one percent of all memorials to expellees are stones (73).
93 Additional honor groves in Schaafheim, Hessen, and Bad Heilbrunn, Bavaria, memorialize both fallen soldiers and expellees.
94 Other memorials to the expellees and lost territories mourn Germany's postwar divided state: a memorial stone in Cochem, Rhineland-Palatinate, features a map of divided Germany that includes the eastern territories. The inscription reads, "Germany entire should be unified" (Das ganze Deutschland / vereinigt soll es sein).
95 According to Nazi plans, a ring of *Totenburgen* was to stretch along the borders of a new, German-imagined Europe that would reach from the Atlantic to the Ural Mountains in Russia and from Norway to North Africa. Frederic Spotts, *Hitler and the Power of Aesthetics* (New York: Overlook Press, 2002), 116.
96 The dramatic genre of the *Thingspiel* was institutionalized by the Nazis between 1933 and 1937, and sixty-six *Thingspiel* amphitheaters were built in 1934. Henning Eichberg and Robert A. Jones, "The Nazi Thingspiel: Theater for the Masses in Fascism and Proletarian Culture," *New German Critique* 11 (Spring 1977): 134, 137.
97 Lurz, *Kriegerdenkmäler*, 5:209–10.
98 Bernd J. Wagner, "April 1946: Der Horst-Wessel-Stein im Teutoburger Wald wird gesprengt," *Stadtarchiv und Landesgeschichtliche Bibliothek Bielefeld*, April 1, 2021, https://historischer-rueckklick-bielefeld.com/2021/04/01/01042021/.
99 Wagner, "April 1946." A *Findling* was to be erected upon a plot of land on the Baltic Sea to mark the tomb of Reinhard Heydrich, but this plan was never realized (Lurz, *Kriegerdenkmäler*, 5:211).
100 Fuhrmeister, "Erratische Steine," 3.
101 Bert Strebe, "Ahnenstätten arbeiten Vergangenheit auf," *Hannoversche Allgemeine*, December 12, 2017, www.haz.de/der-norden/ahnenstaetten-arbeiten-vergangenheit-auf-XQIJAEMHRQ24B5MFYRHD4GNB4M.html. See also Karsten Krogmann, "Friedhöfe im Oldenburger Land: Wo alte Nazis friedlich ruhen dürfen," *Nordwest-Zeitung*, September 27, 2014, www.nwzonline.de/niedersachsen/wo-alte-nazis-friedlich-ruhen-duerfen_a_19,0,506055321.html#.
102 On the worship of ancestors among neo-Pagans, including the use of *Ahnenstätten*, see Julia Dippel, "Ritualplatz, Ahnenstätte, Kraftort: Neopagane Rezeptionen germanischer Kultplätze," in *Germanischer Kultorte: Vergleichende, historische und rezeptionsgeschichtliche Zufänge*," ed. Matthias Eggeler (Munich: Herbert Utz Verlag, 2016), 315–46.
103 Strebe, "Ahnenstätten."
104 Landsmannschaften are associations of Germans who were expelled from former German territories in the wake of World War I and World War II.

105 Berlin, formerly divided and the capital of reunified Germany, is not represented by a leaf because of its special status.
106 Quoted in Fuhrmeister, "Erratische Steine," 9.
107 Schmidt, *Hünengrab*, 9. Well-known *Hünengräber* include the Sieben Steinhäuser (Seven Stone Houses) of Lüneburg Heath near Fallingbostel, Lower Saxony; the Pöppendorf *Hünengrab* of Waldhusen Forest, near the village of Pöppendorf in Schleswig-Holstein; the seven Lancken-Granitz *Hünengräber* on the island of Rügen; and the *Hünengrab* of Lennépark at Castle Basedow in Mecklenburg-Vorpommern. The Route of Megalithic Culture, which runs for over two hundred miles through the Osnabrücker Land and Weser-Ems regions from Osnabrück to Oldenburg, leads to thirty-three megalithic sites and over seventy megalithic tombs from the Neolithic period.
108 Holtorf, "Life-Histories," 25.
109 Schmidt, *Hünengrab*, 9–11.
110 See "Das Geheimnis der Hünengräber," *Norddeutscher Rundfunk (NDR)*, August 19, 2022, www.ndr.de/geschichte/chronologie/Huenengraeber-in-Norddeutschland-mystische-Orte,huenengraeber101.html. See also Bradley, *Significance of Monuments*, 79–80.
111 Adalbert Kuhn, *Westfälische Sagen und Märchen* (Altenmünster: Jazzybee Verlag Jürgen Beck, 2012), no. 327, Das Hünengrab and no. 342, Hünengrab bei Wunbüttel.
112 Kuhn, *Westfälische Sagen*, nr. 33c, Heidenkirchen.
113 Holtorf, "Life-Histories," 27, 30.
114 Richard Bradley, *Altering the Earth: The Origins of Monuments in Britain and Continental Europe* (1991–92 Rhind Lectures) (Edinburgh: Society of Antiquaries of Scotland, 1993), 129.
115 Loretana de Libero, *Rache und Triumph: Krieg, Gefühle und Gedenken in der Moderne*, Beiträge zur Militärgeschichte, vol. 73 (Oldenbourg: De Gruyter, 2014), 204–5.
116 Bradley, *Altering the Earth*, 120.
117 Stefan Goebel, *The Great War and Medieval Memory: War, Remembrance, and Medievalism in Britain and Germany, 1914–1940* (New York: Cambridge University Press, 2007), 1.
118 Lowenthal, *Past*, 44.
119 In major cities, the preferred style for memorials was either Neoclassicism or figurative representations (Fuhrmeister, "Erratische Steine," 9); see also Lurz, *Kriegerdenkmäler*, 6:206.
120 Fuhrmeister, "Erratische Steine," 9–10.
121 Esther Geisslinger, "Ruhestätte mit bester Aussicht," *Die Tageszeitung*, April 13, 2019, https://taz.de/Ruhestaette-mit-bester-Aussicht/!5585525/.
122 "Projektvorschlag: Ehrenfriedhof Karberg / Schleswig," *Volksbund Deutsche Kriegsgräberfürsorge e.V.*, accessed October 15, 2024, https://schleswig-holstein.volksbund.de/aktuell/projekte/artikel/karberg-schleswig-1.
123 Lurz also describes this memorial as an imitation of a *Hünengrab* (*Kriegerdenkmäler*, 6:206).
124 Pierre Nora, "Between Memory and History: Les Lieux de Mémoire," special issue, Memory and Counter-Memory, *Representations* 26 (Spring 1989): 19–20.
125 "Todesmarschdenkmal," *Sudenburg Chronik*, accessed October 15, 2024, www.sudenburg-chronik.de/Denkmal/Todesmarsch.htm.

126 The four victims are Oswald Feis, Frieda Morgenthau, Adolf Reinach, and Reinach's son Max. Their places of death are Schloss Hartheim bei Linz/Donau, Izbica in East Poland, Gurs in South France, und Auschwitz.
127 Other examples include *Findling* memorials in the city park in Cham, Bavaria (dedicated to the persecuted, deported, and murdered Jews of Cham); at the former concentration camp Neugraben (a satellite camp of Neuengamme, Hamburg), dedicated to Jewish female forced laborers; at the former concentration camp Hambühren (satellite camp of Bergen-Belsen), dedicated to the forced laborers; in Harpstedt (Oldenburg, Lower Saxony), dedicated to the Jewish victims of Nazi persecution from Harpstedt; in Waren (Mürtiz), Mecklenburg-Vorpommern, in memory of the Waren synagogue; and at the former concentration camp Ellrich-Juliushütte (satellite camp of Buchenwald/Mittelbau-Dora).
128 The memorial site also includes a reception hall; stelae inscribed with the names, dates of death, and areas of deployment of the German soldiers who died while deployed overseas since 1993; and a sacred memory space called the "Ort der Stille" ("Place of Silence").
129 "Der Wald der Erinnerung," *Bundesministerium der Verteidigung* (Frankfurt am Main: Zarbock, 2021), accessed October 15, 2024, www.bmvg.de/resource/blob/5261476/5197b46abf805362a5fe2afc9cf4ee15/der-wald-der-erinnerungen-data.pdf.

CHAPTER FIVE

1 Rudolf Simek, "Continental Germanic Religion," in *The Handbook of Religions in Ancient Europe*, ed. Christensen Lisbeth Bredholt, Olav Hammer, and David A. Warburton (Durham, UK: Acumen, 2013), 297.
2 Simek, "Continental Germanic Religion," 298.
3 Few memorials after 1918 mention the Kaiser; exceptions are memorials of conservative military units such as the memorial at the Saint Johannis church in Nuremberg, dedicated to soldiers who died for "Kaiser und Reich/König u. Vaterland"; Meinhold Lurz, *Kriegerdenkmäler in Deutschland*, vol. 6, *Bundesrepublik* (Heidelberg: Esprint-Verlag, 1987), 318.
4 *Mahnmale* are memorials warning of the consequences rather than celebrating the glory of war. Mourning and grief first became common tropes on war memorials in the modern period; Reinhart Koselleck, "Kriegerdenkmale als Identitätsstiftungen der Überlebenden," in *Geronnene Lava: Texte zu politischem Totenkult und Erinnerung*, ed. Manfred Hettling, Hubert Locher, and Adriana Markantonatos (Berlin: Suhrkamp Verlag, 2023), 27.
5 Moshe Halbertal, *On Sacrifice* (Princeton, NJ: Princeton University Press, 2012), 8, 15–16.
6 On the ethics of the gift and the obligation to receive and reciprocate see Marcel Mauss, *The Gift: Expanded Edition*, selected, annotated, and trans. Jane I. Guyer (Chicago: Hau Books, 2016). Making a sacrifice to god is actually returning rather than giving, since the offeror gives to god what god had originally given as part of his bounty; such sacrifice is thus a "symbolic recycling of the gift to its origin" (Halbertal, *On Sacrifice*, 11).

7 Halbertal, *On Sacrifice*, 13.
8 Halbertal, *On Sacrifice*, 16.
9 *Opfer*, as Wenk explains, has three meanings: victim, casualty, and sacrifice. Silke Wenk, "Sacrifice and Victimization in the Commemorative Practices of Nazi Genocide after German Unification—Memorials and Visual Metaphors," trans. Matthias Schneider and Herbert Mehrtens, in *Sacrifice and National Belonging in Twentieth-Century Germany*, ed. Greg Eghigian and Matthew Paul Berg (College Station: Texas A&M University Press, 2002), 202.
10 Halbertal, *On Sacrifice*, 59–60. Current scholarship discusses martyrdom as a literary genre rather than merely an objective reality. While martyrs of the early Christian church and of Hellenistic Judaism were indeed individuals who died for their faith, the representation of their martyrdom in literature consistently draws on certain recurring characteristics: martyrs are described, for example, as experiencing visions before their deaths and as making affirmations of their faith while dying, in addition to other symbolic aspects. The literature of martyrdom thus reveals itself to be a literary genre possessing a number of clichés rather than a history of objective accounts. See Daniel Boyarin, *Dying for God: Martyrdom and the Making of Christianity and Judaism* (Stanford, CA: Stanford University Press, 1999), 116.
11 Halbertal, *On Sacrifice*, 62.
12 Lurz, *Kriegerdenkmäler*, 6:316.
13 War memorials became increasingly common in the wake of the French Revolution and the Wars of Liberation. In the case of World War I and World War II memorials, not only fallen soldiers but suffering women and children also became worthy of commemoration Reinhart Koselleck, "Einleitung," in *Der politische Totenkult: Kriegerdenkmäler in der Moderne*, ed. Reinhart Koselleck and Michael Jeismann (Munich: Wilhelm Fink Verlag, 1994), 12.
14 Lurz, *Kriegerdenkmäler*, 6:324.
15 Lurz, *Kriegerdenkmäler*, 6:323.
16 Lurz, *Kriegerdenkmäler*, 6:320.
17 Halbertal, *On Sacrifice*, 2, 33.
18 Halbertal, *On Sacrifice*, 29.
19 Halbertal, *On Sacrifice*, 33.
20 Dennis Phillips, "Most Ruthless Buried at Bitburg," *Chicago Tribune*, May 5, 1985, www.chicagotribune.com/1985/05/05/most-ruthless-buried-at-bitburg/.
21 George Mosse, *Fallen Soldiers: Reshaping the Memory of the World Wars* (New York: Oxford University Press, 1990), 202.
22 Mosse, *Fallen Soldiers*, 211.
23 Halbertal, *On Sacrifice*, 7.
24 Walter Burkert, *Homo Necans: The Anthropology of Ancient Greek Sacrificial Ritual and Myth*, trans. Peter Bing (Berkeley: University of California Press, 1986), 3.
25 Burkert, *Homo Necans*, 3, 9.
26 Carole M. Cusack, *The Sacred Tree: Ancient and Medieval Manifestations* (Newcastle upon Tyne: Cambridge Scholars, 2011), 17. For a discussion of homologies between trees, worlds, human beings, and horses, the concept of the hippodrendon, and the myth of Wodan's self-sacrifice on Yggdrasil in light of these homologies, see Cusack, *Sacred Tree*, 17–25, 157.

27 Simek, "Continental Germanic Religion," 295.
28 Simek, "Continental Germanic Religion," 295–96.
29 Ken Dowden, *European Paganism: The Realities of Cult from Antiquity to the Middle Ages* (London: Routledge, 2000), 182.
30 Dowden, *European Paganism*, 180, 184.
31 Dowden, *European Paganism*, 21, 171, 181–82. Dowden notes that the Alamans decapitated and sacrificed horses, cows, and other animals to gods as well as trees, streams, hilltops, and gorges (52).
32 Dowden, *European Paganism*, 182.
33 Dowden, *European Paganism*, 185.
34 Bruce Lincoln, *Myth, Cosmos, and Society: Indo-European Themes of Creation and Destruction* (Cambridge, MA: Harvard University Press, 1986), 41.
35 Bruce Lincoln, *Death, War and Sacrifice: Studies in Ideology and Practice* (Chicago: University of Chicago Press, 1991), 7. See also the "Purusha Sukta" in *Rig Veda* 10.90.
36 Lincoln, *Myth*, 42.
37 Dowden, *European Paganism*, 292.
38 Dowden, *European Paganism*, 276; Malcolm Todd, *The Early Germans* (Oxford: Blackwell, 1992), 105.
39 Dowden, *European Paganism*, 186, 276.
40 Dowden, *European Paganism*, 276–79.
41 Dowden, *European Paganism*, 162.
42 Dowden, *European Paganism*, 277, 290.
43 Lincoln, *Myth*, 45–46.
44 Cornelius Tacitus, "Germany," in *Voyages and Travels Ancient and Modern*, The Harvard Classics Series, trans. Thomas Gordon (New York: P. F. Collier & Son, 1910), 114–15.
45 Lincoln, *Myth*, 50.
46 Todd, *Early Germans*, 105.
47 Lincoln, *Myth*, 47. "Purusha" in the *Rig Veda* also means "Man."
48 For a discussion of the connections between the self-sacrifice of Wodan on a tree and the story of the crucifixion of Christ, see Cusack, *Sacred Tree*, 130–33, 142–45, 155.
49 In Cusack's telling, Wodan gained power over the runes through his self-sacrifice (Cusack, *Sacred Tree*, 155).
50 Burkert, *Homo Necans*, 29, 33.
51 Dowden, *European Paganism*, 169–70.
52 Lincoln, *Myth*, 47.
53 Lincoln, *Myth*, 47–50.
54 Burkert, *Homo Necans*, 15.
55 Burkert, *Homo Necans*, 20.
56 Burkert, *Homo Necans*, 18–20, 47.
57 David Pan, *Sacrifice in the Modern World: On the Particularity and Generality of Nazi Myth* (Evanston, IL: Northwestern University Press, 2012), 101–2.
58 Burkert, *Homo Necans*, 18.
59 Burkert, *Homo Necans*, 16, 21.
60 Burkert, *Homo Necans*, 22–23.
61 Burkert, *Homo Necans*, 35.
62 Burkert, *Homo Necans*, 18–20.

63 Burkert, *Homo Necans*, 37.
64 Burkert, *Homo Necans*, 45.
65 Burkert, *Homo Necans*, 38–40.
66 Burkert, *Homo Necans*, 47.
67 Mosse, *Fallen Soldiers*, 53–57.
68 Mosse, *Fallen Soldiers*, 59–60.
69 Mosse, *Fallen Soldiers*, 64–65.
70 Mosse, *Fallen Soldiers*, 7, 73.
71 Mosse, *Fallen Soldiers*, 78.
72 Lurz, *Kriegerdenkmäler*, 6:315–16.
73 Mosse, *Fallen Soldiers*, 3–4, 7.
74 Mosse, *Fallen Soldiers*, 6–7.
75 Mosse, *Fallen Soldiers*, 21–22.
76 The admonishment to future generations to imitate the fallen was a classic sentiment on war memorials commemorating the Wars of Liberation as well as the late nineteenth-century Wars of German Unification. A typical phrasing is "Den Gefallenen zum Gedächtnis, den Lebenden zur Anerkennung, den künftigen Geschlechtern zur Nacheiferung" ("To the fallen in memoriam, to the living with acknowledgement, to future generations for emulation"), authored by August Böckh for Friedrich Wilhelm III (Koselleck, "Kriegerdenkmale," 29).
77 Otto Binswanger, *Die seelischen Wirkungen des Krieges* (Stuttgart, Berlin: Deutsche Verlags-Anstalt, 1914), 21.
78 Binswanger, *Die seelischen Wirkungen*, 21–22. "In the course of the last year and on the outbreak of the war, I had been treating a whole series of young men with weak nerves: anxious, timid, vacillating, weak-willed individuals whose consciousness and feelings were determined only by their own ego and who exhausted themselves in complaints about their physical and mental pain. Then the war came. Their morbid sickliness fell away from them at a stroke, they reported for service—and all have so far proved their worth"; quoted in Doris Kaufmann, "Science as Cultural Practice: Psychiatry in the First World War and Weimar Germany," *Journal of Contemporary History* 34, no. 1 (January 1999): 128.
79 Binswanger, *Die seelischen Wirkungen*, 18.
80 Binswanger, *Die seelischen Wirkungen*, 27.
81 Halbertal, *On Sacrifice*, 5, 68.
82 Pan, *Sacrifice*, 94–96.
83 Halbertal, *On Sacrifice*, 90–91, 104.
84 Halbertal, *On Sacrifice*, 108.
85 Arthur Schopenhauer, *The Basis of Morality*, trans. Arthur Brodrick Bullock (London: Swan Sonnenschein, 1903), 278–79.
86 Halbertal, *On Sacrifice*, 115–16.
87 Pan, *Sacrifice*, 113–14.
88 Pan, *Sacrifice*, 117–19.
89 Halbertal, *On Sacrifice*, 104.
90 Pan, *Sacrifice*, 114, 138–39.
91 "From a Speech by Himmler before Senior SS Officers in Poznan, October 4, 1943," Yad Vashem Shoah Resource Center, www.yadvashem.org/odot_pdf/Microsoft%20Word%20-%204029.pdf.

92 Greg Eghigian, "Injury, Fate, Resentment, and Sacrifice in German Political Culture, 1914–1939," in *Sacrifice and National Belonging in Twentieth-Century Germany*, ed. Greg and Matthew Paul Berg (College Station: Texas A&M University Press, 2002), 107.
93 Eghigian, "Injury," 101–3.
94 Eghigian, "Injury," 104, 106.
95 Eghigian, "Injury," 109.
96 Insa Eschebach, *Öffentliches Gedenken. Öffentliches Gedenken: Deutsche Erinnerungskulturen seit der Weimarer Republik* (Frankfurt am Main: Campus Verlag, 2005), 47–48, 185.
97 Eschebach, *Öffentliches Gedenken*, 193.
98 Eschebach, *Öffentliches Gedenken*, 186.
99 Konrad H. Jarausch, "Normalisierung oder Re-Nationalisierung? Zur Umdeutung der deutschen Vergangenheit," *Geschichte und Gesellschaft* 21, no. 4 (October–December 1995): 572.
100 Aleksandr Solzhenitsyn, *The Gulag Archipelago, 1918–1956: An Experiment in Literary Investigation*, trans. Thomas P. Whitney (1–4) and Harry Willets (5–7) (New York: Harper Perennial, 2007), 77–78.
101 Halbertal, *On Sacrifice*, 63–65.
102 Halbertal, *On Sacrifice*, 78–79.
103 Mosse, *Fallen Soldiers*, 3.
104 The phrase used was "gebaute Metaphern"; Reinhart Koselleck, "Denkmäler sind Stolpersteine," in *Geronnene Lava: Texte zu politischem Totenkult und Erinnerung*, ed. Manfred Hettling, Hubert Locher, and Adriana Markantonatos (Berlin: Suhrkamp Verlag, 2023), 298.
105 Examples include memorials at the former concentration camps of Neuengamme ("Le Deporté" by Françoise Salmon), Dachau ("International Monument" by Nandor Glid), and Mauthausen ("Slovenian Memorial" by Jože Bertoncelj).
106 James E. Young, "Memory and Counter-Memory," special issue, Constructions of Memory: On Monuments Old and New, *Harvard Design Magazine* 9 (Fall 1995), www.harvarddesignmagazine.org/articles/memory-and-counter-memory/. The close connection between war memorials and new wars is commented on by Koselleck in a discussion of Nazi Germany's destruction of Warsaw's Tomb of the Unknown Soldier, where he points out the common pattern that captured enemy arms are used for the erection of war memorials, which are themselves in the next war melted down in order to create new weapons; Reinhart Koselleck, "Die bildliche Transformation der Gedächtnisstätten in der Neuzeit," in *Geronnene Lava*, 160–61.
107 Bill Niven, *Germans as Victims: Remembering the Past in Contemporary Germany* (Basingstoke, UK: Palgrave Macmillan, 2006) and Bill Niven, "From Countermonument to Combimemorial: Developments in German Memorialization," *Journal of War & Culture Studies* 6, no. 1 (February 2013): 75–91. See also *Memorialization in Germany since 1945*, ed. Bill Niven and Chloe Paver (New York: Palgrave Macmillan, 2010), for a discussion of innovative Holocaust memorials blurring the boundaries between memorials and art installations, exhibitions, documentation centers, graveyards, history paths, archives, and libraries. The Grafeneck Euthanasia Center in Gomadingen, Baden-Württemberg, for example, functions as both

memorial to the victims of the Aktion T4 forced "euthanasia" program and home and workplace for mentally ill and disabled persons.
108 There are exceptions: Käthe Kollwitz's *Trauernde Eltern* 1914/18 (*Grieving Parents*), located in the German war cemetery of Vladslo, Belgium, is a notable example of a memorial that thematizes grief over death itself, rather than commemorating soldiers who "died/sacrificed themeslves for" a greater cause (Koselleck, "Kriegerdenkmale," 38).

CHAPTER SIX

1 Karl von Seeger, *Das Denkmal des Weltkriegs* (Stuttgart: Hugo Matthaes Verlagsbuchhandlung, 1930), 32–33. The original German reads, "Die Jugend, ... die vielleicht nie wiederkehrt, war durchlodert von den Flammen freudiger, opfervoller Hingabe ... Ihr Todesgesang war das Lied von Deutschland und die brausende Hymne vom Rhein ... Er nimmt sein Schicksal ernst, ja er liebt es, und ist am stolzesten dann, wenn es ihn vernichten will."
2 Franz Grillparzer, *Das goldene Vließ* (Stuttgart, 1822; Projekt Gutenberg-DE, 1994), www.projekt-gutenberg.org/grillprz/vliess/argont22.html.
3 The Memorial to the Expellees at the Theodor-Heuss-Platz in Berlin (1955) also features a large fire bowl. The flame was lit by German expellees from the east and was designed to burn until Germany was reunified; Silke Wenk, "Sacrifice and Victimization in the Commemorative Practices of Nazi Genocide after German Unification—Memorials and Visual Metaphors," trans. Matthias Schneider and Herbert Mehrtens, in *Sacrifice and National Belonging in Twentieth-Century Germany*, ed. Greg Eghigian and Matthew Paul Berg (College Station: Texas A&M University Press, 2002), 206. The dedication reads: "Freiheit / Recht / Friede" ("Freedom / Justice / Peace").
4 Reinhart Koselleck, "Einleitung," in *Der politische Totenkult: Kriegerdenkmäler in der Moderne*, ed. Reinhart Koselleck and Michael Jeismann (Munich: Wilhelm Fink Verlag, 1994), 9.
5 Edgar Wolfrum, "Geschichtspolitik und deutsche Frage: Der 17. Juni im nationalen Gedächtnis der Bundesrepublik (1953–1989)," *Geschichte und Gesellschaft* 24 (July–September 1998): 383–84.
6 Clemens Tangerding, "Für Deutschland gestorben," *Deutschlandfunk*, November 18, 2012, www.deutschlandfunk.de/fuer-deutschland-gestorben-100.html, 5–7.
7 Stefan Goebel, "War Memorials (Germany)," in *1914–1918-online: International Encyclopedia of the First World War*, ed. Ute Daniel, et al. (Berlin: Freie Universität Berlin, 2014).
8 Adolf Rieth, *Denkmal ohne Pathos: Totenmale des zweiten Weltkrieges in Südwürttenberg-Hohenzollern, mit einer geschichtlichen Einleitung* (Tübingen: Verlag Ernst Wasmuth, 1967), 15.
9 Koselleck, "Einleitung," 9.
10 Reinhart Koselleck, "Kriegerdenkmale als Identitätsstiftungen der Überlebenden," in *Geronnene Lava:. Texte zu politischem Totenkult und Erinnerung*, ed. Manfred Hettling, Hubert Locher, and Adriana Markantonatos (Berlin: Suhrkamp Verlag, 2023), 12, 21–23.

11 Koselleck, "Einleitung," 11.
12 Reinhart Koselleck, "Die bildliche Transformation der Gedächtnisstätten in der Neuzeit," in *Geronnene Lava*, 156.
13 Koselleck, "Einleitung," 12.
14 Koselleck, "Kriegerdenkmale," 26, 44; "Die bildliche Transformation," 161. In 1793, Koselleck reports, the Prussian king Friedrich Wilhelm II erected in honor of victorious Hesse a memorial in Frankfurt that was the first *national* (rather than local, urban, or bourgeois) memorial to list the names of and thus equally commemorate all fallen soldiers as well as officers (although names were still listed by rank). Shortly thereafter, in the wake of the Wars of Liberation, the Prussian king declared that plaques listing the names of all fallen soldiers were to be displayed in all churches in Prussia (Koselleck, "Die bildliche Transformation," 156). After World War I, the names of fallen German soldiers were no longer listed by rank but rather alphabetically or by date of death (12, 14–15). See also Reinhart Koselleck, "Der Unbekannte Soldat als nationalsymbol im Blick auf Retterdenkmale," in *Geronenne Lava*, 207–35. Although a memorial to unknown soldiers was not erected in Berlin in the post–World War I period, in 1969 the remains of an unknown soldier and a concentration camp victim were buried under the Neue Wache in Berlin, where they remain to this day.
15 George Mosse, *Fallen Soldiers: Reshaping the Memory of the World Wars* (New York: Oxford University Press, 1990), 20.
16 Tangerding, "Für Deutschland gestorben."
17 These words, part of the inscription, were written by August Boeckh (1785–1867).
18 The other two panels of the memorial offer similar inscriptions, namely: "Aus der Amtsgemeinde Schildesche zogen 5 459 für Heim und Herd in den Kampf" and "684 besiegelten ihre Treue zum Vaterland in ungleichem Kampfe mit dem Tod."
19 Similar is the World War I memorial inscription "Im Felde unbesiegt" ("Undefeated in the field of battle"), as seen on a memorial in Oerlinghausen, North Rhine–Westphalia.
20 Libero notes that no one objected to the memorial's defamation of the Jews during the process of planning the memorial (although twenty-five Jews lived in the town at the time); Loretana de Libero, *Rache und Triumph: Krieg, Gefühle, und Gedenken in der Moderne*, Beiträge zur Militärgeschichte, vol. 73 (Oldenbourg: De Gruyter, 2014), 158.
21 Insa Eschebach, *Öffentliches Gedenken: Deutsche Erinnerungskulturen seit der Weimarer Republik* (Frankfurt am Main: Campus Verlag, 2005), 15.
22 Mosse, *Fallen Soldiers*, 39.
23 Stefan Goebel, *The Great War and Medieval Memory: War, Remembrance, and Medievalism in Britain and Germany, 1914–1940* (New York: Cambridge University Press, 2007), 257.
24 Goebel, *Great War and Medieval Memory*, 254.
25 An example is the legend of Barbarossa (Holy Roman Emperor Frederick I), according to which the emperor was not dead but rather sleeping in a cave in the Kyffhäuser mountains of Thuringia and would someday awaken to rescue Germany from its troubles. During the nineteenth century, Barbarossa was imagined as returning to unite Germany.
26 Goebel, *Great War and Medieval Memory*, 254.

27 Angela Sumegi, *Understanding Death: An Introduction to Ideas of Self and the Afterlife in World Religions* (New York: Wiley Blackwell, 2014), 51, 81.
28 Mosse, *Fallen Soldiers*, 102.
29 In particular, a sketch of a *Heldengrabmal* (hero's tomb) by Rupert von Miller (1916).
30 Libero, *Rache*, 59.
31 Seeger, *Denkmal*, 34.
32 M. S. H. (Sinclair) Hood, "*Tholos* Tombs of the Aegean," *Antiquity* 34, no. 135 (September 1960), https://doi.org/10.1017/S0003598X00029331.
33 Stocker—like many other German sculptors of World War I memorials—was a repeat exhibitor at the *Große Deutsche Kunstausstellung* (Great German Art Exhibition) in Munich's Haus der Kunst (House of Art), a venue for Nazi-supported art between 1937 and 1944.
34 Libero, *Rache*, 75.
35 Greg Eghigian, "Injury, Fate, Resentment, and Sacrifice in German Political Culture, 1914–1939," in *Sacrifice and National Belonging in Twentieth-Century Germany*, ed. Greg and Matthew Paul Berg (College Station: Texas A&M University Press, 2002), 92–94.
36 Even depictions of soldiers in lying postures often contained hints of revanchism. Schlafender Krieger (Resting Warrior) by Friedrich Lommel (1883–1967) lies in an old *Tresekammer* (a former repository for documents) of the Unser-Lieben-Frauen-Kirche in Bremen, renovated by Otto Blendermann in 1924 into a World War I memorial chapel. Lommel's fallen soldier wears an overcoat and helmet; his right hand clasps a sword, its tip extending beyond his feet, suggesting readiness for future military action. A World War I and World War II memorial in Bünde, North Rhine–Westphalia, depicts a soldier in a half-crouching position; one hand is pressed to his heart and the other claps a grenade—a hint of future vengeance.
37 James E. Young, "The Terrible Beauty of Nazi Aesthetics," *Forward* 109, April 25, 2003, https://forward.com/news/8694/the-terrible-beauty-of-nazi-aesthetics/; Frederic Spotts, *Hitler and the Power of Aesthetics* (New York: Overlook Press, 2002), 109.
38 Libero, *Rache*, 229–30.
39 Famous Nazi monuments include Munich's Feldhernnhalle (Field Marshals' Hall), the graves of Horst Wessel and Herbert Norkus, and the Albert-Leo-Schlageter Memorial. Many lesser-known memorials from the Nazi period still exist: a World War I memorial by sculptor Hugo Knittel (1888–1958), erected 1937 in the city garden (Alois-Herth-Anlage) of Furtwangen, Baden-Württemberg, still faces France. It features three soldiers: one crouches, grenade in hand; one grasps his gun; a third—missing from the waist up due to vandalism in 1977—stands erect, his left leg flung forward. Formerly, he stood ready to fling a grenade. The former thirty-two-foot-high Freikorpsdenkmal (Freikorps memorial) designed by Ferdinand Liebermann (1883–1941), erected in Munich-Giesing (1942), depicted a naked figure with a snake in his arms, recalling the mythic figure of Hercules, who, as an infant, strangled two snakes sent by the goddess Hera to kill him in his cradle.
40 Stefanie Schäfers, "Schlagetersiedlung," *Die Ausstellung Schaffendes Volk, Düsseldorf 1937*, accessed October 17, 2024, http://schaffendesvolk1937.de/schlagetersiedlung/.
41 Jo Achim Geschke, "Reeser Platz: Was wird aus dem Nazi-Denkmal? Ausführlicher Bericht zum Workshop," *Düsseldorfer*, November 21, 2018, https://the-duesseldorfer.de/reeser-platz-was-wird-aus-dem-nazi-denkmal-ausfuehrlicher-bericht-zum-workshop/.

42 Mosse, *Fallen Soldiers*, 212.
43 The former prisoners assembled two piles of the corpses of those who had died since liberation of disease and malnutrition; the corpses were flanked by wreaths and placed in the courtyard of the camp crematorium. These piles reconstructed a pile of corpses left behind by the SS (Rudy Koshar, *From Monuments to Traces: Artifacts of German Memory, 1870–1990* (Berkeley: University of California Press, 2000), 209–10).
44 East German memorialization embraced three forms of memorials: first and most important, memorials at former concentration camps (Buchenwald, Sachsenhausen, and Ravensbrück); second, other camps and sites of resistance; and third, monuments, streets, and buildings. An example of a memorial to resistance in former West Germany is the bronze memorial statue of a young man with his hands bound by Richard Scheibe (1953), located at the Bendlerblock German Resistance Memorial Center (Stauffenbergstraße Memorial) in the former West Berlin and erected to honor the five officers who led the July 20, 1944, plot against Hitler and were executed there. See also the Memorial to the Victims of the Hitler Dictatorship at Plötzensee Prison (1952), also in former West Berlin.
45 Designed by Gunter Demnig, each Stolperstein consists of a brass plaque memorializing a single victim of the Nazis and is embedded into the pavement in front of the victim's last residence of choice. The first fifty Stolpersteine were placed, illegally, in Berlin-Kreuzberg in 1996. Today, over ninety thousand Stolpersteine have been installed across twenty-eight countries.
46 Gilad Margalit, *Guilt, Suffering, and Memory: Germany Remembers Its Dead of World War II*, trans. Haim Watzman (Bloomington: Indiana University Press, 2010), 141–43.
47 Margalit, *Guilt, Suffering, and Memory*, 61–63, 75.
48 Margalit, *Guilt, Suffering, and Memory*, 68.
49 Moshe Halbertal, *On Sacrifice* (Princeton, NJ: Princeton University Press, 2012), 47.
50 Gertrud Schiller, *Iconography of Christian Art*, vol. 2, *The Passion of Jesus Christ*, trans. Janet Seligman (Greenwich, CT: New York Graphic Society, 1972), 179.
51 Schiller, *Iconography*, 179.
52 Meinhold Lurz, *Kriegerdenkmäler in Deutschland*, vol. 4, *Weimarer Republik* (Heidelberg: Esprint-Verlag, 1985), 172; Meinhold Lurz, *Kriegerdenkmäler in Deutschland*, vol. 6, *Bundesrepublik* (Heidelberg: Esprint-Verlag, 1987), 223.
53 See Wenk, "Sacrifice and Victimization," 204–6.
54 In response to protests, chancellor Helmut Kohl allowed a brass plaque engraved with the names of persecuted groups (based on part of a famous speech by president Richard von Weizsäcker in 1985) to be mounted at the entrance to the memorial.
55 Stephen Kinzer, "Berlin Journal; The War Memorial: To Embrace the Guilty, Too?" *New York Times*, November 15, 1993, https://timesmachine.nytimes.com/timesmachine/1993/11/15/121793.html?pageNumber=4.
56 "Ich gebe wieder das was ist: das Wirkliche und Wahrhaftige," www.ernst-barlach-stiftung.de/ernst-barlach/plastiken/pieta/.
57 There are dozens of other Pietà-themed memorials in a variety of other towns and cities across Germany. See Lurz, *Kriegerdenkmäler*, 6:223–26.
58 Koselleck, "Die bildliche Transformation," 152.
59 Jacobus de Voragine, *The Golden Legend* (Princeton, NJ: Princeton University Press, 1993), 238–41.

60 Halbertal, *On Sacrifice*, 59.
61 Meinhold Lurz, *Kriegerdenkmäler in Deutschland*, vol. 5, *Drittes Reich* (Heidelberg: Esprint-Verlag, 1986), 232.
62 Koselleck, "Die bildliche Transformation," 152. A Saint George–themed memorial in Warsaw (erected 1788), for example, depicts the Polish king Jan III Sobieski as Saint George, suggesting that the king has taken on the rescuing and sanctifying role of the saint. Other memorials feature Generals as Saint George (152, 154). World War I and World War II memorials depict Saint George exclusively as a simple soldier (154).
63 "Den Tapferen Kriegern 1914 + 1918 / In Dankb. Erinnerung / Markt Schwaben."
64 Saint George memorials also stand in Beuren, Baden-Württemberg; Kempen, North Rhine–Westphalia; Berlin-Potsdam; Hammelburg, Bavaria; Körbecke/Möhnesee, North Rhine–Westphalia; Ebersberg, Bavaria; Sandbach, Baden-Württemberg; and Munich, in the Saint Bennokirche. Saint George statues are particularly common in the Palatinate (Pfalz) region in Germany, for example, in Sankt Martin, Haardt bei Neustadt, Lauterecken, and Mußbach (Lurz, *Kriegerdenkmäler*, 4:232).
65 Lurz, *Kriegerdenkmäler*, 6:234.
66 Other examples of Saint George memorials featuring Saint George in the act of killing the dragon appear in Lautrach, Bavaria, and Herdringen bei Hüsten, North Rhine–Westphalia.
67 Lurz, *Kriegerdenkmäler*, 6:234–35.
68 Hermann Hesse and Thomas Mann, *The Correspondence of Hermann Hesse and Thomas Mann, 1910–1955*, ed. Anni Carlsson and Volker Michels, trans. Ralph Manheim (New York: Harper & Row, 1975), 59.
69 Mosse, *Fallen Soldiers*, 217.
70 While the memorial was absent from the city park in 2014–15, Oppenau artist Tim Otto Roth and Miriam Seidler set up an art installation consisting of an LED-display board, upon which the names of the fallen were projected.
71 "Unseren Toten 1914–1918 / 1939–1945" ("Dedicated to our dead 1914–1918 / 1939–1945").
72 The Iron Cross is an ancient Teutonic symbol used as a military decoration since the early nineteenth century. King of Prussia Friedrich Wilhelm III adopted the Iron Cross as a medal in 1813, and it was issued during both world wars. The Iron Cross is now called the Ehrenkreuz der Bundeswehr für Tapferkeit (The Bundeswehr Cross of Honor for Valor) and is the highest military decoration of the Bundeswehr. It was awarded to four German soldiers for the first time since 1945 in July 2009 by chancellor Angela Merkel, sparking a debate.
73 The statue was stolen in May 2017, and has yet to be recovered. See "Memorial 116 Panzer Division "Windhund," *Traces of War*, accessed October 17, 2024, www.tracesofwar.com/sights/734/Memorial-116-Panzer-Division-Windhund.htm.
74 "Möge diese Gedenkstätte . . . die Welt zum Frieden mahnen."
75 Jürgen Salm, "Umstrittenes Gedenken an die Eifel-Schlacht," *Deutschlandfunk*, June 13, 2017, www.deutschlandfunk.de/geschichte-des-huertgenwaldes-ums trittenes-gedenken-an-die-100.html.
76 Salm, "Umstrittenes Gedenken an die Eifel-Schlacht."
77 Karin Heiß, "Debatte um Kriegerdenkmal in Waldkirch: Soll die Nazikunst weg?" *Badische Zeitung*, October 31, 2014, https://bz-ticket.de/debatte-um-kriegerdenk mal-soll-die-nazikunst-weg--93819424.html.

78 From George Bernard Shaw's *On the Rocks: A Political Comedy*, Project Gutenberg of Australia, eBook # 0300561h.html, https://gutenberg.net.au/ebooks03/0300561h.html.

CHAPTER SEVEN

1 Translation of title: "Ask God to Render the Soul for a Short Time Again Free from Pain." A copy of the original *Mordwange* by Hans-Peter Jaeger from Stralsund was erected in 1999 at its original spot in Grün Kordshagen in a vegetable patch; Hartmut Schmied, *Geister, Götter, Teufelssteine: Sagen—and Legendenführer Mecklenburg-Vorpommern* (Rostock, Germany: Hinstorff, 2016), 62–63.
2 Achim Timmermann, *Memory and Redemption: Public Monuments and the Making of Late Medieval Landscape*, Architectura Medii Aevi, 8 (Turnhout, Belgium: Brepols, 2017), 180.
3 "Im Jahre des Herrn 1490 zwei Tage nach dem Fest Invocavit starb Bruder Detmarus Muurdorp. Betet für ihn."
4 "Alle die hier gehen, ich bitte sie, ein Kleines stehen und bitte Gott, kurze Zeit mache die Seele von Pein wieder frei."
5 Schmied, *Geister, Götter, Teufelssteine*, 62–63.
6 Reinhart Koselleck uses an additional word, *Schandmal* (a monument of shame), to describe the monuments that perpetrators of crimes (for example, insurgents) were sometimes forced to erect by the communities in which they lived; Reinhart Koselleck, "Die Widmung: Es geht um die Totalität des Terrors," in *Geronnene Lava: Texte zu politischem Totenkult und Erinnerung*, ed. Manfred Hettling, Hubert Locher, and Adriana Markantonatos (Berlin: Suhrkamp Verlag, 2023), 326.
7 Joseph Telushkin, *Jewish Literacy: The Most Important Things to Know about the Jewish Religion, Its People, and Its History* (New York: William Morrow and Company, 1991), 541.
8 Early Christian literature contains two Greek words that refer to repentance: *metanoia* (to change one's mind) and *metameleia* (regret).
9 Lindsay Jones, ed., *Encyclopedia of Religion* 2nd ed. (Detroit: Macmillan Reference, 2005), 7755.
10 Jones, *Encyclopedia of Religion*, 594.
11 Jones, *Encyclopedia of Religion*, 595–96.
12 Jones, *Encyclopedia of Religion*, 596.
13 Telushkin, *Jewish Literacy*, 542.
14 Charles Taylor, *Sources of the Self: The Making of Modern Identity* (Cambridge, MA: Harvard University Press, 1989), 27.
15 Linda Radzik, *Making Amends: Atonement in Morality, Law, and Politics* (Oxford: Oxford University Press, 2009), 21.
16 Radzik, *Making Amends*, 75–76, 86.
17 Radzik, *Making Amends*, 16, 22, 82.
18 Köber places the earliest penance crosses in the early Middle Ages; Heinz Köber, *Die alten Steinkreuze und Sühnesteine Thüringens* (Erfurt, Germany: Stolzenberg, 1960), 7.
19 Paul Frauenstädt, *Blutrache und Todtschlagsühne im Deutschen Mittelalter. Studien*

zur Deutschen Kultur- und Rechtsgeschichte (Leipzig: Verlag von Duncker & Humblot, 1881), 155.
20 Wolfgang Haubrichs, "Wergeld: The Germanic Terminology of *Compositio* and its Implementation in the Early Middle Ages," in *Wergild, Compensation and Penance: The Monetary Logic of Early Medieval Conflict Resolution*, Medieval Law and Its Practice, vol. 31, ed. Lukas Bothe, Stefan Esders, and Han Nijdam (Leiden: Brill, 2021), 94.
21 Frauenstädt, *Blutrache*, 89.
22 Harald Siems, "Observations Concerning the 'Wergild System': Explanatory Approaches, Effectiveness and Structural Deficits," in *Wergild, Compensation and Penance*, 38, 42.
23 Siems, "Observations," 39.
24 Siems, "Observations," 39.
25 Marcel Mauss, *The Gift: Expanded Edition*, selected, annotated, and trans. Jane I. Guyer (Chicago: Hau Books, 2016), 170.
26 Mauss, *Gift*, 171–72.
27 Mauss, *Gift*, 172–73.
28 Bernhard Losch, *und erschlugen sich um ein Stücklein Brot: Sühnekreuze in den Landkreisen Schwäbisch Hall und Hohenlohe* (Schwäbisch Hall, Germany: Hällisch-Fränkenisches Museum, 2001), 22.
29 Losch, *und erschlugen sich*, 22–23; Bernhard Losch, "Steinerne Versöhnungsdenkmale—Recht und Religion," *Schwäbische Heimat Magazin für Geschichte, Landeskultur, Naturschutz und Denkmalpflege* 65 (2014): 53.
30 Losch, "Steinerne Versöhnungsdenkmale," 50.
31 Frauenstädt, *Blutrache*, 88, 91–92. This system was only effective when the bonds of kindship were sufficiently strong as to obligate the families of perpetrators to fulfill obligations of restitution to the families of victims (88). Timmermann points out that the redress of a crime during the Middle Ages "was primarily the affair of the injured party or his or her relative, and only in the second instance one of the courts, which mostly acted as background mediators" (Timmerman, *Memory and Redemption*, 169).
32 Köber, *Die alten Steinkreuze*, 15; Frauenstädt, *Blutrache*, 124.
33 Timmermann, *Memory and Redemption*, 169.
34 A penance cross in Unterthingau, Bavaria, is said to have been erected as part of an atonement contract between perpetrator Matheiß Völk and the survivors of his victim, blacksmith Matheiß Stainer, who was stabbed to death in 1630. In addition to the cross, Völk was obligated to support Stainer's widow and three children. Thomas Pfundner, "Unterthingau," *Suehnekreuz.de*, accessed October 17, 2024, www.suehnekreuz.de/bayern/unterthingau.htm.
35 Losch, "Steinerne Versöhnungsdenkmale," 50.
36 Losch describes these required masses and vigils as grand and solemn, requiring at least thirty priests and an entourage of at least thirty men. The perpetrator dressed in penitential robes and carried a broken or upside-down candle (Losch, "Steinerne Versöhnungsdenkmale," 51).
37 Köber, *Die alten Steinkreuze*, 10, 14; Losch, "Steinerne Versöhnungsdenkmale," 51–52; Losch, *und erschlugen sich*, 22.
38 Frauenstädt, *Blutrache*, 154.

39 Frauenstädt, *Blutrache*, 97n18, 127–28.
40 Losch, "Steinerne Versöhnungsdenkmale," 50.
41 Losch, "Steinerne Versöhnungsdenkmale," 51–52.
42 Losch, "Steinerne Versöhnungsdenkmale," 50.
43 Approximately seventy atonement contracts from the fourteenth to the seventeenth centuries still survive in German archives (Losch, *und erschlugen sich*, 23).
44 Losch, "Steinerne Versöhnungsdenkmale," 53.
45 Losch, "Steinerne Versöhnungsdenkmale," 54.
46 Losch, "Steinerne Versöhnungsdenkmale," 49.
47 Losch, "Steinerne Versöhnungsdenkmale," 54.
48 Losch, *und erschlugen sich*, 26.
49 Frauenstädt, *Blutrache*, 154.
50 Losch, "Steinerne Versöhnungsdenkmale," 52.
51 Losch, *und erschlugen sich*, 23.
52 Bernhard Losch, *Sühne und Gedenken, Steinkreuze in Baden-Württemberg: Ein Inventar* (Stuttgart: Theiss Verlag, 1981), 102.
53 Thomas Pfundner and Ulrich Schuster, "Betzigau," *Suehnekreuz.de*, accessed October 17, 2024, www.suehnekreuz.de/bayern/betzigau.htm. See also the penance cross in Oy-Mittelberg, Bavaria, erected for two brothers who killed each other while drunk. The inscription reads, "1539/Caspar Müller/Georg Müller," Thomas Pfundner, Ulrich Schuster, and Albert Mayr, "Oy-Mittelberg," *Suehnekreuz.de*, accessed October 17, 2024, www.suehnekreuz.de/bayern/oy.htm.
54 Timmermann, *Memory and Redemption*, 22.
55 "Dieses Kreuz wurde errichtet zur Sühne für den Tod des Bischofs von Straßburg, Konrad von Lichtenberg. Er fiel im Kampf gegen die Stadt durch die Hand eines Freiburger Metzers am 29. Juli 1299. Zur Erhaltung seines ehemaligen Zustandes neu gefaßt durch die Stadt Freiburg i. J. 1903." Timmermann mentions a likely corresponding atonement contract of January 30, 1300, between the Freiburg's count and citizens (Timmermann, *Memory and Redemption*, 173).
56 Losch, *Sühne und Gedenken*, 221–22.
57 Thomas Pfundner, "Illerbeuren," *Suehnekreuz.de*, accessed October 17, 2024, www.suehnekreuz.de/bayern/illerbeuren.htm.
58 Peter Roth, "Heimatgeschichtliche Beilage zum Amtsblatt der Gemeinde Aitrach," January 2021, accessed October 17, 2024, www.gemeinde-aitrach.de/files/content/Downloads/Download%20Aktuelles/Heimatbeilagen/Heimatbeilage%20Januar%202021.pdf.
59 Nadet Somers und Dieks Nagelhout, "Valwig / OT von Cochem," *Suehnekreuz.de*, accessed October 17, 2024, www.suehnekreuz.de.
60 Losch, *Sühne und Gedenken*, 71, 81. Peter Hartig, "Obersontheim (II)," *Suehnekreuz.de*, accessed October 17, 2024, www.suehnekreuz.de/bw/obersontheim.htm. Timmermann cites eight crosses that match preserved atonement contracts: The *Bischofskreuz* of Betzenhausen; the *Bernauer Kreuz* of Berlin; the *Sühnestein* of Ustersbach, Bavaria; the *Mönchskreuz* of Erfurt, Thuringia; the *Mordwange* of Rostock; the *Vasmer-Kreuz* of Bremen; the *Sühnekreuz* of Heidingsfeld, Bavaria; and the *Hochkreuz* of Lappersdorf, Bavaria (Timmermann, *Memory and Redemption*, 173–79).
61 "Stadt Würzburg—Sühnebildstock" accessed October 17, 2024, www.wuerzburg.de

/themen/kultur-bildung-kulturangebot/stadtarchiv/touristische-leitsystem-heid ingsfeld/infotafeln/index.html (#16 Sühnebildstock).
62 Timmermann, *Memory and Redemption*, 147–48.
63 Three examples of *Scheibenkreuze* may be found in Blumenfeld (Tengen), Baden-Württemberg (fifteenth century) (Losch, *Sühne und Gedenken*, 261); Ehra-Lessien, Lower Saxony (sixteenth century); and the *Glockenstein* in Rade, Lower Saxony, so named due to the following legend: in 1430, a bell founder apprentice was murdered by his master because the latter envied his apprentice's casting of the Wittingen church bell, made in his absence; Robert Ache and Werner Müller, "Rade," *Suehnekreuz.de*, accessed October 17, 2024, www.suehnekreuz.de/nieder/rade.htm.
64 Timmermann, *Memory and Redemption*, 31–32.
65 Ernst Deeke, *Lübische Geschichten und Sagen* (Lübeck: Dittmer'sche Buchhandlung, 1890), 252–53.
66 Timmermann, *Memory and Redemption*, 178–79.
67 Erich Sauer, "Unterfarrnbach / OT von Fürth," *Suehnekreuz.de*, accessed October 17, 2024, www.suehnekreuz.de/bayern/unterfarrnbach.htm.
68 Köber, *Die alten Steinkreuze*, 15.
69 Achim Leube, "Geschichte Rügens," accessed October 17, 2024, www.geschichte.ruegens.de/ein-mord-vor-500-jahren-aus-der-geschichte-gustows-und-ruegens/.
70 Hartmut Schmied, *Die schwarzen Führer, Mecklenburg-Vorpommern* (Freiburg: Eulen Verlag, 2001), 144–45.
71 Losch, *und erschlugen sich*, 29.
72 Losch, *und erschlugen sich*, 27.
73 Jack Zipes, "Breaking the Magic Spell: Politics and the Fairy Tale," *New German Critique* 6 (Autumn 1975): 123.
74 Losch, *und erschlugen sich*, 26–27.
75 For example, the *Pestkreuz* in Buchen, Baden-Württemberg, engraved with what appears to be a jar of ointment, is perhaps a reference to Rochus von Montpellier, patron saint of doctors and pharmacists (Losch, *Sühne und Gedenken*, 262).
76 Losch, *und erschlugen sich*, 27.
77 Losch, *und erschlugen sich*, 54.
78 Losch, *und erschlugen sich*, 26–27.
79 Robert Ache and Detlef Sommer, "Wellmitz (I–IV) / OT von Neißemünde," *Suehnekreuz.de*, accessed October 17, 2024, www.suehnekreuz.de/brandenburg/wellmitz.htm.
80 Sven Gerth, Uwe Stößel, and Heike Apel, "Chemnitz," *Suehnekreuz.de*, accessed October 17, 2024, www.suehnekreuz.de/sachsen/chemnitz.htm.
81 Köber, *Die alten Steinkreuze*, 5. Losch notes that such markings in some cases do indeed indicate the weapons used in homicides (Losch, *und erschlugen sich*, 25).
82 Uwe Stößel and Holger Bär, "Schlettach," *Suehnekreuz.de*, accessed October 17, 2024, www.suehnekreuz.de/bayern/schlettach.htm.
83 Volker Rumpf, "Wollrode / OT von Guxhagen," *Suehnekreuz.de*, accessed October 17, 2024, www.suehnekreuz.de/hessen/wollrode.htm.
84 Köber, *Die alten Steinkreuze*, 5; Losch, "Steinerne Versöhnungsdenkmale," 52.
85 See also the *Wagnerkreuz* of Schömberg, Baden-Württemberg, engraved with a roofer's hammer or pickaxe and the handle of a scythe, late sixteenth / seventeenth century (Losch, *Sühne und Gedenken*, 202).
86 Losch, *Sühne und Gedenken*, 192.

87 Gernot Werner, "Möglingen," *Suehnekreuz.de*, accessed October 17, 2024, www.suehnekreuz.de/bw/moeglingen.htm.
88 Losch, *Sühne und Gedenken*, 36.
89 Losch, *und erschlugen sich*, 95.
90 Hollenbach (Mulfingen), Baden-Württemberg (Losch, *und erschlugen sich*, 144).
91 Losch, *und erschlugen sich*, 28.
92 Losch, *Sühne und Gedenken*, 283. On the front of the cross are engraved the name of the deceased and his date of death; on the reverse side appear his profession ("hunter") and the word *Mordplatz* (site of the murder).
93 Typical phrasing is some version of: "Dort soll vor langer Zeit jemand umgebracht worden sein" ("Someone is said to have been killed here long ago").
94 Losch, *und erschlugen sich*, 96.
95 There are dozens of such legends: one example is the penance cross in Unteraspach (Ilshofen), Baden-Württemberg (Losch, *und erschlugen sich*, 68).
96 Losch, *und erschlugen sich*, 26–27.
97 Hermersberg (Niedernhall), Baden-Württemberg (Losch, *und erschlugen sich*, 148).
98 Simmetshausen (Blaufelden), Baden-Württemberg (Losch, *und erschlugen sich*, 42).
99 Lauenhain (Mittweida), Saxony (two butchers); Neckarwestheim, Baden-Württemberg (a butcher and a shepherd) (Losch, *Sühne und Gedenken*, 54); Herrentierbach (Blaufelden), Baden-Württemberg (two peddlers: *Krämerskreuz*) (Losch, *und erschlugen sich*, 41).
100 Respectively, Westgartshausen (Crailsheim), Baden-Württemberg, and Brettheim (Rot am See), Baden-Württemberg, on the road to Hilgartshausen (Losch, *und erschlugen sich*, 48, 93); Weipertshofen (Stimpfach), Baden-Württemberg (Losch, *Sühne und Gedenken*, 88); Billingsbach (Blaufelden), Baden-Württemberg (Losch, *und erschlugen sich*, 40).
101 Mellrichstadt, Bavaria; there are key-shaped grooves or engravings on the top of the cross. Armin Glückert, "Mellrichstadt (I)," *Suehnekreuz.de*, accessed October 17, 2024, www.suehnekreuz.de/bayern/mellrichstadt.htm.
102 Losch, *und erschlugen sich*, 117.
103 In Hirschfelden (Michelbach an der Bilz), Baden-Württemberg (engraved with the date of 1659), and Bossendorf (Schrozberg), a vagrant and policeman are said to have killed each other (Losch, *und erschlugen sich*, 78, 100).
104 Leopold Hessek, "Hüffenhardt (I)," *Suehnekreuz.de*, accessed October 17, 2024, www.suehnekreuz.de/bw/hueffenhardt.htm.
105 Losch, *Sühne und Gedenken*, 166.
106 A second version tells of three brothers who fell in love with the same local girl and killed each other during a fight over her; their elderly father collapsed in grief over their corpses, Ute Fuhrmann and Rainer Vogt, "Zerbst I–III," *Suehnekreuz.de*, accessed October 17, 2024, www.suehnekreuz.de/anhalt/zerbst.htm.
107 Losch, *Sühne und Gedenken*, 185.
108 Losch, *und erschlugen sich*, 52.
109 For example, in Michelbach am Wald (Öhringen), Baden-Württemberg (Losch, *und erschlugen sich*, 151).
110 Haverbeck (Hameln), Lower Saxony (with reliefs, perhaps, of hammer and nails), Andreas Martin, "Haberbeck / OT von Hameln, *Suehnekreuz.de*, accessed October 17, 2024, www.suehnekreuz.de/nieder/haverbeck.htm; and also Tilbeck,

North Rhine–Westphalia (from 1164), Benno Lux, "Tilbeck," *Suehnekreuz.de*, accessed October 17, 2024, www.suehnekreuz.de/nrw/tilbeck.htm.
111 Paul Basler, "Sparow / OT von Nossentiner Hütte," *Suehnekreuz.de*, accessed October 17, 2024, www.suehnekreuz.de/mv/sparow.htm.
112 Losch, *und erschlugen sich*, 44, 67, 70. Respectively, Mittelbach (Blaufelden), Baden-Württemberg; Rückershagen (Gerabronn), Baden-Württemberg; Gaggstadt (Kirchberg an der Jagst), Baden-Württemberg. See also Herrenberg, Baden-Württemberg (Losch, *Sühne und Gedenken*, 10). Tales of two shepherds killing each other are especially common.
113 Losch, *Sühne und Gedenken*, 211.
114 Robert Ache, "Ringelbach / OT von Oberkirch," *Suehnekreuz.de*, accessed October 17, 2024, www.suehnekreuz.de/bw/ringelbach.htm. An alternate legend tells of a murderer who, finding only shoe nails on the man he murdered and planned to rob, hammered the nails into the body of his victim.
115 Schmied, *Die schwarzen Führer*, 159–60.
116 Losch, *Sühne und Gedenken*, 167.
117 In Dimbach (Bretzfeld), Baden-Württemberg, a cross is said to mark the spot where a girl murdered the object of her unrequited affections. A pruning hook is engraved on the cross (Losch, *und erschlugen sich*, 127).
118 Unterheinriet (Untergruppenbach), Baden-Württemberg (Losch, *Sühne und Gedenken*, 57).
119 "Polditz," *Suehnekreuz.de*, accessed October 17, 2024, www.suehnekreuz.de/sachsen/polditz.htm.
120 Kemmeten (Künzelsau), Baden-Württemberg (Losch, *und erschlugen sich*, 138).
121 Losch, *und erschugen sich*, 83.
122 Losch, *Sühne und Gedenken*, 114–15.
123 Losch, *und erschlugen sich*, 75. The cross bears the engraving of a colter.
124 Armin Glückert, "Euerdorf," *Suehnekreuz.de*, accessed October 17, 2024, www.suehnekreuz.de/bayern/euerdorf.htm.
125 Robert Ache, "Gräfenhain (I)," *Suehnekreuz.de*, accessed October 17, 2024, www.suehnekreuz.de/sachsen/graefenhain.htm.
126 Losch, *Sühne und Gedenken*, 98.
127 Detlef Sommer and Günter Wetzel, "Schwarzkollm," *Suehnekreuz.de*, accessed October 17, 2024, www.suehnekreuz.de/sachsen/schwarzkollm.htm.
128 The *Blutstein* (blood stone) or *Bluthochzeit* (blood wedding) in Westernbach (Zweiflingen), Baden-Württemberg (Losch, *und erschlugen sich*, 165); and Ladenburg, Baden-Württemberg (Losch, *Sühne und Gedenken*, 181–82). Also, Thorsten Pirkl and Barbara und Gert Künzl, "Altenfeld / OT von Gersfeld," *Suehnekreuz.de*, accessed October 17, 2024, www.suehnekreuz.de/hessen/altenfeld.htm.
129 "Milkel (I)," *Suehnekreuz.de*, accessed October 17, 2024, www.suehnekreuz.de/sachsen/milkel.htm. A second example of a murder / suicide is said to have occurred in Bad Zwesten. Volker Rumpf, "Bad Zwesten," *Suehnekreuz.de*, accessed October 17, 2024, www.suehnekreuz.de/hessen/badzwesten.htm.
130 H. P. Probst and Volker Rumpf, "Krofdorf-Gleiberg / OT von Wettenberg," *Suehnekreuz.de*, accessed October 17, 2024, www.suehnekreuz.de/hessen/krofdorf.htm.
131 Schmied, *Die schwarzen Führer*, 150–51.
132 Losch, *und erschlugen sich*, 97.
133 Steinbeck, North Rhine–Westphalia. A second example of a legend involving

one shepherd killing another pertains to a penance cross in Blaufelden, Baden-Württemberg (Losch, *und erschlugen sich*, 39).

134 Losch, *und erschlugen sich*, 147.
135 Losch, *und erschlugen sich*, 161.
136 Thorsten Pirkl, "Gudensberg (I)," *Suehnekreuz.de*, accessed October 17, 2024, www.suehnekreuz.de/hessen/gudensberg.htm.
137 H. P. Probst, "Flensungen / OT von Mücke," *Suehnekreuz.de*, accessed October 17, 2024, www.suehnekreuz.de/hessen/flensungen.htm.
138 Robert Ache, "Hirschfelde (II)," *Suehnekreuz.de*, accessed October 17, 2024, www.suehnekreuz.de/sachsen/hirschfelde.htm.
139 Poppenreuth (Fürth), Bavaria. An alternate legend tells of a girl who died here because she spit out the host. Erich Sauer, "Poppenreuth (I) / OT von Fürth," *Suehnekreuz.de*, accessed October 17, 2024, www.suehnekreuz.de/bayern/poppenreuth.htm.
140 Losch, *Sühne und Gedenken*, 181.
141 Armin Glückert, "Morlesau (I) / OT von Hammelburg," *Suehnekreuz.de*, accessed October 17, 2024, www.suehnekreuz.de/bayern/morlesau.htm.
142 Peter Hartig, "Nordenberg (III) / OT von Windelsbach," *Suehnekreuz.de*, accessed October 17, 2024, www.suehnekreuz.de/bayern/nordenberg.htm.
143 Franz Höreth, "Thanheim / OT von Ensdorf," *Suehnekreuz.de*, accessed October 17, 2024, www.suehnekreuz.de/bayern/thanheim.htm.
144 Benno Lux, "Saerbeck (II) / OT Middendorf," *Suehnekreuz.de*, accessed October 17, 2024, www.suehnekreuz.de/nrw/saerbeck.htm.
145 Eutendorf (Gaildorf), Baden-Württemberg, and two crosses (sixteenth / seventeenth century) in Oberrot, Baden-Württemberg (Losch, *und erschlugen sich*, 63, 82).
146 Thomas Pfundner, "Greith / OT von Halblech," *Suehnekreuz.de*, accessed October 17, 2024, www.suehnekreuz.de/bayern/greith.htm.
147 Leopold Hessek and Rudolf Wild, "Unter-Abtsteinach (I) / OT von Abtsteinach," *Suehnekreuz.de*, accessed October 17, 2024, www.suehnekreuz.de/hessen/unterabtsteinach.htm.
148 Leopold Hessek and Rudolf Wild, "Stallenkandel / OT von Wald-Michelbach," *Suehnekreuz.de*, accessed October 17, 2024, www.suehnekreuz.de/hessen/stallenkandel.htm.
149 Paul Basler, "Nankenhof," *Suehnekreuz.de*, accessed October 17, 2024, www.suehnekreuz.de/bayern/nankenhof.htm.
150 Volker Rumpf, "Ortenberg," *Suehnekreuz.de*, accessed October 17, 2024, www.suehnekreuz.de/hessen/ortenberg.htm.
151 Robert Ache, Detlef Sommer, Günter Wetzel, und Claus Dieter Weinert, "Boragk (Altenau) / OT von Mühlberg," *Suehnekreuz.de*, accessed October 17, 2024, www.suehnekreuz.de/brandenburg/boragk.htm.
152 Thorsten Pirkl, "Neunstetten (I–VI) / OT von Herrieden," *Suehnekreuz.de*, accessed October 17, 2024, www.suehnekreuz.de/bayern/neunstetten.htm.
153 Barbara und Gert Künzl, "Bad Salzschlirf (I)," *Suehnekreuz.de*, accessed October 17, 2024, www.suehnekreuz.de/hessen/badsalzschlirf.htm.
154 Armin Sopp, "Stockhausen," *Suehnekreuz.de*, accessed October 17, 2024, www.suehnekreuz.de/hessen/stockhausen.htm.
155 Dörte Bleul, "Dahlowitz," *Suehnekreuz.de*, accessed October 17, 2024, www.suehnekreuz.de/sachsen/dahlowitz.htm.
156 "Petersbuch," *Suehnekreuz.de*, accessed October 17, 2024, www.suehnekreuz.de/bayern/petersbuch.htm.

157 *Bußkreuz*, Muggensturm, Baden-Württemberg (Losch, *Sühne und Gedenken*, 155).
158 Wittau (Crailsheim) and Öhringen, Baden-Württemberg (Losch, *und erschlugen sich*, 50, 149).
159 Fichtenberg, Baden-Württemberg (Losch, *und erschlugen sich*, 53).
160 Heimsheim, Baden-Württemberg (Losch, *Sühne und Gedenken*, 207).
161 Köber, *Die alten Steinkreuze*, 6.
162 I would like to thank Franz Piendl for helping me obtain this image.
163 Alfons Listl, et al., "Das eiserne Handl," *Niederbayerische Hefte*, 107: Kelsgausagen (Regensburg: Leonhard Wolf, 1962), 9.
164 Benno Lux, "Saerbeck (I)," *Suehnekreuz.de*, accessed October 17, 2024, www.suehnekreuz.de/nrw/saerbeck.htm.
165 Losch, *und erschlugen sich*, 164.
166 Losch, *Sühne und Gedenken*, 208. Other *Hängerle* legends accompany crosses in Nußloch, Baden-Württemberg (*Gräfelskreuz*, sixteenth century) (Losch, *Sühne und Gedenken*, 185); Wohlmuthausen (Forchtenberg), Baden-Württemberg (Losch, *und erschlugen sich*, 131); and Hermersberg (Niedernhall), Baden-Württemberg (Losch, *und erschlugen sich*, 147).
167 Detlef Sommer, "Tremmen," *Suehnekreuz.de*, accessed October 17, 2024, www.suehnekreuz.de/brandenburg/tremmen.htm.
168 Ute Fuhrmann and Rainer Vogt, "Zerbst (I–III)," *Suehnekreuz.de*, accessed October 17, 2024, www.suehnekreuz.de/anhalt/zerbst.htm.
169 Albert Veit, "Hengersberg," *Suehnekreuz.de*, accessed October 17, 2024, www.suehnekreuz.de/bayern/hengersberg.htm; and Pflaumloch (Riesbürg), Baden-Württemberg, sixteenth century, limestone, called *Schwedenkreuz* (Losch, *Sühne und Gedenken*, 130–31).
170 Möglingen, Baden-Württemberg (Losch, *Sühne und Gedenken*, 36).
171 1702, Rudolf Wild, "Battenberg," *Suehnekreuz.de*, accessed October 17, 2024, www.suehnekreuz.de/rhein/battenberg.htm.
172 Edmund Schiewer, "Warle (I)," *Suehnekreuz.de*, accessed October 17, 2024, www.suehnekreuz.de/nieder/warle.htm.
173 Johannes Znotins, "Mittelhembach (I / II) / OT von Schwanstetten," *Suehnekreuz.de*, accessed October 17, 2024, www.suehnekreuz.de/bayern/mittelhembach.htm.
174 Hartmut Blaszczyk, "Mechtshausen / OT von Seesen," *Suehnekreuz.de*, accessed October 17, 2024, www.suehnekreuz.de/nieder/mechtshausen.htm.
175 Irene Thompson, *A to Z of Punishment and Torture* (Brighton: Book Guild, 2008), 183.
176 Jacob Grimm and Wilhelm Grimm, *Deutsches Wörterbuch von Jacob und Wilhelm Grimm*, vol. 5 (Leipzig: S. Hirzel, 1855), 70.
177 The monikers *Judenstein* (Jew's stone) or *Judenkreuz* (Jew's cross) are common for such memorials.
178 H. P. Probst, "Ruppertsburg (I–III) / OT von Laubach," *Suehnekreuz.de*, accessed October 17, 2024, www.suehnekreuz.de/hessen/ruppertsburg.htm.
179 Losch, *Sühne und Gedenken*, 146.
180 Gunter Marx, "Sandebeck (I)," *Suehnekreuz.de*, accessed October 17, 2024, www.suehnekreuz.de/nrw/sandebeck.htm.
181 Paul Basler, "Oberkonnersreuth (I) / OT von Bayreuth," *Suehnekreuz.de*, accessed October 17, 2024, www.suehnekreuz.de/bayern/oberkonnersreuth.htm. See also

Mittelbach (Blaufelden), Baden-Württemberg, where two "Gypies" are said to have killed each other (Losch, *und erschlugen sich*, 44).
182 Volker Rumpf, "Leubach / OT von Fladungen," *Suehnekreuz.de*, accessed October 17, 2024, www.suehnekreuz.de/bayern/leubach.htm.
183 Sven Gerth, "Gersdorf," *Suehnekreuz.de*, accessed October 17, 2024, www.suehnekreuz.de/sachsen/gersdorf2.htm.
184 (Ruppertsburg (Laubach), Hesse). Additional examples may be found in Schönnen (Erbach), Hesse; Weisenheim am Sand, Rheinland-Pfalz; and Honings (Hetzles), Bavaria.
185 Barbara und Gert Künzl, "Wechterswinkel (III) / OT von Bastheim," *Suehnekreuz.de*, accessed October 17, 2024, www.suehnekreuz.de/bayern/wechterswinkel.htm.
186 Benno Lux, "Lembeck," *Suehnekreuz.de*, accessed October 17, 2024, www.suehnekreuz.de/nrw/lembeck.htm.
187 Lembach (Großbottwar), Baden-Württemberg (Losch, *Sühne und Gedenken*, 34).
188 Losch, *Sühne und Gedenken*, 36.
189 Armin Sopp, "Stockhausen," *Suehnekreuz.de*, accessed October 17, 2024, www.suehnekreuz.de/hessen/stockhausen.htm.
190 Émile Durkheim, *The Elementary Forms of Religious Life*, trans. Karen E. Fields (New York: The Free Press, 1995), 412–13.
191 Robert Hertz, *Death and the Right Hand*, trans. Rodney Needham and Claudia Needham (Glencoe, IL: Free Press, 1960), 94.
192 Losch, *Sühne und Gedenken*, 298; Losch, *und erschlugen sich*, 164.
193 Köber, *Die alten Steinkreuze*, 6.
194 Benno Lux, "Lembeck," *Suehnekreuz.de*, accessed October 17, 2024, www.suehnekreuz.de/nrw/lembeck.htm.
195 Paul Basler, "Neuhaus / OT von Windischeschenbach," *Suehnekreuz.de*, accessed October 17, 2024, www.suehnekreuz.de/bayern/neuhaus.htm; Barbara und Gert Künzl, "Frischborn / OT von Lauterbach," *Suehnekreuz.de*, accessed October 17, 2024, www.suehnekreuz.de/hessen/frischborn.htm; Murrhardt, Baden-Württemberg (Losch, *Sühne und Gedenken*, 40–41).
196 Erich Sauer, "Priesendorf," *Suehnekreuz.de*, accessed October 17, 2024, www.suehnekreuz.de/bayern/priesendorf.htm, and Gaggstadt (Kirchberg an der Jagst), Baden-Württemberg (Losch, *und erschlugen sich*, 70), respectively.
197 Leopold Hessek and Rudolf Wild, "Krumbach / OT von Limbach," *Suehnekreuz.de*, accessed October 17, 2024, www.suehnekreuz.de/bw/krumbach.htm.
198 Rot am See, Baden-Württemberg (Losch, *und erschlugen sich*, 92).
199 Johannes Znotins, "Deinschwang / OT von Lauterhofen," *Suehnekreuz.de*, accessed October 17, 2024, www.suehnekreuz.de/bayern/deinschwang.htm, and Robert Ache, "Dittigheim / OT von Tauberbischofsheim," *Suehnekreuz.de*, accessed October 17, 2024, www.suehnekreuz.de/bw/dittigheim.htm.
200 Jochen Früh, "Waldkirch (IV) / OT von Waldshut-Tiengen," *Suehnekreuz.de*, accessed October 17, 2024, www.suehnekreuz.de/bw/waldkirch.htm.
201 Benno Lux, "Emsdetten (I–III)," *Suehnekreuz.de*, accessed October 17, 2024, www.suehnekreuz.de/nrw/emsdetten.htm; Martin Wittwar and Uwe Stößel, "Orferode / OT von Bad Sooden-Allendorf," *Suehnekreuz.de*, accessed October 17, 2024, www.suehnekreuz.de/hessen/orferode.htm.

202 Gaggstadt (Kirchberg an der Jagst), Baden-Württemberg (Losch, *und erschlugen sich*, 70).
203 Gesine Weber and Rudolf Wild, "Langen (I / II)," *Suehnekreuz.de*, accessed October 17, 2024, www.suehnekreuz.de/hessen/langen.htm.
204 Rechenhausen (Gerabronn), Baden-Württemberg (Losch, *und erschlugen sich*, 66).
205 Steinbach (Schwäbisch Hall, Baden-Württemberg) (Losch, *und erschlugen sich*, 112).
206 There are a few exceptions: a memorial cross for a curate killed by a wasp sting in 1962, for example, stands in Neustadt (Breuberg), Hesse. Volker Rumpf, "Neustadt (I) / OT von Breuberg," *Suehnekreuz.de*, accessed October 17, 2024, www.suehnekreuz.de/hessen/neustadt.htm.
207 Hans-Günther Morr, *Steinkreuze, stumme Zeugen alter Schuld: Inventarisierung der überbrachten Flurdenkmäler, mit Sagen, Märchen, und Erzählungen aus dem Odenwald* (Weinheim: Edition-Diesbach, 2009), 29.
208 Losch, *Sühne und Gedenken*, 181.
209 See legends of crosses in Demitz-Thumitz, Saxony (for a cross removed and smashed); Bossendorf (Schrozberg), Baden-Württemberg (a cross shifted to a new site); and Steinbach an der Jagst (Frankenhardt), Baden-Württemberg (a cross walled up within a stable) (Losch, *und erschlugen sich*, 61).

CHAPTER EIGHT

1 William E. Mann, "Augustine on Evil and Original Sin," in *The Cambridge Companion to Augustine*, ed. Eleonore Stump and Norman Kretzmann (Cambridge: Cambridge University Press, 2001), 45. Respectively, Augustine's *De natura boni contra Manichaeos* 36 and *De libero arbitrio* 2.20.54.
2 Many of the memorials that identify with and mourn victims have been discussed as examples of "countermonuments"—memorials of the 1980s and later that undermine the traditional goals and aesthetics of monuments; James E. Young, "The Counter-Monument: Memory against Itself in Germany Today," *Critical Inquiry* 18, no. 2 (Winter 1992): 267–296. A few examples include Sol LeWitt's Black Form—Dedicated to the Missing Jews (Hamburg, 1989); Gunter Demnig's Stolpersteine (Stumbling Stones); Jochen Gerz and Esther Shalev-Gerz's disappearing Monument against Fascism in Hamburg-Harburg (1986); and Horst Hoheisel's Aschrott Fountain memorial in Kassel (1985). See James E. Young, *The Texture of Memory: Holocaust Memorials and Meaning* (New Haven: Yale University Press, 1993). Other studies of countermonuments include Noam Lupu, "Memory Vanished, Absent, and Confined," *History and Memory* 15, no. 2 (Fall/Winter 2003); Cecily Harris, "German Memory of the Holocaust: The Emergence of Counter-Memorials," *Penn History Review* 17, no. 2 (2010); Quentin Stevens et al., "Counter-monuments: The Anti-Monumental and the Dialogic," *Journal of Architecture* 23, no. 5 (2018): 951–972.
3 Ernesto Bonaiuti and Giorgio La Piana, "The Genesis of St. Augustine's Idea of Original Sin," *Harvard Theological Review* 10, no. 2 (April 1917): 163, 165. A "lump" or "mass" of "sin, clay, condemnation / damnation, and of the condemned/ the damned."

4 Mann, "Augustine," 47.
5 George P. Fletcher, "The Storrs Lectures: Liberals and Romantics at War: The Problem of Collective Guilt," *Yale Law Journal* 111, no. 7 (May 2002): 1568.
6 John Carroll, *Guilt: The Grey Eminence behind Character, History, and Culture* (London: Routledge & Kegan Paul Books, 1985), 156–58.
7 René Girard, *Violence and the Sacred*, trans. Patrick Gregory (Baltimore: The Johns Hopkins University Press, 1977), 275, 300, 302.
8 Girard, *Violence*, 77, 94.
9 Peter D. Clarke, *The Interdict in the Thirteenth Century: A Question of Collective Guilt* (New York: Oxford University Press, 2007), 1.
10 Clarke, *Interdict*, 57–58.
11 H. Seyer, "Mord mit Folgen," in *Archäologie in Deutschland* 3 (July–September 1995): 41; Andreas Conrad, "Berlin: Schuld und Sühnekreuz," *Tagesspiegel*, October 24, 2012, www.tagesspiegel.de/berlin/schuld-und-suhnekreuz-2222353.html.
12 Achim Timmermann, *Memory and Redemption: Public Monuments and the Making of Late Medieval Landscape*, Architectura Medii Aevi, 8 (Turnhout, Belgium: Brepols, 2017), 176.
13 A half share of the town of Limburg belonged to the Electorate of Trier, an ecclesiastical principality of the Holy Roman Empire, since 1344.
14 Paul Frauenstädt, *Blutrache und Todtschlagsühne im Deutschen Mittelalter: Studien zur Deutschen Kultur- und Rechtsgeschichte* (Leipzig: Verlag von Duncker & Humblot, 1881), 49–50.
15 Bernhard Losch, "Steinerne Versöhnungsdenkmale—Recht und Religion," *Schwäbische Heimat Magazin für Geschichte, Landeskultur, Naturschutz und Denkmalpflege* 65 (2014): 52.
16 Charles Taylor, *Sources of the Self: The Making of Modern Identity* (Cambridge, MA: Harvard University Press, 1989), 27–28.
17 Taylor, *Sources of the Self*, 34–35.
18 Fletcher, "Storrs Lectures," 1509–10.
19 Linda Radzik, *Making Amends: Atonement in Morality, Law, and Politics* (Oxford: Oxford University Press, 2009), 176.
20 Radzik, *Making Amends*, 185–86.
21 Fletcher addresses the following: Germany's unusual law regarding treason, according to which anyone—not only German citizens—may be charged with treason; Germany's law of return for nationals born abroad; the wording of Germany's Basic Law, which refers in several places to German "nationals" (rather than "citizens") ("Storrs Lectures,"1535–37).
22 Fletcher, "Storrs Lectures," 1522–26, 1537.
23 Fletcher, "Storrs Lectures," 1541–42.
24 Dan Diner, "Negative Symbiosis: Germans and Jews After Auschwitz," in *Reworking the Past: Hitler, the Holocaust, and the Historians' Debate*, ed. Peter Baldwin (Boston: Beacon Press, 1990), 253.
25 Fletcher, "Storrs Lectures," 1569.
26 Fletcher, "Storrs Lectures," 1569.
27 Quoted in Katharina von Kellenbach, *The Mark of Cain: Guilt and Denial in the Post-War Lives of Nazi Perpetrators* (New York: Oxford University Press, 2013), 15–16.
28 Kellenbach, *Mark of Cain*, 18.

29 Founded 1958 by the Evangelical Church in Germany under the leadership of Lothar Kreyssig, *Aktion Sühnezeichen* is known for its international volunteer programs in countries that suffered under German occupation, as well as in Israel and the United States.
30 Radzik, *Making Amends*, 85–86.
31 Roy Brooks, "The Age of Apology," in *When Sorry Isn't Enough: The Controversy over Apologies and Reparations for Human Injustice*, ed. Roy Brooks (New York: New York University Press, 1999), 3.
32 See Susan Neiman, *Learning from the Germans: Race and the Memory of Evil* (New York: Farrar, Straus and Giroux, 2019).
33 When founding the Claims Conference, representatives make clear that "no amount of money 'can make good the destruction of human life and cultural values,'" or "atone for the systematic annihilation of the Jewish people," www.claimscon.org/about/history/.
34 Stefan Engert, "Confessing the Holocaust: The Evolution of German Guilt," in *On the Uses and Abuses of Political Apologies*, ed. Mihaela Mihai and Mathias Thaler (New York: Palgrave Macmillan, 2014), 100–101.
35 Ulrike Jureit, "Opferidentifikation und Erlösungshoffnung: Beobachtungen im errinerungspolitischen Rampenlicht," in *Gefühlte Opfer: Illusionen der Vergangenheitsbewältigung*, ed. Ulrike Jureit and Christian Schneider (Stuttgart: Klett-Cotta, 2010), 21.
36 Engert, "Confessing the Holocaust," 97.
37 The study was organized by the Psychological Institute of the University of Hanover and sponsored by the Volkswagen Foundation. The members of the group included Olaf Jensen, Torsten Koch, Sabine Moller, Erika Rothärmel, and Karoline Tschuggnall. In all, 2,535 stories were collected and analyzed.
38 Harald Welzer, *Grandpa Wasn't a Nazi: The Holocaust in German Family Remembrance* (New York: American Jewish Committee, 2005). Original publication: Harald Welzer, Sabine Moller, and Karoline Tschuggnall, *"Opa war kein Nazi": Nationalsozialismus und Holocaust im Familiengedächtnis* (Frankfurt am Main: Fischer Taschenbuch Verlag, 2002).
39 See Gilad Margalit on the discourse of victimization (suffering, hunger, expulsion, abuse by victors) in family memories of the Nazi years: Gilad Margalit, *Guilt, Suffering, and Memory: Germany Remembers Its Dead of World War II*, trans. Haim Watzman (Bloomington: Indiana University Press, 2010), 290–93.
40 Harald Welzer, "Collateral Damage of History Education: National Socialism and the Holocaust in German Family Memory," special issue, Collective Memory and Collective Identity, *Social Research* 75, no. 1 (Spring 2008): 297–301.
41 Heidi Behrens and Sabine Moller, "'Opa war kein Nazi' and die Folgen: Zurück an den Anfang der Gedenkstättenpädagogik?" *Gedenkstättenrundbrief* 121 (September 2004): 18.
42 Welzer, "Collateral Damage," 312.
43 See Margalit, *Guilt, Suffering, and Memory*, 76, 285.
44 Welzer, "Collateral Damage," 310.
45 Welzer, "Collateral Damage," 313.
46 Katja Iken and Eva-Maria Schnurr, "Unser Gedenken ist in Ritualen erstarrt," *Spiegel Geschichte*, September 15, 2022, www.spiegel.de/geschichte/holocaust-und-die-deutsche-erinnerungskultur-unser-gedenken-ist-in-ritualen-erstarrt-a-f9fe9ae3

-4ebc-4390-ab16-121650fc52d6. See also Aleida Assmann, *Das neue Unbehagen an der Erinnerungskultur: Eine Intervention* (Munich: Verlag C. H. Beck, 2013).
47 Jureit, "Opferidentifikation," 13, 24.
48 There are exceptions, including the Topography of Terror, the House of the Wannsee Conference, and the Eagle's Nest.
49 Jureit, "Opferidentifikation," 30, 36.
50 "The Jewish nation remembers and will always remember. We seek reconciliation as human beings. Precisely for this reason we must understand that there can be no reconciliation without remembrance.... 'Seeking to forget makes exile all the longer; the secret of redemption lies in remembrance.'" Bill Niven points out that "the countermonument's agonized representation of fissures and spaces may express the wish for them to be filled, so that history can move forward once more"; Bill Niven, "From Countermonument to Combimemorial: Developments in German Memorialization," *Journal of War & Culture Studies* 6, no. 1 (February 2013): 84.
51 Jureit "Opferidentifikation," 38.
52 Jureit "Opferidentifikation," 42.
53 Jureit "Opferidentifikation," 22–23.
54 Jenny Hestermann, Roby Nathanson, und Stephan Stetter, "Deutschland und Israel heute: Zwischen Verbundenheit und Entfremdung," *Bertelsmann Stiftung*, September 2. 2022, www.bertelsmann-stiftung.de/de/publikationen/publikation/did/deutschland-und-israel-heute-zwischen-verbundenheit-und-entfremdung.
55 Seventeen percent of Germans were undecided. Thirty-three percent disagreed with the statement (1 percent said they did not know or didn't respond). In comparison, fourteen percent of polled Israelis agreed with the statement (66 percent disagreed; 21 percent were undecided).
56 Jureit, "Opferidentifikation," 27. See Silke Wenk, "Sacrifice and Victimization in the Commemorative Practices of Nazi Genocide after German Unification—Memorials and Visual Metaphors," trans. Matthias Schneider and Herbert Mehrtens, in *Sacrifice and National Belonging in Twentieth-Century Germany*, ed. Greg Eghigian and Matthew Paul Berg (College Station: Texas A&M University Press, 2002).
57 Martin Walser, in his acceptance speech for the Peace Prize of the German Book Trade (Frankfurt, 1998), famously declared the memorial to be the "monumentalization of shame"—a "soccer field- sized nightmare" and example of "negative nationalism"; ("Erfahrungen beim Verfassen einer Sonntagsrede"; Martin Walser, *Ich vertraue: Querfeldein: Reden und Aufsätze* (Frankfurt am Main: Suhrkamp, 2000), 36. The far-right politician of the AfD, Björn Höcke, expressed what appeared to be—at least superficially—similar sentiments about the Berlin Holocaust Memorial in January 2017. In response, eleven months later activists built a minuscule replica of the Berlin memorial outside Höcke's house in Bornhagen. It is also worth noting that Eisenman never intended for the memorial to be an expression of guilt. In an interview with *Spiegel Online* published on May 9, 2025, Eisenman testifies to the contrary, saying that he hopes that "this memorial, in its absence of guilt-making, is part of the process of getting over that guilt." Thank you to the anonymous reviewer who brought this to my attention.
58 Jureit, "Opferidentifikation," 28–29.
59 For a striking contrast to the memorials of reconciliation discussed here, consider Slovakian sculptor Martin Hudáček's two works, Memorial for Unborn Children (Slovakia; a replica stands at the Holy Spirit Catholic Church in Fresno, California)

and Memorial for Unborn Children II (Wroclaw, Poland; replicas stand in the Resurrection Cemetery, Madison, Wisconsin, and in Svidnik, Slovakia). These memorials, popular with pro-life advocates, depict, respectively, a grieving mother being approached by her aborted baby, who reaches out to her in forgiveness, and a father and mother being approached by a likewise forgiving, older girl child (four years old)—the father reaches out his hand to the child while also comforting the mourning mother. Here, reconciliation and healing come not from the offender's decision to "turn toward" the good but rather through the merciful forgiveness granted by the harmed party—here, the aborted child.

60 The original sculpture upon which Reconciliation was based, titled Reunion (1977), was erected at the University of Bradford in Yorkshire to mark the establishment of a Faculty of Peace Studies. Reunion, in turn, was based on a smaller sculpture from 1955.

61 Bob Crowther, "Josefina de Vasconcellos (1904-2005): Sculpting for Peace and Reconciliation," *British Art Journal* 21, no. 2 (Autumn 2020): 28-30.

62 I would like to thank Pfarrer Jürgen Dolling for sharing with me photographs and informational materials about this memorial.

63 These words appear in relief on a metal plaque at the memorial site: "Möge Intoleranz und Menschenverachtung verwandelt werden in die Verwirklichung von Versöhnung."

64 The Gospel of John 1:1: "In the beginning was the Word, and the Word was with God, and the Word was God"; John 1:14: "And the Word was made flesh, and dwelt among us . . ."

65 See Björn Mensing, "Evangelische Versöhnungskirche in der KZ-Gedenkstätte Dachau und ihre Anfänge (1967-1984)," in *Verständigung und Versöhnung nach dem Zivilisationsbruch? Deutschland in Europa nach 1945*, ed. Corine Defrance and Ulrich Pfeil (Brussels: Peter Lang, 2016), 194, 197. Members of the Protestant church in Dachau as well as the pastor of Dachau-Ost, Dr. Daum, did not support the building of the new church. Mensing notes other problematic aspects of the church's history, including requests of Oskar Zeiss, retired general secretary of the Protestant youth group in Würzburg and active in the Dachau Reconciliation Church from July to August 1967, to have all "terrible photos" of atrocities and medical experiments removed from the camp museum, arguing that no nation displays its "darkest history" for others to see, and that such displays would only foment hate. Instead, Zeiss suggested an exhibit on the resistance movement be added (Mensing, "Evangelische Versöhnungskirche," 198).

66 Mensing, "Evangelische Versöhnungskirche," 194-5.

67 Heinrich Bauer, Walter Joelsen, Björn Mensing, Klaus Schultz, and Christian Topp, eds., *Evangelische Versöhnungskirche KZ-Gedenkstätte Dachau*, 2nd ed. (Augsburg: LaySa Mediendienstleister), 21.

68 Mensing, "Evangelische Versöhnungskirche," 195.

69 Bauer et al., "Evangelische Versöhnungskirche," 23.

70 Mensing, "Evangelische Versöhnungskirche," 200-201.

71 Bauer et al., "Evangelische Versöhnungskirche," 3.

72 Pages 15-17 of Bauer et al., "Evangelische Versöhnungskirche," summarize the Protestant church's response to Nazism, including the formation of the Bekennende Kirche (Confessing Church, founded 1934), and admits the failures of the

Protestant church, including the fact that the political turn in 1933 was greeted by most Protestants with enthusiasm and theologically legitimized by a number of Protestant theologians, and even that the Bekennende Kirche limited its opposition to National Socialism in most cases to the regime's treatment of Christianity and the Protestant church.

73 Bauer et al., "Evangelische Versöhnungskirche," 3.
74 See Silke Wenk, "Sacrifice and Victimization in the Commemorative Practices of Nazi Genocide after German Unification—Memorials and Visual Metaphors," trans. Matthias Schneider and Herbert Mehrtens, in *Sacrifice and National Belonging in Twentieth-Century Germany*, ed. Greg Eghigian and Matthew Paul Berg (College Station: Texas A&M University Press, 2002), for an analysis of the memorial's location. See Rudy Koshar, *From Monuments to Traces: Artifacts of German Memory, 1870–1990* (Berkeley: University of California Press, 2000), 107–9, 258; Bill Niven, *Germans as Victims: Remembering the Past in Contemporary Germany* (Basingstoke, UK: Palgrave Macmillan, 2006), 4–6; Margalit, *Guilt, Suffering, and Memory*, 223–24, 250. See also Siobhan Kattago, "Representing German Victimhood and Guilt: The Neue Wache and Unified German Memory," *German Politics and Society* 16, no. 3 (Fall 1998): 86–104.
75 Kollwitz created the original in 1937 to express her grief over the death of her son Peter in World War I. The version in the Neue Wache is five times its original size.
76 Koshar, *From Monuments to Traces*, 258. Kattago notes that given the different interpretations of the Nazi past in the former East and West Germany, "victimhood provides the most common commemorative theme" (Kattago, "Representing German Victimhood," 101).
77 In Weizsäcker's speech, the first victims named were the six million murdered Jews; here, Jews are listed after the following: the people who suffered through war, the citizens who were persecuted and lost their lives, those killed in action in the world wars, and the innocent who lost their lives as a result of war in their homeland, in captivity and through expulsion.
78 Reinhart Koselleck, "Mies, medioker und provinziell," in *Geronnene Lava: Texte zu politischem Totenkult und Erinnerung*, ed. Manfred Hettling, Hubert Locher, and Adriana Markantonatos (Berlin: Suhrkamp Verlag, 2023), 271.
79 Reinhart Koselleck, "Bilderverbot. Welches Totengedenken?" *Frankfurter Allgemeine Zeitung*, April 8, 1993, 33.
80 Reinhart Koselleck, "Die bildliche Transformation der Gedächtnisstätten in der Neuzeit," in *Geronnene Lava*, 173.
81 Additional memorials of reconciliation are being planned but not yet erected, including the Memorial to Polish Victims of Germany in Berlin, approved by the Bundestag on October 30, 2020 (www.bundestag.de/dokumente/textarchiv/2020 0/kw44-de-deutsch-polnische-geschichte-798198), or have failed to be realized, as in the case of the German-Danish Reconciliation Memorial proposed by Danish sculptor André Stilling for the town of Dybbøl, on the site where a Prussian memorial from 1872, dedicated to the triumph of Prussian and Austrian troops during the German-Danish war, once stood before it was destroyed by the Danes in May 1945. The memorial project was abandoned due to popular, local resistance to the idea. See Frank Jung, "Nej tak zum symbolischen Händedruck," www.shz .de/deutschland-welt/schleswig-holstein/artikel/nej-tak-zum-symbolischen-haend edruck-41194809.

82 Horst Hoheisel, "Das Denkmal muß auf die Täter verweisen," *taz*, February 6, 1996, https://taz.de/Das-Denkmal-muss-auf-die-Taeter-verweisen/!1472878/.
83 Reinhart Koselleck, "Vier Minuten für die Ewigkeit: Das Totenreich vermessen—Fünf Fragen an das Holocaust-Denkmal," in *Geronnene Lava*, 291. See also Reinhart Koselleck, "Die Widmung Es geht um die Totalität des Terrors," in *Geronnene Lava*," 325–31. Koselleck uses the terms *"Opfermale"* and *"Tätermale"* to distinguish between memorials that speak for the victims from the victim perspective and those that recall the crimes of the perpetrators, and insists that the line between the two be respected. "As Germans," Koselleck admonishes, "we may under no circumstances assume the role of the victims (or play that role) by erecting a Holocaust memorial as Jews, naturally, can do in countries around the world" ("Die Widmung," 327).
84 In his project Die Tore der Deutschen (The Gateways of the German People), Hoheisel projected the parole from the entry gate to Auschwitz, "Arbeit macht frei," onto the Brandenburg Gate on Holocaust Remembrance Day, January 27, 1997: "If the Germans celebrate their Brandenburg Gate as a national symbol, they should never forget the other gateways they have also built—the gateways to the concentration camps"; Horst Hoheisel, "'The Long Shadow of the Past' in the Short Light of the Present,'" *Magazine of the European Observatory on Memories*, December 10, 2018, https://europeanmemories.net/magazine/the-long-shadow-of-the-past-in-the-short-light-of-present.
85 Gerz's other memorial projects include 2146 Stones—Monument against Racism / The Invisible Monument in Saarbrücken (1993) and his Monument against Fascism in Harburg (Hamburg) (with Esther Shalev-Gerz, 1986). See Jochen Gerz and Esther Shalev-Gerz, *Das Harburger Mahnmal gegen Faschismus / The Harburg Monument against Fascism* (Stuttgart: Hatje Verlag, 1994). For a study of Hoheisel's and Gerz's work, see Kristine Nielsen, "Monumental Attack: The Visual Tools of the German Counter-Monument in Two Works by Jochen Gerz and Esther Schalev-Gerz and Horst Hoheisel," *Images* 9, no. 1: 122–39. For a study of the Berlin memorial competitions, see Claus Leggewie and Erik Meyer, *"Ein Ort, an den man gerne geht": Das Holocaust-Mahnmal und die deutsche Geschichtspolitik nach 1989* (Munich: Carl Hanser Verlag, 2005). See Wenk for a discussion of proposals that sought to use the Jews and their culture to "articulate the German self" by appropriating the signs of the victims (Wenk, "Sacrifice and Victimization," 216–20).
86 Hoheisel, "Das Denkmal." Although his Berlin memorial project remains unrealized, Hoheisel's and Andreas Knitz's conceptually related project Crushed History—Zermahlene Geschichte (1997–2003), which began with the public demolition of former Gestapo barracks and prison in Weimar, was realized. A description of the project may be found on the website of Hoheisel & Knitz, www.knitz.net. The Jewish Museum of New York City also offers a short description of the project here: thejewishmuseum.org/collection/33058-crushed-history-zermahlene-geschichte.
87 I would like to thank Daniel Trujillo and Diana Edkins for helping me obtain this image.
88 Hoheisel, "Long Shadow."
89 Wenk, "Sacrifice and Victimization," 215.
90 Hoheisel, "Long Shadow."
91 James E. Young, "Memory and Counter-Memory," special issue, Constructions of Memory: On Monuments Old and New, *Harvard Design Magazine* 9 (Fall 1995):

13, www.harvarddesignmagazine.org/articles/memory-and-counter-memory/. See James E Young, *At Memory's Edge: After-Images of the Holocaust in Contemporary Art and Architecture* (New Haven: Yale University Press, 2000), 92–93, for a brief discussion of Hoheisel's Brandenburg Gate proposal.

92 Ofer Aderet, "Israeli Sculptor Gives Rare Tour of His Book-Burning Memorial in Berlin," *Haaretz*, September 7, 2014, www.haaretz.com/jewish/2014-09-07/ty-article/a-rare-look-inside-berlins-book-burning-memorial/0000017f-e0e8-d9aa-afff-f9f8f0010000.

93 Richard Brody, "The Inadequacy of Berlin's 'Memorial to the Murdered Jews of Europe,'" *New Yorker*, July 7, 2012, https://www.newyorker.com/culture/richard-brody/the-inadequacy-of-berlins-memorial-to-the-murdered-jews-of-europe. Brody notes that the Holocaust memorial "separates the victims from their killers and leaches the moral element from the historical event, shunting it to the category of a natural catastrophe."

94 Jochen Gerz, "Rede an die Jury des Denkmals für die ermordeten Juden Europas," November 14, 1997, https://jochengerz.s3.eu-central-1.amazonaws.com/Rede-an-die-Jury-des-Denkmals_Jochen_Gerz.pdf, 3.

95 Gerz, "Rede an die Jury," 4.

96 Gerz, "Rede an die Jury," 2–3.

97 "Warum. Warum ist es geschehen? Denkmal für die ermordeten Juden Europas / Memorial to the Murdered Jews of Europe," *CR* 127 (1997), https://jochengerz.eu/works/warum-warum-ist-es-geschehen-denkmal-fuer-die-ermordeten-juden-europas.

98 Gottfried Knapp (1977) states: "If today for convenience's sake the museum keyword 'Exit' hangs over doors that once led directly to a certain death... then the thoughtless analogy with reference systems, distorted through this discrepancy, takes on a macabre dimension"; EXIT Materialien zum Dachau-Projekt, *CR* 38 (1972/1974), https://jochengerz.eu/works/exit-materialien-zum-dachau-projekt.

99 EXIT Materialien zum Dachau-Projekt, *CR* 38 (1972/1974), https://jochengerz.eu/works/exit-materialien-zum-dachau-projekt.

100 In "Das Aufkehren der Scherben," Francis Lévy discusses similarities between modern life and life in the camps, including the labeling of human beings in modern societies from birth forward (19, 28) as well as medical experimentation on prisoners; Francis Lévy, "Das Aufkehren der Scherben," in Jochen Gerz and Francis Lévy, *EXIT: Das Dachau-Projekt* (Frankfurt am Main: Verlag Roter Stern, 1978), 20, 24.

101 Gerz and Lévy, *EXIT*, 137.

102 I use this term here in the sense in which it has been used to describe Alfred Hrdlicka's *Gegendenkmal* (opposition or countermemorials) to the battle-glorifying 76th monument (Richard Kuöhl, 1936) in Hamburg: Hamburger Feuersturm (Hamburg Firestorm, 1985) and Fluchtgruppe Cap Arcona (Fleeing the Cap Arcona, 1986). Thank you to the anonymous reviewer who helpfully pointed out the irony of the fact that the first *Gegendenkmal* was, in truth, not really a *Gegendenkmal* at all in the sense that both Hamburg Firestorm and Fleeing the Cap Arcona memorialize those who died—both Germans and victims of Nazi persecution—as a result of Allied bombings.

103 Neo-Nazis have for years gathered in Dresden to stage mourning marches on the anniversary of the city's bombing; in the early 2000s, Dresden saw marches with as

many as six thousand participants. The anti-Nazi platform "Dresden Nazifrei" and other progressive groups work hard to organize blockades and counterprotests.
104 The memorial was financed privately through the estate of Dr. Helga Barbara Petzold, who personally experienced the Dresden bombing.
105 The entire speech, "Das Schmuddelkind," can be found at "Das Schmuddelkind," *No Excuses!* (blog), February 7, 2015, https://noexcuses.noblogs.org/das-schmud delkind/. I would like to thank Thomas Baumann-Hartwig for sharing an image of the Schmuddelkind with me.
106 "Schmuddelkind."
107 "Schmuddelkind."
108 "Nest-befouler": a pejorative term used to describe one who denigrates one's own "nest"—be it country, family, community, etc.
109 "Schmuddelkind." Details of the complicity of Dresden citizens are listed in the speech.
110 "Schmuddelkind."
111 "Schmuddelkind auf dem Heidefriedhof: Bildhauerin Chodakowska kündigt rechtliche Schritte an," *Dresdner Neueste Nachrichten*, February 9, 2015, https://www.dnn.de/lokales/dresden/schmuddelkind-auf-dem-heidefriedhof-bildhau erin-chodakowska-kuendigt-rechtliche-schritte-an-LVATQQ7J2ECWPA2GH G22NWIO7E.html.
112 "Stellungnahme zur Aktion "Schmuddelkind." *No Excuses!* (blog), February 11, 2015, https://noexcuses.noblogs.org/stellungnahme-zur-aktion-schmuddelkind/.
113 Oguibe is also the creator of the *Biafra Time Capsule* (Athens, 2017), among other works.
114 *documenta* is a series of contemporary art exhibits that takes place in Kassel every five years. In 2017, *documenta 14* took place in both Kassel and Athens under the direction of Adam Szymczyk.
115 The Königsplatz is the site where Goethe was famously denied a hotel room at first because he was mistaken for a Frenchman after speaking French with an innkeeper.
116 All statements directly attributed to Oguibe come from an interview with artort. tv titled *Documenta 14 Artist Olu Oguibe and the Obelisk. Documenta 14 Artist Olu Oguibe and the Obelisk*, September 1, 2017, https://artort.tv/allgemein/documenta -14-artist-olu-oguibe-and-the-obelisk/.
117 Reinhart Koselleck, "Einleitung," in *Der politische Totenkult: Kriegerdenkmäler in der Moderne*, ed. Reinhart Koselleck and Michael Jeismann (Munich: Wilhelm Fink Verlag, 1994), 9.
118 Cited in a statement by Nigerian artist Ugochukwu-Smooth Nzewi on the *documenta 14* website, www.documenta14.de/en/artists/13571/olu-oguibe.
119 Bonaventure Soh Bejeng Ndikung, "Exposing the Question the Answer Hides: The Lives and Afterlives of Olu Oguibe's *Monument for Strangers and Refugees (2017)*," *Frieze* 219 (May 2021): 150–51.
120 "Ideologisch polarisierende, entstellte Kunst"; Andreas Hermann and Werner Fritsch, "documenta-Kunstwerk Obelisk: Die AfD spricht von 'entstellter Kunst.'" *Hessische/Niedersächsische Allgemeine (HNA)*, August 17, 2017. https://www.hna.de/kultur/documenta/documenta-kunstwerk-obelisk-afd-spricht-von-entstellter -kunst-8601756.html.

121 The goal was six hundred thousand Euros; 126,000 Euros were raised. Dorian Batycka, "Dispute Erupts over Artist's 'Monument for Strangers and Refugees' in Germany," *Hyperallergic*, March 31, 2018, https://hyperallergic.com/445282/olu-oguibe-monument-for-strangers-and-refugees-dispute-kassel-documenta/.
122 Catherine Hickley, "Documenta Obelisk, Dismantled Last Week, to Remain in Kassel After All," *Art Newspaper*, October 12, 2018, www.theartnewspaper.com/2018/10/12/documenta-obelisk-dismantled-last-week-to-remain-in-kassel-after-all. Oguibe cites the height and color of the obelisk, the size and gilding of the inscriptions, and platform where Kassel citizens could sit and wait for the train.
123 Hickley, "Documenta Obelisk."
124 Hoheisel, "Long Shadow."
125 Frank-Walter Steinmeier, "Berlin: Day of Remembrance for the Victims of National Socialism," January 29, 2020, www.bundespraesident.de/SharedDocs/Reden/DE/Frank-Walter-Steinmeier/Reden/2020/01/200129-Gedenken-Bundestag.html.
126 Joseph Telushkin, *Jewish Literacy: The Most Important Things to Know about the Jewish Religion, Its People, and Its History* (New York: William Morrow and Company, 1991), 543.
127 Praising the humanitarian impulse behind Germany's acceptance of refugees does not deny the benefits of immigration to Germany with its shrinking and aging population.
128 Telushkin, *Jewish Literacy*, 543.
129 "Welcoming culture" is a phrase denoting a welcoming attitude toward foreigners and immigrants. Since 2015, the term refers primarily to providing assistance to refugees.
130 "September fairy tale" recalls *"ein deutsches Sommermärchen"* ("a German summer fairy tale"), used to describe the World Cup of 2006 (the motto was "Die Welt zu Gast bei Freunden" / "A time to make friends") and a reference to Heinrich Heine's satiric poem "Deutschland: Ein Wintermärchen" ("Germany: A Winter's Tale, 1844").

CONCLUSION

1 "Der Kopf des Soldaten" (Langendreer), *Bochumschau*, www.bochumschau.de/kriegerdenkmal-soldaten-kopf-bochum-langendreer-2019.htm. See also "Einst kommt der Tag da alle Welt . . ." *Bewegung in Bochum*, January 23, 2011, www.bo-alternativ.de/2011/01/23/einst-kommt-der-tag-da-alle-welt/.
2 Other examples of memorial soldiers beheaded include a World War I memorial in Leverkusen-Rheindorf, North Rhine–Westphalia, by Walter Koch, erected 1939. The crouching German soldier poised to fling a hand grenade, bearing the inscription "1914–1918: Euer Tod, Unsere Kraft" ("Your death, our strength") has been beheaded at least three times, most recently in 2019. Hermann Hosaeus's Monument for the Fallen Soldiers of the Garde Pioneer Batallion at the Garnisonkirche in Berlin (1929), too, has been both vandalized with graffiti and beheaded. When photographed by photographer Vladimir Pomortzeff, a pineapple sat on his shoulders in place of the missing head. Vladimir Pomortzeff, "The Woe of the Vanquished," https://pomortzeff.com/german.
3 The memorial stands by the Bundeswehrverwaltungszentrum München (Army

Administrative Center Munich), Dachauer Straße 128; it was dedicated in 1923 to memorialize the fallen soldiers of the Bavarian Railway Troops, destroyed in 1945, and reerected in 1962. The original inscription was: "Sie glaubten zu sterben für Deutschlands Ruhm und Ehr" ("They believed to be dying for Germany's glory and honor"). In 1935 National Socialists changed the inscription to "Sie starben für Deutschlands Ruhm und Ehre." When the memorial was reerected in 1962, the National Socialist version of the inscription was preserved.

4 Sven Rieber, "Mahnmal der Unehre: Protest gegen Kriegerdenkmal," *Merkur*, March 2, 2015, https://www.merkur.de/lokales/muenchen/wolfram-kastner-protestiert-gegen-kriegerdenkmal-4776498.htmlRieber.

5 Bill Niven, "From Countermonument to Combimemorial: Developments in German Memorialization," *Journal of War & Culture Studies* 6, no. 1 (February 2013): 86, www.knitz.net/index.php?option=com_content&task=view&id=29&Itemid=32&lang=en.

6 Bund für Umwelt und Naturschutz Deutschland (German Federation for Environment and Nature Conservation). See their website for information on the Green Belt project, www.bund.net/gruenes-band/. BUND is seeking UNESCO World Heritage Site status for Das Grüne Band. See also the BUND's seven-volume book series *Vom Todesstreifen zur Lebenslinie—Mensch und Natur am Grünen Band Deutschland* by Reiner Cornelius (Niederaula, Germany: Auwel-Verlag, 2005–12) for descriptions of natural treasures as well as histories of the border regions.

7 Melanie Kreutz, "Ein lebendiges Denkmal für Freiheit und Demokratie," *Politik und Kultur* 6/20 (June 2020): 23.

8 Among dozens of examples are Kirsten Grieshaber, "Plaques for Nazi Victims Offer a Personal Impact," *New York Times*, November 29, 2023, www.nytimes.com/2003/11/29/arts/plaques-for-nazi-victims-offer-a-personal-impact.html; Michael Imort, "Stumbling Blocks: A Decentralized Memorial to Holocaust Victims," in *Memorialization in Germany since 1945*, ed. Bill Niven and Chloe Paver (New York: Palgrave Macmillan, 2010)"; Kirsten Harjes, "Stumbling Stones: Holocaust Memorials, National Identity, and Democratic Inclusion in Berlin," *German Politics & Society* 23, no. 1 (Spring 2005); and Mary Rachel Gould and Rachel E. Silverman, "Stumbling upon History: Collective Memory and the Urban Landscape," *GeoJournal* 78, no. 5 (2013).

9 "Children's transport": "A series of rescue efforts between 1938 and 1940 . . . [that] brought thousands of refugee children, the vast majority of them Jewish, to Great Britain from Nazi Germany." US Holocaust Memorial Museum Encyclopedia, https://encyclopedia.ushmm.org/content/en/article/kindertransport-1938-40.

10 Keystones; figuratively speaking, something bringing closure.

11 Anecdotes are cited from TEDx talks by Demnig in Stuttgart ("Die Stolpersteine: Geschichte und Zukunft," 2012) and Cologne ("Stolpersteine: Spuren und Wege," 2013).

12 http://tedxkoeln.de/language/en/speaker/demnig-gunter/.

Index

Abhörung des Waldrandes (*Listening to the Edge of the Forest*, Dieter Appelt), 71
Adenauer, Konrad, 264–65, 268
Adenauer-de-Gaulle memorial (Berlin), 268
das Ahnenerbe, 308n117
Ahnenstätten, 111, 128–29, 319n102
Akedah, 144
Akkermann, Theo, 215
Aktion Sühnezeichen Friedensdienste (Action Reconciliation Service for Peace), 263, 271, 342n29
Algermissen Memorial to the Victims of the World Wars, 198
Alt-Mariendorf cemetery WWI memorial (Berlin), 175
Altdorfer, Albrecht, 61
Alternative für Deutschland (Alternative for Germany), 284–86, 318n81, 343n57, 348n120
Anselm, Archbishop of Canterbury, 222
antisemitism, 64, 265–66
Appelt, Dieter, 70–71
Arbeitsgemeinschaft jüdisches Leben (Committee on Jewish Life), 138
Arminius (Hermann), 28–32, 50, 69, 107, 149, 161, 300n68, 308n135l; as symbol, 33
Arndt, Ernst, 66
Arnim, Achim von, 64, 298–99n29
Arnold, Wilhelm Heidwolf, 186
Artamanen-Gesellschaft, 64
ash tree, 17, 36, 39, 44, 49, 51–52, 55, 63
Assmann, Aleida, 4, 9–10, 27–28
atonement, 2, 9, 13, 218–53; via Christian memorials, 258–60, 268–71; collective, 258–61; medieval, 224–29; secular 260–61, 263–64; of West Germany, 263–65
atonement contracts (*Sühneverträge*), 219–20, 224–32, 235, 259–60, 332n31, 332n34, 332n36, 333n43, 333n55, 333n60
Augustine, Saint, 254–55
Austro-Prussian War (1866), 91, 97, 118, 170, 180, 296n9; memorials to, 91, 97, 118, 180, 296n9
autochthony, 18–19, 22–23, 63–66, 85–86, 92, 107, 114, 125
axis mundi, 21, 33–37, 50, 61

Babisnauer Pappel, 53–54
Bagdons, Friedrich, 176
Bandel, Joseph Ernst von, 32
Barbarossa, Emperor, 33, 60, 327n25
Barlach, Ernst, 200
Barmen-Elberfeld WWI, WWII memorial, 210
Bataille, Georges, 159
Battle of Teutoburg Forest, 27–30, 32, 34–35, 67, 69, 107, 149–50, 300n59, 301n94, 308n135
Beer Hall Putsch, 164
Ben-Gurion, David, 264
Benjamin, Walter, 4, 33
Berlin Holocaust memorial competitions, 274–75, 277
Bernau, Nikolaus von, 258
Beuys, Joseph 41
Bielefeld / Schildesche WWI memorial, 174

Bindl, Andreas, 198
Binswanger, Otto, 158–59, 342n78
Bischofswiesen memorial chapel, 202
Bismarck, Otto von, 65, 114, 314n7
Bismarck oaks, 98
Bismarck towers, 105, 132, 314n7
Bitburg incident, 147
Bleeker, Bernhard, 178
Bochum WWI memorial, 289
Boitiner Steintänze, 103–104
Borchmeyer, Dieter, 72, 76
Bradley, Richard, 2, 21, 45, 47, 105, 118, 120, 134
Brandenburg Gate, 274–76, 346n84
Brandt, Willy, 265
Brentano, Clemens, 22, 85, 298–299n29
Brod, Max, 102
Bruner, Jerome, 2, 295n1
Buchenwald concentration camp and memorial, 93–94, 195, 289, 329n43
Büdelsdorf WWI, WWII memorial, 168
Bund der Vertriebenen (Federation of Expellees), 123, 318n81
Burkert, Walter, 148, 154–56, 211

Cain (Book of Genesis), 144, 201, 217
cairn, 60, 108, 113
Calder, Alexander, 137
Canetti, Elias, 40, 68, 85
Carolina Penal Code (Constitutio Criminalis Carolina), 229
CDU (Christlich Demokratische Union Deutschlands) (Christian Democratic Union of Germany), 272, 318n81
Celtis, Konrad, 30–31
Charlemagne, Emperor, 61, 234, 316n47
Cimbri (tribe), 149
Claims Conference (Conference on Jewish Material Claims Against Germany), 263–64, 342n33
Columbiadamm Cemetery WWI memorial (Neukölln, Berlin), 1
community (ethnic) (*Volksgemeinschaft*), 10, 17, 19–21, 34, 42, 47–48, 54, 64, 67, 90, 106–8, 123, 159, 161, 163, 216, 299n36
Conwentz, Hugo, 75–76
Council of Trent, 221

countermonuments / countermemorials, 165, 276, 340n2, 343n50, 347n102
"Crushed Brandenburg Gate" memorial proposal (Horst Hoheisel), 274–77
cult of the fallen solider, 137, 148
cultural memory, 1–4, 8–10, 124, 133, 289–90, 296n23
culture: transmission of, 8–10, 13

Dachau Church of Reconciliation, 270–71, 344n65
Dachau concentration camp and memorial, 278–80, 344n65
Dammann, Hans, 173–174, 287
Darmstadt-Waldkolonie war memorial, 210
Darré, Richard Walther, 69, 129, 298n11
Deidesheim memorial to Jewish victims of Nazi persecution, 138
Demnig, Gunter, 291–93, 329n45, 340n2
Denkmalschutz, 193
Denkmalsturz, 289. See also memorials, vandalism of
Deusen (Dortmund) WWI memorial, 204–5
Deutsche Turnerschaft, 31. See also Turner
Deutches Baumarchiv, 76
Das Ding (The Thing), 82, 142, 150–51, 154
documenta 14 (art exhibition), 283–84, 348n114
Doehler, Gottfried, 60
Dolchstoßlegende (stab in the back conspiracy theory), 175, 301n104
dolmen, 11, 60, 104–5, 131, 136
Dorflinde (village linden), 95
Dorrenbach, Franz, 1
Dresden: memorialization of bombing, 280–82
Düesberg, Rudolf, 64–65
Durkheim, Émile, 47–48, 90, 106, 251
Dußlingen war memorial, 179–80

Eberhard, Franz Xaver, 204
Eckfeld war memorial, 198
Eden, Garden of, 50, 255
Effelder memorial to expellees, 14–16, 21, 41–42
Ehlers, Alfred, 168

Ehrenhaine (honor groves), 139–41, 166. See also *Heldenhaine*
Eichen (*Oaks*, Arnulf Rainer), 70
Eichendorff, Joseph Freiherr von, 59–60
Einheitsbäume (unification trees), 44, 74–75, 98–101
Eisenman, Peter, 267, 343n57
das Eiserne Händl, 247–48
Eliade, Mircea, 25, 81
Elkan, Benno, 195
entartete Kunst (degenerate art), 6, 200, 284
Erfelden WWI memorial, 173–74
Erhardt, Werner, 99
ethnie, 20–21, 29, 104, 106–8
Evans, Christopher, 4, 105
"EXIT: Das Dachau Projekt" (Jochen Gerz), 278–80, 347n98, 347n100
EXIT-Deutschland, 99
expellees (Germans and ethnic Germans), 14–15

Fallersleben, August Heinrich Hoffmann, 206
Familienverbandes der Windhunde (family association of former Windhund members and relatives), 214
Findlinge (glacial erratics), 103–116, 118, 120–22, 126–27, 132, 166, 316n32, 316n45–46, 321n127; as memorials to divided Germany, 129; as memorials to expellees, 111, 115, 123, 125–26, 139; as monuments to reunification, 129–31; as memorials to wars of German unification (1864–71), 114, 118, 120, 131; as memorials to Wars of Liberation (1813–14), 114, 116, 118; as WWI memorials, 111, 114–20; as WWII memorials, 115–17, 119–20, 123
Finsterwalder, Eberhard, 178
forest, 10, 13, 44–45; and autochthony, 23–25, 31, 63–67; eternal, 39–40, 46, 67–69; in folk psychology, 16–17, 40–42, 53–55; myths of, 18–22, 36, 107, 304n50; in pagan practice, 26–27; postwar symbolism of, 69–72; primeval, 17–20, 25, 27, 34, 37, 52–53, 57, 60, 63–64, 79–83, 87, 107, 305n65; qualities of, 46; and rebirth, 37–38; sacred nature of, 25, 61–63; as symbol, 53; as testimony, 45–46; *Volk* theories of, 68–69. See also trees
Franco-Prussian War (1870–71), 54, 90–91, 114, 118, 120, 131, 164, 170, 172, 176, 180, 182, 206–7, 296n10; memorials to, 90–91, 114, 118, 120, 131, 172, 176, 180, 182, 206–7, 296n9
Frazer, James George, 48, 112
Friedenseichen (peace oaks), 44, 90–92
Friedensengel (*Angel of Peace*) WWII memorial (Mannheim), 195
Friedenslinden (peace lindens), 44, 82, 85, 90–92
Friedrich, Caspar David, 59, 62, 110, 127
Fuss, Fritz, 187

Die Gartenlaube—Illustriertes Familienblatt (*The Garden Arbor—Illustrated Family Journal*), 38, 77–79, 97, 302n116
de Gaulle, Charles, 268
Gedenkbäume (memorial trees), 97
Gedenkkreuze (memorial crosses), 230, 252
Geertz, Clifford, 34
Gefallenenhain (grove for the fallen), 89
Gegendenkmal, 165–191, 280, 347n102
Gelöbnis treuester Gefolgschaft (Vow of the Loyal Followers, 1933), 210
Gemeindelinde (community linden tree), 85
genocide, 124, 261–262
Georg-August-University Göttingen, WWI memorial, 214–15
George, Saint: legend of, 202–3
Gerichtslinde (court linden), 95
German Unity Day, 268
Gerz, Jochen, 275–77, 280, 346n85
Gießen WWI, WWII memorial, 186–87
Girard, René, 159, 257
Goebel, Stefan, 9, 11–12
Goebbels, Joseph, 162–63
Goethe, Johann Wolfgang von, 38, 45, 57–58, 306n77, 348n115
Goethe Oak, 93–94
Gondenbrett WWI, WWII memorial (Saint Dionysius Catholic Church), 200
Göring, Hermann, 68–69

Goths, 142
Grabbe, Christian Dietrich, 32
Griethausen WWII memorial, 209
Grimm Brothers, Jacob and Wilhelm, 22, 36
Groening, Gert, 87
Große Deutsche Kunstausstellung (Great German Art Exhibition, 1937–44), 328n33
Großholthausen WWI, WWII memorial, 168–69
groves, 23; culture of 80–83; depictions of, 62; and memorials, 37, 111, 113–15, 121, 135, 166, 168, 178; and myths, 18, 64, 107, 150–51; pagan, 35–36, 48, 80–82, 150–51; and ritual, 19, 36, 80–82, 144, 150–51, 303n21; sacred, 13, 52–53, 73, 80–82, 94, 150–52. *See also* Heldenhaine (heroes' groves)
das Grüne Band (Green Belt), 290–91
die Grünen (The Greens), 41, 193
guardian trees (*Schutzbäume*), 95
guilt, collective: theories of, 255–63; Germany, 261–63, 265; in Hebrew Bible, 256–67
"Der gute Kamerad" ("The Good Comrade"), 206, 212, 215

Halbertal, Moshe, 144, 159–62, 164, 203
Halbwachs, Maurice, 9
Haller, Ingo, 214
Harsewinkel WWI, WWII memorial, 209
Heidefriedhof (Dresden), 280
Heilig, Wilhelm, 174
Heimat, 4, 17, 23–25, 42, 65, 90, 93, 96, 112, 137–39, 145–46; in memorial inscriptions, 14, 16, 112, 124–25, 136, 145–46, 166–68, 174, 183, 215
Heimatschutz (homeland protection) 20, 75
Heimatverein (homeland association), 317n58
Heine, Heinrich, 37, 61, 349n130
Heldenhaine (heroes' groves), 44, 74, 80–90, 97, 100–101, 107–8, 111, 114–15, 118, 120–21, 126, 135, 140, 166, 311n52, 319n83; legacy of, 88–89
Henselmann, Josef, 180–181
Hercynian forest, 19, 45–46
Herder, Johann Gottfried von, 14, 37, 62

Hermannsdenkmal (Hermann monument) 31–34, 132, 161, 301n82
Hermunduri (tribe), 149
Hess, Rudolf, 99
Hesse, Hermann, 38, 73
Himmler, Heinrich, 66, 93, 162, 298n11
Hitler, Adolf, 33, 101, 147, 161–62, 188, 196, 210, 276
Hitler oaks, 98, 101
Hochkreuze (high crosses), 238
Hofgarten war memorial (Munich), 178–79
Hoheisel, Horst, 273–78, 285, 290, 340n2, 346n84, 346n86, 347n91
Hohensyburg Castle war memorial, 176–78
Hölderlin, Friedrich, 14, 38, 69
Holocaust, 40, 165, 262–263, 265–66, 325n107; memory culture of, 264–67, 274–78, 286
Holy Roman Empire, 229
Hosaeus, Hermann, 186
Huckarde (Dortmund) WWI memorial (Saint Urbanus Church), 212
Humboldt, Alexander von, 45, 57–59, 75
Hümmel WWI, WWII memorial, 198
Hünengräber (giants' graves), 106–10, 113, 115, 320n107; depictions of, 60, 110–111; legends of, 314n6; memorials and monuments, 11, 104–5, 108–9, 111, 115–16, 122, 126, 131–41, 290, 314n6
hunting (ritual of), 154–56, 211
Hürtgen Forest, battles of, 214
Hutten, Ulrich von, 30

interdicts (High Middle Ages), 257–59
International Criminal Court, 261
Israel, 264, 342–43
Ivenack Oaks, 43–44, 47

Jaeger, Hans-Peter, 200
Jenenser Studenten (Students of Jena), 92
Jewish WWI soldiers, 191
Joanni, Theodor, 202
Job (Book of Job), 224
Jupiter Oak, 61

Karberg memorial hall (am Haddebyer Noor), 136–38

Karl der Große, 60
Kaisereichen (Kaiser oaks), 97
Kaiserlinden (Kaiser lindens), 85, 97
Kemmerich, Josef, 215
Kerken WWI, WWII memorial, 215
Kersting, Georg Friedrich, 92
Kiefer, Anselm, 41; *Varus*, 69
Kindertransport (Children's Transport), 350n9
Kleist, Heinrich von, 32, 301n94
Kley / Oespel (Dortmund) WWI memorial, 192–93
Klophaus, Rudolf, 193
Klotz, Clemens, 187
Klug, Hanns Joachim, 198
Knappe, Karl, 178
Knittel, Hugo, 212
Kohl, Helmut, 272, 276, 329n54
Kolbe, Carl Wilhelm, 59
Kollmar, Wilhelm, 191
Kollwitz, Käthe, 272–73, 326n108, 345n75
Koselleck, Reinhart, 7, 12, 165, 171–72, 204, 273–74, 325n106, 331n6, 346n83
Krumm, Erwin, 215
Kuöhl, Richard, 193, 317n59, 347n102
Kyffhäuser (Barbarossa) monument, 132
Kyffhäuserbund, 200

Landsmannschaften, 129, 319n104
Lange, Willy, 82–90, 100, 107–8, 118, 120, 126
Langenberg WWI, WII memorial, 213
Langendreer WWI memorial, 287–89
Lappersdorf war memorial, 207
Latteyer, Karl, 206
Law of Reparations (West Germany), 265
Lebensbaum (tree of life), 58
Lebensmale (living memorials), 73–102
leges barbarorum, 225
Lehmann, Albrecht, 53, 96
Lehmbruck, Manfred, 179
Leibzeichen, 228
Lenz, Johann Baptist, 198
Liegender Krieger WWI memorial (Wanne-Eickel), 186
lieu de mémoire, 2, 7, 34, 138, 295n5, 316n46
lindens, 38, 44, 48, 74, 94–96, 311n52; healing powers of, 56; Kaditz linden, 77–78; *Kaiser- und Friedenslinden*, 85, 97; *Marienlinden*, 61, 306n99; in memorials, 85; Prior linden, 78–79; Puch linden, 78–79; *Tanzlinden* (dance linden), 95; as unification tree, 99
Ludendorff, Erich, 6
Lüdenscheid WWI memorial, 187–89
Ludwigshafen WWI memorial, 202
Lurz, Meinhold, 12
Luther, Martin, 60, 95, 97, 101

Mages, Josef (Sepp), 189
Mahnmal, 119, 143, 321n4
Maimonides, Moses, 286
Mainbernheim WWI memorial, 175
Mallon, Hans, 111, 127–128
Mann, Thomas, 210
Männerbund (male community), 154–55, 211
Manu / Mannus, 18, 150, 152–53
Marcks, Gerhard, 195
Margalit, Gilad, 318n86, 319n91, 342n39
Markt Schwaben WWI memorial, 207–8
martyrdom, 144–45, 153, 157, 200, 202–3, 211, 322n10
Mauss, Marcel, 226
megaliths, 60, 105, 108, 122, 132–33, 137–38, 314n1, 315n30, 320n107
Meller, Jakob Wilhelm (Willy), 187
Memmingen WWI, WWII memorial (Mariä Himmelfahrt Church), 198–200
Memorial to the 5th Guards Grenadier Regiment (Berlin, Spandau), 184
Memorial to the 23rd Royal Bavarian Infantry Regiment (Kaiserslautern), 189
Memorial to Homosexuals Persecuted under Nazism, 289
memorial iconography: angels, 201, 234; archangel Michael, 206; camaraderie, 211–17; Christian symbolism, 195–96, 218; coats of arms, 227, 234, 238; crosses, 15; crucifixion, 219, 233–35, 238, 241, 259; enchanted sleep, 175–81; family scenes, 182; Greek and/or Roman imagery, 173–74, 204, 206–7; Jesus, 202; martyrdom, 232; medieval imagery, 176; occupational tools, 238; Passion imagery, 15, 35, 196; Pietà imagery, 196–200, 272–73, 329n57; praying soldiers, 202; sacrifice, 143, 145–147, 157–58, 161–163, 168, 174;

memorial iconography (*continued*)
Saint George, 202–10, 330n62, 330n64, 330n66; *Stahlhelm*, 1, 173, 175, 197, 200–201, 209, 212; *Trotz-Faust*, 184–86, 188, 280
memorial inscriptions, 171–74, 189
Memorial to the Murdered Jews of Europe, 13, 267, 289, 291, 343n57
memorials: of atonement, 218–253; to expellees, 14, 196, 220, 319n94, 326n3; to former eastern territories, 112; Nazi era, 189–194, 328n39; of reconciliation, 268–71; to resistance, 89, 160, 270, 291, 329n44; to unknown soldier, 172, 327n14; vandalism of, 4, 6–7, 48, 119, 207, 217, 232, 253, 284, 289, 349n2, 328n39, 349n2; to victims of Nazi persecution, 138, 188, 195, 197, 255, 272, 289, 291, 321n127, 329n45, 347n102; to wars of unification, 182
memory, 4, 9; post WWII, 89, 290; transmission of, 8–9; victim-centered, 266–268
Merkel, Angela, 98–99, 284–286, 330n72
Military Service Law (1935), 188
Möller, Heinrich, 175
Monument to the Battle of the Nations (Leipzig), 132
Monument for Strangers and Refugees (Das Fremdlinge und Flüchtlinge Monument) (Kassel), 122, 282–85, 293, 349n121
monuments: prehistoric, 45, 47, 315n27; to German unification, 100, 268
monuments / memorials: theories of, 105–6
Mordwange / Mordkreuz, 218–19, 224, 232–35, 241–42, 331n1, 333n60
Mosse, George, 35, 148, 156–57, 211
Mother with her Dead Son sculpture (Käthe Kollwitz, Neue Wache, Berlin), 197
Munich war memorial (Army Administrative Center), 289, 349–50n3
Myth of the War Experience, 148, 156–57
myths, 2, 34–35; of creation, 142, 150–53, 156, 164; Germanic, 88, 150, 153; of groves, 81; of lindens, 94; of nature, 49–52; of origins, 9; 18–21, 25, 60, 102, 105–8, 134, 150–51, 154, 161; of self-sacrifice, 152–53

Nadav and Avihu (Book of Leviticus), 144, 201, 217
Nahanarvali (tribe), 151
Napoleon, 35, 276
Nathe, Christoph, 111
National Socialism, 6, 19–20, 24, 39–40, 45, 64, 66, 68, 87, 93, 122, 126, 134, 156, 193, 217, 265–266
Nazi memorials and monuments, 192, 216, 328n39
Nazi party, 127, 187, 210
Nationales Naturdenkmal (national nature monument), 43, 302n2
Naturdenkmale (nature monuments), 44, 74–75, 79
Naturschutz (nature conservation), 20, 75–76, 302n2
Neolithic period / monuments, 47, 60, 104, 108–9, 113, 117–18, 132, 320n107
neo-Nazis, 89, 99, 128, 193, 347n103
Neu-Isenburg memorial, 185
Neukloster WWI memorial, 174
Neue Wache / Central Memorial to the Federal Republic of Germany for the Victims of War and Tyranny, 197–98, 272–73, 327n14, 345n77
Niebelungenlied, 311n44
Niederwald monument, 132
Niemöller, Martin, 270
Nietzsche, Friedrich, 184
Niven, Bill, 165, 290, 325n107, 343n50
No Excuses (antifascist group), 280, 282
Nora, Pierre, 2, 34, 138, 295n5, 316n46
Norse mythology, 18, 36–39, 44, 51–52, 63, 83
nostalgia, 21–22, 24, 104–8
NPD (National Democratic Party of Germany), 33, 214, 288

oaks, 25, 38, 44, 48, 70, 74, 297n1; Bridegroom's oak; groves, 23, 303n21; healing properties of, 55–56; Marieneiche, 61; in memorials, 84–87; in myth, 83
obelisk, 283
Oberdolling war memorial, 207, 209
Oberhaching war memorial, 182–83

Odenheim WWI memorial, 190
Odin, 17, 36–37, 49, 52, 60, 149, 152. *See also* Wodan / Wotan
Oedipus the King (Sophocles), 257
Oedipus of Thebes, 257
Oguibe, Olu, 282–85, 293, 348n113, 349n122
Ohly, Wilhelm F.C., 206
Ohnmacht und Wille WWI memorial (Stuttgart-Feuerbach), 184
Öhringen war memorial, 209–10
Opherdicke WWI memorial, 213
Oppenau WWI, WWII memorial, 212–13, 330n70
Original Sin, doctrine of, 255

pagan: history, 105, 112; practice and ritual, 17–18, 52, 56, 61, 81–82, 92, 118, 132, 304n48, 316n43; societies, 154
Paleolithic era, 154
Pang WWI, WWII memorial, 201
Paul, Saint, 176, 255
penance, 9; acts of, 223–24; Marienkirche (Berlin), 258–59; sacrament of, 221, 269, 271; West Germany, 264–65
penance crosses, stones, and shrines, 219, 224, 226–253, 331n18, 332n34, 333n53, 333n60, 333n99, 334n63, 335n95, 338n166
pergola, 119, 317–18n67
pilgrimage, 3, 84, 227–29, 231–32, 250, 260, 284, 306n99
Pliny the Elder, 81
Prussian National Monument for the Liberation Wars (Berlin), 173
Puch, Edigna von, 78–79

race (Germanic), 87
Radzik, Linda, 223, 261
Rainer, Arnulf, 70
ransom: in religious discourse, 222
Rebel, Karl, 42
reconciliation, 219–225; rituals of, 228
Reconciliation Sculpture (Berlin), 268, 344n60
Reeser Platz memorial (Düsseldorf), 193–94
Reformation (Protestant), 222
refugee crisis (2014/2015), 283

reorientation: moral, 223, 254, 260–61, 263, 268, 273–86; religious, 254
reparations, West Germany, 264
repentance, 2, 221–22, 224, 228–29, 254, 259, 263, 270–71, 286, 331n8
reunification, of Germany, 111, 272, 276
Rheingönheim memorial, 178
Richter, Ludwig, 61
Richter-Elsner, Fritz, 133, 168, 213
Riehl, Wilhelm Heinrich, 20, 23, 54–55, 65–67
rituals: of killing, 155; of sacrifice, 19, 34–36, 80–81, 142, 144, 146–156, 159. *See also* sacrifice, rituals of
Romanticism, 22, 31, 64
Rostock Mordwange, 259
Rother, Richard, 175
Rousseau, Jean-Jacques, 261
Rowlands, Michael, 8, 10
Rübsam, Josef, 4–6
Ruhr Warrior Memorial (*Ruhrkämpferehrenmal*, Horst), 119

sacrifice: and atonement, 221; betrayal of, 175; and Christian imagery, 195–96; as debt, 1, 3, 11, 143, 146, 163–64, 179, 220; to god, 144, 146, 200–201, 321n6; and Hebrew Bible, 144, 200–201, 217, 257; and hunting, 143, 153–56; iconography of, 11; and imagery of camaraderie, 211, 215; of Jesus, 222; and memorials, 13, 143, 145, 147–49, 158, 166, 168–217; myths of, 11, 142, 150–53, 169, 322n26; pagan, 11, 17, 19, 34–37, 79–80, 142–43, 148–53, 169, 323n31; and Pietà imagery, 196–200; and rebirth, 174, 184–85; and renewal, 163–64; rituals of, 11, 17, 19, 34–37, 64, 79–81, 142–44, 146, 148–53, 168, 203, 257, 301n97, 323n31; and Saint George imagery, 203; and soldier imagery, 168; theories of, 11, 142–46, 158–60, 169; and Third Reich, 161–63; and victimhood, 146–48; and war, 143, 148–50, 156–58, 301n97. *See also* rituals, of sacrifice; self-sacrifice
Sallay, Laszlo, 137
Saxons (tribe), 149, 316n47
scapegoating, 146, 159, 257
Schaffendes Volk (Productive People exhibition), 193

INDEX

Scheler, Max, 184
Schicksalsbaum (fate or destiny tree), 58, 97
Schilking, Heinrich, 60
Schinkel, Karl Friedrich, 173
Schlageter, Albert Leo, 111, 315n30, 328n39
Schmitz, Bruno, 132
Schmuddelkind (Dresden), 280–82
Schoenichen, Walther, 66
Scholz, Stephan, 12, 124, 318n82, 319n92
Schopenhauer, Arthur, 160
Schreitmüller, August, 184
Schulz, Otto, 174
Schutzgemeinschaft Deutscher Wald (Association for the Protection of the German Forest), 40, 99–100
Schwarzbeck, Fritz, 210
Second Schleswig War (German Danish War, 1864), 114, 118, 170, 345n81; memorials to, 114, 118
Seeger, Karl von, 80, 114–115, 158, 167, 179–80
self-sacrifice: for family, 182–83; myths of, 152–53, 322n26, 323n48–49; of soldiers, 1–2, 11, 13, 35–37, 52, 67, 84–85, 89, 97, 142–43, 146, 157–64, 166–68, 172–74, 189, 211, 217, 326n108; theories of, 144–48, and Third Reich, 161–63
Semnones (tribe), 80, 82, 142, 144, 151, 154
Siegfried, 60, 83–84, 87, 89, 94, 122, 311n44
Sigmaringen war memorial, 180–82
Signatures, doctrine of, 57
Smith, Anthony, 17, 20–21, 104, 106
Sophocles, 257
SPD (Sozialdemokratische Partei Deutschlands) (Social Democratic Party of Germany), 193, 214
Spengler, Oswald, 46, 63
Speyer WWI memorial, 206–7
Staffeler Kreuz, 259–60
Stahlhelm (WWI veterans' organization), 200
Steinbach, Erika, 318n81
Stenden WWI memorial, 217
Stocker, Daniel, 184
Stöckl, Anton, 202
Stolpersteine, 195, 291–93, 329n45, 340n2
stone circles and settings, 21, 103–5, 114, 117–19, 122, 135, 166, 314n1

Stralsund Pietà (Saint Johannis Monastery), 200
Sturluson, Snorri, 18, 49
Der Stürmer, 175
Sudenburg Todesmarschdenkmal (Death March Memorial), 138
Suebi (tribe), 154
swastika, 93, 98, 289

Tachill, Artur, 193
Tacitus, 18, 26, 30, 31, 81, 107, 149, 151–52, 300n77; *Annals*, 32, 149; *Germania*, 18, 151
Tag der Heimat (Homeland Day), 124–25
Tannenberg memorial, 176
Tannhäuser legend, 97, 313n101
Taylor, Charles, 223, 260
Teshuvah, 220, 222, 254, 286
Thingspiel, 319n96
Thingstätte / Thingplatz, 127–28
Third Reich, 4, 36, 67, 161, 190, 265, 271, 299n39
Thirty Years' War (1618–1648), 237, 245, 249–50, 318n69
Tholos tomb, 180–81
Tiwaz, 36, 149–50, 152
Todesangel (Angel of Death) WWII memorial (Cologne), 195
totem, 10, 47–49, 90
Totenburgen, 127, 319n95
Totensonntag (Sunday of the Dead), 215
Tränenmeer (Sea of Tears) memorial (Dresden), 280–82
Trauernde Alte (*The Old Woman in Mourning*) WWII memorial (Bochum), 195
Treaty of Versailles, 133–34, 185, 305n61
Tree of Life, 50
trees, 10, 13, 15–16; and burial, 39–40; and death and rebirth, 37–40; depictions of, 37–38; in folk psychology, 17, 38–39; 52–53, 56–57; Goethe's writings on, 57–58; healing powers of, 45, 55–57; in Heldenhaine, 82–90, 101–102; homology with humans, 57–58; Humboldt's writings on, 58–59; as memorials and monuments, 14–16, 20, 25, 38, 44–47, 72–79, 101–102; in modern culture, 39–41; and myth, 29, 37, 49–53; in Norse mythology, 51–52; in pagan culture, 17–18, 25–27, 35–39;

postwar symbolism of, 69–72; and racist thought, 64–66; and rebirth, 39; and ritual, 26, 35–36, 48; as sacred, 2, 17, 25–26, 36–39, 48–49, 50–51, 61–63, 73; and sacrifice, 35–36; as soldiers, 67–69; as testimony, 78; as totem, 47–49; in world religions, 51, worship of, 18, 25, 38–39, 53, 61, 83. *See also* forest; lindens; oaks
tribes (Germanic) 30–31, 36, 48, 53, 80–81, 86, 95, 107, 111, 118, 122, 142, 148–50, 152–54, 156, 159, 161. *See also entries for individual tribes*
Trittau WWI memorial, 116–17, 315n58–59
Tuisto / Yemo, 18, 150, 152–54, 298n9
Turner (Turners), 92. *See also* Deutsche Turnerschaft

Uhlbach WWI memorial, 168
Ulanendenkmal (Uhlan WWI memorial), 133–34
Unfallkreuze (accident crosses), 230, 252
unification (of Germany), 90–91, 93, 114
Unter Bäumen. Die Deutschen und der Wald (*Beneath the Trees. The Germans and the Forest*), 72

Valhalla, 52
Vasconcellos, Josefina de, 268
Vesper, Willi, 210
victimhood, theories of, 146
victimization, discourse of, 124, 163, 319n91, 342n39, 345n76
Volk (German), 10, 14, 19, 24–25, 54–55, 67, 82–83, 92, 107, 114, 305n65; unified, 100
völkisch: movement and ideology, 24, 33, 63–70, 82, 107, 114, 129, 139, 307n107, 308n125
Volksbund Deutsche Kriegsgräberfürsorge (German War Graves Commission), 88, 127, 137–38
Volksgemeinschaft. *See also* community (ethnic)
Volkstrauertag (National Day of Mourning), 116, 121, 288
La voûte des mains (Clasping / Vaulted Hands) sculpture, 268

Wagner, Richard, 60
Wahl, Karl, 190

Wald der Erinnerung (Forest of Remembrance), 139–41
Walddenkmal (*Forest Memorial*, Reinhart Heinsdorff), 71
Waldkirch-Kollnau WWI, WWII memorial, 215–17
Waldsterben (forest death), 41, 53, 96, 305n57, 307n107
Waldvolk, 25, 43, 52–55, 59–61
War of Annihilation: Crimes of the Wehrmacht, 1941–1944 exhibition, 214
Wars of Liberation (1813–1814), 12, 31–32, 49, 91–92, 114, 116, 135, 145, 153, 164, 172, 206, 297n1, 318n72, 322n13, 324n76, 327n14; memorials to, 12, 35, 91, 114, 116, 145, 153, 172, 206–207, 213, 322n13, 324n76
Warsaw Ghetto Monument, 265
"Warum. Warum ist es geschehen?" (Jochen Gerz), 277–78
wayside cross legends, 235–253; blasphemy, fanaticism, and superstition, 244–45, 337n139; crimes of passion, 242–43, 336n117; death by tickling, 249; envy, 334n63; fratricide, 240–41, 333n53, 335n106; gluttony, 246; haunting, 252–53, 340n209; healing, 251–52; homicide, 239–241, 333n55, 335n92, 335n103, 336n112, 336n114, 336n129, 336–37n133; infanticide, 241; Jews, 236, 249, 338n177; natural disasters, accidents, and animals, 246–249, 340n206; plague, famine, and hunger, 237, 245–46; robbery and poaching, 241–42; Roma and Sinti, 236, 249–250, 338–39n181; Thirty Years' War, 237, 245, 249–50; vengeance and punishment, 243–245
wayside memorials, 218–53
Weber, Carl Maria von, 60
Wechs, Thomas, 178
Weimar Republic, 4, 6, 11, 24, 189
Weingarten memorial, 204, 206
Weinheim WWI, WWII memorial (Kaiser Wilhelm I Infantry Regiment No. 124), 190–91
Weizsäcker, Richard von, 265, 267, 272, 329n54, 345n77
Welzer, Harald, 265
Wergild, 220, 225–226, 228
Wessel, Horst, 111, 127–8, 328n39

Wiechert, Ernst, 93–94
Wilhelm I, Kaiser, 32–33, 97, 131
Wilhelm II, Kaiser, 97, 114, 276, 327n14
Wilhelm III, Friedrich, Kaiser, 330n72
Wimmer, Thomas, 178
Windhund memorial (Windhund-Division—116th Panzer Division of the Wehrmacht) (Vossenack cemetery), 213, 330n73
Wodan / Wotan, 36, 60, 94, 149, 152, 153, 322n26, 323n48–49. *See also* Odin
Wolfrum, Edgar, 170
World War I, 4, 11, 24, 31, 35, 74, 88, 97, 164–165, 206; culture of, 156–59, 327n14; defeat in, 76; depiction of, 67; and generation of 1914, 88, 142, 156, 158; and *Heldenhaine* (heroes' groves), 80, 82, 87, 89, 111, 115, 126; and sacrifice, 37, 161, 164–65; soldiers, 35
World War I memorials, 1, 4, 74, 91, 134, 143, 220, 287–89, 327n19; angels, 201; awakening soldiers, 187–89; camaraderie, 211–17; enchanted sleep, 175–181; family scenes, 182–83; fighting soldiers, 192–94, 328n36; *Findlinge* memorials, 114–115, 117, 120–21, 141, 317n66; *Hünengräber*, 131, 133–136; Jesus, 202; Pietà imagery, 196–200; rising and moving soldiers, 185–87, 189–91; Saint George imagery, 203–10, 330n62; sacrificial imagery, 143, 145–48, 153, 156, 167–74; stone settings, 117–19; tree memorials, 97; *Trotz-Faust*, 185–85

World War II, 165, 317n58; atonement for, 255, 263, 290; discourse on, 124; legacy of, 69, 99, 112; memorialization of, 194–95, 220, 253; memory culture of, 263–68; 272–74; and reorientation, 255; and sacrifice, 164–65; 168–69; 170–72; soldiers, 35
World War II memorials, 89, 91, 287–89, 317n59, 317n67, 322n13; angels, 201; camaraderie, 211–17; Christian imagery, 195–96; enchanted sleep, 176, 178–80; family scenes, 182–83; fighting soldiers, 328n36; and *Findlinge*, 115–16, 120–21, 129, 141, 317n66; and *Hünengräber*, 131, 134–38; *Mahnmale*, 143; Pietà imagery, 197–200; rising and moving soldiers, 186, 190–91; and sacrificial imagery, 145–48, 153; Saint George imagery, 207, 209–10, 330n62; and stone settings, 117–19; tree memorials, 97
Würzburg Denkmal der Versöhnung (Memorial of Reconciliation), 268–69
Wynand, Paul, 210

xenophobia, 24, 64, 282, 286

Yad Vashem, 273
Yggdrasil, 17, 36–37, 39, 51–52, 63, 152–53, 322n26
Yom Kippur, 220–221
Young, James E., 12, 93–94, 165
Young Rhineland (*das Junge Rheinland*), 6

JENNIFER HANSEN-GLUCKLICH is professor of German at the University of Mary Washington in Fredericksburg, Virginia. She was born in Baltimore, Maryland and received her BA at Georgetown University and PhD at the University of Virginia. She is the author of *Holocaust Memory Reframed: Museums and the Challenges of Representation*, 2014, and has held fellowships at the Mandel Center for Advanced Holocaust Studies at the United States Holocaust Memorial Museum in Washington DC and with the German Academic Exchange Service (DAAD). She lives with her husband, Ariel Glucklich, and three cats on the Potomac River in King George, Virginia.

www.ingramcontent.com/pod-product-compliance
Lightning Source LLC
Chambersburg PA
CBHW030518230426
43665CB00010B/665